STATE

Democratizing Class Relations

LABOR

in the Southern Cone

CAPITAL

PAUL G. BUCHANAN

University of Pittsburgh Press
Pittsburgh and London

Published by the University of Pittsburgh Press, Pittsburgh, Pa., 15260

Copyright © 1995, University of Pittsburgh Press

Manufactured in the United States of America

Printed on acid-free paper

Library of Congress Cataloging-in-Publication Data

Buchanan, Paul G., 1954 –
    State, labor, capital : democratizing class relations in the Southern Cone / Paul
G. Buchanan.
        p.   cm. — (Pitt Latin American series)
    Includes bibliographical references and index.
    ISBN 0-8229-3910-X
    1. Labor policy—Southern Cone of South America.   2. Industrial relations—
Southern Cone of South America.   3. Social classes—Southern Cone of South
America.   I. Title   II. Series.
    HD8259.S65B83 1995
    331'.098—dc20   95-32215
                                                                           CIP

A CIP catalogue record for this book is available from the British Library.

Eurospan, London

PITT LATIN AMERICAN SERIES

CONTENTS

In memory of

MARGARET DURLAND WACHTER

a special friend,
and to the only part of her legacy that matters to me,
Alejandra and Lorenzo Buchanan

PREFACE

THIS BOOK OWES its genesis to two formative experiences in the life of its author. The first was a childhood and adolescence spent in Argentina, where I witnessed the effects of political instability and authoritarianism, economic exploitation and crisis, social injustice and anomie, sectorial violence and state terror, and from which I developed a sympathy for working-class concerns, for human rights in general, and for left-wing Peronism in particular. Reinforced by experiences gained during sojourns in Brazil, Chile, and Uruguay during the 1970s, this personal interest was transformed into an academic concern during my educational trajectory in the United States. This was the second formative experience, for it was as a graduate student in political science at the University of Chicago that I was introduced to Guillermo A. O'Donnell, Adam Przeworski, and Philippe C. Schmitter, and to a host of other scholars whose work proved inspirational. Using their example and encouragement, I have devoted this study to exploring themes initially broached by my mentors, though I make no claim to being able to do justice to their thought. Although the debt I owe these scholars will become evident in the lines that follow, these mentors are in no way to blame for any errors or inaccuracies that may surface.

Beyond these sources of inspiration, numerous institutions and individuals contributed to seeing the project to its fruition. Financial and logistical support have been provided by the USIS Fulbright Postdoctoral Research Grant Program, the Heinz Endowment, the Naval Postgraduate School Research Foundation, the

University of Arizona School of Behavioral and Social Sciences Summer Research Stipend Program, the University of Arizona Office of the Provost Author Support Fund, the Center for the Study of Foreign Affairs of the Foreign Service Institute, the United States Department of State, the Centro de Estudios de Estado y Sociedad (CEDES) in Buenos Aires, the Instituto Universitario de Pezquisas do Rio de Janeiro (IUPERJ) in Rio de Janeiro, the Kellogg Institute, the University of Notre Dame, the department of national security affairs at the Naval Postgraduate School, and the department of Portuguese at the Defense Language Institute. Portions of the research on the Argentine labor administration were funded by a Mellon summer research grant administered by the Center for Latin American Studies at the University of Chicago. While the support of the above organizations is gratefully acknowledged, it goes without saying that none are responsible for the opinions voiced in this book.

Research assistance was provided by Leslie Carlson and William Krauthammer-Otero at the Naval Postgraduate School and by Anwara Begun, Enke Weber, Tomas Hopkins, Robert Gillespie, Monoar Kabir, Yolanda Cobos-Pons, Mike Kelly, and Linda Bohlke at the University of Arizona. Logistical and material assistance was also provided by Albertine Potter and Irene Dixon at the Naval Postgraduate School, while Denise Allyn, Jan Thompson, and Patricia Morris provided such assistance at the University of Arizona.

In Argentina I benefited from the support offered by Marcelo Cavarozzi, Jorge Balán, and the administrative staff at CEDES; Rolando Costa Picazo, Carlos Newlands, and Oscar "Paco" Riso of the Fulbright commission; John Lamazza of the United States embassy; and Tulio DiBella and Miguel Kenny.

In Uruguay my research was greatly enhanced by the assistance provided by Alfonso Vivo, Dr. Gustavo Caffani, and Dr. Carlos Gitto of the Ministerio de Trabajo y Seguridad Social, and by the courtesies extended by Don José "Pepe" D'Elia and Ruben Villaverde of the PIT-CNT, Romeo Perez of CLAEH, and Mario Lombardi of CIESU.

In Brazil, I could not have conducted field work without the extensive help provided by Marco Antônio da Rocha, Howard Medcaff, and Lolita Anisio of the Fulbright commission; Wallace Keiderling of the cultural section of the United States consulate in Rio; Cesar Guimarães, Amaury de Souza, Luiz Vernek Vianna, and the administrative staff at IUPERJ; Dr. Sandra Valle of the Ministerio do Trabalho; and Flavio Pachowski of the CUT Nacional.

At the Kellogg Institute, I am especially indebted to Albert LeMay, J. Samuel Valenzuela, Erika Valenzuela, Roberto DaMatta, Guillermo O'Donnell, Daphne Shutts, Dolores Fairley, Marylou Fillmore, Caroline Domingo, Scott Mainwaring, and Floreal Forni for their assistance and advice.

I would also be remiss if I did not recognize the support of many friends and acquaintances. At the Naval Postgraduate School I owe a considerable debt to Sherman Blandin, David Burke, Michael Clough, Joseph Sternberg, Irene Dixon, and Albertine Potter, and to several student-colleagues: James "Rusty" O'Brien, Steven Mirr, Frank Thomas Jones, Keith Wixler, Timothy Doorey, Michael Martinez, Michael Flores, Juan Carlos Fernandez, Jorge Jimenez-Rojo, Brett Morris, Thomas Flemma, Al Dorn, and Donald Hanle. At the University of Arizona I owe special thanks to Richard Jankowski, Kathleen Schwartzman, and Donna Guy.

In Argentina I am in debt to my *compañeros* at CEDES: Beatriz Capelletti, Monica Gogna, Andrés Thompson, Alejandro La Madrid, Lucas Rubinitch, Inés Gonzales, Elenor Platte, Maria Matilde Olier, Juan Silva, Gabriela Ippolito, and Juan Carlos Llovet. I am especially indebted to my *familia peronista*, Carlos Acuña and Elsa Lopez, for allowing me to share their lives with gracious understanding and hospitality, and to Daniel and Silvana Cohen, Daniel and Corali Renna, Iris Lestani, and Lorna Lipka-Dillon and family for their unwavering friendship.

In Uruguay, both Alfonso Vivo and Carlos Gitto became friends as well as professional contacts, for which I am especially thankful.

In Brazil, I owe an enormous debt of gratitude to Geri Smith and Thomas Murphy for their friendship and hospitality, and for the many times spent contemplating the more interesting facets of Brazilian life; to Bert and Charlene Strock, who worried about more than my physical comfort here on earth; and to Lolita Anisio, Wallace Keiderling, Peter Swavely, Thomas Glass, and Sonia de Souza.

In the United States, Robert Barros, Jack Knight, Kimberley Stanton, John Bailey, Gary Wynia, Benjamin Schneider, David and Ruth Berins Collier, David Pion-Berlin, Jennifer McCoy, Kathy Gille, Judy Lawton, Larry Appelbaum, Jim Anderson, Steve Baker, Paul Chase, Rick Kozin, Steve Davis, Robin Southern, Kim Holmes, Shelly Pope, Charles Stevens, William Hardwick, Kori Weik, Irasema Coronado, Karen and Giovanni Schifano, and many other friends within and outside the Latin Americanist community offered help and encouragement in one way or another. I owe a special debt of gratitude to my guardian angel, Edith Spencer, and to my editor, coauthor, critic, hiking partner, and *compa* Betts Putnam, both of whom suffered more than anyone else the agonies that accompanied the final stages of this project.

In a very real sense, this is a work born of love and of love lost. Love of things political and things Latin American generated the ambition to undertake the project. The lost love of the person who mattered most to me was the price paid for pursuing this ambition, though her betrayal is a reminder of the frailty of the human spirit and was an extraordinary test of my resolve to finish.

Given the trials that colored the making of this book, I must acknowledge the support of my family, especially my *viejo*, for the many *gauchadas* he has done for me despite our conflicting ideologies. I would also like to recognize my debt to the Wachter family, and especially recognize Beth for the good years shared and the final, bitter lesson imparted. Although I thank all these special people, I owe the most to Alejandra and Lorenzo, who are the reasons I look to a brighter future, and my source of solace in the present.

INTRODUCTION

THIS BOOK ANALYZES ATTEMPTS to institutionalize democratic systems of labor relations in Argentina, Brazil, and Uruguay after the withdrawal of authoritarian regimes in the 1980s. Its fundamental premise is that democratic capitalist regimes are founded on a class compromise between the organized working classes and capitalists that is mediated by the state. However ritualized, mystified, or informal the class compromise may eventually become, it remains the most important variable in explaining the successful reproduction of this form of political and economic organization. Erection of institutional frameworks that promote labor relations systems conducive to maintaining class compromise has been an enduring concern of policy leaders in all democratic capitalist countries, since such institutions promote the ideological and economic bases for the working class's consent to bourgeois rule.

This concern has been evident in the organization of labor relations systems throughout the democratic capitalist world. National labor administration has been the subject of much scrutiny over the last century: it consists of the network of state agencies and of the legislation that regulates the organization, rights, and responsibilities of the organized labor movement; this network also provides the institutional framework for labor's interaction with capital and with public authorities. Capitalists' concern to secure labor's consent has reached such a point that international efforts to promulgate "democratic" and "pluralist" labor relations systems have emerged worldwide, led by the work of the International Labor Organization based in Geneva.

The functions of national labor administration under democratic capitalism are of paramount importance. As part of the state's central administrative apparatus, labor administration is the only government branch that, on an ongoing basis, simultaneously performs ideological, repressive, *and* economic reproduction functions. The distinctions among these dimensions of hegemonic rule will be made clear in the pages that follow. Other state apparatuses may perform either an ideological, an economic, or a repressive function; they may even perform two of these functions; and the parliamentary system clearly has a role to play in all three dimensions. Yet only national labor administration is responsible for the ongoing maintenance and production of working-class consent. This includes seeing to the daily regulation and enforcement of the labor relations regime and meeting the requirements of the evolving contextual parameters that affect the relations — economic, demographic, technological, or political — between labor and capital. For this reason, national labor administration is a malleable vehicle that serves as the institutional core of democratic capitalism in its hegemonic form. It is the organizational nexus within which bourgeois corporate concessions and collective working-class consent are exchanged to sustain the political and economic bases of the regime.

In a country making the transition from authoritarian to democratic capitalist rule, reorientation and reorganization of national labor administration takes on special importance, since it provides concrete proof that the legacy of institutionalized authoritarianism has been eliminated and that the organized working classes are to be reincorporated (or incorporated, as the case may be) as full citizens — that is, as equal collective actors in the political and economic domains of the democratic regime. Given its dual functions (structural and superstructural), national labor administration is one of the primary institutional arenas where the substantive and procedural terms of the hegemonic project underlying the post-authoritarian democratic consolidation process are promoted.

To be sure, many other aspects of the consolidation process are well worth examining — civil-military relations, the role of new political and economic actors and social movements, executive-legislative relations, reform of the judiciary system, the drafting of a constitution, etc. It is equally clear that the importance of national labor administration is directly related to the historical presence of the organized labor movement on the national economic and political scene. In the cases examined here, given the degree to which previous regimes excluded the basic rights of citizens, organized labor constitutes a major actor on all dimensions of the (re)opened sociopolitical contexts of the Southern Cone in the 1980s. In the Southern Cone, national labor administration today plays a critical role in consolidating democracy. As a result, it is a subject worthy of more detailed examination than studies of the transition and consolidation of regimes have devoted to it.

This book is divided into two parts. The first offers a broad discussion of the notions of regime type, regime change, class compromise, and the institutional mechanisms used to achieve such compromise. Particular reference is made to the evolving nature of class relations during regime transitions, the use of neocorporatist versus pluralist modes of interest group mediation, the role of concertative "pacts" as instruments of sectorial negotiation, the historical origins and legacy of labor administration in Latin America, and the relationship of regime type to the organization of the state apparatus in general and to labor administration in particular.

Chapter 1 considers why democratizing class relations is a critical element in the transition from authoritarian to democratic regimes, making particular reference to the impact of different modes of regime change on later efforts to institutionalize a democratic class compromise. Chapter 2 explores the role of the state in promoting and reproducing democratic class compromise, which places the state at the institutional core of the hegemonic system. It then examines the political economy of democratic class compromise, describing the macroeconomic logic and the institutional frameworks deemed conducive to successfully reproducing democratic capitalism.

Chapter 3 describes the basic characteristics of collective labor action under democratic capitalism, showing the strategic postures available to organized labor under this regime type, the collective action problems inherent in working-class organizations, the use of the strike and other suspensions of labor service as instruments of negotiation and sectorial defense, and the structural bases of working-class weakness in capitalist economies. It then analyzes the relationship between regime type and forms of labor incorporation and insertion into the political system, concentrating on the different ways of incorporating interest groups in various kinds of authoritarian and democratic regimes: inclusionary state corporatist, exclusionary state corporatist, societal corporatist, pluralist, and neocorporatist. Finally, it details the relationship between regime type and state organization, arguing that there is an "elective affinity" between specific types of regimes, authoritarian or democratic, and specific forms of state organization, especially as manifested in the structure and functions of core areas of state activity, labor administrations in particular.

Part 2 turns to case studies, offering a historical overview of national labor administrations before reviewing the external and internal dimensions of national labor administrations under the new democratic regimes. Chapter 4 traces the general history and characteristics of national labor administrations in Latin America and the Southern Cone, showing that because of the presence of the state in Latin American labor relations, the state has always played a critical role in institutionalizating class compromise under the new democratic regimes in the Southern Cone. Chapter 5 describes the highly conflictual (and as yet unsuccessful) efforts to institutionalize a democratic class compromise in Argentina, where a combination of the labor movement's political strength, a legacy of Peronist organizational schemes, internal divisions within the current Peronist movement, and the Radical administration's tactical errors, coupled with the inability to stabilize the economy after the authoritarian regime's structural reforms, contributed to an impasse that, if it does not signal the end of attempts to formalize a compromise via concertative or other mechanisms, has certainly delayed that possibility.

In chapter 6 we turn our attention to Brazil, where the process of constitutional reform that ended with the passage of a new Magna Carta in 1988 was one of many interrelated areas in which the labor relations system was reoriented. Here again, despite major advances in overcoming the authoritarian legacy of exclusionary state corporatism and enforced union weakness inherited in 1985, and despite repeated efforts to promote concertative agreements at both the macro- and mesoeconomic levels (i.e. nationally and sectorially), the regime remains unconsolidated. Partisan squabbles, working-class disunity, worsening economic conditions, entrenched authoritarian attitudes, and employer intransigence have all conspired against fully incorporating organized labor into the democratic consolidation process, to say nothing of achieving a durable class compromise.

Chapter 7 examines the case of Uruguay, the exception to the rule in this otherwise bleak landscape, in which the "pacted" nature of the regime transition, coupled with the country's small size, demographic homogeneity, long-term substantive democratic tradition, and history of labor movement militancy provided the conditions for institutionalizing a contingent class compromise that is one of the most important foundations of the new democracy. The Uruguayan case demonstrates that, in addition to other "unique" factors that favored the reincorporation of organized labor into the democratic regime, the preexistence of institutional vehicles for (re)negotiating the material terms of a short-term compromise between organized labor and capital — the Consejos de Salarios established in 1943 and resurrected in 1985 — made possible a quantum leap forward when it came to (re)institutionalizing democratic class relations.

Above and beyond the nature of the party in power (the Colorado Party in Uruguay, the Radicales in Argentina, and the Partido do Movimento Democrático do Brasil [PMDB] in Brazil — all centrist in nature and without strong labor support), this is the variable that best explains the success of Uruguay's labor reincorporation project and the failure of the Argentine and Brazilian projects. Only in Uruguay had conflict resolution among different sectors been institutionalized, based on consensually established procedural mechanisms that all sides could refer to. For this reason, the Uruguayan case study is somewhat longer than the other two.

All the case studies end in 1988, the year before second presidential elections were held in all three countries. The elections of 1989 marked the end of the initial consolidation phase of the new democracies, that is, the end of the immediate post-authoritarian period that saw first attempts at hegemonic projects (if any), the reincorporation of labor, and the institutionalization of class compromise. Given that there occurred a rotation in the executive office in all three countries beginning in 1989, the second phase of this process must receive separate attention. In the interim, I have disaggregated and analyzed the original projects with the purpose of demonstrating how efforts at institutionalization were originally managed in each instance.

The study is state-centered, owing to the primacy of the state apparatus in Latin American labor relations. Recent critics have called for "getting the state back out" of political analysis, but here the alternative seems more sensible. Although the labor movement's problems with collective action, the union's characteristics, and shop-floor politics are all important variables in their own right (and I have attempted to address them where pertinent), all important matters in Latin American labor relations — particularly in post-authoritarian settings like those examined here — remain centered on the state and its policies in the labor field. However *déclassé* or *passé* the state has become as a unit of analysis in certain North American academic circles, in Latin America the realities of labor relations in processes of post-authoritarian democratic consolidation make its study *de rigueur*.

In addition, in focusing on the peak labor organizations rather than on shop-floor or rank-and-file activity, this study recognizes the importance of such organizations in the labor field; the vast majority of workers, even if unionized, do not actively participate in union activities. Hence, although perhaps elitist, agent-centered, and bureaucratic in focus, this approach recognizes the realities of labor movement politics.

Beyond that and the obvious Marxist methodological and theoretical premises (of the neo-Gramscian variety) from which the study embarks, the analysis is quite conventional, examining the major features of the external dimensions (i.e., policies) of national labor administrations (economic, political, and/or social), posing them against the unions' strategic postures, and then relating them to the organizational features, budgets, and personnel that make up the internal dimension of national labor administration in each case. This allows us to get a dialectic and interactive view of attempts to institutionalize the new labor relations systems.

In the conclusion I attempt to draw together theory and case studies in order to demonstrate the importance of national labor administrations as a hegemonic apparatus. I seek to show that in spite of a generalized move away from authoritarian practices, where labor administrations have failed to promote institutional vehicles for achieving class compromise, the process of democratic consolidation remains incomplete or thwarted, while in the lone case where it has succeeded, consolidation has become firmly rooted.

PART ONE

CONCEPTUAL ISSUES

1

CLASS COMPROMISE

AND DEMOCRATIC CONSOLIDATION

IN THE SOUTHERN CONE

THE EMERGENCE AND RESURGENCE of democratic regimes the world over during the last decade have prompted a spate of work detailing differences and similarities between various cases, particularly the conditions and motives for reopening the political arena and the terms and character of the ensuing political competition. Although attention was most recently focused on the demise of Stalinist regimes in Eastern Europe, the literature on transitions from authoritarian rule in southern Europe and Latin America is both sophisticated and extensive.[1] Even so, much less work has been devoted to analyzing the institutional frameworks used to consolidate the nascent democratic systems.[2] This includes the Southern Cone of Latin America, where changes in regime have brought a rebirth of political thought.

The democratic transitions in Argentina, Brazil, and Uruguay provide a unique opportunity to examine on a cross-national basis similar processes of regime change within the same regional and temporal contexts. Although the specifics vary, all three countries witnessed transitions from military-bureaucratic authoritarian regimes to democratic capitalist regimes, and in all three, opposition parties emerged victorious in the electoral competition that preceded the installation of the new regimes. Yet, whereas much attention has been devoted to the frameworks erected by the previous military-bureaucratic regimes to establish and maintain their political domination,[3] little has been written on the institutional networks erected by their elected successors to establish the procedural and substantive bases required to maintain capitalist democracy.[4] That is the object here.

In the Southern Cone, organized labor played a central role in the transition process, constituting the core of a highly mobilized (and previously disenfranchised) mass political movement, which in turn represented a significant portion of the electorate. This book develops a theoretical and methodological framework for examining the organization, role, and strategies of the branch of the state responsible for managing the demands and interests of the organized labor movement under the new democratic regimes of the Southern Cone. National labor administrations in capitalist democracies have institutional responsibilities that make them core hegemonic apparatuses that reproduce bourgeois rule. As the primary agency through which the ideological and structural bases for democratic class compromise between the organized working classes and competing socioeconomic groups are promoted, national labor administration constitutes a crucial actor in any process of democratic capitalist consolidation.[5]

The following analysis distinguishes between *procedural* (i.e., formal) and *substantive* democracy. Procedural democracy is instrumental in that it emphasizes formal party competition and open, competitive elections as the hallmarks of democratic political systems. Substantive democracy operates on three levels to reproduce democratic forms of interaction in society: institutional, societal, and economic.

At an *institutional* level, substantive democracy is reflected in the general organization and specific structure and functions of the state apparatus. There is an ideologically diverse array of competitive — and legally equal — political parties (which may or may not be based on class), and the organization and behavior of collective agents defend and represent the interests of a variety of social groups. The notions of pluralism and polyarchy apply here. Political inclusiveness and competitiveness are guaranteed by substantive arrangements at the institutional level. A combination of procedural rules and institutional frameworks characterize political democracy.

Difficulties in achieving these institutional arrangements are often due to a failure to promote democratic norms, rules, and values at a *societal* level. Substantive democratization involves the inculcation of basic notions of consent, compromise, concession, collective interest, equality, solidarity, individual rights, mutual consideration, egalitarianism, and legitimate exchange in society as a whole. This promotes a general disposition toward negotiated solutions, a (relatively) high degree of political participation and social tolerance, and a broad adherence to the ethical and procedural norms and representative institutional channels that constitute the basic rules and framework of the democratic political "game." This also allows for the organized expansion of civil society and the growth of free expression toward political authorities.

Democratization involves the reforging of collective and individual political identities. The issue is to change socially given (often highly stratified and ascriptive) identities with new political, rationally oriented, autonomous identities unconstrained by socioeconomic status. A dialectical interaction between the political-rational and socio-psychological components of citizen identity is unique to democratic forms of rule.[6] These traits undergird democratic (as opposed to authoritarian) political culture and have a decided impact on post-authoritarian processes of democratic consolidation.

Substantive democracy is also manifest at the *economic* level. It involves a general agreement within society that favors political guarantees for maintaining a minimum standard of living and just compensation for productive labor. Although there is considerable variation on this point, this aspect of democracy is a fundamental component of mature democratic systems.[7]

The degree to which a society has moved toward achieving procedural and substantive democracy on all levels helps distinguish between inclusionary, exclusionary, limited, liberal, and radical democratic political systems.[8]

Those interested in substantive democratization distinguish between "liberal" and "progressive" democratic theory. "Liberal" democratic theory is concerned with preserving individual freedoms and property rights. "Progressive" democratic theory seeks to achieve and reproduce equality in all areas. This implies moving from the macrosystem to the mesosystem, where the internal structures made up of collective agents, political actors, and the state are democratized, and where democratic norms, values, and procedures become integral parts of individual socialization (the micro level). The label *progressive* can therefore be attached to

> any notion of democracy that transcends the protective and defensive notions of liberal political theory [and] is committed to the achievement of societal goals — goals that are established through the process of egalitarian democratic participation and that include the re-distribution, in the name of justice, of society's material resources.[9]

Two broad levels of action are involved in any process of democratization that cuts across the procedural and substantive dimensions. One level encompasses political-institutional conflict, the other civil society.[10] These levels of action correspond to "governed democracy" (representative institutions) and "governing democracy" (popular democracy).[11] Progress on each level can proceed simultaneously or sequentially in either direction; rather than being completely distinct spheres, the two overlap to a considerable degree.

This overlap is most evident at the level of institutional democratization, where the state and organized segments of civil society undergo changes that promote the consolidation of democratic rules and practices in each sector. These levels of action should be complementary and mutually reinforcing: political-institutional democratization without societal democratization is merely form without (social) substance, while societal democratization without political-institutional democratization lacks representative channels for the exercise of political voice. This can lead to a polarization of positions, more radical strategic postures on the part of competing social groups, zero-sum sectorial competition, and eventually, a regime crisis. Institutional democratization is therefore crucial for democratic consolidation, since it is here that the expanded range of demands voiced by civil society are institutionally condensed and equitably mediated.

With a democratic groundswell at the social level, which promotes the horizontal expansion of social networks, dominant and subordinate groups engage in a broad-based — if not egalitarian — vertical dialogue that defines the degree of consent, concession, compromise, and exchange in the relationship between democratic representatives, individual constituents, and the collective agents of competing social groups.[12] This dialogue occurs in an institutional space where the democratic state mediates the demands of competing groups while protecting the basic interests of all. The state's ability to neutrally "hear" the demands of competing social groups broadens its range of democratic activity and increases the ability of political actors to appreciate democratic values and norms as a basis for interaction.

Despite its limitations, procedural democracy can open the door to more substantive types of change. This can be considered a top-down process of redemocratization (or a "transition from above"), in which adherence to procedure clears the way for institutionalizing democratic practices that in turn promote the absorption of democratic values and rules throughout society. In many cases, this form of redemocratization is the designated, if not the natural, successor of authoritarian regimes that have undergone a process of liberalization[13] leading to a political opening (*apertura politíca*).[14]

The departure of the regime that governed Brazil from 1964 to 1985 provides an excellent example of liberalization leading to procedural redemocratization. Having achieved their primary objectives of economic growth and eradication of subversives by 1973, leaders of the Brazilian military-bureaucratic regime embarked on a lengthy period of controlled liberalization that involved a gradual political distension (*distensaõ*) and decompression (*descompressaõ*), followed by an incremental political opening (*abertura*) based on piecemeal procedural concessions. It was only after this announced process of liberalization was well under way (approximately 1979) that broad sectors of civil society began to react and attempt to accelerate the pace of *abertura*.

The interplay between the dynamics of the regime and of society made the transition process extremely uncertain, and resulted in a series of stops and starts tied to strategy reversals, legal maneuvers, and changes in tactical direction on both sides. Owing to these dynamics, the *project* of liberalization envisioned by the authoritarian elite did not coincide with the actual *process* of liberalization. It was nonetheless far closer to what ultimately did occur than any alternative project envisioned by the opposition.

Despite internal divisions and external pressures, the authoritarian elite was generally able to control the outcome of political conflicts so as to preserve its basic agenda, if not its timetable, for transition.[15] Regime transitions of this sort can be seen as fluid political bargains between the authoritarian elite and opposition forces in which the elite holds a dominant (albeit eroding) position until the formal transfer of power.[16]

Top-down democratization can be contrasted with a bottom-up process in which, before the authoritarian regime is formally committed to a transition (though it may have already experienced serious contradictions that exposed the inherent fragility of the dominant coalition), civil society mobilizes and expands the range of its demands while moving to secure a voice in political decision making. Broadly evident in the altered tenor of interpersonal discourse,[17] this form of democratization is politically manifested in the reforging of collective identities and in the formal setting forth, after a period of enforced silence, of a broad range of sectorial demands and interests against those of competing groups, addressed to the principal repository of political power, the state.

Such forms of democratic transition germinate in the political vacuum created by authoritarian collapse or, to a lesser degree, by the process of voluntary withdrawal without gradual or incremental liberalization. A classic recipe for authoritarian collapse is the convergence of internal and external pressures, as Argentina's Proceso de Reorganizacíon Nacional painfully discovered in the Malvinas Islands War of 1982.

In a similar vein, the overwhelmingly negative appraisal of its rule that emerged during the constitutional plebiscite staged in 1980 forced the Uruguayan military-bureaucratic regime to estab-

lish a timetable for prompt democratic elections without first passing through a controlled and protracted period of liberalization.
More restrained than the process resulting from authoritarian collapse, such a transition nevertheless provides an excellent environment for the rapid generation of a substantive democratic
groundswell within civil society. Here, liberalization and democratization occur almost simultaneously, as part of an ongoing
process of formal and substantive political expansion.

In the Southern Cone, much of the substantive move toward
democratic consolidation occurred after the procedural transfer of
political power. In the Brazilian case of liberalization that led to
political opening and procedural democracy, the nature and continued strength of authoritarian actors (particularly the armed
forces) allowed them to exercise dominance throughout the period
of transition and well into the initial phase of consolidation.

Argentina's authoritarian collapse and the Uruguayan military
withdrawal without liberalization left little time to establish democratic institutions prior to the formal transfer of power, despite the
"bottom-up" nature of that transfer.[18] *Per ende*, the primary task of
the new democratic authorities in the Southern Cone was to establish the institutional bases required for democratic consolidation.

Whatever the exact direction and precise contours of the initial
process of democratic transition, a fundamental issue to be
addressed early in the consolidation process is how to overcome
the legacy of authoritarianism. More than just a bad memory, displaced authoritarian regimes leave normative, institutional, and
structural obstacles that present formidable challenges to democratic consolidation. Beyond the persistence of nondemocratic
groups, which actively or passively conspire against the democratic process,[19] institutional vestiges remain in the organization of
the state apparatus and bureaucratic procedures. For example, in
Brazil and Chile, the military's deep penetration into all aspects of
institutional life, from the centralized administrative apparatus to
the educational system, provincial governments, and corporate
boards, guaranteed its presence in political life long after *os gen-
erais* and Pinochet formally left the scene.[20]

The negative effects of authoritarian rule are felt in the modes of interaction and behavioral patterns governing collective interests, political parties, and interpersonal relations. Even where a change to a democratic regime has occurred, it is often difficult to convince citizens that the state embodies and defends the national interest, rather than that of dominant social groups. If zero-sum and maximalist attitudes and strategies persist and dominate in personal discourse and social groups, then compromise and cooperation at a various levels is difficult if not impossible to attain. By itself, no procedural change can alter this.

It is especially difficult to overcome the ethical contradictions involved in "resolving" military violations of human rights, economic misdeeds, and outright corruption under the authoritarian regimes. Throughout the Southern Cone, de facto or even de jure amnesty was granted by the democratic governments to most of those implicated in the atrocities of the military regimes.[21]

Democratic culture refers to the pre-authoritarian presence of democratic practices at the procedural and substantive levels. Pre-authoritarian experiences with substantive democracy give intrinsic rather than instrumental weight to the procedural restoration, as the electoral rite of passage constitutes a form of "secular communion" on the part of civil society that reaffirms the link with the democratic past.[22] Uruguay and Chile might serve as examples of democratic cultures.[23] Beyond the traits mentioned above, a democratic culture can be measured by the degree to which its party system is ideologically representative and competitive — for example, do parties alternate in controlling the executive branch? — the extent to which its collective agents articulate a broad range of social interests, and the degree to which such agents are internally governed by democratic procedures, enjoy procedural equality in addressing the state, and constitute horizontal networks with ties to political parties and other social groups. A democratic culture also includes military subordination to civilian authority, general respect for the rule of law, institutionalized rights of due process, legal equality, and freedom from arbitrary infringements of individual rights.

Authoritarian tradition or *vestiges* refer to the degree to which authoritarian modes of intercourse are ingrained in the fabric of society. This includes the military's independence from civilian control, the arbitrary exercise of power, position, or authority based on ascriptive rationales at any social level, disregard for the rule of equality before the law and procedural rights, the reproduction of inequalities based on economic status, race, ethnicity, language, religion, gender, marital status, sexual preference, or physical or psychological disability, and the predominance of hierarchical modes of social discourse at all levels — family, neighborhood, town, etc. Countries such as Argentina and Brazil are confronted by authoritarianism as a deeply rooted political-cultural tradition. There is little or no substantive democratic ethos to which they can return that can complement and reinforce the move to establish institutional bases for democratic consolidation.

The impact of authoritarian legacies is acutely felt in the state apparatus and in the representation of sectorial interests, particularly in their relations with one another. Favored groups are given privileged access to the authoritarian state, while excluded groups are forcibly suppressed. The state does not mediate or arbitrate (save among certain favored groups) so much as it dictates or mandates (either legally or extralegally) the boundaries of "proper" interaction permissible for social actors. Recent and traditional patterns of state intervention in the field of labor relations in the Southern Cone have borne witness to this fact.

The newly democratic state is bureaucratically unprepared for the functional requirements brought about by the change in regime. This is seen in the immediate post-authoritarian context, where, stripped of its ability to resort to force, "the state lacks effective patterns and capabilities for perceiving, evaluating, and solving the principal questions of society and politics. The characteristics of the social transmitters and the receptor state contribute to this deficit."[24] Promoting institutional channels for transmitting the interests of social groups to *and* within the state, so that social conflicts can be incorporated, regulated, and mediated, is therefore central to democratic consolidation.

An entrenched authoritarian legacy undermines efforts at democratic consolidation long before a regression to authoritarianism begins. Countries where the legacy of authoritarianism is strong at all levels of society, and where nonpluralist (most often state-corporatist) forms of interest group administration have historically prevailed, have "societal equations" that run counter to substantive democratization.[25] This is especially true where procedural democracy followed a top-down liberalization process, or was the product of horizontal agreements among elites. These scenarios are not so much processes of redemocratization as procedural restorations, political-military stalemates, or a continuation of established cycles of elitist control.[26] Thus, democracy may be "liberated" by the procedural transition, but its full achievement is "blocked" by legacies inherited from pre-authoritarian and authoritarian periods.[27]

Although the degree of conservative influence and the threat of regression to authoritarianism depend on the specific circumstances of transition in each case, such influences and threats constitute relatively fixed institutional barriers to short-term substantive democratization. In fact, the combination of top-down liberalization, gradualist transition, elite pact making, corporatist institutions, authoritarian legacies, the need for economic "orthodoxy," initial caution on the part of the government, and the prior lack of democratic socialization in civil society strongly conspires against the short- to medium-term success of democratic consolidation at any level.[28]

Rough calculations of the "societal equation" in the post-authoritarian period allow us to estimate the possibilities of democratic consolidation. If consolidation of procedurally democratic institutions outstrips the inculcation of democratic values and mores at the societal level, the democratic "bias" in civil society will remain weaker than the elitist-corporatist bias and will encourage the formation of a "hollow" democracy based on limited pluralist or corporatist frameworks involving elitist institutions. Such formal democracy without substantive institutional foundations and with limited social substance is a type of rule familiar to many Latin Americans.

Where democratic values outweigh elitist, corporatist, and authoritarian values in civil society, or where they precede or accompany institutional consolidation, progress beyond hollow institutional arrangements can be made.[29] This requires the active participation of grassroots organizations as counterhegemonic agents that promote social support for democratized social relations in general and for institutionalized consensual relations among the state, labor, and capitalist agents in particular.

These factors affect the range of strategic choices available to social and political actors, choices that may or may not dispose them to promote democracy rather than their own interests. Their interaction is strongly influenced by a broad array of conjunctural and structural factors, including the international economic environment, ideological and/or military climate, internal motives and conditions that prompted the reopening of the political arena, the terms and character of political competition, and the actors' organization and resources. Democratic consolidation therefore hinges on a sequence of conflicts over procedural and substantive issues lacking clearly established rules. Once an elected government is in place, sectorial conflicts develop over the rules and guarantees regulating economic and political conflict.[30]

The form of regime change influences the direction of democratic consolidation. In top-down processes of authoritarian liberalization leading to procedural (re)democratization, the consolidation of a democratic regime is often sequential. Gradual institutionalization of procedural democracy (a process ending in open and competitive elections at significant levels and solidified by the peaceful rotation in and out of power of an opposition party) is followed by substantive democratization at the institutional, social, and economic levels.

In the Southern Cone, limitations on substantive change are reinforced by the remedial logic of foreign and domestic capitalists in a context of heavy debt and fiscal austerity inherited from the authoritarian regimes. The structural shifts induced in the national economies by the military-bureaucratic regimes had strengthened these capitalists while simultaneously weakening organized labor's position in the labor market. Since most national investments are channeled through these capitalist groups, democratic governments must be especially concerned with guaranteeing the sociopolitical conditions they demand in order to continue to invest.

This militates against adopting the type of redistribution strategies usually needed to secure the consent of subordinate groups (the so-called Keynesian compromise). Instead, Southern Cone democracies have adopted conservative economic and political strategies that accommodate the demands of the authoritarian elite and their major allies, which has impeded progress in making the socioeconomic reforms required to consolidate substantive democracy.

Post-authoritarian democratic consolidation thus entails a two-phase transformation at the institutional level. First, there is a purgative phase in which the vestiges of authoritarianism are removed from institutional life, both public and private. This opens institutional spaces within which democratic modes of interaction can be promoted throughout society. Attempts to install concertative mechanisms designed to secure economic and political agreements among key social groups are part of this process and will be a major focus of attention here.

The essence of consolidating modern democratic capitalist regimes, then, lies in institutionalizing the democracy of partial regimes.[31] These are the functionally or legally limited interactive networks that constitute the institutional bases of democratic systems. Although analytically distinct, together they comprise the foundation of the national regime. Democratic consolidation thus involves the simultaneous or sequential erection of separate partial regimes into *institutional domains* that encompass state and civil society: the constitutional, clientelist, concertative, electoral, representative, and pressure-group partial regimes. These domains cut across the substantive dimensions of a democracy, already outlined.

Varying in specific content and form, four institutional *complexes* generally mediate the relations of social and political actors: legislative assemblies, political parties, interest groups, and admin-

istrative agencies. The degree to which these relations are constitu-
tionalized also varies. Democratic regime consolidation begins
when consensual rules are accepted and specified for all the partial
regimes that comprise the national political regime. Until then,
regime change is incomplete, locked into what can best be
described as a transitional or "foundational moment."[32]

Each partial regime is made up of *microregimes* regulating sectorial exchanges in core functional areas such as civil-military relations, executive-legislative relations, the political party system, the
labor relations system, interest group administration, etc.

Despite variations, a procedural-institutional minimum — that
is, the minimum rules and institutional factors needed to reproduce political democracy — characterizes all successful cases of
democratic consolidation. Subordination of the armed forces to
civilian authority, competitive electoral schemes within and
between political, economic, and social agents, and equal access to
the state apparatus are some of the institutional factors needed to
reproduce democratic capitalist regimes successfully. This generates the basic threshold of institutionally reproduced sectorial consent and the guarantees underlying a regime's stability and continued existence, giving social substance and legitimacy to otherwise
hollow institutions and procedural mechanisms.[33]

This points to a fundamental moment in the move to democratic
capitalist consolidation. Except where labor-based parties are
important political agents, or where the vacuum produced by the
collapse of authoritarianism leads to a quick electoral competition
for working-class votes on the part of non–labor-based parties,
working-class support is most often sought as a last resort during
the transition from authoritarian to democratic capitalism. It is
rather the consent of the bourgeoisie that is most energetically culti-
vated during the initial transition phase. And yet, for long-term
democratic consolidation, it is working-class consent that must be
secured and reproduced.

The voluntary exchange of consent and concession between
capitalists and labor is what differentiates democratic from
authoritarian capitalism. Under democratic capitalism, collective

action involving the state, labor, and capital institutionalizes the exchange of sectorial consent required for systemic reproduction. Under authoritarian capitalism, collective action is stifled by the state, and sectorial consent is pursued partially if at all.

With regard to the dynamics of collective action implied in democratic consolidation, one fundamental partial regime encompasses the collective action made up of the strategic interaction between the state, labor, and capital, namely, the labor relations partial regime, with its microfacets or components: state-labor, state-capital, and labor-capital interaction. The jurisdiction and responsibilities of the state outlined in the constitutional partial regime promote its formal articulation with all other partial regimes, including the labor relations system, thereby placing the state at the center of efforts to democratize class relations in the post-authoritarian context.

The strategic interaction between the state, labor, and capital under democratic capitalism is fueled by a triple logic of collective action. These are: the relation between the state and labor, between the state and capital, and between labor and capital independent of the state. The need to reproduce the ideological and material bases of capitalist and working-class consent (the dual consent unique to democratic capitalist systems) promotes this logic, as each actor has specific objectives it pursues with regard to the others. What labor wants from the state in terms of public goods it cannot get from capital; what the state wants from capital in terms of investment it cannot get from labor; and so on. The overall need for systemic reproduction leads to overlapping and complementary strategies of accommodation based on a belief in compromise and mutually beneficial exchanges resulting in second-best choices for all sides.

Democratic capitalist reproduction consequently rests on the outcome of an evolving triple logic of collective action within a specific partial regime, based on the need to secure dual contingent consent from a particular combination of economic and political organizations. This not only makes the state the most important actor in the democratic capitalist system (as a principal in two-thirds of the tripartite interactions and as an administrator of the rules governing the remaining third), but also promotes strategies of economic and political moderation on the part of the state and sectorial agents so that they will reach a mutually satisfactory compromise. This is the core of the hegemonic system.

Democratic class compromise reflects the convergence of second-best choices available to capitalists and workers. Capitalists forgo superexploitation and political authoritarianism; workers forgo economic and political militancy that would threaten the capitalist parameters of society. Institutionalized uncertainty in the form of regular elections and other procedural measures guarantee competitive access to government authority. In the economic sphere, a series of institutional arrangements also provides a framework in which the convergence of second-best choices, calculated in terms of material self-interest, can occur.

The risks inherent in adopting best-choice strategies encourage the mutual adoption of second-best options. The risks involved in adopting second-best strategies force regular renegotiation of the terms of the compromise at both the economic and political levels. D. Rostow quotes Bryce to the effect that

> democracy, like any collective human action, is likely to stem from a large variety of mixed motives — [hence] the democratic content of [a] decision may be incidental to other substantive issues. [Moreover,] in so far as it is a genuine compromise it will seem second-best to all major parties involved — it certainly will not represent any agreement on fundamentals. . . . Even on procedures there are likely to be continuing differences of preference.[34]

This is, in effect, a process of compromise and competition based on contingent consent.[35]

If class compromise under conditions of capitalist democracy is to be achieved and maintained, it must rest on institutional foundations that reproduce sectorial agreements on the contingent outcome of political and economic conflicts.[36] Fundamental differences between authoritarian and democratic capitalist regimes are best observed in their respective institutional bases and strategic approaches to problems of collective action.

In the post-authoritarian Southern Cone, the labor movements in question were moving out of situations of weakness — both structural and political — imposed by authoritarianism and toward the stronger exercise of their expanded citizenship rights at both the individual and collective levels. Similarly, the state was moving from a reproductive function befitting a more "naked" type of capitalism toward a more mediatory, redistributive, and conciliatory role better oriented to achieving democratic class relations.

Add to this the varying responses of capital and the intensity of social discourse during the immediate post-authoritarian period, and it becomes clear why democratic institutionalization, especially as it affects the organization and functions of the state apparatus and the collective agents of capital and labor, has provided an arena in which long-suppressed social conflicts are brought to the fore and confronted. The post-authoritarian regime is "a State marked by a struggle that, even under Przeworski's class compromise, attempts to shape the way the compromise is carried out."[37]

While modern democratic transitions require horizontal agreements between political and economic elites, democratic consolidation requires that institutionalized guarantees be extended through the state apparatus to the collective agents of dominant *and* subordinate groups, especially capitalists and organized labor, in order to reproduce the socioeconomic system in consensual fashion (the vertical dimension). Having demonstrated the limits of rule by force, post-authoritarian states such as those of the Southern Cone have an increased appreciation for the intrinsic value of capitalism's "best political shell."[38]

Democratic capitalism is based on a vertical class compromise between socioeconomic groups represented by collective agents that include the state (either as a partner or mediator), as opposed to a horizontal politico-economic compromise with sectorial elites or other dominant social groups. Vertical compromises are formal exchanges of sectorial consent and concession that establish the material and political conditions for maintaining the democratic regime. Although horizontal "pacts" among elites are often necessary for a successful process of democratic transition, achieving an institutionalized form of vertical compromise between class agents is essential for consolidating substantive democracy. Thus the interest in the use of concertative vehicles for securing the incorporation of different sectors.[39]

Institutionalized vertical agreements negotiated between capitalists, democratic authorities (through the state apparatus), and the principal agents of subordinate groups, especially organized labor — the so-called vehicles of consent — are what set democratic capitalism apart from other capitalist regimes. The logic involved in simultaneously securing capitalists' and workers' consent to combine political democracy and capitalism gives a distinctive character to the state and to the types of collective action that characterize the partial regimes revolving around its various branches, including national labor administration. The pursuit of "dual" consent, in other words, shapes the modalities of democratic state action as well as the state's organization.

In South America, the only democracies to survive the authoritarian tides of the 1960s and 1970s were the "pacted" democracies of Colombia and Venezuela. Elite, horizontal pacts relating to the terms for restoring rule by election were paralleled in both countries by deeper, vertical compromises with collective agents of subordinate groups, especially organized labor. The "pact sequence" made up of the Avenamiento Patronal-Obrera, the Pacto de Pruto Fijo, and the Programa Mínimo during the transition and early consolidation of democracy in Venezuela from 1958 to 1962 provides the clearest example of the use and incremental deepening of concertative agreements. The horizontal pacts served as vehicles for procedural transition, while the vertical pact has been, until recently, a more fluid and ongoing (via renegotiation) institutional vehicle for substantive consolidation.[40]

The infrequent use of explicit and formal agreements as transitional devices proves the dangers inherent in the process of regime transition. The lack of agreed-upon rules of the game and the related risks during the transition period make secret, informal, and nonbinding agreements between political leaders attractive. This is because collective agents can renegotiate the terms of these agreements based on shifting assessments of the dynamics at play at different moments in the transition.

Collective actors can simultaneously negotiate on several fronts with different agents, in order to evaluate possibilities and rank tactical and substantive objectives that best serve their requirements for expediency and their long-term goals.[41] Since the state remains under the control of the outgoing authoritarian elite, it can neither mediate nor enforce sectorial agreements. As a result, pacts during this period are highly fluid in nature and subject to a wide range of sectorial interpretations, which adds to the uncertainties involved in each stage of the transition.

The survival of "pacted" democratic regimes in late twentieth-century Latin America depends, in the short to medium term, on their ability to transform initial elite, horizontal pacts into an institutionally founded, vertical class compromise. Such survival over the long term depends on the relative depth and flexibility of the compromise.[42] Elite agreements require ratification by constituents if they are to be substantively democratic, and the number of ratification sites, where citizens express their political will, has to be expanded as well. As Bobbio notes, "If we want to develop an index of democratic development, this can no longer be the number of people who have voting rights, but also the number of sites, distinct from the political sphere, in which the right to vote is exercised."[43]

The constituents' stamp of approval at various ratification sites — firms, in the case of business associations, the shop floor or assembly line in the case of unions, registered primaries or conventions in the case of political parties, and various sites established by other interest groups, social movements, and the like — gives depth to elite agreements. Nationally aggregated, horizontal agreements between political elites or interest group leaders must therefore be encompassing and democratically ratifiable by their respective constituencies if they are to be mutually binding. Only in this measure can depth, verticality, and hence substance in sectorial agreements be achieved. A framework has to be developed in which this process of transformation (or deepening) can occur.

Hence the need for institutional bases for democratic consolidation.

The organization and function of specific branches of the democratic state reflect an institutional effort to lessen the uncertainty about the transition among both workers and capitalists. That is,

> institutional arrangements are crucial to determine the actual level of risk involved. Corporatist arrangements are designed specifically to increase certainty beyond the particular collective agreement or a particular election: they constitute a form of self-commitment of the parties to adhere to some agreed compromise independently of the short-term fluctuations of both economic conditions and of popular will as expressed in elections.[44]

Obviously, this type of corporatist arrangement would have to be inclusionary and societal (or neocorporatist, as the European literature calls it), since exclusionary or strictly state-corporatist arrangements do not reflect a democratic class compromise.

The scenario of democratic transition and consolidation is strongly influenced by the strategies adopted by the labor movement and by its historical location in the political system, which, though varying widely in the cases studied here, uniformly makes sectorial dialogue more acute in all three cases. Previous modes of interest group administration, historical orientation, strategic location, political and economic objectives, ideological unity, organizational structure, and resources combine to form the internal boundaries that define labor's role in and strategic approach toward the move to secure stable institutional bases for the consolidation of substantive democracy.

In countries that have no democratic culture or in which class lines are clearly demarcated, the terms of a class compromise must be made explicit and are codified in laws and other institutional measures enforced by the legally autonomous state. The fluid nature of economic and social factors forces regular renegotiation of the terms.

The successful reproduction of socioeconomic and political

agreements within these institutional boundaries may eventually lead to a "spontaneous" class compromise based "on outcomes that emerge from autonomous choices of strategies and which are self-enforcing under the existing institutional arrangements."[45] This requires a specific organization of the state as the mechanism in which the structural and superstructural bases of class compromise are negotiated, agreed upon, and neutrally enforced in the face of market and political uncertainties.

Under democratic regimes the state apparatus is institutionally aligned in favor of procedural equality and negotiated compromises. That alignment promotes a more equitable distribution of choices and costs to political and economic agents, thereby reproducing (and readjusting) the hegemonic compromise underpinning the regime. This procedurally neutral state position highlights the importance of institutions as vehicles of political and economic reproduction, and their particular significance in processes of democratic consolidation in the wake of the peaceful withdrawal of the authoritarian regime.

Democratic consolidation, as an interactive process, can be considered in terms of game theory, especially regarding issues of concertation and collective action. The consolidation of the democratic regime cuts across the lines dividing the nation, partial regimes, and microregimes, and involves an interlocking hierarchy of multiple-actor, nested games. These games are iterative or extensive-form because payouts may or may not change over time as a result of interaction; they are also asymmetrical, both in terms of different payoff structures and the levels of the actors' resources and information.[46]

One-shot interaction between two actors deprived of critical information (the classic prisoner's dilemma game, PD) may characterize the initial rule-making negotiations or "foundational moment" of democratic regimes, or specific microregime games (civil-military or labor-capital relations, for example) at specific times. But in most cases social games are multiple (N) actor and iterative (or extensive-form) in nature. The "shadow of the future," or the consequences of present interaction, weigh heavily on all actors' strategic calculus. Moreover, regime change differs from regime consolidation precisely in that sectorial choices are so variable, actor positions so fluid, and the range of outcomes so indeterminate. The transition "game" is never completely stabilized. The establishment of consensual rules governing the competition over substantive objectives marks the passage from regime transition to regime consolidation. In the end, the adoption of consensual rules governing sectorial competition among all partial regimes and encompassing all substantive dimensions (with attendant institutional guarantees and sanctions) characterizes successful democratic consolidation.

Developing consensual mechanisms that promote forms of strategic interaction leading to negotiated substantive agreements lies at the heart of democratic regime consolidation. The process of institutionalization regulates and reproduces stable, symmetrical sectorial competition throughout an interlocking hierarchy of extensive-form, multiple-actor, nested games. These games compromise the partial and microregime network that is the foundation of the new national political regime. Institutional boundaries stabilize each partial regime's nested game and the overall national democratic game, and encourage strategies of moderation among collective agents. In turn, interaction on these grounds stabilizes the game and eventually consolidates the regime at all levels.[47]

Modern labor relations in the Southern Cone have already been viewed in terms of informal game theory, specifically as a two-actor prisoner's dilemma game of incomplete information, asymmetrical costs and benefits, and other coordination problems that make zero-sum free-riding or defection strategies the mutually preferred sectorial option.[48] If we consider this strategic interaction problem as a core element of democratic consolidation, it points to the difficulties of achieving a vertical class compromise that is institutionally reaffirmed and guaranteed.

Notwithstanding current obstacles facing attempts to produce formal models of asymmetrical, extensive-form, multiple-actor, nested games, we can conceptualize in abstract (or better perhaps, metaphorical) terms the process of democratic consolidation along such lines. The point here is not to develop a formal model. Instead, this book focuses on examining issues of strategic choice and sectorial interaction that constitute the essence of democratic consolidation games.

Whatever its initial phase, the full achievement of democracy requires substantive change at the institutional level. Establishing the institutional bases of class compromise is crucial for the consolidation of democratic capitalist regimes. The construction of the partial regime network encompassing the political, legal, and organizational bases underlying societal and economic democracy is the subject of the following chapters.

2

THE POLITICAL ECONOMY
AND INSTITUTIONAL BASES OF
DEMOCRATIC CLASS RELATIONS

IN DEMOCRATIC CAPITALIST SOCIETIES the state acts as an institutional mediator and provides the organizational guarantees and framework within which the structural bases of class compromise are negotiated, despite the fact that both the state and society as a whole are structurally dependent on capital.[1] Although its importance in the overall reproduction of capitalism is obvious, the state must remain relatively independent from specific capitalist factions. Being relatively autonomous, the democratic state can constrain capitalist choices by, for example, taxing capitalist consumption for redistributive purposes while offering investment incentives that encourage increased productivity.[2] By doing so, it can secure the working class's ongoing consent to capitalist rule. For this reason, the state, and the range of choices it presents to capital *and* labor, constitute the core of the hegemonic system.

It should be clear that we are considering democratic class compromise and the role of the state in its reproduction in ideal terms. The degree to which either approximates the ideal in practice is often quite low and varies a great deal, in any event. This is particularly so in the Southern Cone, as case studies will demonstrate. Nonetheless, all democratic capitalist regimes with hegemonic aspirations — that is, all those that wish to consolidate and reproduce themselves over the long term — must attempt to move toward this ideal.

Bourgeois democracies remain class-based societies and states because the material benefit of everyone depends on the private investment decisions of capitalists. Since the ultimate mission of the democratic capitalist state is to ensure systemic reproduction at all levels, that state also functions to reproduce capitalism. In that sense, it remains a class state, though states differ in the degree to which they follow the dictates of dominant class interests. Institutionally, it frames the range of choices available to both labor and capital to assure the harmonious reproduction of consent to capitalist forms of economic and political domination. In essence, then, the difference between authoritarian and democratic capitalism is a difference more of degree — of choice, repression, exploitation, and the instrumental use of the state — than of substance.

The state's critical role lies in its ability to promote both the structural *and* the superstructural conditions for the reproduction of democratic capitalism qua hegemonic system.

> The indeterminacy of struggles to realize short-term material interests is the condition for hegemony, since it leads to the organization of wage earners as participants in the struggles over distribution and allows their interests to be realized within some limits. At the same time, capitalist democracy reduces class struggles to struggles over the realization of immediate interests, and generates struggles over those immediate interests.[3]

Yet capitalist hegemony also has ideological bases. This requires that attention be

> focused on the capitalist state as distinct from the capitalist class. The political class consciousness of capitalists manifests itself through a hegemonic system in which the "dominant group is coordinated concretely with the general interests of the subordinate groups." . . . As important as material conditions are as a basis for hegemony, political and ideological conditions are even more important. The hegemonic system is political in that it uses the state apparatus as its central organ. Political class consciousness is the basic underpinning of the hegemonic system, and it coexists with the corporate economic interest that propels the economic machine of the capitalist system.[4]

This form of rule demands that "account be taken of the interests and tendencies of the groups over which hegemony is to be exercised, and that a certain balance or compromise be formed — in other words, that the leading groups should make sacrifices of an economic-corporative kind."[5] At a minimum, it implies recognition of the legitimacy of the interests of subordinate groups, and the incorporation of their collective agents (as subordinate "partners") in the political and economic decision-making processes. The ability to organize in defense of these commodified sectorial interests, and to realize them through nonviolent forms of conflict (elections, collective bargaining, etc.), is regulated by the state.

The dual levels at which hegemony is exercised and reproduced — ideological and material — require an institutional core for the game of sectorial coordination that frames democratic forms of strategic interaction. That core, the vehicle for systemic reproduction, is the state apparatus.

The stability of democratic capitalist regimes depends on how the social accumulation regime and the political regime are articulated over time. Because the fluidity of economic and political factors ensures that there is no "natural" articulation between the two spheres, the state apparatus serves as an institutional bridge that responds to evolving structural and superstructural conditions to ensure the basic conditions of hegemonic reproduction.[6]

Politically, it does so by giving the working masses and their collective agents institutional access, both as citizens and as a class, to government decision-making spheres. Economically, it does so by providing an institutional framework in which sectorial negotiations can occur, and by using public policy to redistribute the social costs of production.

For these reasons, the state mediates between the interests of dominant groups and those of subordinate groups in democratic capitalist societies. In this sense, "the state is an instrument — a provider of economic resources to reproduce the material bases of capitalism in such a way as to assure labor's continued assent to profit."[7]

Democratic class compromise is a product of institutionalized strategic interaction between the state, labor, and capital. "The logic of a tripartite coalition reflects the basic economic need for the state to reinforce the bases of class compromise through public policies. . . . State involvement through public policies is a political-economic strategy to increase the material interests of both labor and capital . . . [because] the consent of both labor and capital is necessary in order to achieve a system of exchange"[8] that is the basis of the hegemonic system.

Institutionally, this means more than universal franchise and parliamentarism. Parliamentary and party-based forms of representation, which formally disassociate state and class, are supplemented by (often corporatist) forms of representation that are explicitly class-based and arise directly out of the social division of labor.[9] This is particularly true for countries with extensive state intervention in the economy and relatively high labor mobilization, as is the case with the three countries under scrutiny here.

Efforts to achieve hegemony extend directly into the workplace, where the more "naked" or authoritarian nature of capitalist domination under Taylorist production has gradually been replaced by more autonomous work schemes that mask exploitation while simultaneously reinforcing workers' ideological consent to capitalist relations of production. Worker participation and codetermination schemes replace quantitative notions of direct capitalist control of production with qualitative notions of "circumscribed autonomy" for labor in the workplace. This both blurs the distinction between capitalist control and labor control and increases productivity.[10]

States reproduce capitalist hegemonic projects both at the point of production and in the political marketplace. Specific branches of the state apparatus handle the day-to-day details of class compromises — or at least of democratic class relations. Other branches shape the broader parameters governing the exchange of working-class consent and capitalist concession.

Since the accumulation of capital is required for economic stability, under democratic capitalism workers consent to the perpetuation of profit (surplus value) in exchange for improvements in their material welfare. Organized and represented by unions, they collectively recognize that the current material condition of all groups is derived from past profit and that future wages and material standards therefore depend on current profits — or more precisely, on the rate of (re)investment of profits. Wages are consequently tied to productivity, since this brings the profit from which (re)investment is derived. For workers, the firm's current profits are therefore a form of delegated investment, since workers are the ultimate producers.

The issue for organized labor is not which economic variable is independent and which is dependent, but rather what current rate of investment provides the optimal economic base for reproducing the workers' consent. A stable rate of investment over time ensures the material conditions for achieving and maintaining a class compromise. Individual rank-and-file members may prefer high immediate payout rates (in the form of wage increases), but the long-term material well-being of the organized working classes depends on the rate of investment, not on current wages. Nonrevolutionary unionism is acutely aware of this fact.

From the workers' standpoint, turning profits into wages is a doubly tenuous proposition. This is because, first, wage bargains are struck before prices are fixed (unless prices are fixed by government decree). This means that wage increases can be translated into price increases without affecting the overall rate of investment or the real wage, simultaneously contributing to the inflationary spiral. Second, such agreements do not guarantee a steady rate of savings and (re)investment conducive to improvements in long-term productivity (and hence material standards of living).

Wages — and the negotiating strategies of unions — only become significant once prices are fixed (either by market competition or by government fiat). Capitalists will thus always prefer to establish wage rates before setting prices and making investment decisions.

Investment decisions should not be left solely to capitalists. Organized labor has a more consistent interest in maintaining sectorial (re)investment levels because, unlike capital (which can be transferred elsewhere, either to other productive activities or abroad), union members have their livelihood at stake when sectorial investment rates are determined. Hence, the working classes need a strong, if not an equal, voice in such decisions, and the democratic state must provide the framework within which that can occur.[11]

For their part, capitalists require some measure of certainty and predictability before they will commit themselves to medium- to long-term investment, especially in infrastructure and research, which require large capital outlays. A few mavericks aside, capitalists are notoriously averse to risk. The need for relative certainty on the part of capitalists is not purely economic: social and political considerations strongly influence investment strategies.

Economic, political, or social uncertainty pushes capitalists toward disinvestment, capital flight, and speculation. Hence, the state must promote the socioeconomic and political guarantees required for investment by institutionalizing class relations in both the economic market (the labor relations system) and the political market (the political party system). In other words, the state must codify the rules of the labor relations partial-regime game.

By institutionally framing the range of sectorial choices, the state must overcome a basic contradiction. In modern capitalist societies, corporate controlling groups (i.e., those who make the strategic decisions of firms) prefer high rates of savings from profit, but members of noncontrolling groups (individual shareholders and lower managers, plus associated members of the middle and lower bourgeoisie and working classes) prefer a high payout rate that allows them to be consumers, thereby maintaining the demand levels that ensure continued economic expansion.[12]

If the state were indifferent toward high individual payout rates (dividend gains for shareholders and wage increases for workers), it would have an adverse impact on corporate savings rates, jeopardizing the cycle of accumulation that forms the basis for future economic and social stability. This implies political problems, which the democratic capitalist state has a primary responsibility to avoid or effectively redress.

As a result, the state has economic and political reasons for promoting a high rate of savings for all groups, no matter what their sectorial preferences, for this ensures the future material conditions required to secure the ongoing consent of subordinate groups to economic policies based on asymmetrical choices. Reform mongering is thus an integral feature of democratic capitalist states, with the measure of reform ultimately linked to the political necessity for structural adjustment.

Under capitalism, owners of productive wealth rely on their firms to realize their material interests over time, but no such security exists for workers. Democratic state managers frame the range of choices available to these controlling groups through institutions, to encourage interest in maintaining high rates of savings and internal (as opposed to externally borrowed) reinvestment.

For controlling groups, this is the preferred government strategy. It is paralleled by state measures that frame the range of choices for subordinate groups to promote savings. Since this is not the preferred strategy for subordinate groups, it represents an asymmetrical choice.

To compensate for this imposed limitation on preferred choices, the state offers corporate concessions to the working classes. Unions need political guarantees to maintain membership and to bargain as economic agents. In fact, "wage earners must rely on political institutions to share in the growth made possible by their past restraint."[13]

Thus the democratic capitalist state adds a political rationale to the economic logic that dictates the need for high rates of saving from profits. The state and capitalists have a mutual interest in securing a stable rate of (re)investment; organized labor has a similar interest, though the motives are different. Under conditions of political democracy, the state, capitalists, and organized labor have strong reasons for attempting to institutionalize stable structural bases for class compromise. At a political level, this is reflected in the organization of the state apparatus and its interaction with dominant and subordinate social groups.

The democratic state offers legal and material inducements and constraints to guarantee these stable rates of (re)investment, regardless of short-term fluctuations in profit. Designed to ensure compliance on all sides, these include differential tax rates as incentives to firms and individuals to save; disincentives for consumption, liquidation, or payouts; and the imposition of (compulsory) occupational pension and insurance fund schemes that amount to mandatory group savings.

Tax policy is thus a crucial element of any democratic class compromise, since it strongly influences mediation of class conflict. For example, tax incentives for high savings (reinvestment), for research and development, or for the use of domestically produced goods, play a crucial role in determining both labor's and capital's interest in how the specifics of class compromise are worked out. The thrust of the state's tax policy and its degree of flexibility structure capitalists' choices in ways that strongly influence the chances of a successful class compromise.

For the working classes and other subordinate groups, state-provided public goods and services such as cost-of-living allowances and social security and other welfare benefits for low-income persons accomplish the same objective, and include the basic right to associate freely and the monopoly of representation awarded to labor's collective representatives. These "concessions" encompass "policies relating to wages, industrial relations, labor disputes, social security, promotion of equal rights, occupational safety and health, protection of migrant workers, conditions of work, participation in the process of economic and social planning, inflation, vocational training, productivity, and protection of the environment."[14] Such services mask or defray the social costs of production. This mitigates labor militancy and promotes wage restraint among workers.[15]

The provision of social security benefits in Latin America has been an indicator of regime type and the approaches of individual regimes toward the working classes. As Malloy and Rosenberg point out,

> both the sequence and quality of coverage were determined by the power of groups to pose a threat to the existing sociopolitical sys-

tems and the administrative logic of the contractual type of social insurance schemes developed within the region. . . . The upshot was the incremental evolution of social security systems that were both highly fragmented and unequally stratified in terms of the quality of programs. . . . These structures, which were often part of a general corporatist approach to labor relations, reflected the goal of established elites to undercut the emergence of a broad class-conscious movement of workers.[16]

In many instances, extension of social security coverage was part of the initial period of labor's incorporation into the national political process and involved union control over state- and employer-financed medical and pension programs. Plentiful resources available to unions through such schemes allowed them to consolidate their organizational bases, thus formally affirming their positions as collective agents. Along with institutionalized and noninstitutionalized forms of graft and corruption, this gave union leaders the power to exercise political leverage, which often extended far beyond their constituencies or their strategic location in the productive apparatus.

The issue of union versus state operation of social welfare networks has been a major point of discussion in writings on modern capitalist political economy. When a state provides welfare and social security benefits that were previously provided by the union, organized labor's membership is eroded because there are fewer incentives to join the union. The source of revenues ultimately influences union strategies regarding the utility and operation of networks for distributing benefits.

Reextending state-operated welfare and social service agencies under conditions of democratic rule contributes to expanding the previously exclusive benefits of union membership to society at large (as the example of Uruguay before the 1960s would suggest). Controlling the union's provision of welfare benefits is therefore central to promoting democratic class compromise in the Southern Cone, and institutional approaches toward social security coverage for organized labor play a large role in determining whether democratic consolidation will be achieved in the region.

Public employment is another important issue in constructing democratic class relations. Because of the proportion of public workers and their level of organization, state approaches in the Southern Cone and elsewhere have been used in the past to absorb surplus labor, promote domestic consumption, and reward or punish the lower bourgeoisie and working classes (depending on whether they were used as incentives, disincentives, or inducements).

State approaches to public employment in the region have become problematic due to the constraints imposed by rationalization and privatization programs in the public sector, which are required to establish debt repayment schedules. Repeated and prolonged union strikes in the public sector protesting government attempts to implement IMF-mandated austerity or privatization programs in all three countries attest to the sensitivity of these issues, and to the myriad difficulties confronting attempts at achieving the sectorial trade-offs required for democratic consolidation in post-authoritarian settings.

Democratic class compromise is best accomplished during periods of economic expansion, when material payouts allow capitalists to profit and workers to be materially rewarded for consenting to continued exploitation. Workers can be rewarded directly, through employer-provided wage and benefit increases, or indirectly, via tax-financed subsidies and benefits provided by the state (this is more often the case in depressed economic climates such as the Southern Cone). Successfully reproduced over several generations, such positive-sum economic outcomes can establish the structural foundations for the move to the Althusserian "moment" when, material concerns having been mollified, ideological reproduction becomes the predominant form of hegemonic control.[17] However, when economies contract, the material payouts available to secure labor's consent drop accordingly. To offset declining profitability, capitalists attempt to lower the wage bill and other labor benefits, further reducing the material grounds for sectorial accommodation. If the state cannot offset these losses, the structural grounds for class conflict increase dramatically.

The historic "depth" of hegemonic ideology and ideological leadership exercised by the ruling classes allows them to mitigate the worst effects of these structural crises, and to ride out the economic down cycles that prove fatal to nonhegemonic regimes (which neither seek labor's consent through material concessions nor exercise any ideological leadership). Yet, however ritualized and mystified, democratic class compromise "in the last instance" rests on concrete material grounds that recede behind the ideological curtain only after generations of successful reproduction. Thus, material conditions ultimately structure the possibilities of class compromise, and by extension, hegemonic rule.[18] Not surprisingly, in unconsolidated democratic regimes, economic contraction often brings about the withdrawal of labor's consent (and a concomitant rise in labor militancy), which precedes the regime's collapse.[19]

The contradiction between having to regulate inter- and intra-class competition while promoting overall capital accumulation and dual (working-class and capitalist) consent pushes the democratic capitalist state to create institutions that reproduce class compromise. This also gives a distinctive character and prominence to the state as the ultimate mechanism of mediation and enforcement. Its need to secure the consent of strategically important interest groups while depriving them of control over some of their material resources, in order to promote the "common good" by redistributing social benefits within capitalist parameters, gives the democratic state a unique dynamic of intervention.[20]

Why does organized labor consent to this type of exchange rather than adopt more militant strategies oriented toward restructuring the socioeconomic and political parameters of society? Co-option and alienation may well weigh more heavily than rationally calculated appraisals of the risks and costs involved in such strategies.[21] But even where working-class alienation is not an obstacle, these risks force organized labor to secure greater participation through "moderately militant" political and economic strategies. In return, institutionalized guarantees of a political voice and economic redress make it inadvisable for workers to pursue revolutionary options.

Such pragmatic or reformist labor postures stem from uncertainty. Even if socialism is a more efficient allocator of society's resources, organized labor cannot be certain that it will be victorious from the violent conflict it will have to engage in to gain control of the state and the means of production. Since the resources available to capital include the state's coercive powers and the assistance of foreign governments, it is more likely that organized labor will lose any such conflict. In the worst-case scenario, the working classes lose on two fronts when they follow a militant strategy. Economically, their material welfare will probably diminish for both punitive and economic reasons in the aftermath of the conflict. Politically, their level of participation will most likely be curtailed or they will be subjected to authoritarian exclusion. The history of the Southern Cone in the 1960s and 1970s — Chile in particular — serves as a point of reference in this regard.

Even so, there are obviously conditions where structural and superstructural crises combine and deepen to the point where the "valley of transition" does, in fact, appear feasible. If workers' material conditions steadily and markedly deteriorate despite their collective moderation (most evident in the union's acceptance of unilateral or government-imposed wage restraint), and if the socioeconomic environment and political system show no signs of being able to accommodate their minimum subsistence needs in the future, workers may approach the threshold beyond which the common benefits gained by economic and political militancy outweigh the personal and collective costs of a violent transition to socialism. When such "organic" or hegemonic crises occur, political democracy gives way to open conflict, Caesarism, and the imposition of one or another form of authoritarianism, i.e., dictatorship, either of the proletariat, the peasantry, or of the bourgeoisie.

In post-authoritarian environments characterized by economic crisis and fiscal austerity, the range of labor's demands that capitalists and government officials perceive as militant (as opposed to moderate) is considerably reduced compared to that of an institutionally consolidated capitalist democracy. In the latter, parameters separating the two types of labor demands are both broad and well-defined: socializing the means of production is unacceptably militant, while tying wage increases to cost-of-living or productivity indexes is not. In post-authoritarian regimes, however, especially when nondemocratic labor relations systems have been the norm, basic demands for wages, security, or benefits are often considered unduly militant. This viewpoint establishes a very narrow range of issues upon which sectorial agreements can be reached.

Under such conditions of structural constraint, with the principal collective actors following diametrically opposed strategies (rising labor militancy, expressed in expanding economic and political demands versus narrowing capitalist and state perceptions of the range of acceptable labor demands, which further limit the range of negotiable issues), sectorial preferences become increasingly oriented toward imposing a unilateral outcome. At that point, the possibility of class compromise is nil. Thus, whatever each democratic government's preferences, the inherited economic structures, such as externally financed transnational oligopolies with the ability to move capital across national borders on short notice, combine with the strategic position and pressing problems of the dominant capitalist agents (especially the amount of privately incurred debt), to give these agents unusual leverage in negotiating with the government and other social groups.

Because they charge interest and control the primary sources of investment (since they serve as conduits for foreign financing and domestic accumulation), these business groups hold disproportionate control over the national productive apparatus. Under such conditions, capitalists have no need for a formal agreement with labor and can instead pressure democratic governments to support projects that allow the bourgeoisie to reassert itself, whereas labor is de facto prevented from exercising all its options. We can then see why authoritarian labor legislation was maintained in both Argentina and Brazil well after democratic regimes were installed. The austerity programs, privatization schemes, and anti-inflationary measures imposed by executive decree in all three nations, which have had a disproportionately adverse impact on the working-class standard of living, can also be understood in this way.

The extent to which structural constraints and noncooperative capitalist strategies impede the achievement of class compromise is conditioned by institutions that filter and ameliorate environmental obstacles to sectorial negotiation in ways conducive to securing labor's consent. The relative success of Uruguay in promoting sectorial agreements on economic issues after 1985 is a case in point, since the return to the tripartite Consejo de Salario system, which had been eliminated in 1968, served as an institutional foundation for labor-capital dialogue, an option not available in either Argentina or Brazil. In all instances, institutions shape the role that organized labor plays in any process of democratic consolidation, since through them labor's range of possible choices and consequent strategies of action are structured.

Where there is an institutionalized range of choices, labor can adopt one of three approaches toward capital and the state: competitive or conflictual, bargaining or negotiated, and concertative or cooperative. Over time, labor may choose to move from one approach to another, depending on the relative success of a given strategy. The first two approaches involve few or no restrictions on the union's freedom of action, and consequently embody relatively high (albeit diminishing) levels of conflict. Conversely, concertative approaches restrict the union's freedom of action within a

Figure 2.1   Labor Approaches to Capital and the State

	Concertation	Bargaining	Contestation
LEVEL OF INSTITUTION- ALIZATION	High	Moderate	Low
OUTCOME	Positive-sum	Even-sum	Negative or Zero-Sum

NOTE: *Direction of arrow indicates increasing degrees of conflict institutionalization; dashes indicate noninstitutional forms of conflict.*

framework of increasingly institutionalized conflict, leading to eventual cooperation. Such approaches can involve consultation or participation. In either case, they represent the highest institutionalized forms of (class) conflict resolution.

The conflictual approach is one of open contest, where labor attempts to improve its position vis-à-vis capital at all costs. It is usually negative-sum, since it is likely to involve a struggle that will impose losses on all sides. Labor, however, stands to lose more than capital. This approach is adopted by the most economically intransigent or ideologically militant unions, which see an intrinsic value in promoting open class conflict via "wars of maneuver," whatever the short- and medium-term consequences. In postauthoritarian conditions such as those examined here, this approach is not likely to enjoy general support.

The bargaining approach is essentially even-sum. It is based on the premise of a fluid exchange of substantive concessions where, within the asymmetrical parameters of the hegemonic "debate," neither side secures appreciable advantage over the other. Understood in terms of pursuing second-best choices, this approach lies at the core of labor collective bargaining strategies in a wide array of capitalist countries, although the autonomy of the negotiations with respect to the state varies considerably from case to case.

The concertative approach can be positive-sum. Both parties believe that mutual gains secured through institutionalized cooperation outweigh the procedural concessions and limitations on freedom of action or on the substantive demands the parties may have to accept. Here the state's roles as mediator, arbitrator, and guarantor are paramount.

Whether or not a government is willing to use the powers of the state to unilaterally impose "agreements" on social groups clearly affects the strategic options available to all groups. For example, "social democratic governments are typically more prepared than conservative or Christian democratic ones to intervene by strongly etatist modes of regulation in the case that voluntary and cooperative agreements among societal actors fail to come about."[22] This "etatist" orientation forces social actors either to look first to the state for initiative and direction when approaching intersectorial negotiations, or conversely, to look to each other in order to reach mutually satisfactory agreements without state interference. The absence of an "etatist" orientation in government broadens the range of choices available to social actors, and hence their array of strategic options, but also increases the chance of destabilization due to noninstitutionalized sectorial conflicts.

In the Southern Cone, recent government approaches have wavered: "etatist" approaches to labor relations and nonintervention in other economic areas have even been combined at times. Whatever the approach, for democratic consolidation to occur, both the state and sectorial groups must be included in — and more important, mutually bound by the decisions of — an institutionalized framework for conflict resolution. In the Southern Cone, the long tradition of state involvement in labor-related policies initially made the "etatist" mode the most favored government approach to sectorial negotiation, regardless of the preferences of collective agents.

Labor's objective in such a scenario is therefore to choose the best strategies for improving its material and political welfare, given the institutional possibilities of the post-authoritarian, procedurally democratic capitalist context. The modern history of Western Europe suggests the usefulness of societal or neocorporatist (as opposed to state-corporatist) frameworks as institutional parameters to promote a range of sectorial choices that is conducive to achieving the structural bases of democratic class compromise.[23] Experience has also shown that such cooperation is most effective with regard to non-wage issues, with wage negotiation most effectively handled via the more conflictual process of collective bargaining.[24]

To demonstrate the range of choices institutionally made available to labor under democratic regimes, I have developed a typology of choices for capital and labor, based on, first, the orientation of the democratic government, and second, the type of labor relations systems in operation.[25] In conceding the state's structural dependence on capital, this model distinguishes between two types

of democratic government: overtly pro-capital (presumably conservative) and nominally pro-labor (presumably liberal). Examples
of the former would include governments controlled by United
States Republicans, British Conservatives, or Latin American
Christian Democrats. Examples of the latter might be governments
controlled by European and Latin American Socialists, Social
Democrats, or Labor Parties. Variations between and among
democratic capitalist governments are reflected in differences in
policy orientation, which influence sectorial preferences regarding
the labor relations system.

Given these differences, three possible labor relations systems
exist: *competitive* or *atomized* (in which labor is unorganized and
workers bargain and sell their labor services as individuals); *pluralist* (in which labor is organized and represented by more than
one collective agent in each economic sector); and *corporatist* (in
which labor is organized into monopolies, and is represented by
one nationally aggregated, state-recognized collective agent).
Using the assumed preferences of labor (left) and capital (right),
we come up with the following matrix of choices:

Figure 2.2 *Matrix of Choice*

Labor Relations System	Prolabor Government	Procapital Government
COMPETITION	3,4[a]	6,1
PLURALISM	2,5	5,2
CORPORATISM	1,6	4,3

[a]*where 1 = most preferred choice and 6 = least preferred choice.*

Labor and capital preferences are not uniform under those governments that "structurally" favor them. This is noteworthy
because pro-labor governments further labor interests regardless
of institutional frameworks, while pro-capital governments do
likewise for the dominant factions of capital. Note that corpo-

ratism is never simultaneously preferred to pluralism by both labor and capital, and optimal outcomes are impossible for the disfavored group.

Neither side always prefers the binding qualities of monopolistic representation of sectorial agents over the judicially limited or free reign of collective interests. This suggests that if the main economic objective of democratic capitalist regimes (regardless of the particular orientation of specific governments) is to reproduce capitalism qua hegemonic system, then corporatist systems of interest group representation, given different degrees of sectorial preference, offer only one of several institutional linkages through which labor and capital can institutionalize a class compromise. Yet, given the historically state-corporatist nature of most Latin American labor relations systems (including two of the three cases studied here) it would appear that, *mutatis mutandis*, the possibility of a neocorporatist administration of class compromise exists in the Southern Cone.

Another scenario can be envisioned in which the government is "objectively" class-neutral and strives to play the role of mediator without an overt orientation toward either side. This would affect the choices available to capital and labor, which would complicate the matrix and increase the range of strategies upon which to base collective action. Such may be the position occupied by democracies that follow authoritarian capitalist regimes in contexts of severe economic crisis. They cannot move too far toward the pro-labor position because of the fiscal constraints imposed by their respective economic problems and the fear of authoritarian regression, yet they have to humanize the national capitalist system in relation to the preceding authoritarian period. Thus, although they ultimately continue to respond to capitalist interests, they must do so in a far more oblique, nontransparent fashion.

However, the opposition of well-entrenched capitalists who see themselves disfavored by "humanizing" economic reform programs places many post-authoritarian incumbents between a rock and a hard place, since any labor consent depends on implementing such reforms. In climates of fiscal crisis and economic austerity, where the state is particularly reliant on capital, structural conditions militate against pro-labor policies. Hence, no matter what their subjective preferences (which can be assumed to be pro-capital), elected government's objective condition in such cases is at best one of imposed procedural neutrality.

This is particularly so when there are various contending factions of capital involved in the equation, each with a preferred (and often opposed) range of policy choices. Here the question of sectorial preferences becomes more complicated, giving more importance to comparisons of the strategies adopted by multiple actors, and more important, to the institutional mechanisms that frame the range of choices that influences strategic interaction. Using the same ranking of preference as before, we can develop another scenario:

"Neutral" Government

COMPETITION	6,1
PLURALISM	3,3
CORPORATISM	1,2

In this scenario, inclusionary "neo"corporatist labor relations systems constitute the mutually preferred institutional alternative for regulating sectorial competition. While sectorial perceptions of unrestricted labor competition are obvious, note that pluralism is viewed negatively by capital and labor alike. The combined weight of the competition between intra- and intersectorial collective agents is perceived as hurting both sides, due to the compounded propensity to free ride in pursuit of short-term gain. In addition, in such cases "neutral" governments must constantly arbitrate the antagonistic demands of different actors in each functional group (employers and workers), as well as between the groups themselves, rather than assuming a preference for one side or the other. This broaches the question of whether a democratic class compromise can be achieved with a "neutral" government in power.

The point is not really to rank the order of possible preferences outlined in a model of labor-capital interaction per se. None of these scenarios challenge the basic exchange sustaining democratic capitalism; they are variations on a common theme. The issue is one of sectorial choice, and specifically the institutional mechanisms that frame the range of choices presented by new democratic regimes to the labor movement in order to promote class compromise.

In that light, we have focused here on efforts to institutionalize vertical political-economic compromises between socioeconomic classes represented by nationally aggregated collective agents. We believe that such arrangements constitute the core mechanism for negotiating the class compromise required for consolidating substantive democracy.

Given this, concertation is a method of conflict resolution oriented toward achieving pragmatically calculated, second-best outcomes for both parties. It seeks to promote even-sum or positive-sum sectorial payouts on economic and political issues, thereby giving rise to a political culture in which confrontation and veto politics are replaced by the logic of compromise and bargaining.[26] It represents a self-binding strategy on the part of actors who wish to avoid the mutually negative conquences of the unfettered pursuit of unilateral preferences.[27]

Three sets of risks confront both workers and capitalists as they negotiate a class compromise. First, there may be a lack of class unity, which makes a monopoly of representation impossible. That is, one side or the other (or both) may lack a single legitimate bargaining agent (or set of agents). This leads to problems of free riding. Such is more likely the case with employers competing within (and even between) various economic sectors, but is also quite possible among workers in different sectors (e.g., between those employed in foreign-owned versus domestically owned firms). Second, the state may be used for partisan purposes that infringe on its autonomy and favor one side to the detriment of the other. And third, there may be larger systemic economic risks normally associated with capitalism (dependent capitalism in this case), aggravated by unemployment, lack of domestic demand, large burdens of foreign debt, increased disinvestment and financial speculation, and very high rates of inflation.[28]

Subject to these risks, democratic class compromise is the product of a specific type of strategic interaction known as tripartite concertation. This is a form of sectorial negotiation between labor, capital, and the state based on notions of equitable, rationally calculated political and economic exchange. The agreements reached via this process are known as "managerial pacts," where the state administers and guarantees the substantive and procedural terms of sectorial agreements. Reaffirmed over time (via regular renegotiation, most often within corporatist frameworks), the utility of this form of ongoing strategic interaction is eventually reflected in the mutual expectations by workers and capitalists that the structural bases of class compromise can — and will — be maintained by those means. This can lead to the generation of a self-enforcing, "spontaneous" class compromise based on rational calculations of sectorial interests (material and political) within ongoing institutional parameters.

The importance of concertation in processes of redemocratization and democratic consolidation is well understood. As Schmitter notes, "particularly important in the contemporary consolidation processes are the efforts undertaken to reach and implement `socio-economic pacts' as a device to reduce uncertainties and expectations in specific policy areas such as wages, prices, investments, and taxation."[29] Not surprisingly, sectorial concertation, as a mechanism that mediates and stabilizes class compromise, has received considerable attention in several industrialized European nations.[30] It also came to the fore as a subject of theoretical and practical interest during the redemocratization of Southern Europe in the early 1970s.[31] With the shift toward democracy in Latin America in the 1980s, it attracted the attention of both Latin American scholars and policy makers, despite obvious differences in context and circumstances.[32]

Not all attempts at tripartism succeed. Cooperation has proved unsuccessful in countries in which labor-based parties constitute the bulk of the opposition, since they prefer to use their autonomous potential for mobilization to pursue preferences in the political market. This was the situation in Argentina and, to a lesser extent, in Brazil and Uruguay, during the first years of the new democratic regimes.

Where successfully established, concertative agreements manage societal demands that might otherwise overwhelm the procedural safeguards of liberal democracies.[33] In Venezuela,

> from 1960 on, one can speak of a tacit agreement among parties, worker organizations, and industrialists to maintain in the country what has come to be called the "labor peace," which has been solidified increasingly through *concertación* (reaching informal agreements so as to avoid public conflict). Without a doubt this constitutes a basic factor in the stability of the present regime.[34]

Such pacts are often an integral part of the process of (re)democratization itself. Known as "foundational pacts," these are political bargains with two distinct sides. On one side is the bargain struck between opposition forces and the outgoing authoritarian authorities, which establishes the terms and rules for the democratic transition. On the other side are the agreements reached among different sectors of the opposition in order to, first, present the outgoing regime with a united democratic platform, and second, allow the elected authorities to operate during the early stages of the democratic restoration within generally accepted guidelines (and possibly within a certain grace period). These *pactos-políticos* may be political party pacts exclusively, in that the parties agree to compete centripally rather than centrifugally, or they may involve the agents of labor, capital, and other sectorial interests as well.

The process of regime transition influences the ongoing character of concertation. Thus, the nature and terms of the foundational pact depend on which side holds the dominant position in the political negotiations leading to democratization. For example, in Uruguay (1984–1985), the evolution of informal negotiations among the opposition grouped in the Intersectorial and Multipartidaria eventually led to the Concertación Nacional Programatica, which represented an effort on the part of the opposition to reach a more formal agreement on the political conditions necessary for democratic transition and consolidation. This allowed opposition groups to confront the outgoing military regime on common ground (at the Club Naval Meetings), and eventually led to agreements on the timing and terms of the transition.[35]

Transitory by nature, foundational pacts provide a precedent that can be used during the process of democratic consolidation.[36] That is, horizontal foundational pacts often pave the way for vertical managerial pacts. Concertation during the last stages of authoritarian liberalization and the initial period of democratization can provide the bases for subsequent efforts to reach substantive sectorial agreements. The scope, subjects, and even some of the principals may change once the democratic regime is installed, but the avenues of communication, forms of dialogue, institutional guarantees, and levels of mutual trust established during the period of transition promote the formal, regularized use of concertation as an institutional linchpin of new democratic regimes.

Concertation among opposition groups can serve as a primary vehicle for regime transition, but, once the procedural restoration of democracy is achieved, it is often supplemented by more traditional vehicles — particularly political parties — as the leading agents of sectorial negotiation. Likewise, prior to the procedural transfer of authority, concertative sectorial agreements — where they occur — are often very broad in scope and general in nature. In contrast, after the transfer of power the scope and terms become increasingly narrow and more issue-specific, if only because of the expansion of the political arena proper.[37] Success with a narrow concertative agenda may pave the way for more universal discussions, though the ratio of success at this broader level is often inversely related to the degree of complexity and scope of issues involved.

In countries emerging from authoritarian rule, the terms of *concertación* are most often formal, in that they delineate and codify the positive-sum rules that are the institutional bases of substantive democracy. This was evident in the political and economic pacts negotiated in Southern Europe during the wave of redemocratization that swept through the region in the 1970s. The process of maintaining such pacts via regular renegotiation of the substantive terms within clear, consensually agreed upon institutional boundaries allows a high level of mutual expectation and trust to develop among the "social partners." The organization of this institutional network, i.e., the state apparatus and organized interests, links the horizontal and vertical dimensions of collective discourse, and in so doing constitutes the bridge between procedural and substantive democracy.[38]

Democratic concertation complements the individual freedoms and partisan politics of liberal democracy by compensating for the disparate organizational resources available to different social groups (at least with regard to their status before the state), and by absorbing collective or sectorial demands that are not assimilated by other institutional features of democratic regimes. Institutionalized concertation diminishes the cost of transactions and the sectorial uncertainties produced by unrestrained political and economic competition. It is designed to forge a new social contract that can overcome the inherently antagonistic positions of propertied and nonpropertied groups in capitalist societies, and can simultaneously strengthen the organization of civil society while diminishing rationally calculated incentives to secure sectorial advantages at the expense of all others.

In post-authoritarian contexts of economic crisis, asymmetries between benefits and costs make sectorial free-riding strategies all the more attractive, creating a prisoner's dilemma scenario that concertation is supposed to overcome. Tempering sectorial urges to defect is thus at the heart of the move to institutionalize concertative vehicles in nascent capitalist democracies.

Institutionalizing a democratic class compromise via concertation is an extensive-form, multiple-actor, forced cooperation game involving three sets of conflicts. The first occurs over the basic rules, terms, and framework governing sectorial negotiations (the procedural conditions of the so-called *diálogo ínicial*); the second over the ongoing institutional guarantees tendered by the state and collective agents that govern negotiations in core substantive policy areas; and the third over the specific terms of particular substantive agreements. Payouts and actors change as the game evolves, but the forced cooperative premise does not.[39] This is how sectorial consent to a democratic class compromise is reproduced at an institutional level.

Concertation is not possible if actors (firms, unions, parties, etc.) are unwilling to pay a price for the certainty, predictability, and security achieved via such mechanisms: sectorial concession is the cost of compromise.[40] As a result, democratic concertation represents a middle ground between the unrestrained freedom of the economic market and the general restraints imposed by a common, consensual government. It is one manifestation of what Offe calls the "mercantilization of politics and politization of markets" under democratic capitalism.[41] In the cases studied here, this "reciprocal contamination" of politics and markets is made all the more pronounced due to the prior histories of state intervention in the economy and the existing climates of economic crisis.

Democratic concertation has been repeatedly used as an institutional solution to the periodic structural and political crises that afflict modern capitalism, whether in the 1930s, the 1960s (in the industrialized nations of Europe), the 1970s (in the emergent democracies of Southern Europe), or the 1980s (in the Southern Cone).

A general condition for promoting concertative agreements is that social agents are locked into situations of "mutual deterrence" in which each is able to impede the direct realization of the other's interests and yet unable to impose its own preferences unilaterally.[42] This serves to alter the sectorial "coordination game" from one of confrontation to one of imposed or forced contingent cooperation, the essence of the democratic class struggle.

This requires overcoming a major paradox. The very existence of an economic and/or of political crisis — especially in a context of repositioning dependent capitalism within the international economy — serves as a significant obstacle to achieving democratic concertation in countries emerging from extended periods of authoritarian rule. In such instances, attempts to institutionalize democratic class compromise fail because of a lack of material or procedural grounds on which to negotiate viable sectorial trade-offs. Instead, extended situations of "mutual deterrence" — the so-called *empate hegemónico* (hegemonic impasse) mentioned by J. C. Portantiero — can, as the modern history of South America has shown, lead to the unilateral imposition of authoritarian solutions that patently favor some groups over others.

The European experience suggests that the economic basis for concertative compromises between the state, capital, and labor is not always the crucial variable, and that the economic logic of the compromise shifts in response to exogenous structural conditions. Thus, the "Keynesian compromises" of the 1930s and 1950s traded wage restraint for guarantees of full employment and price stability, but the structural crises of the late 1960s brought into play a different rationale.

> In so far as wage restraint could no longer be legitimated on the grounds of full employment and price stability, the rationale upon which postwar corporatist structures had rested was effectively removed. Corporatism now had to be legitimated on the grounds that wage restraint would *restore* full employment and price stability, or, even more difficult, on the grounds that it would prevent the situation from getting worse.[43]

The point to be underscored is that concertative, neocorporatist frameworks have been based on a variety of economic justifications, and hence have a fundamental political objective regardless of the specific economic rationale used. That political objective is social peace, particularly in the relations between labor and capital.

The political strength of labor, particularly its ties to national political parties, help make concertation the preferred vehicle for social peace. And where labor is organizationally weak and/or underrepresented by political parties, the stage is set for market approaches to the issue of social justice, complete with social Darwinist pathologies. Neoconservative experiments such as those of the Thatcher and Reagan governments used rising unemployment as an instrument to bring down the aggregate wage bill in order to increase the competitiveness of domestically produced goods and to weaken labor as an organized social agent. Sectorial cooperation was eschewed in favor of the reassertion of capitalist interests, with little regard given to its adverse impact on the subordinate classes. In a sense, this is a nonauthoritarian variant of the socio-economic projects of the military regimes that ruled the Southern Cone in the 1970s.

In the democracies of the Southern Cone discussed here, labor regained a strong political presence, had "organic" links to important political parties, and was difficult to subject unilaterally to market forces (though there was no lack of trying). For this reason, concertative approaches toward class compromise initially seemed attractive to the democracies in that region.

Even so, concertative mechanisms are neither uniform or invariably necessary in maintaining capitalist democracies. Nor do they always coexist with other democratic institutions in a harmonious or egalitarian way. In some instances, the crisis of other democratic institutions creates political conditions that make sectorial concertation appear necessary (e.g., parliamentary deadlock or the fall of a coalition government). In other cases, different types of concertation are evident only in specific areas of economic activity or in subnational political arrangements (at the so-called meso- or microcorporatist level, which constitutes the various partial regimes encompassed within the national political regime). This has often brought with it conflict with the party system and Parliament over the appropriate role and jurisdiction of concertative mechanisms.

In light of this situation, we can discern general typologies of concertative roles in democratic political systems: (1) concertation that complements other democratic institutions; (2) concertation that supersedes other democratic institutions (some believe this has serious authoritarian implications);[44] (3) concertation that is subordinated to other democratic institutions; and (4) concertation that is deemed unnecessary or superfluous in the presence of other democratic institutions (this is the case in the United States, for example).[45] Each variant represents a particular degree of structural differentiation and functional specialization within democratic political systems.[46] In addition, while we will not address the issue here, sectorial concertation can and has been used by authoritarian regimes, though the tone and content of the issues addressed varies significantly from democratic concertation.

As mentioned earlier, concertation implies more than tripartism. Actors involved in concertation can be few or many, and can include representatives of organized labor, important factions of capital, special interest groups such as environmentalists and feminists, ethnic or religious communities, political parties, representatives of national or local governments, and even the armed forces. Moreover, concertation can simultaneously or sequentially involve political and economic issues, can initially occur with or without direct state involvement, and can even take place within the partisan confines of a single dominant party with majority control in the legislative and executive branches (especially where there is heavy sectorial — particularly labor and capitalist — representation in that party).

In terms of the labor relations partial regime, democratic concertation can occur at all levels of production (factory, firm, industry, economic sector, or national economy), and in every geographic or political jurisdiction. In practice, concertative activity often occurs simultaneously at a variety of levels. The degree to which these levels are linked forms the internal vertical dimension of concertative labor relations systems, which "relates to the pattern of participation of individual peak associations in policy-making and implementation, and the corresponding integration of lower organizational levels into corporatist arrangements."[47]

The state's role in fostering this vertical integration is crucial. It takes

the form of progressive legislation and state-fostered managerial practices designed to facilitate union recognition in unorganized sectors and extend union membership in organized sectors; to foster worker participation schemes in company boards and work councils (this time under the direct aegis of the unions); to institutionalize local-level bargaining and shop-steward committees; and to provide a legal framework for qualitative issues (e.g., health and safety), unfair dismissals, and redundancy.[48]

The character of the labor movement and its capitalist counterpart(s) determines the precise flow of information between the apex and bases of the system.

Concertation can be top-down (i.e., sectorial agreements made by national peak associations are successively ratified by affiliated groups at the subnational level), or bottom-up (agreements reached at various subnational levels — shop, sector, region, etc. — are ratified by national representatives).

Both forms of concertation are feasible and have, in fact, been implemented. There is not one standard or "pure" form of concertation. It emerges in a variety of guises depending on the circumstances and issues involved. We will focus here on the national level, given the inherited (exclusionary state-corporatist) structure of the labor relations systems and the need to consolidate democracy institutionally on a national scale in all three countries.

The scope and subject of concertative negotiation can be broad (what G. Lehmbruch, using T. Parsons, calls a "generalized exchange"), or narrow (in Lehmbruch's terms, a "barter transaction"). It can be political, economic, social, or some combination thereof; can involve negotiation on different "tracks" or as part of a comprehensive agenda, with trade-offs possible in either framework; and can even shift over time.

Organized labor's participation in concertative frameworks transcends merely economic concerns. It constitutes a framework within which to negotiate the form and extent of labor's collective representation in the three areas of citizenship, i.e., as a social, economic, and political actor. Only with organized labor exercising the full range of rights inherent in all three areas can a democratic class compromise emerge from concertative exchanges. More generally, all participation by subordinate groups in concertation implies an extension of suffrage that involves a formal recognition of the collective right to full citizenship.

This is not to say that democratic concertation always reflects a seriousness of purpose on the part of those involved. More specifically, concertation can be either formulaic-symbolic or substantive-pragmatic. That is, it can be used to symbolically incorporate specific groups into formulaic discussions of general policy concerns or of the specific rules and issues involved in further concertation, while pragmatic decision making on substantive issues is made elsewhere (in the Parliament, the presidency, other branches of the state, or private entities).

On the other hand, concertation can be used to pragmatically formulate policy and make decisions on specific issues of a substantive nature. Substantive-pragmatic concertation can be conducted informally or formally, and can be bilateral (in this case, social groups initiate negotiations and reach agreements through their collective agents, then present them to the state for ratification), or multilateral (here, the state's role in initiating, mediating, and defining the scope of discussion and rules is much greater).

The state legitimizes democratic concertation at the national level, since it constitutes the superordinate enforcement authority by virtue of its formal mediation of all sectorial interests. As the so-called *rector y garente*, the state provides "the ultimate legal reassurance that what is negotiated is abided, by virtue of the legal rules (including sanctions) to which the groups in question are subjected."[49]

In practice, formulaic-symbolic concertation (as a form of "initial dialogue") commonly provides a means of formally incorporating previously excluded social agents, and has often established the ground rules and agenda within which subsequent substantive-pragmatic concertation occurs. In so doing, it defines the actors, institutional parameters, and thematic guidelines involved in substantive negotiations.

While the benefits of concertation often appear hypothetical and long term, from the onset the costs are immediate and real. Hence, continued interest in maintaining concertative frameworks stems from the ability to deliver on what is agreed upon. Sectorial expectations of the benefits to be reaped must be fulfilled, and the costs of cooperation need to be minimized or equitably distributed.

Since the benefits of cooperation are long term and collective, there are powerful incentives structured into the game for social actors to engage in short-term, self-maximizing strategies in order to shift the costs of compromise onto others. This is acute in crisis economies, where labor suffers a disproportionate burden of the sacrifices imposed by austerity programs (in terms of declining wages and rising unemployment). Hence, the asymmetry in the costs disposes labor toward noncooperation while leaving capital relatively unconstrained in its options.

The problem is compounded by another structural legacy of authoritarianism in the Southern Cone. When industrial real wages lost an average of 50 percent of their value from 1983 to 1988 (Uruguay is the exception), and with unemployment at record levels throughout the region, the ability of organized labor to serve as a viable interlocutor for working-class interests remained uncertain. The Southern Cone's post-authoritarian context saw a structurally weakened labor movement in both the public and private sectors forced to wage basic defensive struggles for maintaining salary levels and employment stability. The costs of economic reform in the 1980s shifted the burden of sacrifice onto the working classes to the point that it made it difficult for unions and employers to engage in the exchange of material concessions required for compromise. This is the material threshold of the organic crisis, the point where the masses may be uncoupled from their traditional vehicles of representation because they are no longer served by their affiliation with them.[50] At that point, the "valley of transition" may well appear crossable.

In the Southern Cone, organized labor periodically withdrew from strategies of moderation and cooperation with concertative efforts, and adopted confrontational postures that allowed it to remain as the collective agent of a restive rank and file. This explains the repeated use of general and industrywide strikes by labor confederations in all three countries during this time.

Successful national-level concertation is thus generally believed to have "a tight relation to the degree of centralization and representativeness of syndical organizations, and the degree of control they have over the bases" (rank and file).[51] Analysts have pointed out that concertative approaches to public policy making most often prosper when labor organizations are highly centralized, bureaucratized, vertically organized, and oligarchical; i.e., when they are cohesive and autonomous enough at the leadership level to exert effective discipline over the rank and file and veto power over government decisions. The capacity to control and to veto, in other words, is the most important resource labor brings to the concertative process.[52]

Principal/agent problems and that of the mutual veto hold true for the representatives of capitalist interests as well, and are often more acute in that sector than among organized labor. The dynamics of profit-oriented competition make self-maximizing irresistible to capitalists, to which can be added the counterposed material interests between various capitalist factions. In such cases, collectively binding concertative pacts have little usefulness.

For both sides, members' calculations of the costs and benefits to be realized via collective, as opposed to individual, action, beyond the degree of organizational centralization per se, determines how well the sector adheres to concertative mechanisms. Stable concertation requires that, along with the ability to deliver material and political benefits, collective agents maintain a significant degree of internal representativeness, since it is the binding quality of legitimate authority that makes them the genuine articulators of sectorial interests. Thus the internal composition of collective agents — particularly their degree of centralization, representativeness, and political unity — is a matter of concern for new democratic regimes, since these factors can either contribute to or detract from the process of democratic institutionalization.

As a result, several conditions must be fulfilled for tripartite concertation between labor, capital, and the state to succeed.

First, *concertación* requires that the government and the regime be accepted as legitimate by the relevant social actors. Second, there must be a reasonable convergence in the overall strategies followed by capital, labor and the state. Third, notwithstanding their contradictory interests in a market economy, labor and capital must agree on a minimum agenda and there must be clear incentives to reach mutually satisfactory outcomes. Fourth, the state must cede part of its decisional authority on issues of economic policy to organized labor and associations representing entrepreneurial interests, thereby attributing public status to private interests. Finally, in exchange for this attribution of public status, business and labor "offer the state their political power, guaranteeing the state consensus and mobilizing their own resources to assure the legitimation, efficiency, and efficacy of state action."[53]

We should note that even when strategies and agendas were similar and political legitimacy undisputed, the question of the state ceding authority on issues of economic policy to private interests was particularly troublesome in the Southern Cone. The institutional reforms required for the state to cede its superordinate position ran counter to the structural exigencies of the moment (another authoritarian legacy), thereby undermining the chances for substantive institutional change.

The underlying objective of democratic concertation is ultimately reciprocal and equitable, if not symmetrical, sectorial control. Each party attempts to ensure that the competitor does not free ride, by evaluating the self-discipline and enforcement capabilities of the other actors, be they collective agents or the state. This analysis is designed to equalize the position of each sectorial agent involved in concertation and therefore to lower transaction costs for all. As Rolando Pietraveno, head of the Consejo Argentino de la Industria (CAI), the association for small and medium-size businesses in Argentina, noted, "what is needed is an equality of effort . . . when concertative approaches are adopted, transfers that affect the sectors with less relative power must be avoided."[54] In other words, sectorial equality within institutionalized parameters, which lowers transaction costs and promotes mutual restraint, lies at the core of democratic concertation.

The strategic variable here seems to be not the absolute degree of bindingness within an association, but the *equivalence of the effectiveness of control between two associations*, or one association and the state. The decisive variable would thus appear to be not the absolute power of associations to bind and control their members, but the *equal distribution of such power* among associations whose members interact and make contracts with each other. In other words, control will work on the basis that there is some well-founded expectation that control within the group of relevant "others" will work too.[55]

This is congruent with the dual character of concertative discourse. One side is made up of a dialogue between collective agents that are equal at a procedural level in their relations with each other and with the state. The other side is constituted by the dialogue between principals and agents, i.e., between constituent "bases" and organizational leadership. Democratic concertation also involves two varying levels of autonomy of decision-making authority on each side and the specific organizational attributes of different collective agents, which may or may not contribute to the extension of powers of mutual control. Inclusionary (neo)corporatist frameworks are designed precisely for this purpose.

In the Southern Cone, the historical pattern of interest group intermediation and state intervention, though variable and often based on the state rather than on society, offers institutional preconditions for erecting inclusionary corporatist mechanisms. In practical terms, this means replacing the bifrontal, segmental, and state-corporatist modes of interest group administration that characterized the military-bureaucratic regimes with inclusionary, societal, (neo)corporatist, or pluralist modes of intermediation among interest groups. This was the central premise underlying attempts to restructure the labor relations systems throughout the Southern Cone in the 1980s.

Examples of the variety of initial concertation can be drawn from recent experiences in the Southern Cone. In Uruguay, the scope of the Concertación Nacional Programática (CONAPRO) was initially very broad, and included representatives of a wide range of social sectors. Among the issues on the original agenda were economic policy in general, education and cultural programs, health, housing, and social security policies, civil rights questions, and a general review of the laws and decrees enacted by the outgoing military government. Discussions of economic policy included: considerations of the foreign debt; internal debt in agriculture, industry, and commerce; tax policy and public spending; economic reactivation and sectorial employment programs; monetary policy; exchange rates; and the role of foreign investors. The civil rights concerns addressed included amnesty for political prisoners, the return of political exiles, the reestablishment of constitutional guarantees on individual freedoms, and the possibility of prosecuting military personnel charged with human rights violations during the previous regime.

The actors involved included all major political parties (the Colorado Party, the National or Blanco Party, the Frente Amplio, and the Unión Civil), as well as most of the important social groups (including the labor movement, represented by the PIT-CNT, the student movement, the cooperative movement, and representatives of business engaged in industry, commerce, and agriculture, especially the Camara de Industria and Camara de Comercio). At its own request, only the private banking sector was excluded from the initial composition of CONAPRO. The groups came together on their own initiative, and without the sponsorship or mediation of the state (they were originally brought together to formulate a coordinated strategy against the outgoing authoritarian regime).[56]

This type of concertation can be contrasted to that attempted in Argentina by the Alfonsín administration. Initiated by the executive branch in 1984, the Consejo Económico y Social (CES) was initially limited to discussions of wage and price levels within the boundaries of the austerity measures imposed by the IMF-backed Austral Plan. Participation was originally extended only to the representatives of organized labor (in this case, the CGT), business (including the Union Industrial, Confederación General Económica, Camara de Comercio Argentina, and the Confederación General de la Industria), and interested branches of the state (particularly the Ministry of Economy and the Ministry of Labor).

In both cases, the original schemes underwent important modifications. In the Uruguayan case, a "political group" made up of representatives of the political parties came together to discuss a more select range of issues and eventually became the executive body of CONAPRO, to which was subordinated, in more of a consultative capacity, a directorate made up of the representatives of business and labor (with all the other groups excluded). Shortly thereafter, once the electoral government was inaugurated, CONAPRO virtually ceased to exist, superseded by the renewal of party-led discussions. Sectorial negotiation reverted to a more horizontal dialogue between traditional political elites, with its vertical dimension subsumed under these interests.[57]

In Argentina, on the other hand, the scope of discussion within the CES was tentatively expanded, at the initiative of labor, to include the terms for refinancing debt and investment policy, and parliamentary representatives of major political parties (Peronists and Radicals) were subsequently invited to participate in the negotiations. Eventually abandoned in favor of techno-bureaucratic approaches toward the administration of interest groups within the executive branch, partisan competition, and informal types of concertative bargaining, the CES nevertheless established the basic agenda for ongoing sectorial dialogue and at least one concrete tripartite vehicle, the Consejo de Salario Mínimo, Vital, y Móvil (council on minimum wage).

In Brazil, the results of state-sponsored concertation were far less significant than initially hoped. Key actors in tripartite and bipartite negotiations adopted noncooperative postures based on self-interested strategies dictated by structural and conjunctural conditions, which stymied any possibility of generalized agreement. This failure underscores the importance of exogenous factors and the enhanced and mutual veto power actors exercise in such arrangements.[58]

Throughout the Southern Cone, attempts to institutionalize tripartite concertation sponsored by the International Labor Organization (ILO) or promoted by the Labor Ministry have been paralleled and often overshadowed by more ad hoc, semiregular discussions led by the president or by formal and informal parliamentary negotiations on labor-related questions or broader economic issues. The different levels at which this sectorial dialogue was pitched, coupled with the lack of clear and binding parameters defining the role and relationship of its different dimensions, have impeded the move to provide stable concertative frameworks as institutional foundations for class compromise.

The lack of clear sites for decision making, agreed-upon substantive themes, and common negotiating instruments had a strong impact not only on specific concertative efforts but also on sectorial strategies in general. That is because, along with influencing the terms of substantive debate, "strategic behavior involves the ability to influence where decisions will be made, and to shift resources and attention between different areas. Power is measured not only in the ability to influence the outcome of decisions, but also in the ability to determine the arena of decision making and to insure that decisions taken there will have authority."[59]

Sectorial agents in the new democracies of the Southern Cone found it necessary to sequentially or simultaneously pursue discussions on substantive themes with different branches of the state apparatus. Divisions within the executive branch (particularly economic policy-making agencies and labor administration), between the executive and legislative branches, and within capitalist and labor organizations caused considerable variation in the strategic outlooks regarding the possibility of class compromise in Argentina and Brazil. Only in Uruguay, with its pre-authoritarian democratic tradition, the dominance of the Colorado Party in the executive branch and legislature, and an ideologically united labor movement, did the parallel use of both approaches take shape in a coherent manner.

The central position occupied by the state in any nationally aggregated process of democratic concertation should not disguise the fact that it does not operate as a uniform actor. The state has multidimensional features that cause it to replay external political conflicts internally, which prevents it from being inherently or uniformly disposed toward specific approaches to the issue of concertation. As A. Flisfisch aptly points out, even if capital and labor are nationally aggregated and centrally organized, "the state is state apparatuses plus government, and government has to do with parties, which are two or more. In this case the situation is clearly multi-personal."[60]

State approaches toward concertation are complex. Consider the role played by the Southern Cone's political parties in the immediate post-authoritarian period. In Uruguay, one dominant party (the Colorado Party) exercised control over both the executive branch and the legislature; in Argentina, a tenuous and hotly contested bipartisan dialogue between the government party and its main opposition (the Radicales and Peronistas) occurred; and in Brazil, initiatives were advanced by factions within and outside a seriously divided government party (the PMDB).

Organizational symmetry between the state apparatus and collective agents, to say nothing of the strategic orientation of each side, is therefore not an assured characteristic, particularly in contexts such as the Southern Cone. Here again, authoritarian legacies have a negative impact. Beyond the problems associated with authoritarian legislation and the arbitrary powers it confers on the state apparatus, important branches of the state, especially the armed forces, continue to be bastions of antidemocratic sentiment. That may make them committed, in whole or in part, to impeding progress in reaching sectorial agreements that contribute to the process of democratic consolidation.

Finally, the extent to which society as a whole is organized determines whether concertation can be used as a viable form for democratically mediating social group interests. If most of society is unorganized and unrepresented by collective agents of one type or another, the possibility that concertation (even if narrow in scope) will have relevance, much less a significant impact, drops considerably. This problem is accentuated in most Latin American societies by the tradition of state-corporatist modes for mediating various interests. Even when they are efficient and inclusionary, these modes perpetuate anti-egalitarian processes of power distribution among social groups.

This question is applicable to the cases under discussion here. Although, in Latin American terms, Argentina, Brazil, and Uruguay represent comparatively well-organized societies, vast sectors of their populations remain without collective voices to represent them (for example, in Brazil less than 17 percent of the economically active population is unionized). This is yet another negative legacy of the previous authoritarian regimes, which used economic policies and repression to disrupt collective identities and restore the primacy of market relations in their societies.

What democratic concertation between representatives of the minority of organized sectors in such societies can do is provide the means for taking policy-making authority (broadly or narrowly construed) out of the hands of a technocratic or class elite and into the hands of a (however slightly) broader array of collective agents. Extended further, democratic concertation can be seen as "an economic and political project that attempts to promote popular participation at all levels."[61] If for no other reason, this represents a significant advance toward more equitable processes of national decision making, and a major step toward democratic institutionalization.

The unique attributes and characteristics of the democratic capitalist state are evident at every level of organization. The organization of the state as an institution and the policies it pursues express a specific class compromise. This includes establishing or strengthening institutional mechanisms for representing interest groups, articulating and redressing demands, integrating sectors and negotiating among them, monitoring and enforcing laws, making forecasts and providing information about the economy, and more general mechanisms of adjustment and support, all of which add complexity to the state's mission and endow it with a distinctive democratic character. Depending on historical and contextual factors, it will most likely be an autonomous and interventionist state, with a particular set of features specific to the regime that are conducive to establishing the structural bases of democratic class compromise.[62]

Administering organized labor's interests democratically

begins with a state apparatus that organizationally promotes the "renewal of collective bargaining, which constitutes an important source of regulation. [Upon this] is assembled a montage of institutional frameworks, in a formalization of corporatist participation . . . [that with regard to] labor conflicts [involves] approaches towards social security and other nodal elements of labor administration."[63] In effect, from the lowest to the highest forms of organized interaction with civil society, the democratic state apparatus displays unique features unseen under other regime types.

In summary, under democratic capitalist regimes, most of the state apparatus (or at least those branches with domestic responsibilities) serves as a vehicle for maintaining class compromise, just as, under authoritarian regimes, a large part of the state apparatus serves as an instrument for class domination. While the particulars of the state's role in promoting and maintaining the compromise may vary significantly among different types of stable democratic regimes (for example, between federal, unitarian, consociational, and parliamentary systems), this role is likely to be a crucial factor in countries where democracy has been absent for long periods. With this in mind, we can turn our attention to the branch of the state that plays a leading institutional role in the labor relations systems of three Southern Cone countries.

3

LABOR COLLECTIVE ACTION, REGIME TYPE, POLITICAL INCORPORATION, AND THE STATE

Labor Collective Action

Whatever its logical basis, whether it is cooperative or conflictual, collective action is a mainstay of political life. This fact is not lost on organized labor as it confronts political authorities (represented by the state) and capitalists under a variety of regime types. However, the attempt of organized labor — as of any large, diverse, and nationally aggregated social group — to speak uniformly with one collective voice is often difficult to achieve, especially in political climates where such unity is officially discouraged or where economic conditions do not favor recruiting new members or improving bargaining positions. This is all the more onerous when opposing groups do enjoy cohesiveness or the protection of the regime in power.

Not surprisingly, a resurgence of collective action is an essential aspect of democratization. This is because democratic "consolidation involves a public definition of substantive issues and an institutional specification of policy spaces which brings *organized interests* to the forefront."[1] Hence the importance of "peak associations" that organize (some might say divide) civil society into segments along functional, ethnic, religious, or class lines in order to represent them.[2] Central among these are the collective agents of labor and capital, for they represent key players in the move to establish a democratic class compromise.

Group size and relative organization, the structure of conflict, and the nature of the goods desired all inform actors' approaches toward collective action. The organizational problems of workers are affected by the organizational capacities and goals of capitalists and the state.[3] Yet the specific logic of collective action is different for labor than for capital,[4] to say nothing of the logic underlying the state's strategic posture toward labor-capital interaction. Thus, in order to overcome the conflicts that would otherwise inevitably arise, the process of institutionalizing democratic class relations requires the presence of nationally aggregated, symmetrically organized collective agents with overlapping strategic outlooks, who exercise binding authority over their affiliates, and of a state apparatus capable of mediating between them in a neutral way.

Subordinate socioeconomic groups in capitalist societies, lacking individual resources when compared to propertied classes, are heavily reliant on their collective agents for the defense and representation of their common interests. Only through collective action (organized or not) can these groups influence policy making. However, whereas spontaneous, relatively unorganized collective action such as demonstrations, riots, or wildcat strikes may have a significant impact at a given moment, the long-term, coherent, and systematic representation and defense of subordinate group interests requires a collective agent capable of negotiating — rationally or "irrationally," as the case may be — with the collective agents of propertied groups and the state. This is because "it is the ability to organize which largely governs the degree of participation in the decision-making process, which in turn facilitates the access of most of the underprivileged groups to the goods and services that are available to the community."[5]

The rationality underriding collective action has both a subjective and an objective dimension. An "objective" situation or context is assessed from the particular vantage point of a given actor (based on the actor's values and ethics, as well as class, etc.) Once the actors have assessed the situation and formulated objectives, they move to "objectively" achieve them in the most expedient manner possible (through cost/benefit analysis, the "lesser evil" approach, carrot-and-stick tactics or whatever is considered the most advantageous approach to the situation in question).

Organized labor represents the collective means by which the working classes address their common concerns, defend their general interests, and present their specific demands before employers and the political authorities that control the state. As such, it occupies a leadership position in expressing the economic and political desires of the working classes in general.

This role is especially important given the dissimilar impact of systemic events, particularly felt in the interaction between business and labor organizations. "In general, sensitivity to macro-problems is unequally distributed among associations of economic actors, which means that only those problems will find easy resonance in the negotiations of collective actors which are perceived to affect them to roughly equal extents."[6]

For instance, employers may have an indirect interest in the infant mortality rate among the working class because of its impact on future labor supply and worker morale, while rank-and-file employees have a direct and immediate interest because it is their children who are dying. Likewise, environmental and health issues connected with the workplace are perceived differently by workers and employers, as are stock market fluctuations, monetary policy, and protectionist legislation. The different kinds of interest expressed in each case make it improbable that both groups will agree to negotiate a common response to these problems unless trade-offs are involved. Yet subjects such as wage policy, employment levels, investment trends, productivity, pricing of domestic staples, etc., either singly or as trade-offs, constitute potential grounds on which to negotiate mutually satisfactory agreements. There must, however, be collective agents for this to occur.

As such, organized labor's interests extend beyond immediate economic concerns. More than a "labor aristocracy," organized labor is the most politically and economically articulate sector of the working classes; hence its leadership role. According to a former Argentine labor leader,

> syndicalism must fulfill a double function that promotes the advancement of the working class and the people in general. . . .

[That is,] it is charged with revindicating the economic, political, social, and cultural rights of workers and, from its specific position, simultaneously marshals energies to ensure that political power is exercised by the people.[7]

To understand why this is so, we must clarify the logic and purpose behind union organization.[8]

The formation of labor unions is originally defensive. It is a form of collective action *cum* identity formation that is mediated by the nature of the relationship established with the specific adversary in question, namely, employers (capitalists). Unions first organize as a collective response to and protection against the vulnerability of the individual's employment relationship. Unorganized workers are vulnerable on two fronts: first, to employers' whims and prerogatives and to negative market factors (scarcity of product demand, oversupply of labor, technological change, etc.); and second, to competition by peers, who bid down wages in their search for employment. Initial organizing thus occurs as a form of defensive, voluntary collective action to this twofold vulnerability; it attempts to limit workers' competition for employment while simultaneously insulating the employment relationship from capricious employers or adverse market conditions.

With initial organization achieved, labor unions move to become a form of compulsory collective action by expanding their membership bases. From a collective action standpoint, union membership would ideally become a mandatory requirement for admission into certain trades (closed shops). Monopoly of representation provides a major step toward maintaining wage and employment levels. The quest for continued material benefits and other payouts (higher wages, full employment, pensions and benefits, etc.) requires that unions constantly attempt to maintain limits on competition among workers in specific functional areas by universalizing the requirement for union affiliation.

Union strength derives from its control of the labor supply. Organizing is designed to improve returns in relation to competitive (i.e., unorganized) levels. However, the more union organization occurs, the more difficult it is to organize the next higher level. Union power and membership benefits are derived from the proportion of the labor force organized in given productive sectors (i.e., union density), but the costs to unions are derived from their absolute size. Thus union density, not size per se, is what unions try to achieve via organization. As a result, there is a constant tension between the inclusionary and exclusionary features of labor unions, which is reflected in varying approaches toward membership recruitment, benefit distribution, and the like.

Union concerns have grown dramatically beyond their original scope to include working conditions and safety ("job control" issues), wages, labor force stability, employment standards, health, welfare, and pension issues, social security policy, productivity and investment objectives, sectorial protection strategies, and national economic policy. Union objectives are procedural, involving control over work, and substantive, involving returns from work. Trade-offs are made between the two categories and it is often necessary to achieve procedural objectives in order to make substantive gains. Calculating a preference between the two types of objectives lies at the heart of labor's bargaining strategies.

The political economy influences but does not determine labor's strategies. In neoliberal or monetarist economic systems characterized by economic climates of recession or fiscal austerity, such as those of the Southern Cone, organized labor assumes a defensive stance that emphasizes employment stability and the enforcement of protective labor legislation. In expansionist Keynesian or welfare state economic systems, labor shifts to an offensive posture that pushes wage increases and the expansion of formally codified labor rights.[9]

Union organization is also directly and indirectly affected by the changing structure of production. Shifts in capitalist forms of production and in the attendant relations of production change the way capitalist agents, and in turn, labor unions, are organized. The evolution of collective agents for capital and for labor in response to structural changes thus occurs as a means of defending the material and political interests of each group in the changed milieu.

In early or "primitive" stages of capitalist development, where the scope of production is limited and small productive units are the norm, shop-level craft unions emerge to confront the employer in the workplace. Labor relations occur segmentally within each firm, with few alliances between firms or sectors being formed among different craft unions (the exceptions are certain cottage industries that use the same type of craftsmanship).

Advances in capitalist techniques of production and the corresponding changes in the structure of production and in the social relations of production lead to broader forms of association. With the expansion of economies of scale based on Fordist and Taylorist schemes, the routinization and commodification of labor lead to the emergence of industrial unions that group workers by productive sector. In Europe, the rise of industrial unionism led to the adoption of corporatist schemes for representing interest groups (both within society and before the state), in which nationally aggregated "peak associations" with a monopoly on sectorial representation negotiated the terms of class compromise, often via concertative frameworks.[10]

Shifting union organization is a response to *both* the changing structure of production and the capitalist organizational capabilities derived from that change, since there is a need to maintain organizational symmetry in the face of these structural and organizational changes.

> The central dynamic of the monopoly stage of capitalism is located in the contradictory effects which capital accumulation has on the working class. While increasingly subordinating labor to capital, capital concentration simultaneously increases the strength of the working class by concentrating and centralizing it and thus developing its collective industrial power and solidarity.[11]

Although this oversimplifies the dynamics by which capitalist development leads to working-class power through organization, it points to a key issue: under conditions of an increasingly competitive, diversified, and interdependent international division of labor within the capitalist world system, organized labor is a crucial ingredient in national economic success. This has given urban labor throughout the world the roots for its expansion as a class, as well as the need to promote the organizational growth and centralization of its collective agents.

The enlarged scope of labor's concerns (even in countries where addressing these concerns is illegal) has added a new focus and another dimension to labor strategy, even if it has not overcome labor's basic defensive orientation. The expansion of labor's concerns introduces an additional actor upon which unions press their demands: the state. Political rights are necessary if workers (and their collective agents) are to effectively voice and defend their economic interests, and the state is the institutional guarantor of those rights. As a result, unions embrace political demands that reaffirm their legitimate economic role before both employers *and* the state.

This is especially true on the Iberian Peninsula and in Latin America, with their strong histories of state-corporatist labor relations.[12] Under these systems, based on Roman law or code law, there is an encompassing body of written legislation covering all contingencies and administered by nonjudicial authorities. The state is the only entity that can expand or delete provisions in these codes, implement and enforce them, and enact provisions that apply to specific cases via the law and the state apparatus. Thus the state is far more important in labor relations and working conditions than is direct bargaining between capital and labor. Here, labor legislation includes the basic right to be recognized as the legitimate agent for any group of workers or capitalists, without which no agreements have legal standing.

Where there is extensive state involvement in labor relations, workers' organizations primarily address their demands and grievances to the state rather than to employers. Unions are "political" because of the legal system in which they operate, regardless of ideological persuasion. This has been particularly true in the Southern Cone, where labor movements received their initial boost to prominence from the state.[13]

Even in those countries where the state's formal role in the economy and the labor relations system is circumscribed, unions divide their demands between employers and the state, and have thus come to adopt a variety of overtly political positions. In fact, the modern role of the state in national economic decision making has made labor's political focus inevitable regardless of legal context.

As a result of this additional actor upon which to focus (to say nothing of the state's structural concern with administering labor interests and demands), organized labor becomes an economic and political agent. This "dual nature" (to use A. Touraine's phrase) is most evident in ideologically militant unions, which for strategic reasons consider the overall political role played by organized labor to be more important than its economic function.

The political role assumed by umbrella labor confederations allows affiliate unions to concentrate attention on industry-specific economic and work-related issues. Conversely, national labor confederations serve as "amplifiers" of local union demands, giving broader voice and support to the specific claims being made by individual affiliates. In so doing, they serve as agents of class consciousness, collective solidarity, and sectorial mobilization, rather than as national economic agents of a particular occupational category.

These different functions stem from an organizational problem specific to labor. While owners and managers of the productive apparatus organize as employers (employer associations) *and* as producers (trade associations), unions organize the labor market, i.e., as employees, in defense of their material interest as a class, as sellers of labor power. This poses a fundamental dilemma. If unions are allowed to organize around production issues specific to their sector or industry, that is, as producers (for example, through "company" or "business" unions, work councils, or industrial federations, etc.), they behave like firms in that sector, differentiating their interests from those of workers employed in other firms or sectors, or from the interests of workers as consumers and citizens.

Conversely, if unions retain the traditional position of class interest, they abrogate their right to involve themselves in production decisions at the industry, sector, or firm level. They concede their structural subordination to capitalist domination of the labor market and microeconomic management issues, in order to concentrate on the demand aspects of the labor market equation.

The heterogeneity of interests within production has traditionally made unions shy away from production issues in favor of class interests in the labor market, but there is a constant tension between the two positions.[14] Issues of industrial subsidies, taxation, tariffs, regional development, import quotas, etc., clearly have an effect on working-class interests. Hence, even if the specific impact differs by sector or industry, labor always has an immediate interest in production-related issues. In order to resolve the tension between the two bases of interest representation, organized labor under democratic capitalism increasingly has allowed for union autonomy at the sectorial or industry level on economic issues, while retaining confederational umbrella organizations as national political vehicles of the working classes in toto.

Such is the case in Uruguay, where the decentralized, functionally heterogeneous yet ideologically homogeneous and principal-oriented nature of the labor movement, operating in a pluralist labor relations system, prompted national labor confederations to act much like political parties rather than economic agents (as is currently the case with the PIT-CNT). In Argentina and Brazil, national labor confederations formally discharge both tasks, although the political roles of the Argentine CGT and the Brazilian CUT, CGT, and USI are the more visible (if not the more effective) functions of each.

Sectorial economic grounds for politization differentiate the unions' strategic position at each level. This may lead unions to adopt complementary strategies at the confederational, federational, sectorial, and industry levels; on the other hand, it may generate conflicts between these levels, as entrenched interests at one level attempt to limit the autonomy or prerogatives available to unions at other levels.

The expansion of labor's original objectives and focuses of attention, which brought its dual economic and political roles into play, has brought to light another dimension in the strategy of modern unions. This dimension is offensive or proactive rather than defensive or reactive, and involves expanding citizenship rights to previously marginalized, subordinate, or disenfranchised groups. While ultimately subordinate to the fundamentally economic concerns of all unions, this proactive approach has become a driving force behind labor's political activities. Labor initiatives in a wide array of policy areas therefore constitute a core element in so-called progressive political agendas (some democratic, some not) to which are joined a variety of similarly "progressive" concerns such as those involving environmental associations, civil rights organizations, and other groups that occupy subordinate positions in capitalist societies. Because of its strategic location in production, organized labor often absorbs and represents the interests of these other subordinate sectors or even becomes their direct agents.

This points to the most far-reaching role that organized labor can play: that of a counterhegemonic agent for social change. In the words of one Latin American unionist, "democratic unions are an axis of freedom and a bridge toward progress because they are vehicles for social justice and a training ground for autonomy and social and political respect." To that end, a primary task of such unions lies in "promoting national development and economic cooperation programs" that bring about "the emancipation of all workers by means of their participation in all decision-making organs." As a result, "workers and their institutions must take the initiative in forging a new social contract"[15] via institutionalized bargaining along class lines.

Although the counterhegemonic position of labor unions has failed to materialize in most instances, the role of the union infrastructure (press, social and sports facilities, educational activities, etc.) in promoting proletarian culture and values is critical to any working-class political agenda. Moreover, labor's ability to fulfill this role is part of the process of horizontal expansion of social networks, an integral part of the societal phase of consolidating substantive democracy. We need only think of the importance of the union of Catholic base communities and trade unions in exploiting the Brazilian *abertura* to understand the significance of this alliance.

The dual political and economic roles played by organized labor are a way of overcoming the artificial division of working-class identities prevalent under democratic capitalism. The separation of the social and political identities of working-class people is codified in institutional arrangements that endow individuals with rights as "citizens" in the political sphere while limiting them to the role of producers and consumers (as wage earners) in the productive sphere. Under this scheme, unions are considered economic agents, while political parties, usually not based on class (but dominated by the interests of the propertied classes), serve as the political agents of the "citizenry."

Under the right conditions, labor unions can overcome these obstacles and serve as the vanguard of the counterhegemonic movement in capitalist societies. To do so, union leadership must be uncompromisingly militant in its anticapitalist ideology (strategically, not tactically), and must be drawn from the rank-and-file base (as organic rather than traditional intellectuals); union organizations must be unified, centralized, strategically focused, and tactically coordinated via democratic principles of rank-and-file representation; and rank-and-file workers must be class conscious and well represented throughout the union hierarchy. Under these conditions, the labor movement is the most "organic" of working-class agents — rooted in production, democratically governed, class-based and acting as a political vehicle for socioeconomic change.

These labor unions can engage in an incremental "war of position" to gradually improve workers' positions in the political and economic markets. This means that, when the anticapitalist orientation and united organizational bases of the labor movement are understood by all sides, unions can negotiate the best pragmatic or moderate economic bargains vis-à-vis employers while simultaneously pushing progressive causes through their ties to militant parties and social movements in the political system. Thus construed, the labor movement presents a solid front before the state and capital, obstructing capitalists' attempts to divide and conquer the working class via selective co-optive techniques. Of the labor movements studied here, only the Uruguayan movement approximates this model.

It is true that, when these conditions are not satisfied, labor unions in capitalist societies are susceptible to economism, co-option, corruption, or capitalist domination (as in the case of so-called business unions). This has been the rule more often than the exception in Latin America and elsewhere. Ironically, it is under these conditions that militant class-based parties become the vanguard of the counterhegemonic movement. The failure of labor unions to realize their counterhegemonic potential, in other words, forces militant parties to act as the primary (yet admittedly second-best) counterhegemonic apparatuses. Otherwise, militant parties take their strategic direction and tactical cues from labor unions, not vice versa. This contradicts every tenet of Marxist thought on the subject of vanguardism, which may explain why orthodox approaches stressing the role of the party as a vanguard have been singularly unsuccessful in advancing working-class interests throughout the democratic capitalist world.[16]

With a dualist strategic posture, organized labor is a vehicle through which workers can forge a united identity, both collective and individual, as citizens and workers. Through such unions, workers recapture a holistic notion of self that incorporates both the political *and* the economic dimensions of citizenship. "The cleavage between the social and the political is in reality a characteristic of capitalist society proper and an important element in the reproduction of this form of social domination. It is for this very reason that, from very early on, the labor movement has attempted to overcome this artificial division, linking (material) revindications with the political. The main labor centrals throughout the world have a clear political orientation."[17]

Union objectives can therefore be classified along the following lines: *political* or *predominately political* (such as electoral support for a party or candidate, revolutionaries, etc.); *wage issues*, including raises, rates and overtime schedules, etc.; work-related *"social"* or *benefit claims*, including working conditions and hours, health, life, and accident insurance, leave policy, unemployment compensation, retraining programs, and the like; *union defense and participation*, including union presence on the shop floor and/or in management councils, the role of shop stewards, union representation on grievance boards and in stock option programs, and related measures of organizational defense; and finally, *solidarity* concerns, including support for other unions, environmental defense, defense of unionists abroad who are subjected to repression or to violations of trade union rights, support for human rights in general, and other nonlabor and union-specific concerns that are deemed worthy of attention.

Local union concerns are usually limited to wage, benefit, and union defense issues, with political and solidarity objectives assuming a position of secondary importance. After all, the "bread and butter" issues represent the original, defensive rationale behind union organization. However, as we move toward the national level, political and solidarity issues assume larger roles.

Regardless of its potential as a counterhegemonic agent, organized labor is not always progressive, egalitarian, and oriented toward the common good and the improvement in position of subordinate groups in society. In practice, unions often adopt egotistical, exclusionary, corrupt, or authoritarian positions, preferring to pursue narrow, self-serving material or political interests rather than communitarian ideals or the objective needs of the working classes. Clientelism and patronage often supersede democratic mechanisms of internal representation, and this works against the universal and egalitarian articulation of rank-and-file interests. This has often been the charge made against Argentine and Brazilian labor.

Organizational requirements lead to the creation of bureaucratic hierarchies within unions. These may generate internal interests that are different from, and even opposed to, those of the rank and file (what might be called the unholy marriage between Weber's and Michel's notions of complex organizations). Defending the inerests of the union, in other words, may not be synonymous with defending the interests of the rank-and-file.

Under authoritarian capitalist regimes, the tendency toward internal conflict between different levels of union bureaucracy is often reinforced and encouraged. This adds to the obstacles to successful democratization at the institutional level. Thus the principal-agent problem for organized labor has two sides. One involves union leaders' responsiveness to membership concerns; the other involves members' compliance with directives from the leadership. The congruence of interests on the part of leaders and members is never assured, which makes their relationship extremely tenuous at times, and always contingent on material and political rewards.

It has been suggested that the same contradictory logic of collective action is shared by pluralist and neocorporatist systems. Most obvious under pluralist systems, collective action problems also beset democratic corporatist systems of concertative intermediation among interest groups, where

> branch organizations of an encompassing neocorporatist business or labor organization have an incentive to push for the interests of their own branch, even when this is not in the interests of the clients of the encompassing organization as a whole. . . . If, as is sometimes the case, the encompassing organization is a federation of partly independent organizations, the organizations in separate sectors can break away with less difficulty than if they are simply branches.[18]

Since the disarticulation of organized labor at the national level was a primary objective of each of the outgoing authoritarian regimes, and since capitalists in all three countries have nationally representative peak associations speaking for them, it should be apparent that achieving the task of speaking with one voice through peak associations — whether labor confederations or political parties — remained fundamental for organized labor during the processes of democratic consolidation. For this reason, the level at which collective bargaining is conducted has been of crucial significance for organized labor, since it can either strengthen or weaken the negotiating position of its peak associations. The new democratic regimes could propose legislation that fixed collective bargaining at the plant, firm, industry, sectorial, or national level. This not only influenced labor strategies, it also provided a strong indication of how each regime wanted to incorporate (or not) organized labor into the process of democratic consolidation.

Labor's response and its own initiatives in this area tell us much about its organization, objectives, orientation, and strategies in each country. Its strategies are based on a collection of egotistical, altruistic, and ideological preferences among both its leaders and members, which makes the issue of internal control (i.e., rank-and-file solidarity and self-discipline) all the more problematic. Nonetheless, organized labor's objectives and roles make it a potentially important actor in any process of democratic consolidation. The question of whether it becomes one hinges on the structural context and institutional conditions that frame the range of choices it is presented with during the initial stages of this process. This is as much a product of initiatives on the part of the regime and market factors as it is of the internal dynamics of the labor movements in question. There is, in effect, a dialectical process of interaction between these internal and external elements that together condition the role organized labor can play in processes of democratic consolidation.

In broad terms, four types of unionism can be identified. These types of labor organization are generally related to the way labor is inserted or incorporated into the political system. They can be identified by the combined objectives of the leadership and the rank and file. Where both union leaders and members orient their strategies around long-term anti–status quo political objectives, we speak of a "militant," "revolutionary" or "opposition" unionism. Where the rank and file pursue immediate economic objectives while the leadership is oriented by longer-term political considerations, we speak of "dualist" unions. Where both the rank and file and the union leadership share immediate economic concerns, we refer to "business" unions. Finally, where the rank and file have longer-term political preferences but the leadership concentrates on immediate economic objectives, we have "official" or "integration" unionism, which has most often been associated with labor relations systems of the state-corporatist type.[19]

There are seldom "pure" types of unionism. Moreover, unions are not static. Union logic, organization, and objectives evolve in response to endogenous and exogenous factors. The way organized labor is integrated into the political system thus has much to do with the type of unionism found in specific instances.

The expansion of the concerns, focuses of attention, roles, and strategic objectives of organized labor complicates the ability of unions to fulfill many of their primary functions. Unlike the interests of capitalist associations, union objectives cannot be reduced to easily quantifiable, "objective," material terms such as protection of profit. They cannot be pursued in isolation from members' other basic needs (since many of these stem from the employment relation). They are subject to members' differing perceptions of their subjective and objective interests, and to problems in collecting information.

The subjective aspect of working-class rationality is grounded not only in material self-interest (the structural dimension), but also in the social relations of the rank and file (familial, ethnic, racial, religious, class, occupational, generational, etc.). After all, workers are not just the fundamental producers of wealth but also consumers of goods and pursuers of cultural activities. Life outside the workplace has as much, if not more, influence than life at the workplace. This leads to contradictions, such as workers' acceptance of increased alienation in production in exchange for a greater subjective good outside the production process (e.g., consumption, family time), or more autonomy in the private social sphere.

As A. Gorz points out, democratic "capitalism owes its political stability to the fact that, in return for the dispossession and growing constraints experienced at work, individuals enjoy the possibility of building an *apparently* growing sphere of individual autonomy outside of work."[20] Individual and group interpretations of this socially given reality constitute the ideological dimension of subjective rationality. Hence, individual and collective subjects often use two parallel logics in approaching issues of strategic interaction, which, in the case of working-class organizations, makes collective action on the part of the union all the more complex.[21]

Intrinsic and extrinsic factors influencing the subjective dimensions of collective action by the working class make it all the more difficult to pursue coherently. The shift from socially given identities to democratic, political identities is not easy even when unionization is successful. It is even less assured during a shift from authoritarian to democratic capitalist rule, particularly where hierarchical modes of social discourse have historically predominated. As a result, workers adopt iterative approaches toward ordering preferences based on the interplay of subjective and objective assessments. These in turn produce cost/benefit analyses of material and nonmaterial objectives that may be discounted over time. These analyses may be rational or irrational. Different subjective and objective perspectives among workers and their agents often lead to deficiencies in coordinating the union's strategic behavior, and to fundamental asymmetries in relation to capitalists' capacity to engage in strategic interaction. This complicates the task of the labor movement, and adds importance to the institutional range of choices presented to it.

In principle, under democratic capitalism this range of institutionalized choices is quite broad. In authoritarian capitalist regimes, by contrast, the unions' range of choices is more narrow; even the right to organize is often suspended, or at least controlled by the regime. Depending on external conditions and legal frameworks, unions under democratic capitalism are confronted with a continuum of choices, ranging from open conflict to institutionalized cooperation. This is because

> in a democracy conflicts have outcomes, since democracy is a system by which they can be terminated. . . . Particular institutions, such as elections, collective bargaining, or the courts, constitute mechanisms for terminating, even if at times only temporarily, whatever inter-group conflicts emerge in a society. In the absence of collective bargaining arrangements, strikes are terminated only when one of

the sides can no longer afford to continue the conflict.... Moreover, in the absence of such institutions, conflicts which are important to group interests often become terminated only after a physical confrontation. Democracy allows such conflicts to be terminated in a previously specified manner, according to explicit criteria, and often within specified time.... Conflicts are organized: their outcomes are related to the particular combinations of strategies pursued by various groups ... [and yet] there is no reason to suppose that the ordering of outcomes upon a configuration of strategies is so strong that each combination uniquely determines the outcome. Conversely, the same outcomes may be associated with multiple configurations of strategies.[22]

Institutionalized forms for resolving sectorial conflicts significantly influence the strategic approaches by the various sectors. In particular, highly institutionalized frameworks such as democratic corporatist concertation affect trade union policy with "the introduction of capitalist growth criteria within the formulation of union wage policy, the central aspect being the recognition that profit is the condition for future economic growth, including that of wages. . . . Macro-considerations for the economy as a whole enter into the formulation of wages policy via union participation in corporatist structures. Thus maintenance of full employment, the avoidance of inflation, even the rationalization and concentration of industry, become explicit concerns of unions in formulating wage demands."[23]

Some institutional frameworks actively promote the mutual exchange of "objective" material logics that underride class perspectives on distributive conflicts under democratic capitalism. Subjective assessments notwithstanding, the institutionally defined range of sectorial choices ensures that all sectors will find objective, material grounds on which to formulate a strategic logic. This is the logic of capitalism, to be sure, but the resulting level of exploitation is institutionally attenuated by political guarantees. These are the institutional bases of a democratic class compromise.

Whatever the approach adopted vis-à-vis capital and the state, organized labor's negotiating position has only one foundation: the ability to withhold the labor services of its members. Unlike commodities (with which it is often confused), labor service cannot be physically separated from the provider. It is one of the few factors of production that can produce more than its own value and is the subject and object of the employment relationship. Labor services are sold by surrendering legal control over something that remains physically in the provider's possession. It is "living" capital, as opposed to "liquid," "fixed," or "inanimate" capital (i.e., money, machines, or property), and is less fluid than these other forms of capital. (Moreover, it is shaped by physiological properties and psychological needs — affective, spiritual, material, etc. — that are the subjective substance of the provider).

Organized labor uses the ability to withdraw the labor services of its members as the most important tool when negotiating with capital and the state, even if it remains a threat held in reserve. From its most extreme form of strikes (political or economic, general or sectorial, industrial or company-specific; staggered, sequential, temporary, long-term, fixed-period, or indefinite) to more moderate versions such as slowdowns, working to rule, the refusal to work overtime, etc., such withholding is the principal method by which organized labor buttresses its negotiating position. It emphasizes the loss that the productive process suffers when union members withdraw their labor service.[24]

This loss is an economic and political concern for both employers and the state. The value of this ultimate "weapon" to labor is all the more evident in post-authoritarian contexts, since strikes and related activities are uniformly proscribed by authoritarian regimes. As part of reestablishing its public identity, organized labor often reemphasizes strikes and slowdowns as the preferred negotiating tools in the newly opened political arenas.[25]

The effect produced by withdrawing labor service depends on whether the action taken supports procedural or substantive issues. "Outcomes are different when strikes concern the very right to organize than when they concern wage demands."[26] In fact, strike strategies are often used as a first step toward establishing unions as viable bargaining agents; strikes can be used as forms of organizing behavior and in forming collective identities.

Labor's structural position, however, makes it doubly susceptible to weakness. First, the power of labor unions stems from the effectiveness of their collective organizations and strategic location rather than their control of productive assets. Second, there is the diminishing ability to guarantee over time rank-and-file adherence to any strike due to a variety of factors — economic, psychological, ideological, organizational, and sociological, in addition to basic material and physical needs — that negatively influence an individual member's perceptions and calculation of the benefits to be gained through such action.[27] In these situations the disjuncture between egotistical and cooperative strategies among the rank and file becomes particularly evident, and egotistical motives generally prevail. In the absence of effective discipline, solidarity among the rank and file becomes particularly tenuous.

Contextual factors also work against the success of withholding labor services. These include the availability of surplus labor and calculations on the part of the rank and file of the chances of successful free riding in the face of the uncertain, nonbinding, and differentiated response from other organized sectors of the working class. Also, the economic situation of firms and the general response of capital combine with the economic and political climate of the time to add to labor's difficulties. For example, firms with lagging sales and large stocks, and those close to bankruptcy, may welcome work stoppages.

For its part, the state is less likely to interfere in a strike that affects all businesses in a given sector equally, preferring to allow the market to determine the terms of an eventual resolution. This does not occur when labor or capital has strong ties to the party system or to the executive branch and can exert pressure in the political arena for a favorable resolution to the conflict. But it is not only withdrawing labor service per se and labor and capital's political power that force the state to act against unions. Rather, it is the fact that capital can refuse to make investments as a response to labor strikes, which presses the state into action. This is because such capitalist responses — in effect, "market coups" or capitalist strikes — threaten to undermine the structural foundations of the entire system.[28] When capitalists vote with their wallets rather than summoning the military, they put a far more effective check on the state and labor in the long run.

A "market coup" is a last resort. Many more "vulgar" options are available. These include purchasing favors and protection from the government, acquiring labor services outside the union, using privately purchased forces of coercion to break the work stoppage, and buying the cooperation of labor leaders.

Other contextual factors significantly influence labor's negotiating position. Recessionary periods, with their attendant declines in production and rises in unemployment, are bad times to press demands by means of strike threats. During such periods, unions often find that they must narrow the scope of their concerns to the original defensive position, i.e., protection of employment and (if possible) wage levels and work conditions. Conversely, periods of economic growth, when demand, productivity requirements, and employment levels are high, offer excellent opportunities for using the threat of withholding labor service as a bargaining tool, particularly in decentralized or pluralist labor relations systems.

The same can be said for the political climate. If the political tenor of the times is, for whatever reason, "antilabor," then labor's chances to exercise a full range of options — especially the threat of strikes — are quite low. This is evident in the labor legislation enacted by different political regimes. Such legislation represents "nothing more than the judicial expression of dominant group ideology."[29]

In Brazil, for example, the labor laws inherited from the military regime expressed a negative view of the usefulness of strikes in achieving working-class objectives, precisely because it was not representatives of the working class but rather the military authorities who drew up the legislation. According to Metalworker Union leaders in São Paulo,

> the law attempted to discipline the strike problem and created [a framework] so rigid that it was almost impossible to declare strike.

... It ... gave a series of advantages to the employer which made striking difficult. ... For a [legal] strike to occur, so many formalities were required that when they were fulfilled there was no longer any reason to strike.[30]

In any event, organized labor's negotiating position is weaker than that of capital in two ways: internally, due to the fragility inherent in maintaining a withdrawal of labor services over time; and externally, because of the adverse effects of a wide variety of contextual factors, which add to the relative strength and range of options available to capital.

For their part, capitalist interests are quite heterogeneous, as is the degree of political influence exercised by different capitalist groups under various regimes and at various stages of accumulation. The strategic importance of individual capitalist factions stems from their location in production and evolves along with the process of accumulation. The economic rise and decline of specific capitalist factions and of the relative power they are able to exercise in defense of their interests before the state and other social groups is rooted in the evolution of the capitalist system, both national and international.

Although, as a class, the bourgeoisie is stronger than labor, it does not universally or perpetually hold a position of absolute dominance. Its heterogeneity and varying degree of influence force it to organize and engage in collective action to better promote its political and economic interests.[31]

There are also finite limits to the state and society's structural dependence on capital as a whole. There is a point, for example, during severe recessions or depressions, when threats of disinvestment lose their credibility because disinvestment would be self-destructive. Moreover, continued threats or incremental disinvestment over time amount to a capitalist version of crying wolf, and eventually state managers and labor discount that reaction. Total disinvestment, except in revolutionary situations where the basic socioeconomic parameters and model of accumulation are being challenged, is not credible either, since it removes the very leverage on which capitalist power is based. Hence, in dependent capitalist societies not facing a revolutionary transformation, those of the Southern Cone, for instance, the structural dependence of the state and society on capital, while real, is filtered through a host of contextual and institutional conditions that give a more fluid character to the interaction between the state, labor, and capital. Thus, in the post-authoritarian context, institutional mechanisms can be constructed to ameliorate labor's relative weaknesses and improve its ability to negotiate rationally calculated sectorial agreements in an equitable manner.

Such institutional channels may be a form of bourgeois co-option, but at present, they are also the most viable means of promoting working-class interests in the Southern Cone. If nothing else, such institutionalization recognizes, after a long period of exclusion, the legitimacy of organized labor as the primary articulator and defender of working-class interests. Of itself, this is an important step toward expanding the notion of citizenship and collective rights needed to overcome authoritarian legacies and advance the process of consolidating substantive democracy.

This is why the strategic posture adopted by the respective labor movements is so important for democratic consolidation in the Southern Cone. How labor is reincorporated into the national political scene will determine the success of current projects for democratic consolidation.

Labor's predisposition to "cooperate" with elected governments in post-authoritarian contexts cannot be assumed a priori, particularly when labor's preferences for egotistical postures are factored in. After a period of exclusion, organized labor in the Southern Cone is reentering the political, social, and economic arenas with its own interests to defend, something that may or may not allow it to find areas of agreement with other actors interested in seeing the new democracies thrive.

Given this, we must assess the character of the three labor movements in question here. Differences in mobilizational capabilities, resource capacity, organization, composition, strategic location, ideology, political and economic platforms, negotiating style, and history within the national political system constitute key variables in the evolution of each state.[32] After taking stock of these variables, we can identify organized labor strategies in four areas — political, economic, social, and organizational — crucial for labor's participation in the process of democratic consolidation. Given their geographic proximity and very different internal characteristics (including the size, composition, and history of their respective labor movements), Argentina, Brazil, and Uruguay present an excellent comparative sample of the strategic postures of labor and the state.

At a *political* level, we must focus our attention on labor's approach toward national politics, including its relationship to political parties, its interaction with the executive branch and the legislature (both in opposition and in support of government policies), and its position with regard to salient political issues (amnesty of military officers charged with human rights violations, constitutional reform, labor and welfare legislation, etc.).

At a *social* level, we need to examine the behavior of the labor movement with regard to other subordinate social groups such as environmentalists, feminists, squatters, etc. The question is whether labor continues to support the interests of these groups (thereby fulfilling its counterhegemonic role) after authoritarianism has been liberalized, or whether it retreats back to a parochial defense of its own interests strictly defined.

On an *economic* level, we need to concentrate on the wage strategies pursued by organized labor to show whether they are formulated and pursued in a unitary, centralized, sectorial, or decentralized fashion. This includes determining whether organized labor is willing to engage in wage trade-offs to guarantee steady rates of investment and job security. In addition, we need to address labor's approach toward minimum wages (in particular occupations and in universal terms), pension benefits, social security, productivity, price indexing, the rationalization of the public sector, the democratization of the workplace (codetermination, workers' councils, etc.) and other macroeconomic issues.

Finally, we must evaluate the (internal) *organizational* strategies adopted by each of the labor movements, especially as they relate to questions of organizational autonomy, bureaucratic centralization or decentralization, compulsory or voluntary affiliation, recruitment efforts, the features of unionization in the public sector versus the private sector, the promotion of counterhegemonic apparatuses (labor schools, alternative media, etc.), and partisan conflict within the union movement (e.g., issues of ideological plurality and minority representation in leadership positions, etc.). This evaluation will clarify what shapes union decision making in the three other strategic areas at a variety of levels (factory, sectorial, federational). After all, the nature of labor strategy in its political, economic, and social dimensions is determined as much by its organization as by the substantive issues involved.

Where there is a pattern of strikes and other methods of withholding labor services, we must evaluate these strategies in terms of how they are used to bolster labor demands in the four strategic areas, particularly the economic and the political. To this we will add an analysis of the rates of adherence in sectorial and general strikes (in terms both of individual unions and the rank and file), the way strikes and slowdowns are called, the demands most consistently voiced at each level, and the overall rate of success of each tactic. In particular, we will determine what types of strike behavior are most successful, and whether the nature of strike activity changes over time (e.g., from general political strikes to sectorial economic strikes or vice versa).

Our focus is on the major labor confederations in each country, specifically the CGT in Argentina, the PIT-CNT in Uruguay, and the CUT, CGT, and USI in Brazil. We believe that national labor confederations, with their broad and heterogeneous constituencies and macroeconomic focus, are more amenable partners for democratic capitalist governments pursuing economic recovery programs (via concertative or other strategies). Centralization, moderation, the symmetry of a perspective that is macroeconomic in scope, and the binding qualities of nationally representative leadership constitute the organizational characteristics favored by democratic governments seeking to incorporate labor into the policy-making process.

This is not to say that all democratic capitalist governments would like to see such organizational characteristics adopted by the labor movement, or that the specific governments in question would not like to see organized labor disarticulated, decentralized, divided, and weakened to the point where it is easily subjected to either market forces or to unilateral controls by the government or employers. Labor critics of government policy make this argument in all three countries: it appears closest to the truth in Argentina and (particularly) Brazil.

By undertaking an analysis of the four different dimensions of labor strategy, we shall develop a picture of labor's collective action that can be linked to the state's approaches toward administering organized labor interests in each country. Taking both sides together, we should be able to assess the objective position labor occupies in the processes of democratic consolidation, the dynamic sectorial interplay and strategic choices that lie at the heart of these processes, the possibilities for the successful incorporation of labor into the new framework, and the overall chances of consolidating the democratic regime in Argentina, Brazil, and Uruguay.

Regime Type and Labor Incorporation as a Political Actor

If class compromise between the organized working classes and capitalists is required for maintaining bourgeois democratic regimes, then an institutional forum must exist in which organized labor is able to formally set out its position against those of competing collective agents. This is especially true for countries such as Argentina, Brazil, and Uruguay, where sustained industrial growth during the postwar period led to the rise of organized labor as a serious political and economic actor.

In fact, by the early 1970s the military hierarchy and dominant factions of the bourgeoisie perceived the rapid growth and political mobilization of organized labor as posing a serious threat to capitalism. Hence the need for an authoritarian reply that could forestall such a possibility.

It is well known that this response had an extremely adverse impact on the economic, political, physical, and spiritual fortunes of the working classes.[33] Thus the ultimate success of the processes of redemocratization witnessed by these countries required the reincorporation of organized labor as a primary political and economic actor on equal footing with other socioeconomic groups, when addressing its collective interests before the democratic state.

The notion of labor incorporation has received serious attention in both Latin America and Western Europe. Broadly understood as a period when the labor movement is awarded an institutionalized presence in the political and economic markets, labor incorporation is believed to be a process that leaves a lasting — and often distinctive — political legacy in the countries where it occurs.[34] In Latin America, the original period of labor incorporation, where it occurred, was between the 1930s and 1950s. It was formalized through legal recognition, the institutionalization of state-mediated collective bargaining, and the extension of social welfare programs that were often managed by the unions and financed by the state.[35]

The circumstances of initial incorporation are clearly conditioning but not determinant. Subsequent economic, political, and social events work to shape the precise evolution of organized labor's institutional conformation and its role in the political and economic systems. A host of other variables have a decided impact on the overall place and role occupied by organized labor after its initial incorporation. These include technological development, demographic change, the evolving international division of labor, and the rise of militant ideological currents.

The term "incorporation" can therefore be expanded to include the three spheres in which the labor movement's participation is felt: *political* (its relations with the political system); *economic* (union collective action and its relationship to the economy); and *workplace* (institutional arrangements governing the relations between workers and managers at the level of the firm). Given the fluidity of these spheres, labor incorporation is not characterized by a single defining moment of a political nature that leaves a lasting legacy. Instead, it is an iterative process that has several "moments" and involves multiple levels of operation. Consequently, it is partial, uneven, and contested, and therefore fragile and transitory.[36] Initial incorporation may influence the relationship between labor, capital, and the state in a significant way, but it is thereafter subject to a variety of other conditioning factors.

Thus, we need to complement our discussion of the type of initial incorporation with a multivariate analysis that incorporates the broad range of intervening factors that shaped the evolution of organized labor's economic and political roles, as well as its institutional presence in the politico-economic system.[37] For instance, we need to look at the specific characteristics and the "historic memory" of each labor movement, the respective particulars of the original incorporation periods and the subsequent evolution experienced by each, and the extent of exclusion to which they were subjected under the preceding military regimes. All these factors had a distinctive impact on the particulars of each process of reincorporation.[38]

J. Samuel Valenzuela has developed a typology for understanding the insertion of labor movements into twentieth-century capitalist political systems based on four interrelated variables. This typology encompasses the historical pattern of consolidating labor organizations, the unity or fragmentation of the labor movement, the nature of ties between labor and party, and the type of regime into which labor is "inserted."[39] This model highlights the fact that the initial process of a labor movement's formation and the political context in which it was originally recognized as a legitimate articulator of working-class interests (i.e., its "incorporation"), have a strong influence over subsequent patterns of labor insertion into modern capitalist political systems.[40]

Based on observations of Western European and South American experiences, Valenzuela identified five general modes of labor insertion into capitalist political systems. Under democratic regimes, there are three modes of insertion: the *social democratic* mode, where a united labor movement is tied to a strong political party (as in Sweden); the *contested* mode, where the labor movement is deeply divided by ideological or partisan differences, which are replicated in party affiliations (as in France); and the *pressure group* mode, in which a functionally or sectorially differentiated labor movement is loosely tied to nonlabor parties or factions thereof (as in the United States). Under authoritarian regimes, there is the *state-sponsored* mode, in which unions and parties are promoted (if not created) by government elites, leaving little room for independent factions (as in the Brazilian Estado Novo and Peronist regime in Argentina of 1946–1955), and the *confrontationalist* mode. In the last, which is found in unstable political systems, the labor movement is generally in opposition and supersedes political parties as the agent of working-class political mobilization (as in Argentina from 1955 to 1973 and in the Novo Sindicalismo movement in Brazil from 1978 to 1985).

Each mode of insertion varies in its individual context and circumstances. For example, the traditional pattern of labor insertion in the Southern Cone shows that "in Chile workers voice their demands through national political parties, in Argentina through powerful labor organizations, in Uruguay as a pressure group on the state bureaucracy, and in Brazil as petitioners within the state corporatist network."[41] Such observations are extremely pertinent to the analyses of the particular dynamics of redemocratization in those countries.[42]

Valenzuela has addressed the role and position occupied by organized labor in processes of transition from authoritarian to democratic capitalist regimes.[43] He claims that while labor mobilization is important for the initial move toward transition to occur, labor's subsequent moderation is equally important in seeing the transition through to a successful democratic conclusion. The sources of variation in the relationship of organized labor to these processes and to their possibilities of success lie in the interrelationship of four variables.

The first is the strength or weakness of the labor movement and the economic context of the transition. The sources of union strength or weakness at the moment of transition have historical-structural as well as political roots, and can be a product of the authoritarian regime alone or of the pre-authoritarian legacy. The second is the centralization or decentralization of the labor movement and its political unity or division. These two factors are of equal importance in determining how labor will act during the transition. The third is the authoritarian regime's treatment of labor and its political allies prior to redemocratization, which has a profound impact on labor's role in that process. The final variable is the modality of the transition (i.e., the form of regime change), and the relationship between the labor movement and the elites guiding the transition. These variables add complexity to the equation. In general, all other factors being equal, elite-managed transitions are more likely to ensure the "proper" sequence of mobilization-moderation on the part of the labor movement, a sequence he deems conducive to successful democratization.[44]

We need to disaggregate labor's position during the transition and post-transition phases to gain a fuller grasp of all the factors involved in its (potential) reincorporation as a full partner in the new democratic regimes.

This type of approach allows us to advance beyond the four broad dichotomies that I. Roxborough identified as the standard forms of conceptualizing Latin American labor movements and their relationship to the politico-economic system: (1) reformist versus revolutionary (i.e., moderate versus militant strategic postures on the part of the unions); (2) oligarchic/bureaucratic versus democratic/pluralist (i.e., labor movements controlled by conservative leaders versus labor movements responsive to the militant rank and file); (3) political versus economic (labor movements oriented toward the state versus labor movements oriented toward bargaining with employers); (4) co-opted versus independent (labor movements supportive of the regime versus labor movements that are autonomous).

As Roxborough notes, this conceptual scheme paints a black-and-white picture of organized labor's position and posture within Latin American political and economic systems, one that often does not accord with reality.[45] There is considerable overlap between many of the ostensibly dichotomous positions. While these broad categories may find substance in specific instances, the use of a more sophisticated, multivariate analysis of the terms of initial incorporation, subsequent insertion and evolution, and the circumstances of reincorporation during the transition and consolidation phases provides a better framework for understanding the forms in which both unions *and* the state approach the issue of institutionalizing democratic class compromise in the reopened political arenas of the 1980s.

Bringing labor into the political system as a legitimate and recognized actor can and has occurred in many different ways. We must be careful to disaggregate the notion of "incorporation" in order to determine the extent to which organized labor is, in fact, fully "brought in" to the political system. There are key differences between regime projects that *incorporate and empower* and those that *incorporate and subordinate*. Projects that are incorporative and empowering bring organized labor into the political and economic arena as an equal, fully developed social partner. On the other hand, regime projects that are incorporative and subordinating are those that, while bringing organized labor into the political and economic game and recognizing its role as a sectorial interlocutor, do so in a way that makes labor subject to the mandates of external forces — the state, an individual leader, a dominant party — for realizing its interests. Such was the case with the inclusionary state-corporatist experiments undertaken by Vargas in Brazil and Perón in Argentina.

A particular regime project may be incorporative and empowering of organized labor in general, but incorporative and subordinating of a particular faction of labor. This has most often been the case with female-intensive sectors of the organized labor force (witness the Rama Femenina of the Peronist Party). The incorporation of laboring men has often occurred at the expense of the subordination of working-class women, even within their common organizations and among their collective agents. Likewise, agricultural labor is often subordinated while urban labor is empowered, most often because of a desire to maintain a steady flow of cheap wage goods to the industrial sector. Such has been the case in Chile.[46]

To the political terms of initial incorporation and subsequent insertion can be added changes occurring in the international and domestic markets and the workplace. Technological progress, the shifting international and domestic division of labor, the introduction of new consumer preferences and consumption patterns, and the more general structural changes associated with macroeconomic shifts in the national and international markets all have a decisive impact on the organization of working-class interests at a national level, and hence play a role in the way labor is (re)incorporated into different processes of democratic consolidation. To understand the impact of macroeconomic changes on the circumstances of labor reincorporation in the current processes of democratic consolidation, we need only recall the structurally induced expansion of the "informal" sector, and the massive entrance of unorganized women and young people into the work force as a result of the "liberal" economic policies of the authoritarian regimes.

Specific political regimes represent particular constellations of economic and social interests, and therefore condition the way market changes and technological progress influence the domestic workplace and the overall tenor of labor relations.[47] Whereas the political may not dominate the economic and the technological absolutely, it is clear that there exists a strong relationship, if not a reciprocity, between the variables in their impact on both the relations of production (i.e., the conformation of the workplace and the work force) and the social relations of production, (i.e., working-class representation and political behavior). The specific interplay of these variables can be said to constitute the core of the hegemonic project of democratic capitalist regimes, for it is through them that the working class's consent to class compromise is secured.

Therefore, the mode of incorporation of social groups and political actors varies according to regime type, and more generally, depends on systemic factors at play during specific phases of national economic and political development.[48] The terms of the initial incorporation and more recent reincorporation, though linked, necessarily differ. For example, the initial process of incorporation experienced by Argentine and Brazilian labor (inclusion-ary but subordinating state corporatist under populist authoritari-anism) cannot be replicated now for a variety of economic, histor-ical, political, and sociological (not to mention normative) reasons.

> It is, of course, only the integrative mode of inclusion that, other things being equal, can on a long-term irreversible basis accommo-date the massive entrance of new participants into the political game without reinforcing any tendencies towards a breakdown of the par-liamentary institutions and the imposition of dictatorial solutions. It is only within an integrative system that the new entrants, given the horizontal, nonpersonalistic mechanisms of inclusion, will reinforce the strength and autonomy of existing collective organisations. Only then can the distribution of political power, on the level of col-lective action, be organised in such a way that extreme polarisation between rulers and ruled is avoided and civil society is strengthened by becoming more resilient to state manipulation — and this type of strengthening, as the English model of political development has shown, presents no threat to the bourgeois order but, on the con-trary, further legitimises it by making it more hegemonic.[49]

It should be clear that the democratic mode of labor incorpora-tion, whatever its specific historical character, has an empowering and integrative orientation that is manifested in a series of institu-tional arrangements evident in the aggregation of social group interests, the type and character of the organizational channels of political and economic representation available to them, and in the organization of branches of the state responsible for administering the contending interests of various social groups. As we shall see, only in Uruguay were there historical parallels (and institutional similarities) between the initial and most recent episodes of labor incorporation.

One concrete manifestation of the democratic mode of incorpo-ration is seen in the role assigned the state in the labor relations system. Strongly interventionist in the area of *individual* worker rights (occupational health and safety, etc.), the state is generally *noninterventionist* in the area of collective rights, being content to mediate and ratify the agreements reached by freely constituted sectorial collective agents. Even so, the question of the relative autonomy of the state *and* civil society under democratic capitalist regimes transcends purely structural transformations or institutional formalities.

Ideally, autonomous, nationally aggregated, yet legitimately representative collective agents of various social groups, in an institutional forum provided and mediated by the equally autonomous democratic state, should negotiate the terms of a democratic class compromise equitably. This requires that both the state and the collective agents of the labor movement achieve some distance with respect to each other *and* with respect to their bases. For the union movement, the issue of autonomy has two dimensions: autonomy in relation to the state and employers on the one hand, and in relation to the rank and file on the other. For the state, the issue is similar, though the actors are different: autonomy in relation to the labor movement on the one hand, and to capital on the other. For all parties to a class compromise, this dual character of autonomy is critical. With an acceptable institutional distance achieved on both sides, the state and labor can offer each other certain benefits. The state offers labor unions welfare legislation, redistributive economic policies, and individual and collective recognition as legitimate bargaining agents for their membership, while the unions offer the state and capitalists domestic order, productivity, and consumption.

The relationship between the state and labor during processes of democratic consolidation can thus be seen as a broad and highly fluid sectorial bargain (here phrased in ideal terms), that operates under consensually established procedural rules. When the *quid pro quo* breaks down, the state must increasingly resort to unilateral constraints and coercion, while the labor movement must resort to more militant opposition (i.e., a frontal war of maneuvers against the state) or accept its own subordination. Attempts at hegemony are replaced by outright domination, and the more "naked" features of capitalism emerge, which are acutely felt in the workplace.

Since both sides are averse to risk, there is a mutual effort to establish grounds for consensus in order to preclude open conflict. This promotes a bureaucratic dynamic within the state and collective agents who are disposed toward institutional arrangements that use them to pursue a negotiated vertical class compromise by means of a socioeconomic concertative sectorial "pact."

Thus, while workers' welfare is the ultimate determinant of labor participation in any class compromise, it

> also brings into play the specific interests of union representatives, their political goals and own needs, their condition as interlocutors and the entrenchment of monopological [*sic*] authority, and the consolidation of their functions of control and active intervention. The opening of avenues of participation — which establish procedures for the regulation of conflict — constitutes a negotiable good in and of itself: it offers guarantees of execution of measures adopted and can make itself felt in the combination of economic and political revindications which offer bases for the development of union power.[50]

In countries where the working classes are relatively large or well organized, and where they have been systemically excluded from the political arena by previous authoritarian regimes, the promotion of class compromise requires that new democratic regimes award importance to the specific demands and ongoing interests of organized labor. As a result, democratic regimes must provide some form of institutional framework within which these demands and interests can be voiced, juxtaposed, and weighed against those of employers and other economic actors, in order ultimately to negotiate peaceful resolutions to sectorial conflicts. This institutional framework is the primary forum in which the structural bases for democratic class compromise are achieved.

The branch of the state that has traditionally been responsible for labor relations has been used as the primary institutional vehicle for promoting democratic class relations in all three Southern Cone countries. This has entailed a major reorganization of the preexisting institutional frameworks and labor relations systems, since those agencies and laws were designed and used by the preceding military-bureaucratic authoritarian regimes as instruments of political domination and economic exclusion that subordinated working-class concerns to those of competing economic and political interests.[51]

The importance of these organizational changes cannot be overemphasized, since they represent changes in the institutional parameters and "policy spaces" that condition the early range of choice available to organized labor when defending its interests against those of competing groups. These early choices influence the subsequent evolution of strategic interaction on the political, economic, and social planes, and "are likely to have a lasting effect on the resources and internal organization of interest associations — which in turn will predispose them to a particular role in different types of democracy."[52]

The institutional range of choices offered collective agents can be considered the essence of the incorporating project of different regimes. Differences in the framing of these choices, both in terms of institutional vehicles and in the specific procedural and substantive options offered, are what allow us to distinguish between the projects proposed by each regime. In turn, the material and normative objectives, degree of cohesiveness, organizational capacity, and resource endowment of various social actors in each of the four dimensions (economic, political, social, and organizational) influences their perception of choices when considering the projects of different regimes. This is what ultimately prompts them to support some regime projects and not others.

Nor are the terms of the original compromise — the "incorporating," "foundational," or "rule-making" pacts, as they are called — immutable or writ in stone. Hence, with regard to organized labor and its role in the process of democratic consolidation "at the political as much as at the industrial level much can be learned of why various labor actors behave the way they do by looking at the logic of their situation, inspecting the means available to them to pursue their goals, and the social context which provides them with a more or less limited set of opportunities and constraints."[53]

For these reasons, the successive, closely linked processes of democratic incorporation and consolidation ultimately rest on a network of institutional factors that frame the range of choices available to social actors, and consequently determine the rational calculation that underlies the strategic interaction between those actors and the state.[54] Thus, the process of democratic consolidation may well be a linked set of iterative, multiple-actor, nested "games," but it is clear that institutional parameters delineate the rules of each game. The sectorial struggle implicit in the process of democratic consolidation is sequential: first, over the rules of the game itself (the procedural minimum); and then, over the terms of the game, once mutually agreed-upon rules have been established (the substantive bases). In this light, democratic consolidation can be considered a process by which the choices of collective agents are gradually framed by consensually established institutional parameters that provide mutually acceptable reciprocal guarantees and control to all actors.[55]

State-enforced organizational frameworks and rules constitute the institutional parameters that determine what forms of collective action are feasible for different social groups and political actors (both public and private). "Given a distribution of economic, ideological, and organizational resources, the manner in which conflicts are organized determines which interests are likely to be satisfied, which are unlikely to be satisfied, and, more importantly, the variety of interests that are at all likely to be satisfied."[56]

This variable range of choices, translated into different types of strategic interaction between collective agents, political parties, and branches of the state, determines the range of possible outcomes, only some of which are conducive to the class compromise required for democratic consolidation (many in fact work against it). The entire process is a highly dynamic or even dialectical continuum, eminently susceptible to reversal, interruption, or collapse. In every aspect — institutional factors, forms of collective action, range of choices, types of strategic interaction, and possible outcomes — the combined processes of democratic incorporation and consolidation exhibit specific characteristics not shared by other regime types.

It is clear that the role and organization of the state influence the range of choices made available to organized labor and other social groups. The institutional framework charged with administering the interests of social groups can be responsive and flexible, unresponsive and rigid, or somewhere between the two. This framework may or may not offer significant differences in the range of choices available to specific social groups at particular times. There is likely to be a complementarity between flexible institutional frameworks and a wider range of choices available to key social groups, and conversely, between rigid institutional frameworks and a more narrow range of choices.

It should be underscored that limits on the range of choices mutually imposed (albeit to different degrees) by contending social actors lie at the heart of notions of relative power, whether economic, political, social, or physical. It is the ability to impose finite limits on other people's range of choices (by, among other things, determining the types of negotiation vehicles and decisional sites used), rather than simply the ability to get others to act in ways contrary to their subjective or objective interests and desires, which defines the relative power exercised over others. In modern societies, such limits on individual and collective choices are imposed by institutions, which not only aggregate and codify the sum total of individual power available in a polity, but also guarantee and reproduce the moral and legal guidelines that serve as the ethical foundations for the ordering of preferences in a society.[57]

The relative power of the democratic state qua superordinate public institution, and the way this power is institutionally manifested and exercised, frame the range of choices that determines whether labor is incorporated into the process of democratic consolidation.[58] The relative power exercised by both labor and capital is also important in this regard, particularly given the need for mutual and equitable control among collective agents and the state in attempting to reach agreements through concertative ventures. This implies the diminution of overtly instrumental manipulation of the state apparatus by dominant social groups or by political elites on the one hand, and the "top-down" manipulation of organizations of subordinate groups by the state on the other. The relative symmetry or asymmetry of power exercised by the state and various social agents, as formally manifested in the institutional range of choices offered social agents, determines the structure of the "game" of democratic consolidation.

Here lies the genius of hegemonic power in democratic capitalism, since, based on the active consent of subordinate groups, it is manifested in the subjective acceptance by these groups of a specific range of choices, framed by basic values — God, motherhood, apple pie, *fútbol*, free enterprise — that ultimately favor and reproduce the interests and position of economically dominant groups who exercise ideological leadership. Unlike authoritarian capitalist domination, the power of capital under democratic capitalism is based on the willing, rather than coerced, "consent" or passive acquiescence of the citizenry. This consent is manipulated, shaped, and molded according to the exigencies of context and circumstance (including forms of resistance by subordinate groups) by a network of ideological institutions (parties, bureaucracies, schools, the media, etc.) that obscure the exploitative class foundations of the capitalist system.[59] Consent may well be a product of alienation, but if so it is a type of acquiescent alienation that is far less dangerous to the socioeconomic status quo than that bred by any rule of force.

Even so, an element of coercion always remains in the calculations of hegemonic power; it is held in reserve as a threat to be used in the event of a systemic ("organic," in Gramsci's terms) crisis. Yet, whereas coercion is the foundation of political power in cases of authoritarian domination (*dominio*), and is thus inherently fragile (since it obeys a form of Newtonian law and wanes over time when used as the sole basis of rule), under democratic capitalism overt coercion is replaced by the inculcation of voluntary, active, and malleable consent on the part of the subordinate group via a broad array of institutions, both public and private (Althusser calls these "ideological state apparatuses").

The incorporation of labor into the process of democratic consolidation requires that the range of choices presented by the state be subjectively perceived *and* objectively accepted by the rank-and-file to be comparatively (if not compensatorially) equal to that of other social actors, particularly capitalists. The institutional framework provided by the democratic state provides the concrete guarantees that such is the case, and that is what allows labor and capital to negotiate as "equals" on the terms of the democratic class compromise. In turn, it is this relatively equal range of institutionally framed choices, and the procedural neutrality of the state in enforcing the terms of choice once they are accepted, which distinguish the incorporating project of democratic capitalist regimes from that of other capitalist regime types. In other words, these are the institutional foundations underpinning the exercise of bourgeois hegemony.

Through the specific range of choices provided by the inducements and constraints set out and imposed by the state, capital and labor are incorporated on procedurally equal terms as the fundamental social pillars of democratic capitalist regimes. Whereas the strategic choice for labor and capital is binary (namely, cooperation or noncooperation), for the democratic capitalist state, strategic options are far more limited (the state may in fact be limited to a single choice), since it has a vested interest in securing and reproducing negotiated sectorial compromises that have state mediation and enforcement as their centerpiece. This is particularly true for the ideological apparatuses of the capitalist state that seek to reproduce sectorial consent to bourgeois rule, especially those with economic functions, such as national labor administrations.

As a result, the democratic state apparatus is organized to frame the institutionalized range of choices made available to major socioeconomic agents in order to promote the convergence of strategic perspectives among them (i.e., on mutually second-best choices). These are the institutional bases of organized consent that underwrite capitalist democracy. Even so, and despite the important issues raised, there are currently no studies that examine the role, structure, and functions of national labor administrations in the processes of redemocratization that have occurred in the Southern Cone. For this reason, I have addressed the issue here.

Regime Type and State Organization

Evidence suggests that the orientation and organization of national labor administrations varies according to the type of capitalist regime.[60] This evidence confirms observations about different macro-organizational characteristics exhibited by capitalist state apparatuses under different types of national political regimes (and the more specific differences evident among the same general regime types).[61] Oszlak and O'Donnell have demonstrated that the organization of the state apparatus in Latin America offers institutional evidence of the type of political regime in power.[62] In this regard, we can conceive of national state organizations — that is, the role, organization, and functions of the state apparatus, both generally and in terms of specific branches in "core" areas of endeavor[63] — as a reliable political indicator of the nature of regimes.[64] As the preeminent institutional actor, the state manifests the social, economic, political, and military objectives of national political regimes, since translating policy objectives into action requires this organizational capacity.

In recent Latin American experiences, the state apparatus shows different organizational features under different regime types. Bureaucratic-authoritarian (BA) regimes adopt pyramidal organizational schemes characterized by hierarchies of parallel (most often military) control. They undertake a program of rationalization, de-concentration, and subsidarization of functional responsibilities, coupled with an efficiency-based management orientation. Financially, BA regimes employ universalist budgetary schemes governed by authoritarian procedures of allocation. In terms of personnel, there is often a virtual "colonization" of the state by active or retired military personnel.[65]

The few democratic regimes that have existed in Latin America display polyarchic (following Dahl's definition) hierarchies within the state apparatus in which bureaucratic power is shaped by public opinion, political parties, and the pressures exerted by representatives of important social groups. Organizational autonomy and decentralization, coupled with a clientelist orientation, are the hallmarks of states controlled by these regimes, though this often leads to the duplication of agencies and overlapping of responsibilities. At a budgetary level, financial autarky and competitive procedures for allocation are the norm. In terms of personnel, there is a clear move toward populating upper-echelon positions in the state apparatus with career public servants, although the clientelist orientation of specific state agencies promotes a relatively high level of turnover among upper-echelon personnel (due to the pressures exerted by "clients" in civil society).

Patrimonial regimes erect radial hierarchies with personalist control channels within the state, superimposing these on a highly formalized (if not sclerotic) bureaucracy subordinated to ad hoc decision-making agencies (the so-called patrimonial "court"). Financial resources are concentrated within the executive branch and subject to the criteria of discretionary allocation. Personnel selection is highly ascriptive in nature.[66]

Recent studies suggest that these general differences are replicated at a microanalytic level within specific branches of the state, although the precise organizational traits in question often vary between different "core" branches of the state (between national labor administrations and health administrations, for example).[67] These organizational differences are linked to changes in the content of public policy and the nature of the regime in power.[68]

Another factor in organizational reforms that promote dissimilar traits in different "core" areas of state activity is a regime change, which has a strong impact on public policy, and on the role, organization, and functions of the national state apparatus. Branches of the state with important domestic responsibilities tend to be influenced by regime change in a direct and immediate fashion.

National labor administrations constitute one such "core" area of state activity in each of the cases examined here. To be sure, the nature of labor's insertion into the economic and political systems and the general character and form of the state in question (federative, unitarian, consociational, laissez-faire, welfare, etc.) both have a strong influence on the institutional frameworks used to administer organized labor interests and secure working-class consent to bourgeois rule. In all cases, however, it is the nature of the regime in power, in this case the specific nature of the democratic regime in power, that determines precisely how these two variables are linked in each instance. Hence, the particularities of regime type constitute the axis around which types of labor insertion and state institutional "forms" revolve. Political regimes determine the institutional frameworks within which the range of sectorial choices (inclusionary or exclusionary, segmental or universal, bifrontal or unitary) are offered.

Two other questions deserve consideration. First, much has been said about the "relative autonomy" of the democratic capitalist state.[69] Under stable democratic regimes, the state in capitalist societies is believed to contain relatively autonomous bureaucracies that are not beholden to specific class interests, and which in fact have particular institutional interests of their own. At worst, these bureaucracies merely disguise the class domination upon which the bourgeois state is founded. At best they allow for a degree of institutional neutrality and flexibility that are conducive to class compromise.[70]

Using functionalist criteria, we can divide the notion of state autonomy to better reflect its different levels of operation. "Formulative autonomy" is the ability of the state to *formulate* policies free from the overt interference of competing sectors of civil society (more subtle pressures and political bargaining serve instead to shape discrete changes within the general parameters established for such policy making). "Operative autonomy" is the ability of the state apparatus to *implement* policies free from these pressures. Though linked, each level of operation is a distinct element in the policy process, and varies considerably in terms of the degree of autonomy achieved. When sufficiently high, both forms of autonomy constitute what is commonly referred to as the procedural neutrality of the democratic capitalist state.

Both types of autonomy imply limits due to the (inter)action of other factors. In addition, there are constraints imposed by "technical" variables such as geography, relative sectorial power, and the availability of resources, variables that are not easily modified or overcome, and that impose a degree of "structural realism" that impinges on state autonomy in any event.

The basic issue is one of relative "permeability." How permeable are the apex of the state or government (at the level of normative autonomy) and specific branches of the state (at the level of operative autonomy) when confronted by the competing pressures exerted by different sectors of civil society? T. Skocpol and others have suggested that the degree of permeability of the democratic capitalist state is low.[71] Oszlak and others have argued that just the opposite is the case in Latin America (hence the "clientelist" orientation of the public bureaucracy). I found this to be partially true in a study of the modern Argentine state.[72]

In Latin America, it has been argued, within the state apparatus, "the power bloc is heterogeneous rather than monolithic, divided by contradictions between factions and institutional orders, and eroded by pressures from other classes, groups, and social movements. Different sectors and branches of the state become seats of power for representatives of nondominant groups competing for control."[73]

Successful democratic concertation involving labor, capital, and the state requires, among other conditions, that the branch of the state responsible for administering the national labor relations system be institutionally attuned to labor concerns and yet neutral in its procedural and substantive position with respect to the collective agents of both groups of social actors. This implies an institutional morphology conducive to fluid interaction between labor, capital, and the state on legally defined procedural grounds, in marked contrast to the strained labor relations that characterized national labor administrations under exclusionary systems such as those employed by the displaced authoritarian regimes.

The democratic state's ability to replicate at an internal or institutional level the positions of the major social groups while distancing itself from immediate capitalist interests constitutes the functional criterion for determining whether it has achieved a higher degree of organizational autonomy than other capitalist regime types. National labor administration is the lead agency where that autonomy is immediately manifest.

The methodological approach that allows us to examine social classes as collections of groups or class factions whose individual logics and agendas differ from one other and from that of the class as a whole (the raison d'être of the Kapitalstate thesis, the state-as-factor-of-cohesion school, and of Olson's rational choice perspective), also allows us to examine the capitalist state itself. The autonomy of the capitalist state is manifested at three levels in both the formulative and operative dimensions. This autonomy can be observed at the level of the capitalist state as a whole (the collection of apparatuses), in the relations among (and permeability of) different state apparatuses, agencies, and branches, and in the relations between each apparatus and the different sectors of civil society.

Often the logic and power of one apparatus (especially the repressive apparatus) can subordinate most or all the others. Charges of organizational predominance or domination have recently been leveled at the economic policy-making branches of the state in all the Southern Cone democracies, since they are considered the "province" of capitalist groups with strong transnational ties, and are thus willing to implement IMF-mandated austerity programs that weaken the economic position of the domestic bourgeoisie and the working classes. Similar charges have been leveled at the military hierarchy in each country, where it is believed to be an ever-present threat to democracy.

The capitalist state apparatus includes different groups and factions that, while sharing a fundamental logic (reproduction of capitalism), also have individual logics that may or may not coincide, and, in fact, often cut across and contradict one another. This is reflected in the varying degrees of autonomy achieved at both the general and specific levels of operation, that is, the autonomy of the collection of apparatuses and of each individual apparatus. As we have already mentioned, certain class factions are often believed to "appropriate" certain state apparatuses, internally replaying, as it were, the larger conflicts that permeate the state as a whole. In this light, we can see that the hierarchies established between competing social groups at the level of civil society under different regimes are paralleled by hierarchies of organizational dominance established within the capitalist state apparatus itself.

This implies that the democratic capitalist state is neither inevitably an arena in which inter- and intraclass conflicts are internally reproduced, nor a forum in which harmonious class relations are maintained over time. Instead, it is the constantly shifting site of an ongoing, dynamic balance between the interests of social classes and factions thereof, involving various degrees and levels of conflict and collaboration that cut across both class lines and the functional boundaries of the formal division of labor that distinguishes individual branches of the state apparatus.

The specifics of this balance, whether weighed more toward conflict or toward cooperation, is a product of the nature of the regime, the composition of the government, the organization and articulation of class agents with the state apparatus, the ideological orientation of these class agents and of government incumbents and state managers, and the influence of cultural variables.[74]

Unlike authoritarian capitalist regimes in which no balance is struck between these sectorial interests, all democratic capitalist regimes must use the state as a device for mediating societal interests. To do this, they shift resource priorities and correct dysfunctions according to the dictates of context and circumstance, either as a substitute for or as a complement to the activities of market forces. Thus, democratic class conflict always involves the state.

Here the role of state managers becomes important: within the democratic state, these professionals, procedurally neutral, sectorially impartial, and detached from any particular class interest, serve as the referees for the class compromise.[75] Rather than representatives of one or the other class (although class representatives can also incorporated into the institutional process), experienced public servants — in the case of national labor administration, most often specialists in labor legislation, conflict mediation, and procedural law — use their expertise to promote a neutral institutional framework in which labor and capital can negotiate the specific terms of the democratic class compromise. Hence, "the strengthening of the state and of its autonomization implies and requires an apparent/real neutrality, efficient to the extent that public personnel think and act according to their own ideological and political categories — categories that act as mediators — and are convinced of their own neutrality."[76]

The orientation of the democratic state is thus apparent at the micro-organizational level. Not only is there a general trend toward increased organizational autonomy and procedural neutrality on the part of state agencies; their very organization reflects democratic orientation as well. Its institutional framework is markedly different from the more centralized and narrowly defined structures displayed by national labor administration under the military-bureaucratic authoritarian regimes that preceded the democratic resurgence in the Southern Cone.[77] It is these organizational changes that we look for when we assess the prospects for the democratization of class relations.

Regime change influences the organization of the state. This change is more likely to be significant and concretely evident in "core" internal areas of state activity such as national labor administration. This is particularly true in Argentina, Brazil, and Uruguay, where the position of organized labor makes it an important social group whose interests are a primary concern of the new democratic regimes. Moreover, stable democratic regimes in capitalist societies require the establishment of institutional bases for a class compromise between labor and capital. To that end, the democratic state must provide an organizational framework within which to equitably negotiate and maintain the substantive terms of the compromise. This requires that the state achieve a significant degree of normative and operative autonomy that allows it to procedurally mediate and foster cooperative, if not concertative agreements between collective agents, and then enforce the substantive terms of the compromise in a class-neutral way. The role and organization of national labor administration is a central element in this process and is therefore critical for the consolidation of the new democratic regimes in the Southern Cone.[78]

Finally, it should be noted that the gap between theory and praxis is seldom fully bridged, and that regime objectives often fall hard on the path toward implementation. For example, informal rules may carry more weight than formal rules; personalities may outweigh bureaucratic structures and regulations; ad hoc, short-term crisis management may replace consistent long-term policy implementation, etc. In the developing world, complex organizations often tend to be an amalgam of traditional and modern practices, where charismatic and technocratic personalities, educational and personal ties, impartiality and bias all have a role to play.[79]

Having acknowledged this fact, and being analytically disposed to factor all of these variables into our assessment, we return to the central issue. The translation of labor policy into practice requires an institutional capacity, and as such is concretely manifested in the organization and functions of national labor administration. This institutional framework conditions the range of choices presented by the new democratic regimes of the Southern Cone to their organized labor movements, which ultimately determines whether such movements are incorporated into the process of democratic consolidation.

PART TWO

LABOR ADMINISTRATION IN
THE SOUTHERN CONE

4

NATIONAL LABOR ADMINISTRATION
AS A STATE APPARATUS

THE ABSENCE OF STUDIES on how organized labor is incorporated into the process of democratic consolidation is particularly notable in light of the relative paucity and general orientation of the literature on labor administration and labor relations in South America. Apart from the works of Victor Alba, Robert Alexander, Davis & Goodman, Julio Godio, Hobart Spaulding, and Howard Wiarda, some of which address the issue only tangentially, little has been written during the past twenty-five years that compares the role and structure of national labor administrations in Latin American countries.[1] Most of these studies, as well as works such as those by Poblete Troncosco, Jorge Difieri, and the International Labor Organization (ILO), are more exercises in prescriptive or descriptive history than analyses of Latin American labor relations systems.[2]

As for the remaining literature, recent works on labor relations in Latin America have concentrated on the corporatist character of the labor relations systems in individual nations, and have seldom ventured to undertake cross-national comparisons.[3] Although they identify differences among the types of corporatist approaches employed, these works have seldom addressed the position of national labor administrations in democracies. Whatever its precise configuration, corporatism has been associated in Latin America with authoritarian rather than democratic rule, despite the fact that European democracies exhibit corporatist traits as well.[4] It has even been suggested that democratic corporatist arrangements increase the probability that class compromises will hold, and hence yield significantly better outcomes than pluralist systems.[5] The authoritarian bias of most of the South American corporatist literature may well reflect the times (since at one point in the mid-1970s, when the literature on corporatism was in full bloom, every country in the Southern Cone, plus Bolivia, Ecuador, Paraguay, and Peru, was governed by an authoritarian regime of one type or another), but it seems less certain that it applies to the institutional frameworks promoted by the new democratic regimes of the 1980s.

As a result, there is no work that either individually or comparatively examines the differences between national labor administrations under the new and old regimes, much less the vital role played by national labor administrations in promoting the class compromise required for democratic consolidation.

The historical development of national labor administrations in Argentina, Brazil, and Uruguay will be discussed in the following chapters. But first I would like to consider the origins and evolution of national labor administrations in Latin America as whole.[6] They trace their origins to the turn of the twentieth century, when labor departments were created in countries experiencing the combined effects of increased urbanization and industrialization, often coupled with massive immigration of blue-collar workers from southern Europe. Immigrants brought with them anarchist, socialist, communist, and anarcho-syndicalist beliefs, and in an effort to stave off the possibility of industrial conflicts, countries with rising urban populations were the first to institute labor departments.

These included Argentina, Chile, and Uruguay in 1907 (Uruguay was the first country to make labor administration a cabinet-level post, in the Ministry of Industry, Labor, and Public Instruction), Mexico in 1912, Brazil in 1918, Peru in 1919, Bolivia and Guatemala in 1925, with the rest of the region following suit during the 1920s and 1930s. With the exception of Uruguay, most of these labor-related agencies were created as dependencies of other cabinet-level portfolios. Many labor agencies originated in the Interior Ministry; this lends substance to former Brazilian president Washington Luis's remark that "the problem of labor is a problem for the police."⁷

Between the 1930s and 1950s, most Latin American labor agencies were elevated to cabinet status as an institutional complement to the move toward labor incorporation, often in conjunction with responsibilities in public health or social welfare. From an agency concerned with collecting statistics, conducting research, or carrying out police functions, national labor administration was gradually transformed into the flagship of social policy. This coincided with the rise of populist movements in the region, the emergence of European-inspired corporatist notions of interest aggregation, and the ongoing wave of industrialization that was gradually transforming the region from predominantly rural-agricultural to urban-industrial.

In all cases, national labor administrations rarely served as a participatory forum for working-class grievances and demands, but were instead used by political leaders as a top-down form of institutional control over the working classes in a way that was preemptive and co-optive. In the Southern Cone legislation was passed in virtually every nation (Uruguay is the notable exception) granting national labor administrations universal powers of union recognition, registration, financial control, approval of personnel, delimitation of union responsibilities and obligations, electoral oversight, and strike authorization, among other things.

All this made national labor administrations the primary referent and determinant of working-class interests within the state apparatus. Depending on labor's relationship with the regime in power, national labor administration assumed either a benign and paternalistic stance toward the organized working classes, or more often, an antagonistic approach, curtailing and limiting (when not coercing outright) rather than supporting and rewarding labor activities at the economic and political levels.

From the late 1960s through the 1980s, many nations redefined the scope of their national labor administrations along more narrow, work-related lines. These changes were inspired by the experiences of more advanced nations, by the increasingly complex division of labor and social relations of production emerging in their own societies, and sometimes by authoritarian projects oriented toward the exclusion and repression of the working classes. National labor administrations were stripped of welfare, health, and social security-related functions, which were placed in other cabinet-level agencies.

Thus, Latin American labor administrations went through three phases of development. The first ran from the turn of the century through the 1930s; during this time, national labor administrations were mostly sub-cabinet-level agencies with narrowly defined responsibilities. In the second phase, from the 1930s through the 1960s, most were elevated to cabinet status and became the centerpiece of national social policy. In the last phase, from the 1960s to the present, national labor administration was stripped of its broader social policy functions and returned to a more work-centered orientation, which in some cases included demotion to sub-cabinet-level status.

This last phase was not simply a return to the past. Through the passage of time and with the evolution of society, the range of labor-specific responsibilities also expanded. By the 1970s national labor administrations had broad responsibilities in the fields of collective bargaining and labor relations, labor norms and regulations, employment policy, occupational health and safety, the economics and demographics of the labor market, and a host of related issues. The incorporation of many of these responsibilities was encouraged by external agents such as the ILO, the OAS, and regional labor groupings such as the Confederación Interamericana de Trabajo (CIAT), Organización Regional Interamericana de Trabajo (ORIT), and the American Institute for Free Labor Development (AIFLD). With ILO's support, national labor administrations also provided the first institutional grounds for tripartite dialogue throughout the industrial relations systems of the region, most notably in Venezuela, Costa Rica, and pre-authoritarian Uruguay.

Regime change has had a decided impact on the fortunes of public labor agencies. When the entering regime was receptive to working-class interests, national labor administration saw an expansion of programs, budget, and services, and incorporated unionists into its personnel. More often, national labor administrations have either been allowed to languish or have been used as an instrument of exclusion and repression. The inclusionary state-corporatist laws, which facilitated the unions' access to benefits and power under sympathetic regimes such as the populist regimes of Juan Perón and Getúlio Vargas in the 1940s, became, with just a minor shift in emphasis, exclusionary instruments of subjugation under the military-authoritarian regimes of the 1960s and 1970s.[8]

Because of the nature of their functions, national labor administrations in Latin America have consistently been among the smallest cabinet-level agencies in both number of staff and size of budget. A 1981 ILO study refers at some length to the underfunding of Latin American labor administrations, noting that, in the nations studied, the average budget in the 1970s amounted to only 1.3 percent of central administrative expenditures, with a mean of just 0.8 percent. No country exceeded 5 percent (Costa Rica, with 4.9 percent, had the highest rate).[9]

The same study refers to the lack of qualified personnel in many countries. This combination of low budgets and lack of personnel reduces the quality and level of services provided by these agencies. Labor administrations are prominent in the public sector because of workers' strategic position, but the nature of their responsibilities ensures that they are given low budgetary and staffing priority by most capitalist regimes. Only populist and social democratic regimes have significantly raised the level of resources and personnel in this area.

Why focus on national labor administrations, as opposed to other branches of the state, as the primary agent for labor incorporation and potential class compromise? Because national labor administration is the institutional nexus where the regime's economic projects can contend with the realities of implementing labor policy.

Cabinet agencies such as ministries of economy are responsible for formulating the broad parameters and long-term orientation of a regime's particular structural project. Other agencies of this sort (such the Central Bank and ministries or secretariats of agriculture, finance, industry, commerce and trade, etc.), each specializing in some aspect of that project, translate and implement segmented elements of the "grand strategy."

Although important in their own right, none of these state agencies receives the feedback generated by the organized labor movement, which represents the work force in public and private enterprises. Translating economic policy into labor policy is the province of national labor administration. Used as an instrument of exclusionary control by authoritarian capitalist regimes, in capitalist democracies national labor administration becomes the main institution for mediating labor-capital conflicts and for reproducing the consent of labor necessary to achieve class compromise.

National labor administration's bureaucratic dynamic is intrinsically amenable to promoting forms of class cooperation such as tripartism. While other state agencies are engaged in tasks connected to the implementation of economic programs, in some parts of Latin America,

> on the side of labour administration there was also [a] marked interest in promoting the participation of the social partners in the elaboration and application of labour policies. It was fully realized that without the support of the organizations directly concerned it would not be possible to implement government policy. How could labour standards be effectively applied, or substantial employment promotion measures be taken, or vocational training be really fostered without the co-operation of the unions and employers who would be the first to be affected by these policies? Tripartism, moreover, served a double purpose: firstly, discussions between the parties and the labour authorities made it possible to reach the minimum degree of social consensus required for production activities to be carried out normally; secondly, tripartite co-operation provided labour ministries with the opportunity of joining forces with organizations of employers and of workers so as to strengthen their

own position vis-à-vis government bodies and the community as a whole and thereby accentuate their role in the process of economic and social development.[10]

In the interest of constructing stable vehicles for sectorial negotiation, transition governments have moved to implement International Labor Organization standards governing the right to association and collective bargaining. As part of the move to secure workers' consent to capitalist reproduction, these standards are designed to alter the social relations of production (and the relations in production, at the workplace) in the uniquely democratic effort to "obscure" the appropriation of surplus value. To that end, ILO representatives work closely with labor administration officials in each country to draft proposed reforms in labor legislation and organizational changes in the labor administration bureaucracy. In all three cases discussed here, the ILO has liaison offices in the Labor Ministry.

Many of the recent approaches toward the use of concertative vehicles in the Southern Cone draw heavily on European experiences (particularly that of Spain). These are specifically translated by state managers who are personally familiar with those processes or who rely on guidelines provided by the ILO and its regional agencies. Most important for those involved, promoting cooperative or concertative labor relations systems codifies the role of national labor administrations as the "technical" and "neutral" enforcer of the formal rules and terms of sectorial agreements. This generates a bureaucratic interest in institutionalizing class compromise.

There are considerable variations in the degree to which national labor administrations in different countries have been able to achieve either this ostensible objective or the autonomy they require. Not surprisingly, in Latin America the most success in this regard has been achieved by stable democratic regimes such as Costa Rica and Venezuela.

National labor administration is the state's network of institutional vehicles that aggregate and administer the interests of organized labor within given national boundaries. Although I use the term interchangeably with "labor relations," "labor relations partial regime," and "labor relations systems," the notion of a national labor administration provides a better sense of the expanded range of state roles and instruments used to manage the demands and interests of the organized working classes. In addition, in using this term, we recognize that the traditional approaches of Latin American states toward organized labor have been heavily weighed toward administering (and even defining) rather than mediating labor interests vis-à-vis capitalist groups.

The broad range of activities of Latin American labor administrations has been underscored by the ILO, which observed that

> in the great majority of labor ministries (in Latin America), in addition to the dependencies that traditionally have constituted their backbone (workplace inspection, labor relations, occupational health and safety), there also function directorates of employment and human resources, social security and welfare, sectorial planning, as well as offices or units dedicated to labor economics, study and research, and international affairs. On the other hand, its geographic coverage has been extended by the establishment of a large number of regional and local agencies designated as directorates, subdirectorates, or delegations, with competence in fields that are under the formal jurisdiction of the central agencies. In some federal states the labor ministry has general competence at the national level while provinces or states enjoy autonomy in the exercise of their various responsibilities and obligations in the labor field.[11]

Although I will examine subnational agencies when and where they are pertinent, I concentrate my attention on *national* labor administrations, because of my focus on the consolidation of national democracy.

Specifically, I will analyze the two dimensions of national labor administration (internal and external) that constitute the national labor relations system. At the external level (outside the state apparatus proper), I will identify the labor strategies adopted by post-authoritarian regimes, and the legal or material instruments used to implement these strategies and to regulate the activities of organized labor. These measure will be related to those that were employed by the previous authoritarian regimes.[12]

At the internal level (within the state apparatus), I examine a number of variables within national labor administration, grouped into three broad institutional categories: organization, budget, and personnel. The internal analysis will focus on organizational hierarchy, jurisdiction, the background of personnel, distribution, turnover, size of budget (both in total amount and as a percentage of central administrative outlays), and internal distribution. This will allow a more precise analysis of the broader role and organization of national labor administrations. In all cases, I will link this role and organization to those used by the previous regimes, in order to discern areas of continuity and change.[13]

These internal variables are important because the organization of national labor administrations shows how public resources and policy responsibilities are distributed within the labor relations system. Budgetary analysis shows where financial authority is vested and where financial emphasis is placed. Personnel data rounds out the picture by identifying the training and roles of those who operate the national labor relations system, their training and social backgrounds.

Together, these individual and organizational resources and strategies all influence the formulation and implementation of labor policy within each regime's general parameters. This policy emerges in decrees, edicts, laws, and resolutions enforced by the Labor Ministry and affiliated agencies. As the formal manifestation of the external dimension of national labor administrations, this legislation sets the range of choices presented by the regime to organized labor. The interaction of these internal variables with the macroeconomic context and with sectorial strategies gives a precise character to the labor relations system in each case. The often overlooked internal dimension of national labor administrations is the organizational base on which the external dimension of a regime's approach toward labor rests.

Our aim is to determine how these external and internal dimensions of national labor administration interact with employers' inducements and constraints to provide an institutional framework for achieving the structural bases of democratic class compromise.[14] Toward this end, the differences between each of the three labor movements, particularly their negotiating strategies, organizational bases, ideological orientations, and relative economic and political strengths, will be related to the different approaches adopted by each of the new democratic regimes.

In addition, we must account for how differences in the type of transition to democracy — managed political opening or *abertura* in Brazil, voluntary military withdrawal from power in Uruguay, authoritarian collapse in Argentina — are reflected in the new labor relation frameworks. Finally, we need to determine whether noncorporatist approaches to national labor administration surfaced along with redemocratization, or whether the character of corporatism changed (e.g. from state to societal corporatism as in the case of many Western European countries). This will allow us to test assumptions about the relation between regime type and corporatism in Latin America, and, more specifically, to identify the nature of national labor administration in each country.

National labor administration under democratic capitalism constitutes a major part of the institutional framework that monitors and enforces (and thereby guarantees) the terms and conditions for ongoing negotiation between the peak associations of capitalists and workers. It offers bureaucratic resources and legal and technical expertise to advise the "social partners" in their quest for mutually satisfactory second-best choices. Branches of the state involved in establishing economic policy perform the same function. But only national labor administration enforces the guarantees in the workplace and material conditions that are required for reproducing the working class's ongoing consent to capitalist relations of production.

The consent of subordinate groups, and particularly that of organized labor, is the distinguishing feature of democratic, as opposed to authoritarian, capitalism. The incorporation of labor into the process of democratic consolidation via material and institutional guarantees is therefore essential for the new regime's success. As a result, national labor administration is unique in the economic, political, and repressive roles it plays in pursuit of this objective.

Under democratic capitalist regimes, national labor administration's ideological roles are twofold. On an economic plane, it must ensure that the procedural and substantive agreements reproduce workers' consent to private ownership of the means of production. On the political plane, it must promote and guarantee the conditions under which workers' consent to democratic forms for articulating interests, bargaining, and redressing grievances is reproduced.

To ensure reproduction in both dimensions, national labor administration must be capable both of making concessions (as inducements) and of exercising coercion (as constraints). It therefore has a repressive role to play as a complement to its ideological functions, which is most often evident in strike legislation and in the labor administration's power to recognize and oversee the unions.

These ideological and repressive roles make national labor administrations a core hegemonic apparatus of democratic capitalist regimes. In addition to developing the cooperative or concertative mechanisms of sectorial negotiation, these roles have made it a major actor in the processes of democratic consolidation undertaken in the Southern Cone in the 1980s.

5

ARGENTINE LABOR ADMINISTRATION
UNDER THE RADICAL GOVERNMENT

THE INAUGURATION OF Raúl Alfonsín on December 10, 1983, closed the book on the darkest chapter in modern Argentine history. In the harshest variant on a repeated theme, from 1976 to 1983 Argentine labor was subjected to a systematic campaign of economic and political exclusion on the part of the military-bureaucratic regime that called itself the Proceso de Reorganización Nacional (process of national reorganization, hereafter referred to as the Proceso). Since Peronist unions represented 90 percent of the organized work force in 1976, the attack on organized labor constituted an attempt to break one of the organizational pillars of the nation's largest political movement. It repeated earlier attempts to eliminate the political power of Peronism after Perón's overthrow in 1955.[1]

The most politically active and economically powerful elements of the labor movement were forced into institutional silence by the legal prohibition on union activities, mass arrests and "disappearances" of union activists, and the military occupation of union facilities by the Proceso. In addition, the exclusion of labor from the state apparatus was evident. This was most clearly seen in the organization and functions of agencies charged with enforcing the executive decrees and emergency laws that gave formal (if legally tenuous) substance to the exclusionary project. Wholesale and systematic use of state terror added a highly coercive incentive for working-class acquiescence to its own subjugation.[2]

Divided and forced underground, Peronist unions reemerged in

1979 to mount the first serious challenges to the Proceso. This process accelerated when the dictatorship began visibly to divide in 1981. A nationwide strike called in March 1982 by one faction of the outlawed Confederación General de Trabajo (CGT) proved to be the triggering event in the decision to reoccupy the Malvinas (Falkland Islands) by force.[3]

As the Proceso began to collapse in the aftermath of military defeat, organized labor actively participated in the transition process as one of the principal collective agents of a disenfranchised mass of citizens representing a significant portion of the electorate. This included a generation of eighteen- to twenty-eight-year-old workers too young to have voted in the 1973 presidential election, whose political socialization had occurred entirely under conditions of social anomaly and class-directed state terror.

Notwithstanding the continuing institutional strength of the union movement, labor's role in the transition was constrained by the divisions between right-wing *ortodoxos* and social democratic *renovadores* in the Partido Justicialista (PJ) and by the different tactics used to confront or accommodate the Proceso. With the suspension of collective bargaining, military intervention in the union-administered health and welfare benefit programs (Obras Sociales), and the repression of union activities in general, Argentine unions in 1983 were serving more as political vehicles and symbols of a divided resistance than as effective economic agents.

The restoration of labor's political role thus had to precede the reassumption of its economic role. Yet the existence of a skeletal organizational network tied to production allowed unions to lead the Peronist movement at a time when the PJ was rearticulating its ideological and bureaucratic bases.[4] Organized labor remained the *columna vertebral* of the Peronist movement, since it was the only part of the movement with direct roots in production and an uninterrupted — albeit often illegal — political presence.[5]

Even so, the labor movement had many obstacles to confront before it could fully reassert its position as a major political and economic actor. Unbowed, reconstituted, but decimated by the political and economic assaults of the Proceso, by 1983 Argentine labor had lost many of the human and material assets that had long been the source of its institutional prominence. That included not only the Obras Sociales but also a virtual cadre of factory-level activists murdered or "disappeared" by the Proceso.

To this was added the socioeconomic dislocation caused by the "neoliberal" economic policies of the Proceso, which adopted a monetarist approach that restored the economic and political primacy of the financial and agro-export sectors at the expense of domestic industry.[6] This contributed to the tertiarization of the labor force — that is, the movement of labor from industry to service-sector employment — at the same time that union membership and real wages were declining. During the Proceso, union membership dropped from over 50 percent to less than 30 percent of the economically active population. Membership in commercial and service industries surpassed membership in industrial unions, reversing a forty-year trend.[7] In addition to resorting to multiple employment strategies and moving to more individualized forms of economic activity in the so-called informal sector,

> union composition moved away from the predominance of large industrial unions defined by productive sector toward smaller commercial unions defined by occupation, further accentuating the disarticulation and decomposition of collective identities among the working classes. Increasing numbers of women and children were incorporated into the work force in order to supplement family incomes, exacerbating the wage differentials within occupational categories.[8]

Thus, organized labor was not the dominant actor in the Argentine transition. Nonetheless, historical and conjunctural reasons — the internal divisions within the Peronist party and the absence of a viable alternative for subordinate group representation — lent particular importance to state-labor relations in the process of Argentine redemocratization.

With the victory of Raúl Alfonsín in 1983, organized labor became part of the legal opposition to the first freely elected and unquestionably legitimate Radical government since that of

Yrigoyen in the 1920s. This posed new challenges for both sides. Organized labor, hoping to recapture its position in the Argentine political and economic systems, wanted to dictate the material and ideological terms of the initial compromises that would secure working-class support for the emergent regime. Capitalists, for their part, expected to do likewise.Given these contending pressures, Argentina's national labor administration would necessarily experience change under the democratic regime.

Historical Background

Under the first Argentine constitution of 1853, no provisions were made for administering working-class interests within the national state apparatus.[9] In the 1870s, with the rise of agro-export industries in the port cities of Buenos Aires and Rosario, incipient industrialization attracted immigrant labor from southern Europe.

By the end of the century, what had originated as an immigration question in the 1870s was now an issue of production and was therefore of increasing concern for the political elite. Formal institutionalization of the Argentine labor administration followed in 1907, when the Dirección General de Trabajo was created in the Interior Ministry. In 1912 it was reorganized and renamed the Departamento Nacional de Trabajo (DNT), continuing to operate as part of the Interior Ministry until 1943.[10]

Anarcho-syndicalist and Marxist ideologies came with immigrants from peripheral Europe and took root in the burgeoning mass of urban workers employed in the dynamic export sector and its infrastructure industries. Labor-capital conflicts over organizational and material issues intensified throughout the first two decades of the twentieth century. This led to clashes in the streets of Buenos Aires, culminating in the Semana Trágica riots of January 1919.[11] As a result, the labor question became a matter of concern for the state, for reasons both of internal security and economic prosperity, and the Interior Ministry was assigned the task of policing the national labor relations system.

Through the efforts of labor administration to codify collective bargaining, labor "peace" was tenuously achieved by the late

1920s.[12] In the wake of the Depression, the move to import-substi-
tution industrialization (ISI) in consumer durables — a process
begun in the late nineteenth century in the sector producing
footwear and other domestic goods — altered the structural position of labor while simultaneously giving it tremendous potential
as a political force.[13] Treating urban working classes as producers
and consumers for the first time, the increasingly interventionist
state adopted a logic of import substitution, adding superstructural emphasis to the structural critique of the comparative disadvan-
tage of agro exports later made famous by the ECLA and the
dependencia schools.[14] ISI brought material benefits to organized
labor, which helped assure its economic acquiescence and political
docility, a tacit expression of labor's consent to capitalist rule.

In spite of selective political repression and continuing ideological divisions between the anarchist and socialist unions, both
industrial employment and union membership increased
significantly during this period, the latter reaching 20 percent of
the economically active population by 1936. The move to "easy"
import substitution industrialization in consumer durables also
altered the character of organized labor, shifting the bulk of the
work force from transportation and commerce to industry (where
union membership tripled between 1936 and 1945). In 1936 there
were 370,000 union members nationwide, and by 1945 the number had risen to 528,000. The number of affiliates rose to 877,000
in 1946, a 58 percent increase in one year, and by 1951 the number
of union members reached 2,334,000, or roughly 40 percent of the
work force.[15]

Juan D. Perón arrived on the Argentine political scene in the
early 1940s, marking the end of an era in which the state played
down labor interests. A new period of state-labor relations began.
Having served in Italy during Mussolini's tenure long enough to
observe firsthand the adroit use of state-corporatist legislation to
control and manipulate the labor movement, and having seen
Getúlio Vargas adopt and use the Italian fascist labor codes to construct the Brazilian Estado Novo in the late 1930s, Perón asked for
the directorship of the DNT when government positions were dis-

tributed following the 1943 coup. Once installed, he used his office to construct the organizational bases of the mass political movement that was later to bear his name.

On November 27, 1943, a month after Perón was named DNT director, the department was elevated to the rank of Secretaría de Trabajo y Previsión (STP), with a status analogous to that of a ministry.[16] With the promotion came a broad expansion of the former department's domain into a variety of labor-related areas, including legal, health, pension, and social security programs. This expansion was accomplished by incorporating responsibilities previously assigned to other regional, provincial, or federal agencies. It was the first time the state had assumed a leading role in Argentine labor relations.[17]

Perón used the increased powers of the STP to cultivate union support for his political project, which culminated in his being elected president in 1946.

> With Perón at its head, the Secretaría de Trabajo y Previsión was granted both executive and judicial functions, and expeditive powers not subject to recourse. . . . The operative rule was the worker was always correct, and the Secretaría always sided with the workers. This approach helped perpetuate a mythos around the Secretaría. . . . Perón had only one objective: to capture the sympathy and support of the masses. Laws were dictated regarding the registration and legalization of unions depending on their degree of support for the authorities. Unions that supported the regime were awarded registered status; others were not.[18]

Organized labor's subordinated incorporation was based on an inclusionary state-corporatist framework in which unions and national labor administration were linked vertically through a centralized organizational hierarchy dominated by partisan adherence to Perón and his personal ideology, *justicialismo*. Perón's use of state-corporatist labor legislation and of the expanded powers of national labor administration established the foundations for the state's enduring dominance in labor relations. This power extended beyond his tenure, and, modified in its strategic orientation, served as the legal basis for labor's exclusion under the military-authoritarian regimes that periodically came to power after 1955. The legacy of state-corporatist administration of the interests of organized labor became an enduring institutional trait and confronted the democratic regime installed in 1983.[19]

By 1954, all welfare and comptroller responsibilities had been transferred out of the Labor Ministry into other cabinet-level agencies. The course of state intervention was thus set in the direction of the oversight of organized labor. This allowed subsequent regimes to use national labor administration as an instrument for labor's exclusion.

It should be noted, however, that the formal control exercised by the state did not necessarily mean de facto control. Witness the labor militancy and factionalization that met the attempts of Onganía's military-bureaucratic regime (1966–1970) to bifrontally incorporate cooperative elements of the labor movement while simultaneously repressing others.[20] Violent resistance within the labor movement in turn split the regime into factions. This occurred outside institutional parameters and represented a period dominated by outright class conflict, when there was no possibility for labor incorporation or class compromise.

Internally, the years following Perón's ouster in 1955 saw numerous changes in Argentina's labor administration.[21] The period saw numerous shifts, relocations, and reassignment of agencies within the national labor administration system. Budgetary allocations varied widely among the regimes that alternated in power over the next thirty years. Organizational hierarchies were compressed or expanded, depending on each regime's objectives regarding public administration in general and labor relations in particular. Rationalization of the central bureaucratic apparatus of the state was a constant theme voiced by all regimes, although the political objectives of each lent a particular character to the type of reforms attempted.

The military-bureaucratic regimes of 1955–1958, 1962–1963, 1966–1973, and 1976–1983 used exclusionary state-corporatist approaches that were bifrontal and segmental in nature to limit the state's provision of public goods while expanding the coercive functions of virtually all branches.[22] The limited democracies of 1958–1962 and 1962–1966 (both Radical governments) were most concerned with defining administrative tasks in technical terms and decentralizing those tasks within the entire state apparatus. Bureaucratically, they placed most emphasis on establishing procedural neutrality and on grounding administrative decision making in legislation, particularly regarding interest group mediation. The Peronist regime of 1973–1976 attempted to restore the original apparatus used by Perón from 1946 to 1955. Thus, the state's development and that of national labor administration responded to the pendular oscillations in power between different political coalitions manifested in the cycles of regime change that characterized postwar Argentina.[23]

What did not change greatly over time was the interventionist role of national labor administration. Except for the 1963–1966 Radical government, Argentine labor administration exhibited state-corporatist traits under all three regime types (populist, limited democratic, military-bureaucratic), regardless of whether it was well or poorly funded, whether it included or excluded unionists, military officers, or career bureaucrats, and even whether or not it had cabinet status. It remained organized, with minor and temporary modifications, along the lines established by Perón in the 1940s: bureaucratic oversight of the labor movement was vertical and centralized. This responded to a continuing governmental logic that saw state control of the union movement, rather than neutral mediation, as the state's primary responsibility in labor relations. The advent of democracy in Argentina in 1983 thus required a fundamental shift not only in the external dimension of national labor administration, but also in the bureaucratic logic and organizational features that were its institutional foundation.

The External Dimension

The formal boundaries of the strategic interaction between the state and labor during the Alfonsín administration were marked by the labor legislation introduced by the government on procedural and substantive grounds, the strategies adopted by the labor movement as initiatives or responses to government action, and the political interplay among labor, capital, political parties, the executive branch, and Congress on specific economic, political, and social issues. The post-authoritarian labor relations partial regime was reconstituted on these grounds.

The Radical administration understood the importance of union democracy and of labor's incorporation into the process of democratic consolidation, but it confronted serious structural and institutional obstacles that limited its strategic options. Along with an economy in crisis and a labor movement in political opposition, the democratic regime installed in 1983 inherited the institutional remnants of the Proceso's exclusionary labor program, where the militarized Labor Ministry and direct intervention in unions obviated many of the tasks normally assigned to national labor administration. This effectively reduced the formal scope of its activities to little more than redrawing exclusionary labor legislation and enforcing labor's subordination in other ways.[24]

Beyond the immediate authoritarian legacy, there were other formidable obstacles. Not the least of these was the vertical organization of the CGT, labor's umbrella organization, established during the first Perón regime (1946–1955). Along with the military hierarchy, the CGT was the Radical government's foremost political adversary. State-labor negotiations were thus prone to stalemates and logjams over seemingly minor procedural issues, as contending labor factions linked unnegotiable substantive claims to any discussion of procedural frameworks in order to attract rank-and-file support, while partisan conflict between Peronists and Radicals stymied the possibility of agreements between the parties in Congress.

For practical and ideological reasons, the process of democratizing the unions and incorporating labor was considered a central element in a larger project of social transformation oriented toward replacing authoritarian institutions, associational life, and social attitudes with their democratic equivalents. An entrenched authoritarian legacy and zero-sum strategic outlook made this a complex and delicate task. Thus, the move toward democratic institutionalization was "fundamental not only for the Government, but for the entire country as well, since long periods of autocratic rule prompted different social operators to also [employ] autocratic types of behavior."[25]

Reorganization of the network for mediating social group interests was crucial for revitalizing Argentine society and for preventing future authoritarian regression. In the words of Alfonsín,

> We must help give birth to a new union that will have material and economic power, but which must have, fundamentally, human content. The new union must be organized from the bottom up, reaffirming its roots among the rank and file and in the interior of the Republic. It will be a union in which leaders emerge as a genuine expression of the rank and file, without the deformations that historically have given rise to the interference of the State, parties, and business, in which electoral processes will be controlled by the Judicial branch, thereby guaranteeing fairness, in which there will be ample participation with an adequate expression of minority views and in which no discrimination of a political, religious, or racial character will be admitted.[26]

The move toward union democracy and labor incorporation had to be accompanied by a similar process of democratization within the state apparatus. This implied reforming the entire labor relations system in accordance with the project of social transformation. According to Labor Minister Hugo Barrionuevo, the labor relations system was "inadequate, antiquated, and contradictory" and needed to be overhauled via a four-part program that included

> a restructuring and democratization of labor relations; an updating of its legal status, which includes repealing authoritarian and ineffectual norms but not automatically returning to previous laws; defining the labor instruments that will accompany economic policy and the modernization of the productive apparatus; and promoting greater efficiency in the Ministerio de Trabajo y Seguridad Social.[27]

Social transformation and democratic consolidation required that the labor movement be reformed at two organizational levels: substantively, at the level of representation (involving greater ideological and functional plurality and proportionality in the CGT hierarchy); and procedurally, in terms of institutionalized guarantees (open, competitive elections, secret ballots, and impartial oversight in all unions).

The move toward decentralizating and diversifying the unions was designed to alter a framework that had been in place since 1949. The traditional union structure was considered ill suited for linkage with the pluralist or societal (neo)corporatist labor relations framework envisioned by the Radicals. However, the vertical union framework constituted the labor movement's major source of strength, as it allowed for the regular mobilization of human and material resources on behalf of working-class and partisan interests under one unified Peronist banner.[28]

La columna vertebral had historically been the primary agent voicing the economic and political revindications of Argentina's working classes. Yet its organizational strength was accompanied by strong authoritarian traits supported by widespread corruption, venality, and coercion by labor leaders. This led periodically to a violent divorce between the interests of the rank and file and those of the bureaucracy.[29]

The obstacles to democratic institutionalization of state-labor relations thus came largely from the vertical union framework that had allowed organized labor to survive during the years of exclusion. This framework continued to be seen by many as the last line of collective defense for Argentina's working classes.

The Radical government wanted to preserve the CGT as the single peak association of the Argentine working class while restructuring its internal organization through legislation encouraging the representation of independent and minority union factions. The move toward union democracy involved erecting pluralist or inclusionary state-corporatist framework that fostered pyramidal hierarchies of democratic representation in the constituent unions. Eventually, this was to be reflected in an ideologically and functionally diverse array of openly elected labor representatives exercising legitimate decision-making authority at the level of a national confederation, where their status as legitimate bargaining agents would be codified by the state.

It was hoped that an internally democratized labor movement would become more interested in using concertative vehicles to negotiate the terms of a democratic class compromise on nonpartisan, "rational" economic and political grounds. However, Peronist union leaders saw the government's efforts as nothing more than an attempt to divide and conquer the labor movement for purely partisan advantage, something earlier Radical governments had attempted without success.

Using the need to replace the existing authoritarian labor legislation as an opportunity to rewrite the union charter, the government initially attempted to prevent the resurrection of pre-Proceso labor legislation that would have formally reestablished the vertical union framework. This attempt ended in failure in February 1984, when the Senate rejected by one vote a draft bill of a new law of professional associations that would have required minority representation at all levels of activity and a decentralized federational structure based on shop-floor union democracy and factory-level collective bargaining.

After this setback, the government attempted to switch tracks to normalize through elections the representational status of a wide array of unions under the supervision of the International Labor Organization. It believed that only after the representational status of unions was normalized could progress in redrafting the law of professional associations be made.[30] As we shall see, the government's switch in tactics and the subsequent delay of the labor legislation reform bill had the unintended effect of strengthening links between the unions and Parliament.

Union elections held in November 1986 saw three Peronist union factions in fierce competition for control of the CGT's decision making. All were eventually awarded key bureaucratic posts in the CGT hierarchy, thereby holding each other and the secretary general in check.

Below the national level, there was a trend toward electoral pluralism, increased competition — even if this was primarily between Peronist factions — and minority representation within the 1,412 unions and 75 federations that constituted the Argentine labor movement. Some of the most significant advances along these lines occurred in unions where there had been heavy intervention during the Proceso.[31] As Ranis notes,

> Union elections since 1983 have been fairer than in the past. They have followed correct timetables, usually encompassed more than one competing list, have been marked with fewer irregularities than formerly and demonstrated more internal open politicking among alternative aspirants. These multiple, open-ended elections are a new and promising internal union phenomenon stimulated by the general climate of democracy during Alfonsín's tenure in office.[32]

The cleavage between orthodox and renovating Peronists and the emergence of viable non-Peronist unions did not prevent the defeat of Radical labor reform proposals in Congress. Nor did it keep unified labor from supporting the subsequent labor reform bill, drafted by the Peronists, that confirmed organized labor's traditional prerogatives. After extensive congressional review and debate, this much-delayed bill became law in January 1988, and legally reaffirmed the vertical union structure[33] It also included clauses ratifying ILO convention 154, which promoted autonomous collective bargaining in the public sector, extended wage agreements to all employers whether or not they were parties to the negotiations, and which codified autonomous collective bargaining at the level of the industry (federation) rather than the firm (as employers and the government would have preferred).[34]

Limitations on state mediation, the government's ability to invoke "economic emergency" clauses to suspend collective bargaining, and the reassertion of the Labor Ministry's responsibility for ratifying wage agreements as law had the compound effect of reinforcing the organizational framework that had been the traditional source of Argentine labor's strength. That helped strengthen labor's economic bargaining position overall, even as it helped accelerate the collapse of the Radical plan for economic stabilization.[35]

Parallel to the effort to reorganize the union movement through legislation was the move to introduce a new strike law. Mandatory authorization by the state for "legal" strikes in Argentina had precedents dating back to the turn of the century, and had been used for both inclusionary and exclusionary purposes.[36] The Alfonsín government initially wanted to narrow the range of legal strike activity to strikes of a strictly economic or professional nature. It specifically wanted to declare so-called political strikes illegal as well as those used to modify existing collective bargaining agreements ex post facto. Political strikes were believed to be a partisan tactical ploy to destabilize the government by thwarting the implementation of economic and social policies, thereby increasing social tensions. Others were considered violations of trust and breaches of contract.

For many official observers, the thirteen general strikes called by the CGT during Alfonsín's tenure were political. This view overlooks the increasing number of strikes at the factory level and among entire productive sectors that occurred over material rather than political issues from 1984 to 1988. With an average of more than seventeen strikes a month, or over five hundred strikes a year in the private sector, and dozens of extended strikes by workers in key state agencies (including public bank clerks, hospital employees and teachers, telephone, mail, and utility workers, and civil service personnel in the centralized administrative agencies), withdrawing labor services once again became labor's preferred vehicle for making material as well as political demands.[37]

Strikes in Argentina have always been directed as much against the state as against employers.[38] In addition, prohibitions on ill-defined political strikes — whatever economic merit they are judged to have — have been used by every Argentine regime in this century. Therefore, regulating permissible strike activity was an extremely sensitive issue. The task fell to Congress, which moved to define the specifics of the new strike law based on recommendations made by the executive branch. Congress attempted to forge a multiparty consensus on a new strike law that was palatable to the labor movement. This was far easier to advocate than to accomplish. The CGT and its congressional backers successfully resisted the government's proposals to circumscribe the right to strike, and all restrictions on strikes were eventually dropped as part of the labor legislation package passed in 1988.[39] The price for incorporating labor into the democratization project was to restore its traditional organizational hierarchy and remove all restrictions on the right to strike. Both concessions were initially considered anathema to that project.

The composition of Congress also reflected the institutional incorporation of the labor movement. Committee assignments in policy areas relevant to labor concerns were almost evenly distributed between Radicals with labor connections and Peronists of various persuasions. This was also true for positions on the Special Commission on Labor and Social Security Codes.[40] This made the passage of legislation favorable to labor's interests easier.

The delaying tactics of the government in reforming labor laws had the effect of directing labor's attention away from the executive branch and toward Parliament, where labor legislation packages were drawn up and considered. The reemphasis on labor-party linkages to secure passage of the labor reform bill reinforced the Peronist coalition in Congress, and in so doing allowed it to better play the role of loyal parliamentary opposition. Given the administration's increasing penchant for managing macroeconomic policy by executive decree, organized labor found that adopting a strategy oriented toward Parliament better advanced its interests.

It therefore broke with the strategy oriented toward the executive branch, which had been in vogue since 1943, and helped promote democratic institutionalization by supporting more balanced roles for the executive branch and Congress in formulating labor policy and overseeing the labor relations system. The passage of a labor legislation package that reaffirmed many of labor's organizational prerogatives cemented the focus on the parliamentary arena.

The government also tried to encourage labor's participation in tripartite vehicles. Relevant policy areas included public employment, where the CGT (as majority representative of 60 percent of public employees who were organized) was invited to share its views with the government and the private sector on the impact that rationalization and "privatization" efforts, implemented and conditioned by the need to service the foreign debt, would have on the public work force. That included discussion of possible ILO-sponsored, tripartite-managed vocational training programs to ease the transfer of labor to other economic sectors.[41]

These discussions were particularly contentious, since Argentine capitalists offered little in the way of employment alternatives for displaced labor, and no prospect for a long-term solution to the economic crisis. The sacrifices imposed on the public sector by the conditions for debt repayment were therefore disproportionately levied on the labor force in ways that went beyond real wage losses or the elimination of public services. This fact was not disguised by advocating tripartite "reconversion" vehicles.

A more pragmatic use of tripartite vehicles occurred with respect to union-operated social security and health programs. Obras Sociales, the union-operated social welfare fund with financial assets of at least $2.5 billion, provided health and insurance coverage for 60 percent of the population; it had been taken over by the military during the Proceso. Before that, it had been used by Peronist union leaders as a political patronage system geared toward the material gain of those involved.[42]

The CGT wanted to return to the status quo ante the Proceso, while the government preferred to centralize administration of the Obras Sociales under one public agency, the Instituto Nacional de Obras Sociales (INOS). Tripartite negotiation was considered the most appropriate means for reaching a satisfactory agreement on the future organization of the health and welfare system administered by the unions.

The tripartite commission that studied normalizing the Obras Sociales included representatives of the CGT and of the Union Industrial Argentina (UIA). By provisions of the December 1983 authorizing decree, this commission was formally incorporated into the administration of INOS.[43] We shall see later that this was part of the trend toward bureaucratic decentralization established within the state apparatus.

Congress created a special commission on Obras Sociales with sectorial and party representation divided equitably; below the national level, tripartite commissions made up of local unions, specific employer groups, and provincial or municipal authorities were formed to evaluate individual Obras Sociales.[44] Sectorial disagreements and the worsening economic crisis prevented the regular functioning of many subnational tripartite agencies — except, ironically, those responsible for the Obras Sociales. The success of this organization in an otherwise disharmonious picture was due to the fact that the Obras Sociales were the one part of Argentina's labor relations partial regime that had used a tripartite administration from its inception, however corrupted that system might have become.

By the end of Alfonsín's term, a compromise was reached according to which unions regained control of their respective Obras Sociales but agreed to periodic review and regular oversight on the part of INOS. This compromise was worked out in Congress as part of the move to pass the 1988 labor reform bill, and was based in part on the recommendations of the various tripartite commissions. Most important, with the reaffirmation of union control over the Obras Sociales, the government's social policies took a back seat to its other endeavors in the labor field.

The government's symbolic interest in tripartism was most evident in Argentina's increased participation in ILO networks. In addition to the invitation extended to the ILO to oversee elections normalizing the unions in 1986 and to participate in preparing vocational retraining programs, the ILO's presence was felt heavily in the Ministerio de Trabajo y Seguridad Social (Ministry of Labor and Social Security, or MTSS), where ILO delegates served as advisers to the minister of labor. In addition, Argentine delegations to International Labor Conferences were made up of senior representatives of the Ministry of Labor, other government agencies, various employer groups (particularly the Union Industrial and Conferencia General Económica) and high-ranking CGT functionaries (including the secretary general and other leading syndical figures).[45]

The most important tripartite vehicle offered by the Alfonsín administration, and which most closely resembled the archetypical notions of *concertación*, was the Conferencia Económico y Social (CES). Announced by the president in 1984, the CES was designed to provide a framework in which representatives of key peak associations of industrial capital (the UIA) and labor (the CGT) were joined by representatives of the branches of the state directly connected to each (the ministries of economy and of labor) to address a broad range of macroeconomic and social issues.

The CES was seen as the lead agency in a concertative network that would provide a wider range of institutionalized sectorial articulation and integrative mechanisms. Nine working groups — on agriculture, reform of the financial sector, tax reform, foreign debt, industrial conversion, exports, income policy, price control, and social security — were established in the CES in late 1984, and the government eventually proposed creating twenty-two such working groups. In parallel, a National Minimum Wage Council was established as a tripartite committee to formulate overall wage policy, which, despite episodic defections by both labor and business, continued to function throughout Alfonsín's tenure.[46] Institutionalization of these national-level tripartite vehicles was considered an advance over the ad hoc, informal discussions that had hitherto taken place.[47]

In practice, labor's ability to negotiate issues and participate in concertative vehicles was much more limited than the role stipulated for it in the initial proposal, which included discussion of social security, income, vocational training, and public employment policy, as well as more specific issues related to investment policy, debt refinancing, the price of domestic staples, and wage restraint in an inflationary climate. The economic crisis prompted the government to adopt a *dirigiste* approach to economic policy, thereby excluding many of these issues from concertative negotiation.

Also on the CES's proposed agenda was social welfare reform. The government proposed to reform the system on the basis of "three principles: generation of more resources for the system; a broadening of welfare services and improved redistribution of major resources; and government participation in accounting procedures."[48] Since this involved basic issues of taxation, income, and government jurisdiction in an environment of austerity, it included discussion of greater participation by both labor and capital in administering public enterprises and various agencies charged with providing for the public good.[49] All this was seen as falling within the purview of the CES, which would elaborate projects of reform and reorganization, subject to parliamentary debate and ratification.

The CES began work on August 7, 1984, with a narrow range of short-term tasks deemed particularly appropriate by the government for tripartite consideration. When meetings were called, the government presented an agenda for discussion, with labor and capital invited to respond.

By charter, the social partners never set the CES's agenda, nor could they call a general meeting of the CES. As a result, sectorial enthusiasm for the CES waned quickly, giving way to ad hoc bipartite initiatives, sectorial deal making, and purely superficial efforts to restart the tripartite dialogue. In fact, joint statements issued by the UIA, CGT, and their sectorial allies denounced the government's unilateral application of macroeconomic policy, its failure to raise wages, cut taxes, and promote investment, and continued delay in passing legislation reestablishing autonomous collective bargaining at the factory level.[50]

In response to the failure to secure a binding national tripartite agreement on economic policy, Radical leaders used the special prerogatives awarded to the presidency by the emergency laws of the Proceso to control key economic variables as part of the anti-inflation plan, while in Congress the two party blocs debated the merits of the labor reform package. The government was limited to trying to secure labor's agreement on a reasonable range of salary increases within the parameters outlined in the Austral Plan and in subsequent plans for economic stabilization adopted as of 1985.

Using the laws of the Proceso, the Alfonsín administration reserved the right to impose salary increases by executive decree. The Radicals hoped that labor and capital would agree to autonomously negotiate limited "bands" of salary increases within minimum "floors" and maximum "ceilings" established quarterly by the government, according to the predicted rate of inflation.[51] Employers were expected to agree not to raise prices during the time contracts were in effect, and labor would agree to refrain from taking subsequent "measures of force" over the terms.[52] As contracts expired, wage "bands" would be redefined. At such times, a limited range of price increases was anticipated, tied to a diminishing inflation rate. Alfonsín and his advisers hoped that this experience would provide the basis for future collective bargaining in a wide array of sectors once the economy had stabilized.[53]

Through short-term use of a highly interventionist approach to macroeconomic management, the Radical administration wanted to foster material agreements and institutional networks that would free labor and capital from wage and price concerns while they autonomously negotiated other substantive terms of the class compromise.

The objective of this concertative approach was made explicit by both economic and labor policy makers. According to a 1984 memorandum prepared by the Ministry of Economy, "It is the intention of the Government to adopt, as soon as circumstances permit, a policy under which wage determination in the private sector would be left to direct negotiation between management and labor."[54] In broader perspective, one labor minister considered the government's approach an important part of democratic consolidation, since it proposed to "exploit the potential for social autonomy in the face of excessive state intervention [in order to] undo rigidities that block economic functions. . . . Rather than anti-syndical or anti-business, the government's proposed reforms are designed to define the protagonistic roles that both social sectors should have in a democratic society."[55]

Nonetheless, the Radical approach to tripartite concertation at the national level failed. After several walkouts, the CGT formally abandoned the tripartite dialogue in June 1986, after another series of government-ordered salary readjustments. Even when confronted with the subsequent failure of the Austral Plan, the administration continued to impose wage and price ceilings by decree until 1989. Other attempts to reach some type of *pacto social* foundered on the shoals of sectorial intransigence, economic stagnation, and political competition within the labor movement and between Peronists and Radicals.

Labor reverted to its use of strikes as a political weapon, repeatedly testing its will against the government's. The effect of this confrontation was ultimately a standoff, debilitating and discrediting both sides. Yet the push for tripartite negotiation produced some substantive advances, most often the product of piecemeal deals (*arreglos*) arranged between the government, employers, and various union factions. This seeming contradiction is best explained by the extremely divided and conflictual internal situation within the CGT at the time of the transition, a situation that was anything but normal.

The CGT was already divided on strategic and generational grounds in 1979, during the initial process of authoritarian decomposition.[56] The major short-term effect of internal struggles was the defeat of the Peronists in the 1983 elections, since over 50 percent of unionists opted to support non-Peronist candidates rather than their traditional political patrons.

The Alfonsín government initially supported the *renovador* challenges to the *ortodoxo* "mafia" within the Peronist Party and labor leadership. In 1983 Alfonsín campaigned against the *ortodoxo* leadership, trumpeting the connections between *ortodoxos*, right-wing death squads, the military regime, and their crystallization in a purported *pacto militar-sindical* in the event of a Peronist victory. Labor conflict continued, both between different sectors of the Peronists and among the many independent labor unions.

By 1988 non-Peronist unions totaled 20 percent of Argentina's union membership, and included strategically important sectors such as public teachers, health workers, commercial bank employees, and employees in nontraditional private enterprises.[57] Many of the independent unions had especially strong ties to the most militant factions of the non-Peronist parties, including the Franja Morada faction in the Radical Party, particularly strong among university student groups (the intellectual counterparts of the younger generation of labor), the *militante* wing of the Intrasigentes, the Trotskyite Movimiento Al Socialismo (movement toward socialism, or MAS) and the Cuban-oriented Partido Obrero (Workers' Party, or PO). The presence of the last two groups and the rise of union currents associated with the Communist Party caused some *ortodoxos* to voice concern that they were being used to "smuggle Montoneros back into the labor movement."[58]

The thirteen general strikes called by the CGT during Alfonsín's tenure produced mixed success, as attrition took its toll on both labor and the state. The government's position was eroded over the long term and ultimately crippled by successful sectorial resistance to its program for economic stabilization and projects of constitutional reform. However, the lack of substantive gains and the continued decline of real wages (which by 1988 had fallen 50 percent relative to the last year of the Proceso) also hurt the CGT leadership, particularly its secretary general, Saúl Ubaldini. As a result, the confrontationalist posture eventually gave way to the "dialoguist," "pragmatist," or "opportunist" deal-making posture of the "15," a group of strategically important unions (textiles, plastics, utilities, metalworkers) with orthodox Peronist leaders grouped within the "62 Organizations," which were influential unions oriented toward negotiating sectorial agreements regardless of regime.

The ongoing impasse between the CGT and the Radical administration allowed the dialoguist "15" to interject its "pragmatic" (as opposed to "ideological") project into labor's discourse with the government. By reaching independent agreements with the government and employers at a time when Ubaldini was at his most confrontational, the "dialoguist" unions undercut the secretary general's position as the main spokesman for labor. More generally, union free riding continually thwarted the attempts by the CGT to portray a "monolithic" labor front on issues of economic and social policy.[59]

By 1987, fatigued by the standoff with the CGT, the Radical administration welcomed the overtures of the *ortodoxo* unions, and in March of that year moved to formally incorporate the "15" into government by naming one of its leading representatives as labor minister: Carlos Alderete, secretary general of the Luz y Fuerza power workers' or utility workers' union. The attempt at the partial and segmental co-option of labor via *cogestión* (or administrative pluralism, in the words of Vice President Victor Martínez) was made to placate a strategically important and cooperative current among the unions while simultaneously isolating the confrontationalist wing, thereby exploiting the divisions between *renovadores* and *ortodoxos* within the labor movement. This was designed to secure labor "peace" while weakening the Peronists on the eve of the September 1987 mid-term elections, a short-term tactical move based on political expediency rather than a genuine interest in incorporating labor.

The move to incorporate a cooperative and strategically important faction of the unions and the simultaneous exclusion of the *ubaldinista-renovador* labor coalition, which was politically confrontational and oriented toward Parliament, failed to achieve either government objective. Instead it proved counterproductive. Sectorial conflicts moved into the state apparatus and were internally replayed under institutional conditions that were heavily biased in favor of the "heterodox" (though in fact increasingly orthodox) policies of fiscal restraint, monetary reform, and social austerity advocated by Minister of Economy Juan Sourrouille.[60] This served to strengthen the impression that policies of economic stabilization and market adjustment dictated by the IMF framed the government's strategic approach to labor.

In June 1987, the wage agreements that had been delicately negotiated by Alderete a month earlier broke down; in September, a dissatisfied electorate voted against the Radicals. Peronist *renovadores* scored significant victories in congressional and gubernatorial elections, increasing the number of parliamentary representatives and key provincial governorships, including that of Buenos Aires. Thus, while failing to achieve its tactical objectives (beyond temporary peace on the labor front), the Radical approach toward co-opting segments of the labor movement further polarized the internal politics within the Peronist union movement, and, in another twist, set the stage for the approach toward labor adopted by Carlos Menem once he assumed the presidency in 1989.

The ultimately counterproductive "divide and conquer" strategy used on contending Peronist factions in the unions was part of the Radicals' failed attempt at incorporating labor. A two-pronged approach toward negotiations, calling for concertation but overseeing piecemeal agreements, was designed to exploit the fact that, because of internal conflicts within the CGT and the delay in normalizing its status through elections, organized labor initially had not one spokesman "but close to 500, which was also the approximate number of outstanding collective bargaining agreements inherited from the dictatorship."[61]

By 1987, after much disagreement between sectors about salary adjustments, the economic team headquartered in the Ministry of Economy assumed full responsibility for formulating a government income policy. In a spirit of cooperation, hoping for rewards down the road, most unions initially opted to negotiate within the government's wage guidelines. According to official figures, within the limits of the 1986 adjustment packages, "57 percent of all private workers were able to have their salaries adjusted, as 70 unions representing 2.3 million people reached agreements."[62] Virtually all contracts contained "social peace" clauses that proscribed strikes for the duration of the agreement. Thus individualized deal making as a "survivalist" strategy was most useful in this environment of economic crisis.[63]

Although factionalized, organized labor did share a macroeconomic perspective that saw the root cause of Argentina's malaise in the structural constraints imposed by its dependent capitalist insertion into the world market, with the immediate obstacle to stabilization being the crushing burden of debt manipulated by the transnational finance elite. Accustomed to the Peronist policy of inclusionary state corporatism, unionists also shared a belief that labor's participation in the government's economic policy making was part of a project of national revitalization that would promote autonomous national growth and redistribution of income. The unions viewed tripartism as the preferred form of "economic and social concertation with a strong state which can vehemently maintain its national goals and objectives, and which can creatively insert the country in the world on the basis of a redefinition of the types of articulation linking it with international financial agencies and creditor banks."[64] Beyond that, the unions' strategies on economic issues differed, even though all were opposed to government policy.[65]

On the other hand, the importance of having the support of influential unions had long been understood by Argentine governments, regardless of their orientation toward labor.[66] Even critics of the Radical government saw the value of the "divide and conquer," deal-making strategy used on strategically important groups such as the metalworkers, whose union "carries out a directive function in the industrial economy. It serves as an example for other unions, sweeping by virtue of demonstration effect other occupations of a diverse nature, and determines labor cost levels and prices in a number of related activities."[67]

Such strategic acceptance by the unions of the need for government-decreed salary adjustment packages eased the way for accepting the decree in related economic sectors. At least temporarily, the "deals" offered mutual benefits to both sides: the government gained support within the CGT, while the "dialoguist" faction saw its position strengthened vis-à-vis the "confrontationalist" bloc. Abetted by the challenges of non-Peronist unions, competition intensified within the CGT, since the very representativeness of its leadership was now open to question.

The differences between the strategies of various unions ultimately rested on internal competition for rank-and-file support. The contending strategies were based on different notions of political leverage derived from opposed perceptions of the advantages of cooperative versus confrontational approaches to a non-Peronist democratic government within a macroeconomic "coordination game" of scarcity.[68] Both union factions constantly maneuvered for rank-and-file support so as not to be outflanked by members' demands; this led to episodic moments of unified labor opposition to government economic policy. But the pragmatic approach attempted to improve the immediate material conditions of affiliates, while the confrontationalist approach attempted to question the entire rationale behind the Radical government's program of stabilization. As a result, state-labor relations during the Alfonsín administration were based on securing tactical advantages that permitted immediate political or economic objectives to be achieved rather than on establishing through consent the procedural terms and institutional bases for a longer-term class compromise.

Limited concertative bargaining was nevertheless undertaken in both the public and private sectors during the first three years of the democratic regime. A commission for salary adjustment, made up of representatives from the Ministries of Labor and Economy, the Secretariat of Public Affairs, the Secretariat of Public Enterprise Control, the Civil Service Union, and the State Workers Association established rates of readjustment for various civil service categories.[69] Similar arrangements were used in the private sector, with union and employer representatives joining officials at the Ministry of Labor in mediated discussions of the permissible range of wage and price increases in each productive area. In 1987, roughly half of the new agreements concerning the private sector were reached through tripartite negotiation, while the other half were reached in bipartite fashion, without state mediation (and most often outside the government's wage guidelines).

In this sense, the government's objective of restoring the autonomy of labor and capital was partially achieved. Yet it had the counterproductive effect of contributing to the inflationary cycle, as unions and firms increasingly ignored government wage and price guidelines and passed the costs of salary agreements to consumers, thereby shifting the burden of enforcement onto an inefficient state bureaucracy. Confronted with a weak state with limited capabilities for enforcement, labor and capital opted for maximalist (if not "survivalist") short-term strategic postures that ignored the call for sectorial restraint and cooperation with the government. Instead, autonomous cooperation without restraint among sectors and outside government guidelines increasingly characterized the labor relations partial regime, testifying to the near feral state of economic behavior seen toward the end of Alfonsín's tenure.

Despite this situation, the Radical government believed that piecemeal acceptance of salary adjustment decrees, direct labor-capital negotiations, and the increased factionalization of the Peronist union leadership were having a salutary effect on the labor relations system, and were in fact the first steps toward incorporating Argentine labor into the democracy. According to one assistant secretary of labor, under Radical policies it was "possible to abandon [the practice of] centralized intervention in salary negotiations, and move on to a system of autonomous negotiation. The very nature of labor conflicts changed. Rather than superpolitical confrontations without resolution, a move was made toward a situation that is more typical of any industrial society, where the negotiators are the principals in labor relations, and where the State assumes a secondary role."[70]

Divisions within the labor movement allowed the Alfonsín administration first to take the initiative in determining the nature of the strategic interaction between the state, labor, and capital. While ultimately incorporative and positive-sum in conception, this approach sought to reinforce a decentralizing and diversifying trend, both economic and political, within the CGT. In this respect, it shared a policy approach with the military-bureaucratic regime that had preceded it, since each side considered the elimination of the vertical, Peronist-dominated union framework a necessary condition for the successful implementation of labor policy. The difference between the two approaches, however, was more substantial: the Radical approach was essentially inclusionary, and thus based on a positive view of the role labor could play in Argentine society, while the military-bureaucratic exclusionary approach was based on an utterly negative assessment of labor's contribution to the country.

The external constraints that characterized the politico-economic "coordination game" — namely, structural crisis and fierce partisan competition — made effective use of concertative vehicles impossible. Short-term deal making eventually became the preferred strategic option for the government, important labor factions, and leading business groups. As a result, state-labor relations in Argentina remained in flux throughout this critical historical juncture, as the quest continued without resolution for a (re)incorporative vehicle that would be different from the initial populist-authoritarian, inclusionary, state-corporatist framework.

Nonetheless, the external orientation of national labor administration underwent important changes that contributed to changing the labor relations system. The administration consciously attempted to demonstrate a strong interest in revitalizing its role in promoting occupational health and safety, thereby reaffirming its technical neutrality and clientelist orientation in the field of labor, after years of authoritarian bias, neglect, and exclusion. This was designed to show organized labor that national labor administration under the Radicals was committed to fair enforcement of the relations in production, thereby establishing the institutional bases for further cooperation between labor and the state.[71]

We should note one final irony. While Argentine capitalists had plenty to offer in supporting social transformation and democratic consolidation, their interest in the project and their reliability as social partners was doubtful. Instead, a large portion of the financial and industrial bourgeoisie (to say nothing of the landed elite) believed that their material self-interest lay in maximizing short-term gains and investing elsewhere.[72] Employers' lack of interest in concertative approaches to democratic consolidation can be evoked in the words of a president of a large national firm: "Concertation is completely useless. It is impossible to do. Everyone agrees with the objectives, . . . everyone signs the pact, but nobody abides by it. Concertation can be useful when everything is practically solved, with a country already stable."[73] Confronted with such a perspective, and unable to enforce the terms of any compromise, the government was largely unable to promote national-level concertative approaches to democratic consolidation.

Even though domestic (re)investment is essential for achieving a lasting class compromise, the Radical government could not provide effective incentives and disincentives to encourage Argentine capitalists to invest at home or to adopt moderate long-term strategic postures. Adverse structural conditions militated against the government's project in ways that transcended the field of labor relations; the economic interests that cut across different sectors combined to form the most damaging sectorial resistance and ultimately undermined the Radical government.

The Alfonsín administration attempted to explore several new avenues for promoting democratic class relations in Argentina. We have seen how it approached the external dimension of national labor administration in pursuit of this elusive goal. We now turn to its approach to the internal dimension, where we might be able to discern longer-term success or significant change. This internal dimension is made up of the organization of the state apparatus, particularly the branch directly responsible for administering the labor relations system.

The Internal Dimension of National Labor Administration

ORGANIZATION

Shortly after assuming office, the Radical government reorganized the state apparatus, replacing the authoritarian law of ministries passed in 1981.[74] The new law of ministries (Law 23,023/10, December 1983) reduced the number of cabinet-level portfolios to eight. The rationale behind this reorganization was twofold. The government wanted to remove the legacy of institutional authoritarianism that was the cumulative effect of the preceding populist and military-bureaucratic regimes. In addition, it wanted to promote a form of national state organization that reinforced democratic practices in government and similar modes of interaction in civil society. Because of the state's traditionally authoritarian role in labor relations, this required a major overhaul of its organizational framework, including the administrative reform of the Labor Ministry and its subordinate agencies.

All labor-related activities, including responsibilities for workers' welfare, were placed under the jurisdiction of the Ministerio de Trabajo y Seguridad Social. This ministry was responsible for implementing — but not formulating — labor policy nationwide.[75] Among the primary duties of the MTSS outlined under the new laws were: registering and regulating the activities of officially recognized unions; mediating and arbitrating labor disputes; approving and mediating collective bargaining agreements; enforcing safe working conditions; and administering union-related social security programs.[76] The new duties of the MTSS reaffirmed the corporatist and interventionist character of Argentina's labor administration.

The organization of the MTSS, however, reflected the government's intention to "democratize" the public sphere on an institutional level. This was manifested in efforts to compartmentalize and horizontally diversify both its internal tasks and its external responsibilities involving direct contact with the labor movement. These efforts were divided between two administrative clusters defined in terms of their functions, each headed by a secretariat that was directly responsible to the minister of labor and social security.[77] The Secretaría de Trabajo (Secretariat of Labor) was charged with all administrative functions related to labor-capital relations on procedural and immediate substantive issues, while the Secretaría de Seguridad Social (Secretariat of Social Security) was responsible for overseeing labor-related social welfare tasks as part of the broader institutional foundation of a democratic labor relations system (i.e., those involved in the social relations of production).

This added another "political" rung high on the bureaucratic ladder, confirming the propensity of postwar Radical governments to expand the state apparatus in terms of functional responsibilities. The rationale behind this expansion was simple. Where the Proceso had narrowed the scope of functional responsibilities of national labor administration to monitoring the relations in production, the democratic regime reemphasized the social relations of production. While the labor relations cluster continued the organizational format inherited from the Proceso, responsibility for social security was restored to national labor administration by the Radical government and was grouped into an organizational cluster oriented toward providing health, education, and welfare services.[78]

Because the bulk of labor-state interaction during the first three years of Alfonsín's administration revolved around issues addressed by the cluster concerned with labor, the cluster addressing social security was more insulated from political pressures, and hence more autonomous. This gave the external dimension of Argentina's labor administration a dual character, based on the different level of autonomy achieved by the two external branches.

The primary emphasis of state-labor relations shifted from overseeing the union (its role under the Proceso) to enforcing laws and monitoring the workplace (its function under the Radical government). The shift in organizational emphasis was designed to reinforce the administration's attempt to project a technical, legalistic, and politically neutral identity of national labor administration in the interest of creating some institutional basis for state-labor cooperation. Here the state envisioned itself as the impartial mediator or arbitrator of the microfoundational features of the social relations of production and of the relations in production. Muted and couched in legalistic and neutral, pluralist ideological terms, the repressive function of national labor administration shifted to employers, while labor was viewed as a (potential) client rather than an adversary. After years of an overtly coercive approach to labor, this represented a quantum leap, though not an entirely novel shift.[79]

The MTSS was given national jurisdiction in an effort to better administer the demands of interest groups organized along strong federational lines. Where feasible, the Radical government preferred to allow municipal and provincial authorities to take precedence when addressing labor issues within their jurisdictions. This reversed the approach taken by both the populist and the military-bureaucratic regimes, which used the regional delegations as instruments of centralized administrative oversight and subordinated local labor administrations to them.

The MTSS under Alfonsín had no formal responsibility for formulating labor policy. That task fell to the president and Congress and their respective advisory bodies, with specific issues being addressed by the tripartite organizations. The MTSS's staff discussed labor policy with the CES, officially classified as part of the executive branch. From these emerged (albeit sporadically, depending on the attitude of individual participants at particular moments) specific decisions, which were implemented by the MTSS.

This arrangement was designed to encourage labor and capital to voice comprehensive demands within the confines of the CES, with more specific concerns handled by a technically and legally defined network of specialized state apparatuses. It was believed that agreements reached in the tripartite forum could be implemented dispassionately, without partisan interference, by neutral and autonomous state agencies. Following this logic, the MTSS became the primary instrument through which the salary adjustment packages adopted by in the CES in 1985–1986 were ratified in the agreements reached in a variety of economic sectors.

The return of democracy in 1983 brought with it another attempt at a neutral, technically defined approach to national labor administration, which had historical precedent in previous periods of Radical leadership. Rather than merely repeat the cycle, this approach used tripartite mechanisms for formulating policy as major vehicles for incorporating labor. In this sense, it was not only vastly different from the labor projects of the preceding authoritarian regimes; it also represented a departure from previous democratic practices in Argentina.

BUDGET

An analysis of the general budgetary picture under the Radical government indicates the regime's approach toward national labor administration. By classifying labor administration as part of the social welfare budget, the state moved it out of the economic management category, where it had been placed by the Proceso. This shift harked back to the budgetary classification schemes used by both populist regimes and limited democracies, which favored classifying labor administration in terms of clientelism and public service rather than production.

Although low compared to other state agencies, figures from 1984 to 1988, which varied from 0.7 to 0.97 percent of the central administrative budget, represent the highest percentage of expenditures allocated by the central administration to Argentina's labor administration in over thirty years (that is, since the last budget formulated by the first Peronist regime).[80] Given that the Proceso established historical lows in funding for labor administration, public health, and social welfare,[81] this shift had enormous political significance. It even surpassed the labor administration budget of the corrupt second Peronist regime, which relied heavily on gross political patronage within the labor movement. If nothing else, such budgetary reemphasis was institutional evidence of the Radicals' understanding of the importance of incorporating labor into the process of democratic consolidation.

The distribution of funds within national labor administration reflected the thrust of its approach to the labor relations partial regime. Most of the funds allocated to the Secretariat of Labor went toward personnel expenditures in decentralized agencies such as regional delegations. This reversed the distribution of personnel allocations in national labor administrations under the Proceso.[82] Beyond the regional delegations, the majority of funds went toward personnel costs in centralized agencies of the cluster concerned with labor questions, where the majority of central administrative employees were located. The emphasis was especially visible in agencies charged with enforcing labor legislation and in occupational health and safety agencies.

Accounting procedures were tightened considerably throughout the MTSS under the democratic regime as a result of fiscal reforms and increased parliamentary oversight. The amount of discretionary funds available to any one agency (the so-called *Cuentas Especiales sin discriminar)* was reduced and made subject to extraministerial oversight mechanisms.[83] The distribution of funds remained constant throughout Alfonsín's tenure, though the total allocated to national labor administration declined toward the end of his term. By 1989 expenditures in this area were close to the median for the previous thirty years, reflecting the limits of budgetary reemphasis in a climate of economic crisis and in view of labor's opposition to the government.

PERSONNEL

Under Alfonsín, slightly more than 3,100 employees (on average) worked in national labor administration, down from more than 3,700 during the Proceso. The personnel emphasis placed on decentralized liaison agencies such as the regional delegations was another reflection of the Radicals' commitment to federalism and to administrative pluralism within the state apparatus. It stood in marked contrast to the centralizing designs for labor administration that were historically favored by both populist and military-bureaucratic regimes. For example, under the Proceso, 3,439 of the 3,749 employees working in the labor administration in 1981 were members of the central administrative apparatus, headquartered in the Labor Ministry in Buenos Aires.[84] The Radicals' effort to decentralize administration of the labor relations partial regime ran counter to the ongoing logic of administrative centralization that characterized state-labor relations throughout the postwar period and represented a significant break with the historical thrust of national labor administration.

The number of civil servants employed in the MTSS and related agencies was relatively low compared to that in other state branches, and the majority were occupied in mid-level technical, management, or administrative positions. The level of functional expertise formally required for employment in the MTSS was relatively high and employees thus comparatively well remunerated.[85] The public good that national labor administration provided was its expertise.

Criteria for selecting personnel in the "professional" category stressed prior experience or education in the field of labor, particularly labor law and occupational health and safety. Political affiliation — whether "dialoguist" Peronist or Radical — also weighed heavily in the recruitment of upper-echelon personnel. Ascriptive recruitment practices were most evident in the cluster of externally oriented agencies that had direct contact with unions. In this cluster, some positions were purely political.[86]

The political nature of many of the "professional" appointees represented the government's recognition that developing a cooperative, if not clientelist relationship with organized labor required "specialized" partisan contacts that transcended the guidelines for recruiting civil servants based on experience or education.[87] The character of Argentine labor, the backbone of Peronist opposition, made political rapprochement between Argentine labor administration and CGT affiliates as important as the neutral enforcement of legally defined labor rights at the level of production.

A significant aspect of this institutional framework was the proliferation of nonelected representatives of the social partners within the CES. For the most part, these sectorial appointees were labor lawyers or specialists in labor-related issues of social security and health, and served as the permanent staff and executive body of the CES. Outnumbering the elected representatives of capital and labor as well as cabinet and other upper-level officers, these appointees, divided proportionately among the three partners, made up the core of state managers responsible for supervising and mediating concertative negotiations. The fact that they were appointed was supposed to place them beyond partisan concerns and factional disputes. This ostensibly endowed them with a measure of autonomy in formulating the terms of sectorial agreements which, when added to the operative autonomy of the branches implementing them, gave the state sufficient distance — and thus an objective view — vis-à-vis both labor and capital when administering the terms of those agreements.

The sex distribution pattern within the MTSS shows relative equality between men and women in the total number employed, but men were disproportionately represented in the "professional" category, while women occupied the majority of clerical and service positions. Given the importance of political contacts and the fact that CGT leaders were overwhelmingly male and patriarchal in orientation (particularly the *ortodóxos*), that is not surprising. Such gender discrimination was more obvious in external, labor-connected agencies such as the Dirección Nacional de Trabajo and Dirección Nacional de Asuntos Gremiales (the labor relations and union affairs directorates) than in the branches of internal administration or social security.

The government's intention to promote neutrality and impartiality in national labor administration was also not always evident in the appointment of the MTSS's upper-echelon personnel. The high turnover in the position of labor minister attests to the extreme difficulty in administering this critical policy area. Beyond the overtly partisan nature of the post and its subordination to the minister of economy during the Alfonsín years, as the "hinge" between the state, capital, and labor, the labor minister was vulnerable to the combined effects of centrifugal pressures exerted by competing sectors in a crisis-ridden economic environment. Below the cabinet level, turnover rates were lower and usually confined to upper-echelon positions occupied by political appointees such as the secretaries, technical secretaries, undersecretaries, and national directors in the external clusters.

Political appointees were also found at the level of national director and general director, with civil service guidelines governing personnel recruitment and retention below that level.[88] Expertise in labor affairs and/or legal training in labor relations dominated the backgrounds of incumbents below the cabinet level.

Significant parts of the labor movement saw the appointment of "operators" sympathetic to labor in a positive light. Many unionists considered MTSS personnel as their main allies within the executive branch. "Syndical sources estimate that two positions exist . . . on matters of labor policy: that of officials in the Labor and Interior Ministries, which are flexible in regards to the salary question, and which are not compatible with the rigid posture of the Ministry of Economy."[89] Thus, "Barrionuevo and Troccoli [former interior minister, who also had strong ties to labor], among other officials, are considered to be more *permeable* by syndical demands."[90]

This clientelist orientation translated into conflicts within the cabinet on basic questions such as wage adjustment policy, with labor administration representatives reproducing labor's demands in the cabinet and attempting to coax labor to accept the government's logic of stabilization, while the branches involved in economic policy did the same for business.[91] The fact that the Ministry of Economy won out in most policy debates and continued to dictate wage policy throughout Alfonsín's tenure attests to its position of strength within the cabinet, and to the structural power of Argentine business.

Given the importance of personal ties in Argentine politics, the appointment of individuals linked to labor (particularly *Ortodoxos*) constituted a move to give national labor administration a sympathetic yet bipartisan character conducive to sectorial agreements. In this sense it was designed to serve as a complement to the use of *renovador* Peronist *operadores* in the Ministry of Economy, although the situation proved different in practice. Beyond that, procedural neutrality and high levels of experience among upper-echelon personnel were considered integral steps toward establishing a measure of institutional autonomy within national labor administration, since it gave policy implementation in the field of labor its ostensibly neutral character.

Conclusion

The process of institutional democratization still has a long way to go in Argentina.[92] The attempt to consolidate a democratic labor relations partial regime at an institutional level after 1983 shows the difficulties of doing so in an environment of economic crisis superimposed on fierce partisan conflict between a strong labor-backed opposition and a centrist government attempting to surmount the compound authoritarian legacies of the previous four decades. Instead of the triple logic of cooperative collective action based on the mutual adoption of second-best sectorial strategies, reinforced by equitable and efficient enforcement by the state, in Argentina under Alfonsín there was a maximalist logic pitting labor and capital (which were cooperating economically through wage and price fixing) against the state's project of structural adjustment based largely on price and wage restraint. At the same time, uncoordinated initiatives based on partisan objectives and sectorial egotism led to ad hoc tactical alliances, standoffs, and stalemates between Parliament and the executive branch, and a general atmosphere of conflict between the state, labor, and capital in the political sphere.

The irony of this situation is that, along with what Hewitt has called the "cruel dilemmas of development" (that is, the difficult choice between national efficiency in allocating resources versus the equality of distribution and the social representativeness of decision making),[93] there were the added contradictions of democratic consolidation in a context where institutionalizing democratic forms of strategic interaction (unrestricted party competition and autonomous collective bargaining) exacerbated the inherited structural crisis. Here the prospects for democracy were jeopardized by the very institutionalization of pluralist and polyarchical decision-making frameworks, which made mutual political and material payouts negligible.

Although it was a positive step in the process of democratic consolidation, the transition to a Peronist government in 1989 did little to surmount the structural and behavioral problems described above. The move toward a labor-backed party in government should have improved the chances for democratic concertation. Yet the Argentine experience contradicts this, since the Peronist regime of 1973–1976, even though it was led by a charismatic leader in the presidency (Juan Perón himself!) and enjoyed an overwhelming parliamentary majority and control of the CGT and of leading business associations (especially the CGE), failed to institutionalize a concertative tripartite pact, despite the formal enunciation of such a pact and more favorable economic conditions.[94]

Here the second requisite for successful concertation mentioned in the literature comes into play, for it was the absence of powers of mutual control (i.e., capacities for enforcement) on the part of the state and collective agents that obstructed cooperative strategic interaction. Without mutual control, collective action hinged on involuntary self-maximizing (i.e., "survivalist") short-term strategies, both political and economic. With all parties discounting the possibility of mutual benefits over the long term, the interplay between the labor movement, capitalist collective action, state organization, partisan competition, and macroeconomic conditions erected formidable structural and institutional obstacles to democratic consolidation through socioeconomic pacts.

The election of Peronist Carlos Menem offers an interesting postscript to the Alfonsín approach to state-labor relations. Menem allied himself with the "pragmatic" faction of the labor movement and established the basis for a nonpartisan and uniform dialogue between the state and labor during the early days of the Peronist administration.

Menem's administration focused on a fuller incorporation of the "dialoguist" *ortodoxo* faction of labor and the utter exclusion of the "confrontationalist" *ubaldinista* faction. There was also a "deepening" of *cogestión* (coadministration) in the state apparatus. Non-Peronists, including conservatives well connected with the *patria financiera*, were named to key cabinet posts. This was particularly true for the Ministry of Economy, where two directors of Argentina's largest transnational corporation, Bunge y Born, were named ministers in quick succession (the first appointee died shortly after assuming office).

The move to sectorial incorporation showed the new president's remarkable degree of acumen, which was unanticipated by many within and outside the Peronist movement. The pragmatic institutionalization of *cogestión* in business and labor was designed to uniformly articulate branches of the state with the sectorial interests they were directly linked to and responsible for administering, in an effort to promote a coherent approach toward the national crisis.

Yet here is where Menem confounded conventional wisdom and added yet another wrinkle to the process of democratic consolidation. Confronted with a rupture within the Peronist ranks that made it harder to forge lasting agreements among peak associations, Menem reversed course and rapidly pushed through Congress an ILO-supported bill that provided for autonomous shop-level collective bargaining without state interference. To repeat: a Peronist president abandons the state corporatist legacy of his political namesake in favor of the anti-Peronists' preferred labor approach: total pluralism. He then opened the economy by freeing the peso (formerly the Austral) and by embarking on a comprehensive "privatization" campaign in which a multitude of state enterprises, from telephones and power to the national airline, were sold to foreign-dominated private consortiums. This meant a complete rejection of employment guarantees for laid-off workers in the targeted enterprises.[95]

The effect of Menem's economic project was to atomize labor, as each local union adopted a "survivalist" mentality and sought to maximize — or, better yet, preserve — its position in the face of this market-oriented approach toward structural reform. Labor solidarity ran aground on the shoals of rank-and-file self-interest, and the CGT was effectively removed from real decision making. Thus, rather than a full and equal actor, labor under Menem was gradually and at best partially incorporated as a subordinate player in a project that responded to a climate where working-class consent was secured by strengthening the political and social backing of market policies conducive to economic stability. Here class compromise at the collective level was not needed, as individual workers and local unions consented to the new approach by turning their attention toward more immediate, economic objectives.

This is still a zero-sum game, however, ruled by maximalist egotistical preferences. More relevant to our concerns, this type of atomizing pluralism may work in the debased post-authoritarian economic environment of the late 1980s and 1990s, but it is no guarantee of political and socioeconomic stability through the end of the century.

Not to end on a cynical and pessimistic note that many *compañeros* would consider *típicamente Argentino*, let us restate the importance of the split within the Peronist movement for democratic consolidation. The emergence of nonauthoritarian currents within Peronism, including the labor movement, offers an unprecedented opportunity to press the case for institutional democracy. Combined with the traumas of the last decade, generational change, and the emergence of new social movements such as feminism, environmentalism, and pacifism, this may well be the incipient moment for substantive democratic consolidation in Argentina.

The question is therefore: which way is Argentina going to go? Will it return to the melancholy cycle of political instability and violence, like some nostalgic tango endlessly replaying a dance of decline on a well-worn Victrola? Or will it learn from the past and open itself to the possibilities of the future, in which new steps and patterns of interaction encourage an equitable and egalitarian social dialogue? These are the questions that lie at the heart of the Argentine dilemma. For the moment, it remains to be seen whether the country has learned the tune of a new *compás*.

6

NATIONAL LABOR ADMINISTRATION

AND DEMOCRACY

IN POST-AUTHORITARIAN BRAZIL

LIKE TURQUOISE DOMINOES that neither time nor change in the political environment has toppled, the buildings that house the Brazilian state apparatus stand horizontally aligned in neatly symmetrical rows along the Esplanada dos Ministerios, Brasilia's major east-west axis. Viewed from the west, they are an impressive frame for the spectacular architectural features of the Praça dos tres Poderes government complex and provide concrete proof of the genius of urban planning in the Brazilian capital. Grandiose design and formidable appearance notwithstanding, it is the internal dynamics at play within the buildings housing the core of the Brazilian state that lie at the heart of that nation's modern political history. The state apparatus so neatly aligned in the capital offers an architectural manifestation of the character and orientation of the political regimes that have held power since 1960. With that in mind, we examine in this chapter the internal architectonics of one state agency housed on the Esplanada dos Ministerios: the Ministério do Trabalho (Ministry of Labor, or MTb).

While its external edifice forms part of the enduring legacy and lofty aspirations of the national project begun over a quarter century ago, internally Brazil's labor administration reflects the evolution of the national labor relations system during this period. They present an ideal window on the character, orientation, and structural bases of the labor policies of the democratic regime installed in 1985.

Historical Antecedents

Responding to the emergence of new syndical movements associated with waves of immigration from southern Europe, and reflecting the overall orientation of the economy at the time, a National Department of Labor (NDL) was created within the Agriculture Ministry in October 1918.[1] It remained unchanged until 1930, when, in the wake of the Depression, Getúlio Vargas — fully understanding the political capital inherent in working-class support and interested in promoting full-scale industrialization as part of a populist national project of Grandeza — incorporated the NDL into the newly created Ministério de Trabalho, Indústria e Comércio (Ministry of Labor, Industry, and Commerce, or MTIC).[2]

The MTIC remained virtually unchanged for nearly thirty years and became the centerpiece of a state-corporatist system for interest group administration that had few equals in Latin America in scope and longevity.[3]

Vargas's approach to organized labor reflected his nationalist-populist ideology and his keen political opportunism. Capitalizing on the economic crisis caused by the Depression, Vargas used the state-sponsored move toward industrialization as a vehicle for cultivating the support of the emerging urban industrial classes. He maintained that creating the MTIC "constituted the first step towards organizing labor, commerce, and industry throughout the country. . . . With this gesture the Provisional Government fulfills an honor debt that the public authorities owed to Brazilian workers."[4]

Modeled after the Fascist constitutions of Portugal and Italy, Vargas's Estado Novo grouped employees and workers according to function in parallel organizations that were to be complemented by a similarly structured national legislature (which never materialized).[5] Here, state corporatism was both an ideological objective *and* a specific approach to policy making and interest group administration. Although the ideological component of this framework waned after 1945, its institutional features survived virtually intact well into the 1980s, particularly in the field of labor relations.

The structure of interest group representation for organized labor consisted of "first grade" organizations known as *sindicatos* (unions) that grouped employers and workers in each category, trade, industry, and economic sector within a given municipality or geographic area. Autonomous shop-level unions were not permitted. Codified as law in the Consolidação das Leis do Trabalho (CLT), this framework provided that, in states with five or more *sindicatos* in a specific economic category, unions could be incorporated into "second grade" organizations known as *federações* (federations). When there were three or more such federations in one economic category, they could be grouped together under an umbrella "third grade" organization, the (sectorial) *confederação* (confederation).

The original CLT outlined seven types of confederations, representing workers and employers in industry, commerce, land transport, communications and publicity, water and air transportation, credit institutions, and educational and cultural institutions.[6] In addition, the CLT provided for a National Confederation of Free Professions (for lawyers, doctors, engineers, etc.).[7] It did not provide for national confederations encompassing different functional categories, nor did it permit direct links between different types of unions. Public sector employees were barred from organizing or striking under CLT provisions, and intersectorial rural labor associations were actively discouraged.

The territorial decentralization of unions promoted by the CLT formed the legal basis for the exclusionary state-corporatist structuring of working-class interests. This structure was characterized by a decentralizing and deconcentrating orientation manifested in legal constraints on sectorial activities and organization designed to weaken the collective strength of the labor movement.[8] Vargas, and later João Goulart (1961–1964), compounded the weakness imposed on Brazilian labor by using techniques of individual co-option, heavily buttressed by corruption, to secure the cooperation of labor leaders. Compliant sectors of the urban working classes received certain state-provided public goods; co-option was reaffirmed by legal provisions accentuating the dependence of labor leaders on national labor authorities. These measures effectively divorced leaders from rank-and-file workers and made them more amenable to government initiatives and susceptible to political manipulation.

To this was added discretionary enforcement of the CLT's provisions regarding the right to association. The government rigorously limited the organization and activities of the union movement while at the same time adopting a more relaxed attitude toward the "less subversive" activities of employer-producer groups. Thus, from its inception, the orientation and organization of modern Brazilian labor administration was fundamentally exclusionary, based on state control of a structurally weak and divided labor movement.

According to the framework outlined in the CLT in 1985, in order to carry out basic functions such as collective bargaining, *sindicatos* had to be officially recognized by the Labor Ministry. Only one *sindicato* per functional category was granted legal status in each locality. To be awarded recognition, *sindicatos* had to agree to subordinate their professional concerns to the national interest, cooperate with government authorities, and refrain from political activities. The Labor Ministry retained authority to intervene in unions, enforce their "normalization," rescind labor contracts, cancel collective bargaining or make it mandatory, and more generally, supervise all wage negotiations (articles 482, 516, 518–21, 528, 554, 611–15, and 623).

The Labor Ministry was also directed to regulate union statutes and oversee union finances and expenditures. These constraints on the unions' freedom did not end with the delimitation of the powers and authority of national labor administration. For example, the constitution enacted under the Estado Novo outlawed all strikes as subversive. Although this was partially modified during the democratic opening and constitutional reform of 1946 (when strikes in "nonbasic" industries were allowed), broad restrictions on the right to strike continued in force and were vigorously enforced during the military regime.[9]

In exchange for legal recognition, *sindicatos* received 60 percent of a state-mandated union tax on all workers (*imposto sindical*, now referred to as the *contribução sindical*), 20 percent of which was designated for a *fondo social sindical* (union social fund, now known as the *seguro de desemprego* or unemployment insurance fund) administered by the Labor Ministry.

This fund was originally to provide benefits and services to nonunion workers and the working population in general. In practice, it was used as an instrument of patronage and applied to internal national labor administration costs. The unions' reliance on the *imposto sindical* removed incentives to expand membership, since the tax was charged to all workers, not only union affiliates. If no *sindicato* existed in a particular functional area or territory, its share of the *imposto sindical* went to the appropriate state federation. If no federation existed, both shares went to the appropriate sectorial confederation. If no confederation existed, the entire amount went to the *fondo social sindical*. Under this scheme, national labor administration had a vested financial interest in seeing that workers remained unorganized in a broad array of activities.

At the union level, funds from the *imposto sindical* were allotted for health, social security, and educational and cultural services for union members. Using them to finance strikes or other forms of grievance petition was specifically prohibited. These legal restrictions and the effect on the unions' internal focus had a decided impact on the labor leadership. Individual fortunes (material and political) within the labor hierarchy came to depend on the state's largesse and the degree of conformity displayed by each leader. As a result, officially recognized unions became increasingly bureaucratized, supportive of the government, and effectively divorced from their ostensible constituencies.

The Vargas labor codes were designed to assure the acquiescence of the rank and file to a union leadership that was responsive to government dictates. This complemented the decentralizing and deconcentrating organizational tendencies mentioned earlier.

The transition period found remnants of the old labor bureaucracy locked in a struggle with new syndical leaders unbeholden to the corporatist system. The new leaders increased the pace of democratic transition after 1978. The most notable contribution was made by the leader of the metalworkers union and founder of the first independent labor confederation, Luís Inácio da Silva ("Lula"), now a two-time presidential candidate and national leader of the Partido dos Trabalhadores (workers' party, or PT).

In contrast to union structures, national labor administration was initially highly centralized. For thirty years the entire labor relations system had as its core just two agencies, the Departamento Nacional do Trabalho (National Labor Department, or DNT) and the Departamento Geral de Previdência Social (Department-General of Social Welfare, or DGPS), both located in the MTIC.[10]

With the activities of these two agencies, coupled with the role of labor courts, national labor administration covered the full spectrum of union activities. Its organization was, in effect, a reverse image of the decentralized, deconcentrated union structures promoted at an external level. This division of labor was subsequently highlighted and codified by Law 3728 of July 22, 1960, which narrowed the scope and changed the title of the labor portfolio, which then became the Ministério de Trabalho e Previdência Social (Ministry of Labor and Social Welfare, or MTPS).[11]

Because of its internal form and external attributes, from the time of the Estado Novo the state occupied a dominant position in Brazil's labor relations system. Unions had to either conform to the requirements of the CLT or live a precarious or even marginal existence. This is not to say that unions chose conformity in all cases. On the contrary, as of the mid-1970s an independent union movement, the *novo sindicalismo*, rose to become a major sociopolitical actor, following the less successful attempts of opposition unions in the 1950s and 1960s. However, the parallel existence of a growing number of independent or unofficial shop unions alongside the official unions reinforced the structural weaknesses promoted by the corporatist labor relations system and accentuated its exclusionary character. Hence, only a major revision of the CLT in light of the new democratic realities could allow the labor movement to consolidate its organizational bases.

Vargas was astute enough to provide labor with many benefits that otherwise would have been the subject of the unions' bargaining strategies. This gave an inclusionary patina to the labor relations system that helped disguise its exclusionary design. To compensate for the loss of union autonomy and the legal restrictions on the unions' freedom, Vargas instituted a series of measures that obviated many union functions. This also served to reaffirm his benevolent image in the eyes of the working classes. The Lei de Estabilidade (Employment Security Law) was enacted in 1940 to regulate terms and compensation for dismissal from employment. In 1941 the first minimum wage law was passed.

Vargas also created the first nationwide social security network, which gave the unionized working population health protection and pensions. This became the primary responsibility of the DGPS. Therefore it was the populist state that provided organized workers with the first significant advances in terms of welfare benefits and workers' rights. This served to marginalize organized labor as an independent collective agent and political actor. Here the interplay between the inclusionary and exclusionary features of this design becomes clear.

These measures had the effect of making Brazilian workers dependent on external actors — either the state or employers — for defining and promoting their rights, rather than on themselves and their collective agents.

Lack of self-recognized empowerment among the rank and file has been a major impediment to consolidating the labor movement, since such consolidation entails overcoming a form of worker socialization that has deep historical roots.[12] This made Brazilian labor administration an excellent vehicle for cultivating working-class support for individual political ambitions.

In the words of one early observer, the structure created by Getúlio Vargas during the Estado Novo "wove a tight net of governmental control over worker and (to a lesser extent) employer organizations." More specifically, it

> resulted in the Ministry of Labor developing into one of the most powerful institutions of the administration. It was given extensive

control over the trade union movement and the employers' associations established under the CLT as well as over the process of settling disputes between workers and employers. It was also given extensive powers over the enforcement of labor laws. . . . The ultimate goal of the CLT was for all workers and employers to be grouped in one section or another of the structure built on the basis of the CLT.[13]

As a result,

although labor-management relations have evolved considerably since the end of the Estado Novo, they still remain very much under its shadow. The Vargas regime, though it made the unions financially strong, made them organizationally weak, and subject to the dictates of the Ministry of Labor. . . . State paternalism established under the *Estado Novo* was still the most important feature of labor-management relations in Brazil more than a decade after the official end of the Vargas corporate state.[14]

Despite periods of relaxation and varying degrees of actual state control, free unions as such have never "officially" existed in modern Brazil. Instead, since the 1930s all issues of importance to labor relations have been raised, addressed, and resolved within the sphere of national labor administration, no matter what its specific orientation at the time. This is a major obstacle to both union and political democracy.[15]

These exclusionary state-corporatist traits were reaffirmed and strengthened after the coup d'état of 1964. Labor repression was coupled with an anti-labor technocratic orientation within the state hierarchy. On the recommendation of the intelligence services (which maintained a parallel apparatus within the federal bureaucracy), 219 members of the Labor Ministry were purged shortly after the coup (almost all of them unionists), and 505 employees were fired from the Ministry of Public Works. This significantly altered the orientation of two main agencies responsible for administering the interests and demands of subordinate groups.[16]

Externally, an anti-strike law was passed (Lei de Greve N.

4330/June 1, 1964), which replaced the right-to-strike provisions in the 1946 constitution, and which in fact made strikes virtually impossible. As a result, the number of strikes fell from 154 in 1962 and 302 in 1963 to 23 in 1965, 15 in 1966, 12 in 1970, and 0 in 1971. In 1973–1974 there were just 34 strikes and slowdowns (including wildcat strikes). It was not until political liberalization was well under way in the late 1970s that strike activity resurfaced.[17]

Another significant effect of the new orientation was to separate labor concerns from welfare issues within the national state apparatus. In 1967 the Instituto Nacional de Previdência Social (National Social Welfare Institute, or INPS) was created as the lead agency in the health and welfare system, removing most social security and welfare concerns from the purview of national labor administration. This was confirmed in 1970, when the functional responsibilities of the labor portfolio were again narrowed and it was renamed the Ministério do Trabalho (Ministry of Labor, or MTb).

Along with narrowing its scope of authority, the government also reasserted national labor administration's powers of intervention. After 1964 the state intervened in hundreds of unions to "normalize" activities that were deemed to have become excessively political and in some cases downright subversive. These measures illustrate the mechanisms of control at the heart of exclusionary state corporatism and expose the true character of the labor relations system outlined in the CLT.

The orientation of national labor administration began to change as part of the process of political opening or *abertura* initiated in 1974 and led to a significant reorganization of the MTb in 1978. This was tied to the military regime's program of political liberalization, characterized by a gradual, controlled process of *distencão* (distension), *descompressão* (decompression), and eventual *abertura*. These reforms responded specifically to the changing character of both the Brazilian labor market and labor relations in general in the late 1970s.

These changes reflected political factors and the transformations occurring in the international and Brazilian economies.[18] By responding to such changing circumstances with a program of policy reorientation and organizational reform, the outgoing authoritarian regime displayed an adaptive capacity that differed markedly from the practices of other military regimes in the Southern Cone.[19] As a result, the democratic regime installed in 1985 inherited a new organization and functions for national labor administration.[20]

The reforms of 1978 eased the process of democratic transition and consolidation at the institutional level, since the democratic authorities did not have to make comprehensive organizational reforms to adapt the state apparatus to the new realities of an "open" society. With reforms already in place, the new regime immediately moved to formulate external policy rather than reorganize the state bureaucracy.[21]

Nonetheless, the formal external attributes of Brazilian labor administration (its scope of authority and legal responsibilities) were not similarly modified and remained an enduring legacy of authoritarianism. The government refrained from exercising some of its power until the law was changed because, unless modified (rather than simply ignored), these attributes invited unilateral rather than negotiated solutions to labor-capital conflicts.

Whether or not they became *letra morta* under the democratic regime, such unmodified formal attributes ran counter to the process of substantive democratization. A basic change in the government's formal role in the national labor relations system was necessary, as was the will and strength to impose this change. The shift to democratic labor practices had to be reflected in a reformulation of the state's overall role and specific functions within the national labor relations system.

To summarize the historical antecedents to the 1985 democratic transition: Brazil's labor administration exhibited considerable institutional continuity throughout its first fifty years. Beyond the different regimes' rationales for maintaining such a system, the exclusionary state-corporatist administration of working-class interests remained a distinctive, enduring, and quite dynamic *traço estrutural* of Brazilian labor administration.[22] This promoted a form of bureaucratic inertia that was extremely resistant to modifying its external role.

With the advent of the new democratic regime, the popular belief that *nada muda* in the federal bureaucracy could be properly tested, since the regime's very consolidation depended on including labor in the political process. This implied a fundamental change in the role and organization of the state apparatus charged with overseeing that incorporation.

The External Dimension of Brazilian Labor Administration: Labor Policy and Redemocratization, 1985–1987

> Our government, that of the workers and mine, from the beginning made use of the social option and granted priority to the poor. Workers began to participate in decisions. Never have we heard so much in favor of those who work. Not only in the laws passed and actions of the government, but also in our conduct. . . . Participation, dialogue, and cordiality characterize the relations between the government and the working classes.[23]

With statements such as this May Day address of 1986, the democratic government led by José Sarney professed to be fundamentally concerned with promoting the welfare of the Brazilian working classes. The external facet of the government's labor program adopted a three-tiered approach that involved reforming labor laws (including constitutional reform), political and economic measures (including attempts at sectorial concertation), and changes the conduct of national labor administration after April 1985.

The government reaffirmed the need to establish an institutionalized "dialogue" between labor, capital, and the state that would eventually culminate in a formal, concertative "social pact." T o accomplish this, it recognized the legitimacy of multisectorial national labor confederations (the CGT, the CUT, and the USI)[24] to articulate working-class interests, despite the lack of legal criteria for such recognition (the CLT expressly prohibited such organizations). The government then invited all major employers, associations, and labor confederations (both national and sectorial) to participate in tripartite and bipartite dialogues and encouraged similar meetings at the state and local level.

After unsuccessful yearly efforts to place the social pact issue on the congressional agenda, in late 1986 and early 1987 the first national tripartite meetings were held in Brasilia. These attempts were boycotted by the CUT and collapsed in January 1987 after the government refused to agree to labor's demand that it suspend all foreign debt payments. This collapse was exacerbated by an economic climate in which producers withheld basic goods from the market, seeking to circumvent price freezes announced by the March 1986 program for economic stabilization, the Plano Cruzado.

Widespread use of such maximalist sectorial strategies, coupled with the state's incapacity to enforce regulations, led to a full-scale shortage of primary goods. Shortages, which led to the emergence of related pathologies (the proliferation of black markets, corruption, profiteering, hoarding, etc.), became particularly acute in late 1986 and early 1987. They made clear to organized labor that Brazilian capitalists were not disposed to cooperate with the program for economic stabilization, government-sponsored talks notwithstanding. Nor was the democratic government capable of forcing producers to comply.

Organized labor felt it was unilaterally shouldering the burden of sacrifice imposed by the Plano Cruzado (by accepting government-imposed wage restraints) while cooperating in a fruitless tripartite discussion that lacked substantive terms and congressional approval. Faced with this scenario and the subsequent collapse of the Plano Cruzado, labor abandoned the concertative forum and returned to the traditional strategies of sectorial confrontation and party-led alliances under the banner of the PT. This was manifested in a wave of strikes and slowdowns in various sectors throughout 1987 and 1988, and in renewed efforts by the unions to influence debate on reforms of labor legislation in Congress.

The Sarney government responded by holding separate bipartite conferences between the president and leading representatives of capital and labor. Scheduled two weeks apart in late March and early April 1987, the initial bipartite talks were designed to encourage the exchange of sectorial ideas and concerns with government proposals. Hence, the April 4 meetings between the president and organized labor included representatives of all the major labor confederations (including the CUT) and responded "to a plea from the unionists themselves and the claim made by various sectors, during the debates over the social pact, that only the President could bring closer the conflicting interests of labor and capital."[25]

These talks were also designed to reaffirm the mediating role of the executive branch by allowing it to consider the full range of sectorial concerns individually, then to outline the agenda for future tripartite discussion. At the same time, the Constitutional Convention (1986) drafted a new framework within which institutionalized sectorial negotiations could occur.

Few substantive agreements were reached during the April 4 meeting, but initial steps were taken toward establishing an institutional basis for cooperation. The president agreed to include labor representatives in formulating economic policy by establishing a tripartite mechanism for determining the inflation index and corresponding wage readjustment scales. Labor and capital would both be represented by DIEESE (the Departamento Intersindical de Estatística e Estudos Socio-Econômicos, which has acquired a strong reputation for reliable and objective economic analyses). He also agreed that labor would be represented on the Conselho Monetario Nacional (national monetary council), in the directorates of the national shipping line, in other public enterprises, and in a host of state and municipal agencies.[26]

Labor Ministry officials argued that the meetings between representatives of the leading sectorial agents and the president, and regular private discussions hosted by the MTb, were a way for labor, capital, and the state to establish an ongoing sectorial dialogue based on mutual trust and understanding.

The government viewed these dialogues as the precondition for authentic concertation and the formal establishment of an institutionalized social pact. With that accomplished, MTb officials "believed in a negotiated solution" to the impasse.[27] Hence, the bipartite discussions symbolically highlighted the legitimate role played by organized labor as a socioeconomic and political actor, rather than establishing the institutional framework within which concertative discussions of a more pragmatic-substantive nature could occur.

However, the length and abstract nature of these discussions left major sectors of the union movement dissatisfied. The CUT saw them as a diversionary delaying tactic rather than a sincere effort to establish bases for incorporating labor into the process of democratic consolidation. According to Jair Meneguelli, president of the CUT, "From the president and his advisors we have only received a commitment to further dialogue, but without any solution to our wage and social revindications."[28]

The CUT may have understood that the emptiness of these proposals was due to the weakening of the executive branch over the course of the Congreso Constituiente. This forced the CUT to emphasize the position of the PT as the articulator of working-class interests in the most important political forum and to de-emphasize a strategy of concertative sectorial negotiation.

The CGT adopted a more opportunistic approach and did not discount the utility of discussions led by the executive branch. This allowed the government to persist in its attempts to use concertative forums in the effort to find negotiated solutions to sectorial differences. At best, these efforts to establish some form of national-level sectorial concertation served to restrain or delay generalized labor conflicts, rather than to mediate conflicts in a viable way.

Because of the limitations of concertative approaches to democratizing the labor relations system, the government simultaneously operated on two other policy levels that were far more concrete. On the legal level, the core of the government's strategy rested on a labor legislation package that was intended to dramatically modify the right to strike, collective bargaining, and the freedom to associate without state interference. On a socioeconomic level, it pursued policies that would mitigate the impact of austerity measures on the working classes.

The government proposed to lower the number of "essential" industries where work stoppages were prohibited, reduce penalties for illegal strikes, permit certain types of strikes among public employees, and modify the regulations governing the strike votes.[29]

The proposed legislation on collective bargaining promoted autonomous wage negotiations and removed mandatory state arbitration and ratification. State sanction was no longer required to formalize collective bargaining agreements, and the principals could choose their arbitrators. These changes were believed to ease the way for conciliation. Procedural matters (time of response to an offer, requirements for counteroffers, etc.) were also clarified. Wage negotiations could involve *sindicatos, federações,* or *confederações* independently or together, depending on the organization and degree of vertical integration of each sector.[30]

As for the unions' freedom to organize, the government attempted to secure congressional ratification of ILO Convention N. 87, the internationally recognized standard guaranteeing basic rights of association and unionization.[31]

Because of the scope of Convention N. 87 and the fact that it fundamentally challenged the state-corporatist structure of the labor relations system, its ratification entailed a complete rewriting of the collective bargaining chapter of the CLT. The convention was thus the subject of much congressional debate and delay, and the focus of opposition from both business and labor leaders.

As a compromise, the government proposed that all existing labor federations and confederations be maintained, albeit with a more heterogeneous base. Where more than one union represented a functional area of activity, joint commissions would be established for wage negotiations, strike decisions, and other pertinent concerns.[32] This did not require as much rewriting of the CLT as a direct transposition of ILO Convention N. 87 would have done. More important, it provided the legal foundations for a move from the exclusionary state-corporatist labor relations system to some form of inclusionary neocorporatist framework that, if not ensuring a monopoly of representation, would maintain centralized and consolidated national peak associations while making them and their affiliated unions more representative of the rank and file.

The government believed that these legislative reforms would "democratize labor-capital relations in Brazil, modernize relations of production, and put an end to the corporatist structure of the CLT," reversing the historical tendency by which "all governments, since 1937, preferred to preserve state powers of intervention and state paternalism as a basis of support for the union apparatus."[33] National labor administration could then assume a neutral role that increased the autonomy of unions while enhancing the state's mediatory functions.

Organized labor was not enthusiastic about the proposed legislative reforms, especially the effort to ratify ILO Convention N. 87. The CUT generally supported the reforms, though it continued to find the strike laws overly restrictive and pushed for the unqualified right to strike. The CGT and USI, however, were vehemently opposed to the ratification of ILO Convention N. 87. If approved, such legislation would see the gradual elimination over five years of the state-mandated *imposto sindical*, which many "official," and most smaller, unions considered the major source of their patrimony and the means by which they provided social services to their members. (This continues to be their main function.)

Leaders of the CGT and the USI were concerned that the centralizing and concentrating trends promoted in the union movement by the elimination of the *imposto sindical* would in turn result in eliminating their respective confederations, which were already losing members to the CUT. Opponents of the move to ratify ILO Convention N. 87 argued that if smaller unions became extinct, there would be an "elitization" of the labor movement under larger and wealthier unions. Hence a logic of mutual self-preservation fueled the resistance to ILO Convention N. 87 on the part of some sectors of the labor movement. In addition, virtually all major business associations opposed the repeal of the *imposto sindical*, fully understanding the implications of the loss of the state's financial control over the union movement.

Proponents of the legislative reforms believed that eliminating the *imposto sindical* would make union leaders more responsive to the rank and file and would encourage recruitment (since union treasuries would become entirely dependent on members' contributions). With less than 15 percent of the Brazilian work force organized, this left much room for expansion. Moreover, the shop-level, autonomous, and nominally illegal industrial unions of São Paulo that had emerged in the 1970s, and whose leaders dominated the leadership of the CUT and the PT, all shared this view. They considered a heterogeneous, yet vertically unified and centralized labor movement dominated by industrywide federations an asset rather than a liability, especially if their expanded membership base occupied strategic positions in the economy, and if each federation represented and was responsive to rank-and-file interests.

Within such an institutional framework, the working classes would be able to speak with one voice at various political and economic levels (national, state, municipal, federational, industry) and across several substantive dimensions (economic, political, social, cultural, etc.).[34] This would significantly alter the terms of labor's strategic interaction with the state and capital on all fronts. Even so, congressional intransigence, coupled with sectorial opposition to the proposed labor reforms, continually delayed debate on the issue in the Constituiente. Because of the number of substantive and procedural items on the Constituiente agenda, it was nearly two years, until mid-1988, before the labor reform bill was considered and voted on.

The government also offered its own draft of the new constitution, including general provisions promoting basic rights of association and the right to strike. In addition, specific clauses covered the legal rights of all workers, organized or not. These included safe working conditions, a fair wage (unspecified), an eight-hour work day[35] employment stability, employer-provided child care, free and voluntary affiliation with unions of choice, and prohibition of state intervention in the unions. These were complemented by rights to social security benefits and improvements in the general welfare of the least advantaged sectors of society.[36] After much delay, the constitution approved by the Congreso Constituiente on October 5, 1988, ratified nearly all the proposed constitutional reforms regarding labor relations and workers' rights.

There were other encouraging signs that labor was being incorporated into political institutions. Although a distinct minority, several labor-based parties were represented in the Constituiente.[37] Despite the PT's initially narrow political appeal (concentrated in the state of São Paulo and other industrial centers), its rise as the main political mouthpiece for organized labor was viewed as conducive to labor's participation in tripartite vehicles. Obviously, the PT also had a role to play in the concertative process because of the strong links between the CUT and the PT.

The Sarney government realized that legal and political guarantees and institutional representation were of little consequence if the working population continued to be victimized by economic exploitation, material deprivation, and social exclusion — to say nothing of the general climate of fiscal crisis. It showed a desire to incorporate labor by adopting a series of socioeconomic measures, but with limited success.

A major step was the decision to suspend interest payments on the foreign debt, which by 1992 totaled some $121 million. Freed from this burden, the government could direct resources toward increased investment and accelerated economic growth, which it believed was the best means to improve wage rates. The minister of labor was confident enough to declare that "the suspension of interest payments on the external debt to international private banks make possible salary growth."[38]

The Sarney administration thus proposed to continue the trend that saw the rate of investment rise from 17.3 percent of the Produto Bruto Interno (gross domestic product, or PBI) in 1985 to 19.6 percent in 1986. It would have had to rise to at least 21 percent in 1988 to achieve a 7 percent real annual growth rate (this was, however, considerably less than the 25.4 percent average for the 1974–1984 period).[39]

In reemphasizing public investment, the government not only attempted to defray the social costs of production, it also hoped to revitalize the dynamic components of the economy by restoring the confidence of domestic investors, realigning private investment levels to accord with a real growth rate of 7 percent.[40] Needless to say, this project had a decided impact on other economic concerns, particularly employment and the level of real wages. In this regard, the public investment program promoted by the government clearly constituted a structural adjustment mechanism that complemented the other elements of the government's labor strategy.[41]

Unfortunately, even if redirected as envisioned, the government's investment program could not have offset the impact of increased inflation on eroding salaries. Thus, the investment program derived from suspending interest payments to foreign lenders was added to the Plano Cruzado announced on March 11, 1986. Regardless of their initial success and subsequent failure, two elements of the various Cruzado programs pertinent to labor concerns are worth noting.

First, the effort to impose a price freeze on domestic staples indicated that the government did not wish to lay the entire burden of sacrifice imposed by the austerity measures on the working classes. In fact, it pursued expansionist policies, at least initially, hoping they would stimulate domestic demand and improve the material well-being of the wage-earning sectors. The second, complementary measure was the imposition of the infamous *gatilho salarial* (wage trigger) on fixed incomes (including minimum wage and social security payments) and all income from wage labor.

The *gatilho* was to be "pulled" every three months, or whenever the inflation rate exceeded 20 percent. According to the *secretária de empregos e salarios* (secretary of employment and salaries) and eventual Minister of Labor Dorothea Wernek, "salaries must also retain their purchasing power," but only if the economic situation stabilized, since "the trigger better protects purchasing power in the face of low inflation rates."[42] If the price freeze had been enforceable and inflation had been slowed, the *gatilho* could have served as a viable catch-up mechanism to help preserve the value of the real wage.

However, consumption increased at unforeseen rates, and the

rate of inflation increased nearly 20 percent per month in 1987 and 1988, exceeding well over 500 percent for both years and 1,000 percent yearly by 1990. The value of real wages continued to drop despite regular attempts to readjust them. The average loss in real wages was calculated at over 40 percent after the original Plano Cruzado was announced, with a subsequent 38 percent additional decrease following the implementation of phase two of the program, the Novo Plano Cruzado, in mid-1987. Similarly, the minimum wage, which the labor movement continually strove to raise and standardize, fell to its lowest national level in thirty-seven years.[43] The failure to even maintain it in the face of the economic crisis accentuated the conflicts between the Sarney government and unions, and undermined all attempts at concertative interaction.

At best, the *gatilho* served as a partial ameliorative mechanism (or empty gesture) that could not fully compensate for the loss of purchasing power provoked by supply-side inflation. Subsequent rounds of price freezes were coupled with the elimination of the *gatilho*. The Sarney government began a series of (ineffective) six-month wage adjustments after the first ninety-day period of price freezes ended.

Labor denounced the elimination of the *gatilho*, demanded an average 100 percent adjustment in real wages for all sectors, and announced a return to "battle stations" as part of a strategy of renewed confrontation (which was periodically tested by national strikes such as those of late June and August 1987).[44] Thus, it reverted to a basic defensive struggle to preserve real wages and employment.

This retrenchment contrasted with many of labor's achievements over the previous decade and in a sense reversed them. Beginning in 1978, the *novo sindicalismo* became a social and economic actor that crossed class lines: a growing domestic bourgeoisie organized itself into white-collar unions to extend organizational rights, and a growing number of unaffiliated, autonomous shop-level unions emerged in various blue-collar sectors. Their fundamental positions revolved around preserving the presence and autonomy of unions in the factories, thus extending demands to nonwage issues.[45] By 1988, basic survival was the issue.

One positive effect of the unsuccessful wage and price freeze enacted by the various Planos Cruzado was an increasing propensity by unions and employers to engage in direct bilateral negotiations without the state's involvement. Especially in the ABC region of São Paulo, where most of the largest industrial unions were concentrated and where the most dynamic elements of the industrial sector were located, this shift was a standing objective within the labor administration hierarchy, since it moved away from the tradition of state corporatism in labor affairs and toward more pluralistic forms of sectorial interaction. Yet efforts to engage in bilateral talks ran counter to the stabilization objectives of the architects of the Planos Cruzado. After all, the state was responsible for combating inflation, and individual firms and unions often reached agreements whereby wage increases were translated into price hikes that superseded the limits advocated by the Ministerio de Fazenda. Ironically, this established the basis for later attempts to secure long-term, industrywide agreements that would assist the regime's anti-inflationary measures (which enjoyed only brief success under the Collor administration in 1990).

The meetings were initially prompted by the more militant unions associated with the CUT, in a "dualist" strategy of concrete negotiations with employers on bread-and-butter issues and involvement by union leaders in political parties at the national level. In general, these political representations were overtly classist and militant in nature. Even unions that received advice and training from the anticommunist American Institute for Free Labor Development (AIFLD), which was associated with the AFL-CIO, supported the meetings. Only the mainstream faction of the CGT continued its strategic orientation toward the state. Thus, the "old guard" continued to pursue outdated strategies, while new union factions, both Marxist and non-Marxist, came to realize the benefits of direct, independent negotiations with employers, free from the state's interference. In this sense, the labor relations system, regardless of the formal legislative climate, clearly began to evolve away from the corporatist tradition and toward a more pluralist direction.

The government, to portray itself as defending the real wage in a hostile environment, opposed the wage ceilings advocated by capitalists.[46] According to the labor minister, the government attempted to both "avoid inflationary corrosion and award a real wage increase."[47]

Secretary of Employment and Salaries Wernek (later minister of labor) was even more blunt in formulating this view, saying that she saw "the biggest pressures come from price increases that attempt to maintain a determined margin of profit."[48] Although they failed to protect the real wage in the manner envisioned, the price and wage provisions of the programs for economic stabilization were part of the government's (unsuccessful) effort to protect the purchasing power of real wages during the period of economic crisis.

Despite economic drawbacks, some successful complementary measures in a broad range of labor-related social policy areas were implemented, oriented toward the general welfare of the working population. In 1986 the first comprehensive national unemployment compensation scheme was created, the *seguro desemprego*, paid in part by the *imposto sindical* (this change of fiscal policy had significant implications for the internal financing of the Labor Ministry).

Besides addressing basic issues of social justice, the *seguro desemprego* had a positive effect on aggregate demand, the conditions of the labor market, and the investment strategies of employers.[49] A job creation program was also established, using financing from the public sector, which provided 970,000 jobs in 1986.[50] According to Secretary of Labor Plínio Sarti, beyond maintaining wage levels, the labor authorities were primarily concerned with generating employment rather than avoiding strikes.[51]

Here it would seem that the MTb hierarchy shared the basic "defensive" concerns of all unions. However, increasing unemployment hindered the success of the government's job creation program. This program was another partial compensatory device that was overwhelmed by the economic crisis.

The minimum wage might have eventually benefited from an innovative reform measure proposed by officials in the labor administration hierarchy, but was stymied by employer opposition. According to this proposal, all future wage adjustments were to use the dollar as a "reference base" and the minimum wage was to be increased to eventually reach the monthly equivalent of $120 (it is currently roughly equivalent to less than $60 per month).[52] This would have maintained the real value of the minimum wage by tying it to a fixed value in stable currency. The eventual amount would have been both fair and competitive with other national wage scales (for example, the minimum wage in Colombia is also roughly equivalent to $120 per month). This would have had a significant impact on working-class standards of living and the general level of consumption.

Labor also added proposals for a major overhaul of the national social security system that would have extracted less and delivered more to the unemployed, pensioners, and single-parent families. This included raising the employers' share of the three-way contribution to social security, increasing federal support for state welfare programs, and implementing benefit readjustments tied to the rate of inflation.[53]

There was a major, relatively unsuccessful, effort to restructure the provision of basic public goods such as social welfare and public health services once the democratic regime was installed. The overhaul included creating an executive council charged with restructuring national health services and creating and implementing integrated health plans designed to ensure effective federal control of the integration of local agencies into the national public health system.

This resulted in a 6.4 percent increase in federal funds allocated for public health through the end of the decade and signing numerous contracts with state and municipal agencies. The number of participating agencies rose from 132 at the end of 1984 to 644 by the end of 1985 and extended the potential range of health coverage to 70 percent of the population. As a result, admissions to public hospitals and clinics increased 18.07 percent during the same period, paralleled by a 15.56 percent increase in admissions to federally supported university hospitals.

This progress notwithstanding, government initiatives fell short of the social and political expectations generated by the return to democracy in Brazil, since they still failed to provide for the basic needs of a large fraction of the population. To this was added the continued frustration of other reforms such as land redistribution, originally a quite ambitious program. Responding to repression and corruption, migrants thronged to urban areas and a wave of land takeovers and illegal squatting fueled the cycle of violence and mutual resistance.

The third level of operation in the government's external approach to organized labor was the state's administrative actions regarding labor relations. Here the government's approach was characterized by deliberate inaction. Until a new labor charter was drafted by the Constituiente, national labor administration deliberately refrained from exercising its full range of prerogatives. Thus, upon assuming office, the labor minister issued a policy directive that ordered the MTb not to meddle in the internal union affairs and in general to refrain from using its powers of intervention when confronting strikes.

Instead, the MTb tried to get its labor reform package through Congress and encouraged direct negotiations between labor and capital.[54] Important strikes, including those by dock workers, petrochemical workers, and bank employees, were eventually settled via negotiations, often on terms below labor's original demands. Many other work stoppages were directly negotiated by the principals to a mutually agreeable solution, often outside the economic terms recommended by the government.

The policy of government restraint and limited mediation was applied selectively to discourage wildcat or systemwide strikes in essential areas.[55] The attitude of the MTb toward strikes during this period can therefore be characterized as a gradual relaxation of legal restrictions and selective (and relatively mild) enforcement of its powers of intervention, particularly regarding economic strikes in nonessential sectors.

When labor returned to a posture of strategic confrontation, this relaxation encouraged an upsurge in strike activity. Strikes increased 77 percent, from 843 strikes in 1985, to 1,493 in 1986. There were 2,275 strikes in 1987 (a 52.3 percent increase).[56] Nearly half the strikes involved public employees. A confidential intelligence report prepared for the president in 1987 showed the figures to be even higher, with 1,289 strikes in 1985 and 2,282 strikes in 1986.[57] The trend continued apace throughout 1987 and 1988.

The wave of strikes did not overly concern labor authorities. For one thing, strikes were seen as an "escape valve" for accumulated social tensions.[58] For another, they were considered an inevitable part of the process of sectorial maturation in the move toward democratic consolidation. Weaned on a tradition of sectorial confrontation, state paternalism, and government interference, labor unions were still discovering the value of nonconfrontational strategies, even though they were first resorting to the long-suppressed strike activities that were their ultimate weapon.

Hence, while in the late 1970s and early 1980s "decentralized strike activity served to increase the space and scope of collective negotiation as well as extend important labor rights,"[59] a growing familiarity with its most efficient use in the mid- to late 1980s reduced and narrowed its effects. The number of work days lost to strikes actually fell by 34 percent from 1985 to 1986. It fell by almost another 75 percent in the first two months of 1987, compared to the same period in 1986.

This led the government to believe that labor was in fact maturing and that union leaders were more interested in negotiating concrete gains rather than striking for symbolic purposes. The cancellation of interest payments on the foreign debt left the labor movement without one of the main reasons for calling a general strike, and the move for a national work stoppage was resurrected only after the plan to eliminate the *gatilho salarial* was announced. Even then, the response to the general strike called in August 1987 was far below its leaders' expectations.[60]

In general, after 1985 unions found it difficult to use national strikes as instruments of direct political pressure, though political strikes at the state and municipal level had some positive effects. Economic strikes remained far more effective, particularly when used against employers on substantive workplace issues that were strictly defined.

Whatever the motivations, national labor administration's approach to strikes reflected a general belief in Brazilian society that strikes are legitimate means of economic defense and revindication.[61] This congruence with the rising tide of tolerance within civil society made the MTb and its associated agencies look like one of the "more democratic" and "pro-labor" branches of the state apparatus. As such, organized labor saw labor administration as one potential (though not the only) toehold within the state apparatus that could help it in its quest for incorporation into the institutional process.

The government may have deliberately refrained from exercising its full power in order to make Brazilian capitalists more sensitive to labor's concerns. They had long been secure in the knowledge that any mobilization by labor would be decisively opposed by the government (often in the form of outright coercion). This was particularly acute in the decade after the 1964 coup, when repression forcibly imposed labor's silence on a broad range of issues. Legislation under the authoritarian regime prior to 1985 prevented organized labor from fully demonstrating its strength, and employers did not have to negotiate directly or equitably with unions. Thus they were insulated from the social realities that enveloped the labor movement.

The *abertura* initiated in 1974 and the post-1979 labor mobilizations gradually changed that situation until the Sarney government's failure to enforce the authoritarian labor codes encouraged direct and honest negotiating by employers. The state's approach was designed to unseat the confrontational attitudes that ran counter to the cooperative and equitable relationship with labor at all levels of production. Coupled with tripartite and bipartite initiatives and the proposed legal, economic, and political reforms, this administrative approach was part of a larger effort to promote negotiated settlements as the foundation of new democratic labor relations.[62]

Notwithstanding the varied and interlocked nature of this multidimensional labor strategy, the success of the government's external project vis-à-vis organized labor was plagued by a host of problems. Several important sectors in Brazilian society were not inclined to favor reforms in labor legislation, much less workers' incorporation into the political process. For many, labor mobilization (the rising tide of strikes) was associated with rising crime rates, increased use of narcotics, vandalism, delinquency, moral and material corruption, and a host of other social pathologies associated with the libertarianism that, they believed, inevitably accompanied democracy in societies such as Brazil, which had a politically "immature," "uneducated," or "uncultured" general population.

These groups promoted a "tutored" (limited and elitist, if not exclusionary) democracy, which was a motive force in the process of authoritarian liberalization that culminated in the 1985 elections. Influential sectors such as the armed forces, conservative political groups of various stripes, most capitalist associations, and even the right wing of the PMDB held this view. Many business interests went on record to complain about the government's permissiveness and indecisiveness before labor, especially about strikes.[63] Others opposed the reforms in the labor code.

Some of these sectors actively worked to subvert the various stabilization plans and even attempted to extort concessions from labor during the worst moments of the economic crisis. Conservative groups in business and agriculture constantly (and largely unsuccessfully) attempted to complicate the government's strategy in order to return to some semblance of the status quo ante.

As mentioned, these sentiments found echoes within the armed forces and certain government sectors. Within the military hierarchy, labor mobilization was seen as "scary" and was believed to reflect a *modismo de greves* (strike fad) that was *revindicativa demais* (overly demanding).[64] The armed forces arbitrarily exercised their authority to end strikes as a warning to both the government and labor. As a senior military officer reportedly said with regard to the armed forces' dim view of strikes, "if they do not listen to the force of our arguments, then they will listen to the argument of our force."[65]

Military intervention was justified each time on the grounds that a vital economic sector could not be disrupted.[66] More important, none of these military interventions was foreseen, authorized, or condoned by the MTb or TST (the Tribunal Superior do Trabalho, the supreme labor court) — or, for that matter, by any other branch of government dominated by civilians. This points to the precarious nature of both the government's position and its labor strategy (to say nothing of the internal balance of power between civilian and military forces in the Sarney government).

Conservative members of the PMDB and the PDS blamed the Labor Ministry, and Minister Pazzianotto specifically, for both permissiveness toward labor and the failure to reach a social pact. Some even accused Pazzianotto (not entirely without reason) of being more interested in cementing the foundations for a future run at the governorship of São Paulo than in improving the national labor relations system — criticism that dissipated with his appointment to the TST.

Other branches of government, particularly the Ministério de Fazenda and the Central Bank, also openly disagreed with national labor authorities. All this increasingly isolated the Labor Ministry from the rest of the executive branch during Sarney's tenure.

Not surprisingly, large sectors of the labor movement saw the government's "liberal" strategy as a tactical diversion and a procedural veneer designed to mask the continuing authoritarian components of the labor relations system. Their preference for confrontation over cooperation, often couched in strongly ideological terms, further undermined the government's reformist program in the field of labor relations.[67] Moreover, public discontent over the ongoing economic crisis and political inefficiency and corruption shifted labor's attention back to the political market, where the PT and other parties associated with labor have had an increasingly strong electoral presence.

The record of government failure notwithstanding, on an external plane, labor policy shifted significantly under the democratic regime. Minister of Labor Pazzianotto summarized this new perspective as follows:

> On the part of the Federal government there were radical changes in posture. . . . Besides the studies designed to modernize and democratize laws relating to collective bargaining and strikes, the government of the Nova Republica has not made use of old and actual legal provisions that allow it to repress work stoppages and administratively intervene in labor organizations by removing or firing elected union leaders. In essence, practices were abandoned that had been habitual under previous governments, and today no Brazilian union leader feels threatened by the Federal government when exercising his responsibilities.[68]

The primary benefits of regime change have been felt most strongly at the most basic levels of activity — freedom from persecution when pursuing the right to free association and the unfettered exercise of sectorial expression. These benefits remain incomplete, but they are a lasting result of the post-1979 labor mobilization and of government policies after 1985. By its policies and its decision not to enforce certain aspects of the labor laws, the government attempted to extend the benefits of redemocratization beyond the most basic level and throughout the labor relations system. The first government of the Nova Republica moved to broaden the range of choices available to organized labor, simultaneously encouraging the adoption of a more narrow range — concertative participation, union democratization, political expression through parties, and autonomous collective bargaining — which it considered the institutional basis for democratizing class relations.

The Internal Face of Labor Administration, 1985–1987

ORGANIZATION

The responsibilities of the MTb and its dependent agencies at the time of the democratic transition were outlined in article 1 of Decree 81,663/May 16, 1978. They included all issues related to "organized labor, both syndical and professional, workplace health and safety fiscalization, labor market factors, employment, wage, and immigration policy."[69] Thus, labor administration was no longer responsible for social security or welfare. This was a far more restricted role than that envisioned under the original design outlined by Vargas; it reflected the structural and political changes in labor-capital relations that have occurred since the Estado Novo, particularly after 1964.

Each of the six functional areas of labor policy has an organizational "cluster" comprised of several agencies that are horizontally linked and vertically subordinate to the office of the minister. Several other agencies are also directly linked to the minister's office.

A clear division exists between internal support and administrative functions (known as *atividades meios*) and external control, coordination, and oversight activities (*atividades fims*). Internal functions are directed by the secretary general. The administrative department handles internal responsibilities of logistical management and is linked to the federal Sistema de Serviços Gerais (civil services system). The personnel department is connected to the Sistema de Pessoal Civil da Administração Central (Civilian Personnel System of the Central Administration). Before its elimination, the comptroller's office handled all budgetary and accounting duties, which have since been separated and dispersed among other agencies.

The advent of a democratic regime did not substantially alter the formal organization of the MTb. Its external responsibilities have been compartmentalized and subdivided into overlapping functions for formulating and implementing policy. Responsibilities for formulating policies are divided among the various *orgaos colegiados* and the *secretárias*, each of which is the lead agency of an implementation branch.[70] There is no direct link between the formulating and implementing clusters, since the minister mediates between them and has ultimate decision-making authority. There are overlapping areas, where two or more agencies are involved at both levels or where upper-echelon personnel occupy positions in both the formulating and implementing agencies. Even so, a hierarchical division of labor exists between agencies concerned with formulating policy and those that implement policy, and both are encompassed within the external area of *atividades fim*.[71]

Most important, through the Secretária de Orgãos Regionais e Colegiais, the Secretária-Geral Adjunta de Asuntos Jurídico-Administrativos is responsible for financing agencies of the DRT (Directorado do Relações do Trabalho — the Labor Relations Directorate) and most labor inspection agencies formally under the jurisdiction of the SRT (Secretária de Relações de Trabalho — the Secretariat of Labor Relations) and SSMT (Secretária de Segurança e Medicina de Trabalho — Secretariat of Labor Medicine and Safety).[72] In this way, there is independent internal control over financial disbursements in a critical external area.

To improve auditing and fiscal procedures, a Secretária de Controle Interno (Internal Control Secretariat) was created. Coupled with the continued presence of the Departamento de Pessoal and the Departamento de Administracao, decentralizing and compartmentalizing internal management brought with it considerable overlapping of responsibilities — an internal variant of the "bureaucratic rings" F. E. Cardoso has mentioned with reference to the entire Brazilian state.[73]

The external branches, including the Orgaos Colegiados, Centrais de (1) Direção Superior, (2) Regionais, and (3) Autónomos, were not significantly modified under the democratic regime. Instead, the impact of regime change has been most strongly felt internally.

A deliberate internal reorientation has meant that the MTb's mission has shifted from the power to intervene to an emphasis on negotiations and conciliatory functions. Coupled with the political, economic, and legal reforms promoted by the government, the Secretária de Relações de Trabalho (SRT) has achieved the most visible external role within the national labor administration, to became the "major focus" of the new labor relations network.[74]

The combination of internal and external reforms generated a host of sectorial demands — particularly requests for arbitration, mediation, and legal competence — that fall within the purview of the SRT. These mutually reinforcing internal and external pressures pushed the SRT to a position of relative prominence within the MTb hierarchy.

Other external areas also received new emphasis. In all phases, the government's economic programs required the active participation of the MTb in determining wage rates, adjustment schedules, inflation indexes, and employment levels, all of which raised the Wage and Employment Secretariat to a previously unknown position of institutional prominence (both within and outside the MTb). Similarly, increased emphasis on the technical responsibilities of the *fiscais do trabalho* (labor inspectors) reaffirmed the primacy of both the Secretariat of Labor Relations and the Secretariat of Labor Medicine and Safety, which jointly oversee the inspection of the workplace through the regional labor delegations.

Thus, while the external branches continued to display the hierarchical structure delineated by decree in 1978, they underwent considerable shifts in emphasis as a result of the democratic government's labor strategy. Decentralization of functional tasks offered a technically justified complement to the quest for procedural neutrality and reciprocal autonomy in labor relations. This new orientation can be seen as the internal complement of the government's external initiatives in this policy area.

We need to identify and explain the diminished role of one agency. The Divisão de Segurança e Informações (DSI) is defined as an agency of "asistencia direita e imediata ao ministro de estado" (direct and immediate assistance to the minister). It is, in fact, a branch of the Servico Nacional de Informações (national information service, or SNI), the national intelligence service operated by the military, and part of a network that is a carry-over from the intelligence systems that operated within the state apparatus under the military regime.

Its responsibilities — which remain ill defined and therefore difficult to completely ascertain — are oriented toward monitoring strike activity, identifying and cataloguing "subversive" elements and otherwise suspect or dangerous individuals and activities within the union movement, keeping tabs on the MTb's activities and relations with unions, and generally apprising the SNI of ongoing developments in labor relations. In this capacity, it is a branch of the national intelligence service engaged in collecting data, a branch with a very specific mission that goes far beyond elaborating labor-related statistics.

As such, it is responsible less to the labor minister than to the armed forces and the SNI. For example, a confidential report on strike activity prepared by the SNI for the president in 1987 is believed to have originated in the DSI. The fact that data on strike activity presented in its report differed significantly from the official figures issued by the Labor Ministry that year underscores its independence from ministerial control.

The DSI's continued presence after 1985 is evidence of an enduring military interest in labor relations for security reasons and of the military's continuing network of parallel organizations within branches of the state not related to defense. As such, the DSI represents one more enduring authoritarian legacy that has yet to be eradicated from Brazilian institutional life. Even so, compared to the previous regime, the activities of the DSI have been severely curtailed by the new labor authorities, and it is very consciously ignored by the ministerial hierarchy. This deemphasis stands in marked contrast to the active role the DSI played in the MTb during the previous regime and offers additional proof of the changed orientation of the labor administration under the democratic regime.[75]

BUDGET

As an agency without responsibilities for furnishing public goods other than its technical expertise and its services of inspection and mediation, the MTb has consistently received a small percentage of the central administrative budget, on average ranking next to last among all ministries in funding. From 1985 to 1988, the MTb budget averaged 0.3 percent of the total federal budget, and 6 percent of the central administrative budget.[76]

There has been an interesting shift in outlays not related to personnel. Prior to 1986 the bulk of such expenditures were directed toward internal agencies with support and management responsibilities, most often for supplies, furnishings, and the like. However, after 1984 there was a progressive redistribution of these outlays within the MTb, which corresponded to its shift in external orientation. Considerable resources were directed toward improving service at the external level.

Most of these increases occurred in programs such as the Serviço Nacional de Emprego (national employment service), the Programa de Preparação de Mão-de-Obra (occupational training program), and the Programa de Sequrança e Medicina do Trabalho (labor medicine and safety program), and in programs of syndical support.[77] Thus the shift in these outlays corresponded to the increased emphasis placed on improving the range of external professional services offered by national labor administration to its major "client."

One very significant change occurred with regard to the *imposto sindical*. Prior to 1986, and regardless of the original intention, the 20 percent of the union tax designated for the state generally went for internal administrative expenditures within national labor administration. In fact, 41.2 percent of these expenditures in 1984 were financed by the *imposto sindical*, and in 1985 this figure rose to 45.98 percent.[78]

In general, half of the MTb's expenditures on accounts unrelated to personnel traditionally came from the *imposto sindical*. However, with the creation of the Seguro Desemprego as part of the Plano Cruzado, beginning in 1987 the state's entire share of the *imposto sindical* was designated for that fund. In anticipation of these reductions, in 1986 the amount of nonpersonnel outlays derived from the *imposto sindical* fell to 21.4 percent, and as foreseen, in 1987 this figure dropped to zero.[79] In parallel, the Cuesteio do Seguro Desemprego (unemployment insurance fund) rose from 376.6 million cruzados in 1986 to 5.8 billion in 1987, an increase of 1,400 percent.[80]

When the government stopped financing MTb accounts that were unrelated to personnel with the *imposto sindical*, serious disagreements arose over the impact of this move on the autonomy of national labor administration. One line of thought held that the transfer of funds from the *imposto sindical* to the Seguro Desemprego lowered the material need for those outlays within the MTb and associated agencies, thereby increasing labor administration's autonomy from the unions when formulating and implementing policy.

Another line of thought held that the opposite was true, that, by eliminating the *imposto sindical's* contribution to nonpersonnel outlays, national labor administration became more dependent on other branches of the state (especially the Ministério de Fazenda and Congress) for the money it otherwise would have received from the *imposto sindical*. Since outlays remained relatively constant despite the climate of fiscal crisis, MTb officials would be forced to go "com o chapeu na mao" (with hat in hand) to ask Congress and the treasury for additional funds to make up the difference.[81] Thus, the argument goes, while it may be politically expedient to transfer the contribution of the *imposto sindical* to a highly visible public service, and while such a transfer may contribute to the autonomy of the MTb in formulating policy vis-à-vis organized labor, it is not expedient in terms of management because it diminishes the autonomy of national labor administration relative to other branches of the state.

Since Brazilian labor administration has always been relatively autonomous with respect to the working classes, the latter argument seems particularly pertinent. The state's share of the *imposto sindical* does not depend on the number of organized workers formally represented in a productive sector (i.e., union density), but on the total number of workers, organized or not, in that sector. Unions therefore have had little to say with regard to how the funds derived from the *imposto sindical* are disbursed.

The shift of revenues from the *imposto sindical* to the Seguro Desemprego represented a technically defined attempt to put funds drawn from workers back into an immediate and visible benefits program for workers. It was believed that the loss of operative autonomy over internal budget decisions was outweighed by the symbolic and practical benefits of this shift in policy. In any event, it removed the vested financial interest that labor administration had traditionally had in seeing that labor remained unorganized in a variety of productive areas. For this reason, it is a significant step on the road toward democratic consolidation.

In effect, there is a relatively centralized process for making up the budget and a relatively decentralized process for distributing funds. The main agencies involved in making up the budget do not carry out primary obligations in distribution. This division of labor is designed to administer the flow of resources in a more objective and equitable manner within national labor administration, thereby diminishing the possibility of arbitrary or discretionary criteria intruding on the distribution process.

PERSONNEL

By late 1988 there were 12,700 employees working in centralized agencies of Brazilian labor administration (the MTb's *sede central* and the TST), a reduction of 300 in the number employed compared to the beginning of the democratic regime in April 1985.[82] There are, in addition, 8,758 agents employed in the DRTs (regional labor delegations).[83]

The MTb derives its cabinet status from its strategic location in an area of political and economic activity that is a "core" functional concern of the state (this is also true of other relatively small cabinet-level agencies such as Intamaraty, the Foreign Ministry), rather than from the human and material resources it commands. It is the nature of this "core" functional task, as opposed to the range of public goods it provides and the resources it controls, that makes national labor administration equal in rank to far larger branches of the state apparatus.

A large number of employees formally assigned to centralized agencies of the MTb are in fact attached to various *orgãos vinculados*. Most are found in the Serviço Nacional de Formacão Profissional Rural (national rural professional training service, or SENAR), which has 1,756 employees. The majority of employees, however, are engaged in administrative and support functions encompassed within the internal areas of *actividade meio*.

Those employed in the external branches, though a minority,

disproportionately represent the more specialized personnel categories in national labor administration, especially when the Delegaciãos Regionais do Trabalho (DRTs) are factored in.

The distribution of specialized skills is even more pronounced in the DRTs, where the largest personnel category is that of labor inspectors (*fiscais do trabalho*), followed by administrative staff, medical doctors, engineers, and the ubiquitous syndical assistants.[84] Nonetheless, Brazilian labor administration has considerable room for improving the range and scope of its services. For example, in the largest regional labor delegation, in the state of São Paulo (which, along with the DRTs in Rio de Janeiro, Minas Gerais, and Rio Grande do Sul comprise DRT Group 1, the biggest and most important regional delegation), there are 904 inspectors, 66 engineers, and 44 medical doctors out of a total staff of 1,700. Together, this staff is responsible for monitoring 470,000 firms and 6 million workers.[85]

The external responsibilities of national labor administration, both centralized and decentralized, require a relatively high percentage of specialized personnel, even though the total number of agents engaged in such tasks is not the largest portion of those employed throughout the labor administration system. Given the nature of the tasks in question — workplace inspection, occupational health and safety, labor market analysis, the determination of wage rates, labor legislation reform, etc. — this should not be surprising, even when we consider the somewhat nebulous specializations of the syndical assistants. As in most organizations with a specialized function, a large body of support personnel works on behalf of the more specialized employees who discharge the most important tasks.

As a curious sidelight, it is worth noting that of the twenty-nine employees working in the DSI, five are classified as information analysts and one is classified in the unique category of national security mobilization analyst.[86] Although the drop in employment levels was most notable in the DSI, it also occurred in other areas after a hiring freeze was imposed on the federal bureaucracy by the original Plano Cruzado. This reduced the total number of employees compared both to the number employed under the military regime (despite the expanded scope of external activities), and to the size requirements for maximum efficiency, which had been estimated internally.[87] In this regard, national labor administration was one of the few areas of the state apparatus where there was a deliberate attempt to implement a hiring freeze according to the Plano Cruzado's guidelines.

The sex distribution of Brazilian labor administration shows a familiar sexist pattern, with women making up the majority of employees, and generally in middle- and lower-echelon internal management (*actividade meio*) positions, while the few male employees are disproportionately represented in higher-echelon and more specialized positions in external branches. Even so, some advances have been made under the democratic regime. The Wage and Employment Secretariat was headed by a woman who later became minister of labor; several of the minister's main advisers were female; and a handful of women continue to occupy positions as heads of divisions, etc. This may be evidence of a trend toward (sexual) democratization within the national labor administration.

With the advent of the democratic regime, the entire decision-making cadre in the MTb (down to the department level), the so-called confidence — or political — positions, was replaced. The leadership from 1985 to 1988 was occupied by a combination of PMDB adherents and specialists in labor relations, with a pronounced tendency toward backgrounds in labor management issues and politics in the state of São Paulo. Many of these individuals were associated with the most progressive wing of the PMDB.

All the secretaries (branch heads) and the minister of labor had prior professional involvement in labor issues in the state of São Paulo, a characteristic that extended throughout the minister's cabinet, advisory agencies, and certain lower-echelon positions such as that of syndical assistant.[88] This infusion of *paulista* technocrats with PMDB affiliation or expertise in labor affairs continued a longstanding historical trend in which Brazilian labor ministers staffed "political positions" and *cargos de confiança* with long-term professional acquaintances, fellow party members, and even friends and relatives. While obviously parochial and ascriptive, this staffing method, defenders argue, ensures a uniformly coherent and professional ministerial position that promotes concerted and efficient policy formation and implementation in the field of labor relations.

Whether this is true or not, there was a very definite (if self-interested) democratic orientation within the first ministerial leadership. In addition, shared perspectives helped reduce the turnover among upper-echelon personnel in a critical and highly visible area of state activity, despite the climate of economic and political crisis surrounding it. This offered an illusionary appearance of political stability. Virtually the entire labor administration hierarchy remained in office throughout Sarney's tenure, in contrast to the Argentine experience.

The government's "liberal" orientation toward negotiation and cooperation with organized labor was reflected in the appointment of upper-echelon personnel in the MTb and other agencies involved in national labor administration. Their previous backgrounds and experience were considered the first steps toward establishing a bridge between the labor movement and the state; other elements of the government's labor strategy were subsequently constructed on this base.

Paulista origins, practical expertise, a "progressive" or "liberal" approach, and backgrounds in fields related to labor were the main characteristics among upper-echelon personnel in Brazilian labor administration under the Sarney government, and allowed the MTb hierarchy to see itself as procedurally neutral and yet the internal "defender" of labor interests within the state apparatus. This allowed it to exercise a fairly significant level of autonomy in formulating labor policy, although, as we have seen, its autonomy of operation was subject to a number of constraints at several levels.

Conclusion

At both the external and internal levels, the character of Brazilian labor administration has evolved considerably since the advent of the Nova Republica. So far, its tenor has not. Because of organizational changes that themselves reflected the profound structural transformations at play within the Brazilian labor market and the syndical movement beginning in 1978, the altered character of national labor administration under the democratic regime was most visible in its external orientation and strategy toward labor-capital relations. This change took three interrelated forms: there was an attempt, first, to establish a concertative dialogue that might culminate in a social pact involving labor, capital, and the executive branch, however narrowly defined and contingent that pact might be; second, to promote legal, political, and economic reforms that could provide substantive institutional bases for incorporating labor into the process of democratic consolidation; and third, to reinforce in all actors' minds the changed nature of the labor administration and labor relations under democracy by administrative acts of commission or (more important) of omission.

All this may well have been part of a larger hegemonic project designed to establish the consensual foundations for achieving class compromise and eventually consolidating democratic capitalism in Brazil. But this project remains incomplete and ill defined.

At an internal level, the changes brought about by the regime were less obvious in organizational reforms, though a move toward functional compartmentalization and decentralizing administrative responsibilities related to formulating and implementing policy is evident, especially in the internal branches of *actividade meio*. The external functions of labor relations, occupational safety, and wage and employment policy were emphasized, while social promotion and welfare activities were subordinated to programs offered by other branches of the state.

Technical emphasis on more strictly defined labor issues was reinforced by redistributing budgets, which supported the MTb's external mission and reduced its dependence on the *imposto sindical* for its internal administrative expenses. This was also evident in a process of personnel selection that emphasized professional backgrounds in labor relations (most often on the labor side) in the country's most populous and industrialized state.

In this fashion, national labor administration reassumed a position previously seen only under the populist regimes of Getúlio Vargas and João Goulert: that of an institutional mediator between labor and capital (and even between labor and other branches of the state), but this time without the strongly interventionist and paternalist posture promoted by state-corporatist labor legislation. Buttressed by the personal backgrounds of its employees, the budgetary emphasis on technical and legal responsibilities, and procedural neutrality in conflict negotiations, the MTb and associated agencies served as a dual filter for sectorial interests. On one side (or perhaps better, from the top down), national labor administration filtered the expectations and demands of the executive branch and capitalist organizations and presented them for review to the organized labor movement. This parallels the direct interaction between labor, capital, and other branches of the state and is, in fact, designed to soften the tone of such interaction.

On the other side (or from the bottom up), Brazilian labor administration gathered and filtered the concrete expectations and demands of the organized working classes and presented them to the rest of the executive branch and to collective agents of capital. Political demands as such were left to the Parliament, where the PT and other labor-based political parties provided the labor movement with an unfiltered conduit for sectorial expression.

The place where the two perspectives converge is constituted by the debate within the executive branch between agencies that respond to capitalist interests (such as the Central Bank and the Ministries of *Fazenda*, Agriculture, and Industry), and the agency responsible for administering the interests of the labor movement — supported by the input provided by other agencies with direct functional ties to subordinate groups such as the MPAS (the Ministerio de Previsão e Asistença — the Social Welfare Ministry), the MS (the Ministerio de Saúde — the Health Ministry), and the INPS (the Instituto Nacional de Previsão Social — the National Social Welfare Institute). Obviously, the dynamics of the debates rest on conjunctural factors at the macro-, meso-, and microeconomic levels, the responses they generate within different social sectors, the more normative concerns with fairness and equality, and the move toward substantive democratization.

In this regard, the role of the Brazilian state in general and of national labor administration in particular has changed markedly since the pre-1985 period. Even if the state's future orientation remains uncertain, the evolution away from the longstanding Brazilian tradition of the exclusionary, state-corporatist administration of organized labor interests appears to be gradually taking shape. This demonstrates that even in Brazil "as coisas podem mudar" for the better, though much remains to be done. If nothing else, the post-1985 changes in the labor relations partial regime have opened the possibility of a cooperative, if not inclusionary, labor relations system in the future.

7

URUGUAYAN LABOR

ADMINISTRATION, 1985–1988

UNLIKE ITS LARGER NEIGHBORS, Uruguay had one major advantage as it set about reconstructing a democratic order in the wake of the withdrawal of the military regime of 1973–1985. The existence of a longstanding pre-authoritarian democratic tradition with significant historic roots stood in marked contrast to the ingrained authoritarianism found in both Argentine and Brazilian political culture.

This homogeneous "city-state" has 3 million inhabitants, mostly descendants of Italian and Spanish immigrants of the late nineteenth and early twentieth centuries. One and a half million of them congregate in and around the capital city of Montevideo. Uruguay carries intact the Krausian political legacy of *Batllismo*, the political doctrine of the nation's first democratic *caudillo*, José Batlle y Ordóñez, president in 1903–1907 and again in 1911–1915). The unique political structure promoted by this creed — including such features as the *Ley de Lemas*, an electoral law, and the collegial executive body that existed until 1967 — endowed Uruguay with the longest democratic tradition of any Latin American nation. It only began to falter in the 1960s under the combined assaults of long-term economic deterioration, the breakdown of the welfare state, rising popular unrest culminating in urban guerrilla warfare at the hands of the Movimiento de Liberación Nacional-Tupamaros (MLN-T), political deadlocks in an increasingly ossified bipartisan party system, and growing military intervention in domestic affairs. By 1968 Uruguay had entered into a full-fledged "organic crisis," which culminated in the institutional rupture and overt military takeover of 1973.[1]

The plebiscite of 1980 formally marked the failure of the authoritarian regime and its foundational project, with the rejection of proposed constitutional reforms by 57 percent of the population as a whole and two-thirds of those living in Montevideo. The stage was set for the military's withdrawal from power. Although the socioeconomic and political context of 1985 prevented a return to the status quo ante, there was a strong democratic legacy to refer back to, and a pre-authoritarian institutional framework on which to build. Whatever the modifications required by time and circumstance, there was a substantive foundation on which to reconstruct a democratic regime.

Historical Antecedents

The first agency charged with national responsibilities in the field of labor affairs was the Ministerio de Industrias, Trabajo e Instrucción Pública (Ministry of Industries, Labor, and Public Instruction, or MITIP), created by Law 3,147, the Organic Law of Ministries, promulgated on March 12, 1907. After a series of reorganizations, modifications, and name changes, the Ministerio de Trabajo y Seguridad Social (Ministry of Labor and Social Security, or MTSS) was created in 1967. Through executive decree and constitutional reform, its responsibilities incorporated a number of previously decentralized labor and welfare agencies. These included the National Welfare Bank, the Children's Council, the National Alimentary Institute (INDA), and several regional welfare boards, in addition to a number of centralized departments responsible for providing legal advice to workers (the Centro de Asesoramiento y Asistencia Jurídica al Trabajador, for example) and internal administrative, comptroller, inspection, research and international liaison functions.[2]

The basic organizational framework of the MTSS was thus established for the period preceding the democratic transition, though its external attributes and several of its agencies suffered important modifications under the authoritarian regime.

From its creation, the general orientation of national labor administration in Uruguay was interventionist regarding the individual worker's rights and noninterventionist toward collective rights. The state was obligated to look after workers' rights to employment, safe working conditions, hours, pensions, and related issues connected with the welfare of individual workers (hence the organizational importance given to agencies such as the Inspector General de Trabajo y Seguridada Social (IGTSS), but Uruguayan law, including article 57 of the 1934 and 1967 constitutions, guaranteed the free right of association and the right to strike regardless of level of activity, region, public or private nature of employment, political affiliation, and the like. Restrictions were placed only on the use of violence, which was subject to criminal prosecution.

In 1953 Uruguay ratified Conventions N. 87 and 98 of the ILO, which recognized freedom of association as a fundamental human right, thereby granting these conventions the status of national law. Hence union structure in Uruguay is based on a heterogeneous array of shop-level unions loosely grouped in federations according to occupation or ideology, which are in turn tied to umbrella labor confederations that operate as political advocates and amplifiers for the economic demands of the rank and file.

Prior to 1973, Uruguay was the only Latin American country with an uninterrupted history of noncorporatist labor administration, offering proof of the depth of its pluralist foundations and the longstanding institutional bases of the democratic regime. Unlike Brazil or Argentina, it did not exercise the powers of recognition, registration, oversight, or intervention commonly associated with state-corporatist labor relations systems. National labor administration traditionally served as a neutral, technical promotor of basic citizenship rights connected with the workplace,and simultaneously managed the institutional apparatus responsible for defraying most of the social costs of production. This left labor and capital free to negotiate autonomously, sector by sector, the material terms of the class compromise.

Given the virtually unrestricted rights of association written into Uruguayan law prior to 1968, the external attributes of national labor administration were limited to protecting basic working conditions, employment and welfare concerns, labor market research, and mediation services. Its activities were focused on the inspection, advising, and monitoring associated with these tasks and with distributional issues connected with welfare and social security.

The creation of the Consejos de Salarios in 1943 gave greater prominence to mediation services within national labor administration, though not to the extent enjoyed by the traditional services. Mediation was sometimes used in efforts to end strikes, but handling work stoppages was more often left to the contending parties on the one hand and the police on the other.

Thus, organized labor in Uruguay followed an exceptional path, in that its organization and insertion into the political system were not determined by the state. This noninterventionist stance of national labor administration allowed Uruguayan labor to develop in response to two other factors: ideological competition within its ranks and the evolving structure of production in the Uruguayan economy.

Not having to pass through the "filter" of state recognition and regulation, organized labor exhibited a "dualist" posture and its insertion into the Uruguayan political and economic system assumed two parallel forms:

> On one side, it acts as a corporate pressure group within the political system in defense of the working conditions of its affiliates; on the other side, it is inserted in a political opposition sub-system through its ties with the leadership of leftist parties and groups, particularly the Communist Party. . . . Such a scheme combines a "militant" orientation on the part of the [union] leadership — which identified union struggles as part and parcel of the revolutionary struggle — with an "immediatist" (bread-and-butter) perspective on part of the rank and file, which see the union as essentially a pressure group or instrument oriented towards the defense of its corporate interests. . . . The support given by workers to leftist union leaders did not imply their support for leftist parties in

national elections, and their vote continued to be preferentially directed towards the two traditional parties (the National or Blanco Party and the Colorado Party).[3]

This "dualist" posture combined confrontationist and pressure group approaches to insert labor into the political sphere (using some contestative strategies as well) and used a bargaining approach to bring it into the economic sphere. That allowed the union movement to simultaneously pursue its short- and long-term objectives without compromising either. Moreover, this type of labor insertion promoted a dual form of worker participation in political and economic markets: support for Marxist union leaders on the one hand, and electoral support for the two big "catch-all" parties on the other.

The rationale behind the rank and file's perspective was simple. Until recently, the left had little chance of gaining majority power through election in the Uruguayan party system (especially given the electoral rules favoring the large "catch-all" parties). But, as one (non-Marxist) labor administration official mentioned to me, who better than a committed Marxist to defend the material interests of workers?[4] Unable to be co-opted, corrupted, or otherwise swayed by bourgeois inducements, the Marxist leaders of the Uruguayan trade union movement make excellent economic agents for their constituents. This is in marked contrast to Uruguay's larger neighbors, where personal venality among labor leaders often interferes with the realization of working-class interests. In turn, the labor leadership, dominated by the Communist Party (PC), continues to advocate a moderate, electorally based line that focuses on exploiting the problems of the major parties. This approach bore fruit in 1971, when the leftist coalition known as the Frente Amplio won 18 percent of the national vote.

Even so, Uruguayan workers tend to vote for either of the two umbrella parties, depending on which makes a stronger appeal. The limited opportunities offered the left in the party system was one of the causes for workers' support of urban guerrilla activity in the late 1960s, when the combination of long-term economic stagnation and political sclerosis appeared to indicate that the conditions for revolutionary upheaval were ripe.

Regarding the terms of the initial incorporation and later insertion of organized labor into the Uruguayan political system, we need to underscore two fundamental facts. First, the early formation of craft unions under anarchist or socialist immigrant leadership (mid-1800s), the consequent rise of a short-lived national labor federation (the Federación Obrera Regional Uruguaya [Uruguayan regional labor federation, or FORU]) in 1905, and the equally early grant of democratic citizenship rights to workers by the Batlle administrations, gave the labor movement an overt classist nature while simultaneously removing institutional obstacles to workers' full political emancipation. This undermined the rationale for political militancy. During the long period of prosperity brought about by Uruguay's preferential position as an agricultural exporter (which lasted until the early 1950s), this trend was reinforced by labor's militancy on wage issues, which was rewarded through increasing profits and the expanded role of a redistributive welfare state.

Secondly, the move to import substitution industrialization (ISI) begun in the 1930s and 1940s, and the promulgation of the Consejos de Salarios's bi- and tripartite wage negotiating boards beginning in 1943, increased the size of the union movement and at the same time altered its character. Industrialization replaced the craft bases of unionism with a larger enterprise and sector-based action, complemented by union growth, which was fueled by the expanding urban work force in the new industrial sectors.

Thus, by the mid-1950s, though it remained dependent on agro exports for the bulk of its revenues, Uruguay's economy was no longer predominantly based in agriculture, and most of its population was employed in the public and private industrial and administrative sectors concentrated in Montevideo, Colonia, and other cities. In addition, the creation of the Consejos de Salarios made union federations the negotiating agents for workers in each industrial sector. Since collective bargaining was fixed at that level and workers had to be organized to be represented, there was a surge in union membership and in industrial union federations after the law was passed.[5] From that time until the *gólpe* of 1973, rates of unionization in Uruguay were among the highest in the world, averaging well over 50 percent for the entire work force.

Because of these factors, by the 1920s anarchist and socialist influence in the labor movement had begun to wane, and the influence of Marxist-Leninists associated with the PC began a concomitant rise. Strategies of "direct action" involving opposition and confrontation in the workplace and the political arena, advocated by the anarchists and socialists, were supplanted by the "dualist" strategies of the Marxist-Leninists. The PC's influence among union leaders became a persistent hallmark of Uruguayan unionism, tempered only by the presence of adherents to other Marxist variants and a very small minority of Blanco Party sympathizers.

The PC's dominance within the labor movement was officially confirmed by the creation of the Central Nacional de Trabajadores (National Labor Central, or CNT) in 1964, which elected an executive board dominated by the PC. This represented the first successful attempt at the national unification of the union movement since the demise of FORU in the 1920s and provided organized labor with a national spokesperson at a time when political and economic conditions were in clear decline.

The move toward national centralization was an effort to confront both the state and capitalists within the context of a worsening economic climate in which the "dualist" character of the labor movement was being severely challenged from within and subjected to assaults from without. The mobilizational capability that had served so well in defense of labor's economic demands was by then literally spilling into the streets in the form of political violence and wildcat strikes. At the same time that the PC and other moderate leftist groups were putting together the Frente Amplio electoral coalition, radical elements in the unions, joined by similarly radical groups of students and parts of a disaffected middle class, attempted to subvert the political system in order to destroy it.

In response, beginning in 1965 civilian authorities increasingly resorted to the so-called *medidas prontas de seguridad* (prompt security measures), which suspended civil liberties for sixty to ninety days. When this failed, the military assumed a direct role in the antisubversion campaign. By the time of the 1971 elections, Uruguay was a country under a virtual state of siege, and by 1973 not even the trappings of democratic rule were considered viable. The military dissolved Parliament and assumed direct control of the executive branch, retaining a civilian president as a figurehead until 1976.

The role of the state in this process of decline and fragmentation should be noted. The fifty-year era of prosperity in the first half of the twentieth century fostered the rise of a large welfare state that used its redistributive functions to soften class differences and reproduce social consensus about the political system. However, this "sociedad amortiguada" ("cushioned society," in Real de Azua's phrase)[6] was utterly dependent on the welfare state, and the state managers who administered it, for political stability. The welfare state and its managers in turn depended both on tax revenues from agricultural exports and on expansion of the clientelist network that depended on their public goods and services.

During this time, public employment became a major instrument for reducing social tensions and a legitimate form of patronage for both Colorados and Blancos, whether they were in the power or among the opposition. By the mid-1960s the public sector employed 20 percent of the economically active population.[7]

When the era of prosperity ended in the 1950s, the entire system went into crisis. Increases in personal taxes could not compensate for lower export tax revenues, and this led to cutbacks in state-provided goods and services, particularly public health and welfare. Political pressure prevented reducing the overblown public work force, which added to the ossification of the system.[8] Thus, by the mid-1960s the Uruguayan welfare state was in a state of collapse, a bloated shell of its former self, unable to pay its bills or provide basic public services, much less effectively control or ameliorate growing social unrest. Internally, it mirrored that unrest.

Beyond these structural and institutional factors, the radicalization and increased militancy of labor played a significant role in pushing Uruguay toward authoritarianism. In a classic example of O'Donnell's pre-authoritarian "threat scenario," a high rate of labor mobilization, increasing numbers of strikes and other forms of labor conflict (including industrial sabotage), and a proliferation of guerrilla activities, all couched in the discourse of insurrection and revolution, sparked a wave of defensive fear among the rural and urban Uruguayan bourgeoisie. In parallel, the armed forces saw the direct challenge to their prerogatives and the outbreak of generalized disorder in civil society as an assault on the nation's basic values and institutions.[9] Under such conditions, the only recourse they saw was to impose a period of authoritarian exclusion to "sanitize" the body politic by eliminating the radical elements, then to restore some form of "protected" democracy in which the left was excluded and the military enjoyed ultimate veto power.

The worsening economic and political situation after 1957 reached a crisis in 1967–1970, when inflation rates rose to over 100 percent, revenues from agro exports declined in the wake of falling international prices and increased foreign competition, and the inward-oriented strategy of industrialization exhausted the confines of the Uruguayan market. At the same time, the tariff barriers surrounding domestic industry made it uncompetitive in the international market. The GNP fell by 12 percent from 1956 to 1972, and real wages fell by 24 percent in the decade after the crisis began (with public employees losing 40 percent of their purchasing power).

Demographic factors also worked against the possibility of recovery: emigration increased while immigration all but stopped, and the birthrate declined. The overall aging of the population was accompanied by increased demands on the state for public goods it could no longer provide, while at the same time union militancy, particularly among the white-collar public sector hit hardest by the crisis, served notice that overt class conflict had replaced the class compromises of the past.[10]

Confronted with this environment, the Colorado government

installed in 1966 adopted a number of measures to stabilize the economy, restore social order, and increase the efficiency of the political system. The 1967 constitutional reforms eliminated the collegial executive body in favor of a strong presidential system, which, it was believed, would prevent party disputes in Parliament from adversely affecting the pressing administrative tasks of the chief executive. The executive branch was authorized to declare without congressional approval "prompt security measures" that suspended civil liberties indefinitely. These were immediately used to end strikes, close the opposition media, arrest militant syndicalists, and conscript into the army strikers who failed to heed back-to-work orders.

The almost uninterrupted use of the state of siege from 1968 on culminated in the May 1972 declaration of a "state of internal war" by the Uruguayan president. In July 1972, under military pressure, Congress passed a Ley de Orden Publica (Public Order Law), which contained provisions far more stringent than those of the "prompt security measures." In November of that year the "state of internal war" was extended, and in February 1973 a military-dominated Consejo de Seguridad Nacional (National Security Council, or CSN) was established to review all government policy.

In effect, the months before the June 1973 "palace coup" were signaled by an encroaching authoritarianism that set the stage for the *gólpe*. Unlike in Argentina and Brazil, the move to authoritarian rule in Uruguay was evolutionary and incremental rather than sudden. The increasingly "hard" nature of the democratic regime beginning in 1966 (making it a *"democradura"*) gave way to civilian authoritarianism by 1970 (a *"dictablanda"*), which itself deepened into full-fledged military rule in 1973.

Along with increasingly authoritarian political measures, in April–June 1968 a number of economic measures were taken to fight the inflationary spiral and affect other adjustments in the economy. Wages were frozen, the Consejos de Salarios were suspended (until 1985), and bilateral collective bargaining between unions and employers was prohibited. All salary and price adjustments were thereupon fixed by decree.

To fix wage and price rates, a tripartite agency, the Comision de

Productividad, Precios, e Ingresos (Commission on Productivity, Prices, and Income, or COPRIN) was created. This was composed of five representatives from the state, and two each from organized labor and the business sectors (each nominated to a six-person slate from which the executive branch selected two representatives). The COPRIN was mandated to fix maximum and minimum salaries for each occupational sector and to reorder collective agreements according to the dictates of the government's economic stabilization program. This severely limited both the number and scope of collective bargaining agreements. In the eighteen months preceding the establishment of COPRIN there were 440 collective agreements reached and ratified by the government; in the eighteen months following the establishment of COPRIN the number fell to 36. Meanwhile, the domain of collective bargaining was effectively reduced to non-wage issues such as leave and insurance benefits, a situation that was modified only in 1977.[11]

These shifts represented a fundamental change in the way the regime viewed the national reality. "The new labor policies were exactly the reverse of that developed by the modern and democratic Uruguay: withdrawal of legislative protection in the area of individual labor relations, accompanied by attempts at state intervention in the area of collective labor relations in order to restrict syndical activity and collective autonomy."[12] Thus, five years before the formal end of the democratic regime, an era of exclusionary state corporatism in labor relations had begun. This process deepened with the advent of the military regime in 1973 and had serious implications for the role and organization of national labor administration.

On June 27, 1973, the Uruguayan military dispensed with procedural formalities and dissolved Parliament, establishing a military junta behind the facade of a civilian president. The announcement of the institutional rupture was answered by the CNT with a general strike that lasted fifteen days, at which time it crumbled under the combined pressures of government repression and the leadership's indecision (conciliatory statements by a "populist" military faction in the months before the coup led some labor leaders to believe it would bring about a "Peruvian-style" reformist military regime à la Velasco in 1968).

Thousands of unionists were arrested (about one in every thirty adults was jailed for political reasons, the highest proportion of political detainees seen in the world at that time), scores "disappeared," dozens more were killed in open confrontations with the armed forces, and many hundreds more were forced into exile. The military prohibited 15,000 individuals from holding political positions, including virtually the entire labor leadership at the moment of the coup.

After attempting to promote elections that would install pro-regime union leaders, the military hierarchy dissolved the CNT and confiscated all its property, outlawed strikes, and established new regulations governing the organization, scope, and permissible activities of unions. There was no legal basis for these measures, since all civil associations in Uruguay, the CNT and its affiliates included, were constitutionally free to organize and regulate themselves without the need for legal recognition or registration by the state. It was thus technically impossible for the state to "outlaw" what could not be constitutionally legalized.

The military ignored this distinction, and the de facto dissolution of the CNT and its affiliates was accomplished by force. This military intervention was different from that of Argentina and Brazil, however, where the long traditions of state corporatism in labor relations had given the military regimes of the 1960s and 1970s a legal precedent for prohibiting or outlawing various aspects of union activity.

The military regime's project of national reconstruction centered on coupling neoliberal or monetarist economic policies (associated with the "Chicago" school) with a heavy dose of repression of political and collective activity. As in Chile and Argentina, it was believed that market forces would have a better chance of restructuring the Uruguayan economy to be more efficient and internationally competitive in the vacuum produced by fear-induced social and political silence. Freed from the pressures of collective demands emanating from civil society, the architects of the regime's economic strategy believed they could effectively "reinsert" Uruguay into its proper place in the world economy, whereupon a return to some form of "protected" democratic regime could be contemplated. For the labor "question," this logic was quite explicit: neoliberal economics plus military authoritarian politics equaled elimination of Marxists from union ranks, a decrease in organized labor power, and political and economic subordination of the working classes.

In addition to prohibiting strikes and collective bargaining and outlawing and dissolving the most important unions and labor federations, the military regime eliminated all labor and employer representation on COPRIN, despite the fact that government representatives were already in the majority. When the regime authorized dismissal of strikers or those who did not immediately return to work when strikes were outlawed, many employers fired hundreds of workers as "agitators." Over 12,000 workers were fired in the public sector, and between 5,000 and 10,000 in the private sector. Coupled with the jailing of union leaders and other repressive measures against labor, these actions had the effect of disarticulating the organizational cornerstone of the working classes.[13]

The combination of repression and neoliberal economic policies had other devastating effects on the working classes. Between 1973 and 1985 real wages decreased by 50 percent.[14] This severe reduction in purchasing power was paralleled by a 7,500 percent increase in the cost of living.[15] Shifting the burden of economic sacrifice to wage earners was part of a conscious effort to transfer resources from income-earning sectors to business (that is, from wages to profits) in order to increase both capital accumulation and competitiveness in the most dynamic sectors of the opened economy.

Unionization levels dropped markedly as a result of repression, of structural dislocations prompted by opening the local economy to international competition, and of the emphasis on developing new agro-export sectors tied to the international financial community. As real wages decreased, more and more women and children were forced into the labor market (especially the informal sector) to supplement family incomes. Most wage-earning adults had to hold more than one job, and the informal and tertiary sectors grew rapidly. This decreased the number of those identified under the occupational category of "workers" and concomitantly increased those considered "employees" and independents. The number of self-employed (*cuentapropristas*) also increased dramatically, as did the number of emigrants, adding to the erosion of collective identities and class solidarity already threatened in a climate of free-market repression.[16]

The attempted disarticulation and reduction of the economic and political power of the working classes and their organized representatives clearly succeeded by the regime's standards, despite another failed attempt at holding "sanitized" union elections in 1977. However, the intended effects in the other facets of the economy did not materialize. Salaries as a percentage of GNP dropped 15 percent from 1969 to 1979, while social security benefits dropped by 2.5 percent and the percentage of the working population working more than forty-eight hours a week increased from 35.7 percent in 1968 to 51.4 percent in 1980. However, per capita income continued to drop, and domestic private investment fell from 50 percent to 10 percent.[17]

Likewise, although the historically high levels of unemployment seen in 1980–1984 (reaching 15 percent) were mitigated by the combined effect of emigration and the entry of women and youth into the labor force, the state's role in total national investment rose from 22 percent in 1973 to over 40 percent after 1978. Most of this was financed by foreign loans, increasing the level of public debt to record levels (from $500 million in 1973 to over $5 billion in 1984).

There was increased profitability in the industrial sectors, and the growth rate of the GNP averaged between 3 and 6 percent annually between 1974 and 1980, after a long period of decline. However, much of this was channeled into the wave of capital flight that sapped the Uruguayan economy of approximately 3.5 billion dollars.[18] In addition, there was financial speculation in unproductive ventures such as the money market, where capital was circulated among different currencies according to differential exchange rates established by the government (a practice known as the "bicycle" or "merry-go-round"). With the recession of the early 1980s, the speculative trend ended, growth stopped, and the economy declined from 1981 to 1984. Meanwhile, inflation and unemployment continued to rise. Hence, by the time the military was prepared to relinquish government authority, the country was once again in a deep economic crisis, and the working classes were in an even worse position to confront it.

When the MTSS was created, it included a general administration level (the minister's office), the Work and Employment Service, the Center for Juridical Advice and Assistance to Workers, the Directorate of Labor Relations and Salaries (to which the meditation offices responsible for overseeing the Consejos de Salarios were attached), the General Inspectorate of Labor and Social Security, the National Alimentary Institute, the Social Service Institute, and the Children's Council.[19] In general, the competence of the MTSS had been limited to

> formulating, supervising, and evaluating the policies, plans, and activities proper of the labor sector (employment, work, and social security) . . . stimulating increases in employment levels . . . promoting and orienting activities conducive to workers' welfare . . . coordinating, directing, and supervising the administration of social security . . . and planning, organizing, directing, and supervising the functions of employment services . . . along with a specific range of technical assistance and promotion activities.[20]

By 1973, with the state's increasing encroachment on sectorial autonomy, there was a move toward bringing the full range of labor activities under its control.

In August 1973, Decree 622/73 established mandatory union registration, subject to MTSS approval. Without this official recognition, unions could not officially "exist."

Then, in 1974, the MTSS's competence in the area of union oversight and control was substantially modified and expanded and a major move toward state corporatism was quietly implemented.

In July 1974, the responsibilities of the MTSS were redefined to include, among a host of more general provisions, specific competence in the labor relations regime, workers' wages, the labor regime in firms, labor policing, labor conflicts, and promotion and regulation of union organizations. This marked the formal passage from the pluralist to the state-corporatist era of labor administration in Uruguay.[21]

To better carry out the expanded scope of its control responsibilities, the MTSS was reorganized (Law 14,489, 1975), and divided into three central coordinating branches, the Directorates of Labor, Social Security, and Human Resources and Employment.

Agencies connected with housing, food programs, children's issues, and general social welfare were transferred to the newly created Ministry of Housing and Social Promotion.[22] Thus, whereas the scope of Uruguayan labor administration was expanded considerably, its responsibility for providing public goods unrelated to salary was eliminated and transferred to other agencies. This responded to the "efficientist" and "technocratic" logic of the military regime's bureaucrats and reduction of labor administration's role as provider of public goods.

In 1977 and 1978 there were several modifications designed to reinforce labor administration's new role. The clauses in an MTSS proposal at the 1977 Solís reunion of ministers included items that "reaffirmed the principle of the complementarity between labor and capital, in accordance with a solidarity position, which definitively rejects the dissolutionary notion of class struggle" and expressed the intention to "legislate . . . on the statutes and functions of Labor Associations, defining their field of action and excluding all politization."[23] This reiterated the intention of Decree 622 of August 1973, which, in addition to requiring union registration requirements, attempted to outlaw the political activities of unions and to place severe limits on strikes. The decree was openly defied by the labor movement until a wave of repression enforced it.

The intention in 1977 was to go much further than the earlier emergency decree and to institutionalize a new labor relations regime founded on a redefined conception of the unions' "proper" functions. To that end, laws were enacted to formally circumscribe and "correct" labor's proper sphere of action.[24] These laws limited unions to the level of the firm, where they could serve only as bargaining agents on non-wage issues connected with the workplace (with some exceptions); they were prohibited from engaging in political activities. Labor confederations were banned. The intention was to permanently atomize and disarticulate the labor movement in order to weaken it economically and politically.

Organizational modifications in the COPRIN accompanied the move to an overtly interventionist stance.[25] All sectorial representation was permanently eliminated and the remaining representation was split between offices of the Ministry of Economy and the Ministry of Labor.[26]

The delimitation of labor-related functions was coupled with restored social security and welfare assistance responsibilities during the next two years. A general Directorate of Social Security was created within the MTSS and charged with administering the national social security system (Constitutional Decree 9/23, October 1979). As a follow-up, the National Directorate of Social Promotion was created and placed in charge of all social assistance programs.[27]

The delimiting and compartmentalizing trends within the MTSS, which responded to the technical criteria adopted by the regime for reordering the state bureaucracy, did not bring with them increased budgets for national labor administration and its areas of attention. To the contrary, both the MTSS budget and the number of persons employed in the ministry fell as a consequence of the regime's austerity measures in the public sector.

The portion of the central administrative budget allocated to national labor administration, which had traditionally remained around 1 percent, was reduced to 0.5 percent by 1978,[28] a level maintained until democracy was restored. Similarly, the number of employees in national labor administration dropped from the historical average of 1,500 to below 1,000, despite the ostensibly expanded scope of the MTSS's social security and welfare functions, to say nothing of its increased powers of intervention in labor relations proper.

This should not be surprising, since the exclusionary features of the regime's state-corporatist approach toward labor relations entailed eliminating the mediation services of labor administration at the same time that it subordinated the focus on the labor "question" to the dictates of the security apparatus. National labor administration was thus a good place to implement the cutbacks and other austerity measures required by the "rationalization" undertaken in public administration generally.

The rejection of the military's proposed constitutional reforms in the plebiscite of November 1980 marked the beginning of the end of authoritarian rule. In contrast to Chile, where a similar referendum was conducted under outrageously fraudulent conditions, in Uruguay the plebiscite was conducted under relatively open procedures (despite an overwhelming publicity campaign waged by the regime on behalf of its proposals and few avenues of expression for the opposition). Even more amazing, the military accepted the verdict once it became clear.

This points once again to the deeply ingrained democratic tradition in Uruguay: not only were the military unwilling to conduct a fraudulent election that would "legitimate" their rule, but they decided to step down once the unfavorable verdict was returned, even though they were virtually unchallenged in the political sphere at that time. With the outcome of the plebiscite accepted, the military regime voluntarily withdrew from power, after a series of negotiations on the timing and types of participation deemed permissible for restoring an electoral regime.

In sum, the Uruguayan military experiment with exclusionary state corporatism was a historical aberration; like the regime itself, it represented an unfortunate intrusion into an otherwise pluralistic, democratic tradition. The military were immediately excluded from the political landscape once democratic authorities were installed.

The External Dimension of the Uruguayan Labor Administration: Labor Relations and Social Policy, 1985–1988

The military's voluntary withdrawal from power was an extremely contingent process because the armed forces remained united as an institution and their ability to govern society by force was unquestioned. This was not the defeated, demoralized, and divided Argentine military after the Malvinas War, nor the weary, internally contentious, and socially unsupported Brazilian military toward the end of the period of incremental liberalization begun in 1974. In addition to internal cohesion, the Uruguayan armed forces were supported by the financial elite and monopoly sectors of the bourgeoisie, until the impact of the recession of 1980–1982 negatively affected the material interests of these groups as well.

The timing and conditions for the transfer of power, including the scheduling of internal party elections and general elections, the number of political actors allowed to compete in the electoral arena, and the institutional guarantees necessary for the military to relinquish control, was the procedural and substantive terrain on which negotiations with the revived opposition took place. The 1981–1984 period was marked by a series of moves and countermoves by the military regime and the opposition, as each tried to consolidate its position, impose its preferences, and retain the upper hand in the transition.

As the economic crisis brought on by the recession worsened, reaching an unprecedented level by 1983, the military regime's hand became progressively weaker, forcing it to resort to coercive powers to remind the opposition what the transition ultimately hinged on. The military's concessions consisted in accepting leftist participation, via the Frente Amplio, in the transition, granting internal party elections in 1982 (in which anti-regime forces won large majorities in all the major parties), and authorizing certain union activities and a May Day celebration in 1983. However, acts such as the political banning and subsequent arrest of the Blanco Party leader, violent repression of street demonstrations throughout 1983 and early 1984, and outlawing the Plenario Intersindical de Trabajadores (PIT) after the January 1984 general strike, clearly demonstrated the military's continued willingness to use coercive instruments to bolster their position.

Along with the mobilization of students, human rights groups, neighborhood associations, and syndicalists, the most important external elements in the transition were the victory of antimilitary forces in the 1982 primaries and the creation and deliberations of peak associations of unions, parties, and social movements. These took part in a concertative "pact sequence" within the context of the Intersectorial (unions, political parties, social movements, and student groups), Intersocial (social movements and parties), Intergremial (unions), and Multipartidaria (all of the above with episodic defections and reentries). These culminated in the formation of the Concertación Nacional Programatica (CONAPRO) in 1984, and led to the agreements struck with the military authorities during the Club Naval meetings of June to August of that year (Institutional Act No. 19 of August 1984). Coupled with the military regime's concessions, these points of interaction among sectors, with their individual patterns of confrontation and cooperation, mobilization and negotiation, characterized the incremental passage from authoritarianism to democracy in Uruguay.[29]

It is impossible to reconstruct in detail the laborious negotiations involved in this process. However, one can highlight areas of contention and agreement that shaped the evolution of various actors' strategic postures throughout the transition, particularly regarding labor-capital relations in the subsequent democratic conjuncture.

The dynamics of the labor movement's resurgence had a decided impact on the process of democratic consolidation following the departure of the authoritarian regime. After years of enforced silence, unions slowly began to become active again in the wake of the 1980 plebiscite. In 1982, after a number of firm-level unions were formed within the parameters outlined by the authoritarian Law of Professional Associations, a number of union leaders began exploring the possibility of holding a joint May Day celebration the following year. A federational table (Mesa de Federaciones) was created to facilitate these discussions, and despite internal differences between various Marxist factions (in particular, between the Democracia Avanzada and the Izquierda Democrática Independiente), this led to the formation of the Plenario Intersindical de Trabajadores (PIT) in early 1983.

After much internal struggle, the labor movement made a clear attempt to demonstrate its historical and ideological continuity by uniting under the banner of the PIT-CNT (the latter the outlawed national labor confederation). At the end of May 1987, the PIT-CNT held its first extraordinary congress, in which it was formally reconstituted as a confederation of eighty-two unions, with an executive board comprising representatives of forty-two major unions. In the historical tradition of autonomy and decentralization, the PIT-CNT can call general strikes only at the request of a majority of its affiliates. Sectorial strikes can be called only by the sectorial union federation in question, and firm- or industry-level strikes by the respective unions in each case. Thus, the majority of the PIT-CNT's general strike calls during the early phase of the democratic regime (eight in four years), were overtly political in nature, a way of forging class and social consciousness rather than expressing concrete economic demands. On the other hand, the hundreds of sectorial and firm-level strikes called during this period were called solely by the unions in question, mostly as a means of making concrete economic demands, without consultation with or approval of the national leadership.

Unlike the Argentine and Brazilian union movements with their strongly centralized and vertical forms of union structure, the Uruguayan labor movement is organizationally and strategically very much a decentralized, relatively loosely bound collection of ideologically similar unions, where decisions tend to flow from the bottom up rather than from the top down (despite the PC faction's insistent attempts to centralize decision-making authority in the executive board). Again, this points to the strong history of democratic procedure, decentralization of structures of authority, and sectorial autonomy existing in Uruguay's labor movement.

The fundamental feature of the sectorial interaction that culminated in the November 1984 general elections was that all the political parties and most of the organized elements in civil society (with the exception of certain employer groups) were united in opposition to the regime, and all were acutely aware that the restoration of democracy would occur under conditions of severe economic crisis and social disarticulation.

Procedurally, the concertative interaction between 1981 and 1984 was informal, horizontal, transitory, and based on emergency conditions. It constituted a form of fluid defensive action against the "triple threat" of economic crisis, continued military presence, and the otherwise inevitable ideological polarization of the political and sectorial agents. It served less as an institutional channel for mediating political and economic interests than as a device to overcome short-term tactical differences in order to confront the common adversary.[30] Even so, this type of sectorial interaction helped create "an environment of discussion and an interest in discussion among [groups] that had not been in contact for twelve years,"[31] an environment that helped lay the groundwork for the more formal concertative negotiations in the months leading up to the November 1984 general elections.

Against a backdrop of increased popular mobilization and military retreat, the early informal efforts at sectorial dialogue promoted by the Intersectorial, Intersocial, Intergremial, and Multipartidaria assumed more concrete, formal, and public shape with the convocation of the CONAPRO in September 1984. The CONAPRO was a more tightly structured, widely encompassing, and deliberately public vehicle than the earlier groups.

Informal and secret discussions paved the way for establishing a "programmatic" common ground on which elements of the opposition could agree. This helped to moderate sectorial positions and hence facilitate the transition. Among other things, sectors adopted pragmatic, "lesser evil" strategies regarding amnesty for military officers charged with human rights abuses and maintenance of military budgets. In these areas, much of the civilian opposition (particularly the left, including the union movement, which had been hardest hit by the repressive campaign) would have preferred an uncompromising stance. Yet a succession of "quieter" concertative negotiations provided guidelines for consensus upon which CONAPRO established its claim as the vehicle through which the opposition would stake out its position in the months before the November 1984 election.

The CONAPRO was organized around working groups in specific functional areas (labor, health, housing, education, etc.), which reported to an Executive Council. Consultative groups were attached to this council, as were various secretariats charged with administering the logistical issues related to the organization. Each working group, as well as the Executive Council, included representatives of the major political parties (the Colorado Party, the Nacional or Blanco Party, the Frente Amplio, and the Unión Cívica), the PIT-CNT, the cooperative federation, the student association, and other groups with a specific interest in the transition (human rights groups in particular). In addition, various business organizations such as the Chamber of Industry and the Chamber of Commerce were convinced to join, given the inevitability of the transition, their need to capture some "space" in the new regime, and the necessity of setting out their positions against those of the other participants in the CONAPRO project. As could be expected, the most important actors within the CONAPRO were the political parties and the collective agents of labor and capital.[32]

With the Colorado victory in the November election, a political group composed of the political party representatives was created as a superordinate coordinating group for the CONAPRO. The business and syndical representatives were delegated to a reorganized Executive Council. This division was designed to establish the broad parameters and orientation of the new regime's socioeconomic and political program on the basis of a partisan consensus. The objectives announced by the CONAPRO were designed to be general policy orientations rather than specific sectorial compromises to be rigorously followed. This allowed all social actors the opportunity to offer specific interpretations and proposals within those general guidelines.

In broad terms, the CONAPRO was an instance of multipartite concertation involving interaction between political parties and collective agents on one procedural and two substantive issues: first, it was a political pact that guaranteed the terms of the transition and the immediate aftermath of the election; second, it established the principle of intersectorial socioeconomic agreements; and it was a medium- to long-term agreement on the need to study and assess the possibilities of a new national project. Each substantive dimension allowed room for interpretation by the various parties. These differences were to be negotiated and resolved once the new regime was installed. As such, the CONAPRO was first and foremost a procedural agreement on the general outlines of the transition and the immediate post-authoritarian phase, concentrating on general objectives rather than concrete instruments and setting aside the specific substantive discussion and the search for ways to apply the accords until the dictatorship was formally replaced.[33]

The CONAPRO's original scope was thus general and broad. It included economic policy broadly construed, education and culture, health, housing, social security, human rights, civil liberties, amnesty and exile issues, and a review of the laws and decrees passed by the authoritarian regime. Each of these tasks was assigned to a working group, which, after a review of the subject areas, issued policy recommendations to the Executive Council.

The work of the CONAPRO can be divided into two phases, the first from September through November 1984 (from its creation until after the elections), and the second from December 1984 through February 1985 (until the inauguration of the civilian government). In the first phase, agreement was reached on allowing the return of all exiles, on institutionalizing the CONAPRO after March 1, 1985, as an advisory body to the executive branch, restoring the independence of the judiciary, and restoring the autonomy of the universities. Agreement was also reached on the general objectives of reforming economic and social policy. More sensitive debates between labor and capital, such as income redistribution, were left for discussion in the second phase, once election results were known.

One major achievement of the first phase was that it gave the civilian political opposition grouped in the CONAPRO (except for the Blanco Party, which withdrew from talks with the military while retaining its position in the larger body) common ground on which to confront the military authorities and negotiate with them the guarantees required so that the transition could go as scheduled. After months of behind-the-scenes maneuvering, these guarantees were formally exchanged at the Club Naval meetings of August 1984, where the CONAPRO representatives (including future president Julio Sanguinetti of the Colorado Party and representatives of the Frente Amplio) met with members of the military hierarchy to discuss the final terms of the transition and to set an election date. In addition to the ethical compromise on the issue of amnesty for past human rights abuses, there were a number of other concessions, including the proscription of the Community Party and of Blanco Party leader Wilson Ferriera, and guarantees that the military's autonomy and budgets would be maintained. These concessions were made in exchange for complete return to democratic civilian authority, rather than the "protected" democracy the military preferred.

The military's concessions included reducing the National Security Council to a purely consultative agency on military matters only, reestablishing the 1967 constitution, and the freedom to review and reverse virtually all legislation passed by the military authorities during their tenure. In addition, the Frente Amplio was formally recognized as the legitimate political vehicle of the left, which returned it to a place in the institutionalized party system. This *quid pro quo* was a positive-sum game, both in terms of each group's interests and in terms of the restoration of democracy.

On November 25, 1984, the Colorado Party won the national elections with 39 percent of the vote. The Blanco Party ran a close second, with approximately a third of the vote, while the Frente Amplio improved on its 1971 showing by capturing 21 percent of the electorate. Uruguay now has a primarily three-party system, in which the percentage of votes in Congress are roughly distributed 40-40-20 among the major parties, with a very small fraction going to the rightist Union Cívica. Rather than restoring the previous two-party system, the revived Parliament established a renovated coalition system in which the left, through the Frente Amplio, represented the swing votes. This has given added political weight to their concerns.[34]

After the elections, the scope of activities of CONAPRO was narrowed considerably, both in terms of the actors involved and issues addressed. Its orientation became overtly political, as it attempted to establish foundations for workable interaction between the executive and legislative branches in the early days of the new regime. Representatives of labor and capital were relegated to the Executive Council, and other social agents were entirely excluded. Under the new "political" format, the discussions during the second phase produced a document that was broad in its scope, outlining the need for party agreements on economic issues and social policy. This included a call to free all political prisoners and lift all political proscriptions enacted by the military. This document also rescinded the decision to institutionalize the CONAPRO after the new government was installed, because this would have infringed on both the government's and the opposition parties' room for maneuver in the parliamentary forum.

Among the few specific measures adopted by the second phase of the CONAPRO was the agreement to resurrect the Consejos de Salarios as the primary vehicles through which labor-capital negotiations would take place, making them the hub of the labor relations system. Equally important, all the actors in the CONAPRO agreed that the state would have to assume a much larger role in the economy and in social issues in general.

Each political and social actor had its own reasons for wanting an enhanced state role. However, in agreeing on the need to reassert the state's role, these actors not only rejected the neoliberal project but also provided the entering Colorado government with a mandate to use the state to address the pressing socioeconomic problems inherited from the *dictadura*. This became particularly evident in the field of labor relations, and in the role and actions of national labor administration.

It was widely accepted that democratic consolidation could not occur without economic growth, and that a great part of that growth had to be derived from the internal market. Even business interests that had initially welcomed the wage controls of the authoritarian regime were alarmed by the impact of the steep reduction in incomes on domestic sales. Except for the export and financial sectors, capitalists and workers agreed on the need for measures that would increase real wages and thus revitalize the domestic market. The central questions were how to raise wages without renewing the inflationary cycle and who should finance the increases. Here the state's role as macroeconomic manager would be crucial and would in fact become an integral part of the labor policies adopted by the Colorado government.

The labor relations working group in the CONAPRO shaped the labor policies to be adopted by the democratic government. Agreement was reached during the first phase on repealing the military regime's labor legislation, including the 1981 Law of Professional Associations, decrees governing collective bargaining, and legal restrictions on the right to strike.

Agreement was also reached on setting a quarterly system of wage negotiations and on rehiring public servants fired by the authoritarian regime for political reasons. (The same did not occur with respect to dismissals in the private sector, however.)

During the second phase of the CONAPRO, attention focused on the Colorado Party as the future governing party. At the same time, there was a virtual void in the official sphere of labor relations, as the outgoing MTSS hierarchy stopped enforcing the edicts it had promulgated and social actors all but ignored outgoing officials. In addition, an ad hoc group within the CONAPRO labor relations working group mediated the rapid surge in strikes and stoppages during the end of 1984 and first two months of 1985. With the inauguration of the Colorado government on March 1, 1985, the Consejo Superior de Salarios (COSUSAL) began to function as a formal tripartite forum in which sectorial grievances could be aired and conflicts resolved.[35]

I have prefaced the discussion of the Sanguinetti government's policies in the labor field with this extended review of the

CONAPRO and the general circumstances of the transition in Uruguay to illustrate two points. First, unlike Argentina and Brazil, in Uruguay the transition was clearly a "pacted" form of transition: it made guarantees to the outgoing military incumbents, and it gave procedural assurances to members of the opposition, which were necessary to secure their support for the transition. These "bifrontal" agreements established the procedural framework (the terms and the timing) within which the transition and immediate post-authoritarian phase occurred.

In addition, the "pacted" nature of the Uruguayan transition established basic policy guidelines to be followed by the incoming democratic government regardless of the outcome of the November 1984 elections. The tone of these guidelines left much room for interpretation, depending on the orientation of the victorious party. Nonetheless, to promote the regime's consolidation and social stability, all parties and social agents grouped in the CONAPRO formally bound themselves to respect the terms of the transition and abide by the decisions of the new democratic authorities.

The Colorado Party's statement of principles, issued during the electoral campaign, outlined seven policy areas that required priority attention: political organization, socioeconomic policy, labor relations, enterprise democracy, education, municipal policy, and providing public goods.[36] Civil-military relations did not figure among these critical areas.

In socioeconomic policy, the party platform maintained that while the government had primary responsibility for administering policy, fighting the economic crisis and promoting equitable development required a national consensus. To that end, "overcoming the crisis requires the concertation of a great national accord. In the short run, this will be implemented through concertative mechanisms that bring together the different social groups and the state."[37] On labor policy, the party platform

> consider[ed] that the syndical organization is a crucial arena for growing citizen participation. In that sense, it recognizes unions as the legitimate political interlocutors in the conception and execu-

tion of policies which guarantee the effective realization of the rights of their affiliates. It assumes, therefore, the defense of principles of pluralism, internal democracy, and representativeness in the formation and functioning of syndical organizations, as well as their independence from political parties.[38]

Over the short term, the government proposed to restore all trade union rights and freedoms, including the right to strike, the protection of union representatives against dismissal for exercising their union responsibilities (the so-called *fuero sindical*), the right of the public sector to unionize, the immediate rehabilitation of all banned union leaders, and the return of or compensation for all confiscated property belonging to the unions. In addition, the government proposed the rehiring of all unionists fired for political reasons by the dictatorship or, if that was impossible, compensation to the affected individuals. It also proposed the creation of an institute of workers defense as an independent government agency to oversee the protection of workers' rights, the establishment of a labor liaison within the Colorado Party, and the creation of an institute of syndical and labor studies that would study the situation of rural workers, alternative forms of labor organization, and education and training projects for labor.

The Colorados proposed to promote concertative vehicles that would include labor representatives in search of a national accord; they accepted the autonomy of unions in selecting their own representatives to international labor congresses (such as those of the ILO, to which union representatives designated by the government had been sent under the previous regime); and they promised to repeal all authoritarian legislation in labor relations and to substitute a democratic legal framework based on the 1967 constitution. Over the medium term, the government offered to help in organizing rural workers, to secure more active participation on the part of retirees and pensioners in the administration of social security and social welfare programs, to promote worker participation schemes in both the private and public sectors, and to begin a more in-depth review of all legislation connected with individual and collective workers' rights to ensure the most democratic, autonomous, and representative labor relations system possible.[39]

The external dimension of the democratic government's labor policy involved reconstituting the institutional framework within which wage negotiations could occur (within the limits of the government's economic revitalization program) and reconstructing the social security and welfare system and the administrative network responsible for providing public goods in general and health, education, and housing in particular. The government reemphasized the state's role in providing for and protecting the individual rights of the working population, primarily through its labor justice network, its service agencies responsible for legal advice, occupational training, and employment, and its corps of labor inspectors.

In giving priority to these three policy areas, the Colorado government felt that the state's role as agent of social reproduction would enhance the prospects that the working population would be reincorporated as full citizens in the new democratic system. More important, through these areas of activity, the Colorado leadership sought to secure the institutional and material bases of the consent of the rank-and-file working class to their rule, and to confine the confrontationalist strategies of their Marxist representatives to the role of swing votes in the parliamentary arena, under the banner of the Frente Amplio.

With Congress installed on February 15 and the president inaugurated on March 1, 1985, the Colorado government immediately set out to implement the most pressing of these measures. On the day of his inauguration, President Sanguinetti signed into law decrees repealing the authoritarian legislation on labor relations, effectively returning to the legal regime of 1967. This included the full restoration of union rights and property, a return to the policy of *auto-reglmentación* (self-regulation) by which all professional associations established their own internal rules of organization, and the guarantee of a virtually unrestricted right to strike (save in certain "essential services"). A Law of Unionist Employment Security (*fuero sindical*) was introduced (it was subsequently passed by

Congress in 1987) which protected union leaders from dismissal for engaging in union activities. Finally, Sanguinetti signed decrees authorizing wage increases of 13 percent over the wage rate of November 1984, or 85 percent over the rate of January 1984, whichever was larger. He also signed a degree that placed in operation the Consejo Superior de Salarios.[40]

The Consejo Superior de Salarios, which, unlike its predecessor in the CONAPRO, did not have a limited period for its operations, was made up of representatives of the executive branch (the minister of labor and social security and the national director of labor), business (the presidents of the Cámara de Industria, the Cámara de Comercio, and the Cámara de Frutos del Pais), and labor (the leaders of the PIT-CNT). The major change in the composition of the Consejo Superior de Salarios consisted in substituting representatives of the executive branch (that is, agents of the government party) for representatives of the four parties who had served in the CONAPRO labor relations working group. In addition, capital's representation on the Consejo Superior de Salarios was reduced.

The Consejo Superior de Salarios had a consultative function, and its decisions were formally announced as decrees or resolutions of the MTSS. In some cases, such as the across-the-board wage increase passed on March 1, 1985, the executive branch enacted the decree without prior consultation with either Congress or the Consejo Superior de Salarios, to establish the terms of the substantive debate within both Parliament and the tripartite forum. On other issues, especially the institutional framework in which private-sector wage negotiations would thereafter occur, the Consejo Superior de Salarios was given responsibility for proposing the mechanisms to be used.

Labor representatives were partial to the idea of restoring a strict collective bargaining system at the firm and sectorial levels, without state mediation or interference. This was a modified version of the 1943 system. Business, on the other hand, preferred to continue the DINACOPRIN regime, with salaries fixed by the government without sectorial input.

The Colorado government favored returning to the 1943

regime. The Consejos de Salarios, a Colorado invention, represented part of the Colorado legacy that was deemed worth preserving, as a concrete link with the origins of Uruguayan democracy. The sectorial scope of the Consejos ensured that wage increases would respond to industry dynamics, thereby avoiding across-the-board wage increases, which were considered a major cause of inflation. Increases in real wages could be tied to differential cost structures and rates of sectorial productivity and would be the specific product of the negotiating capacities of the various collective agents mediated by the state.

After considerable debate, in March 1985 the Consejo Superior de Salarios (COSUSAL) restored the Consejo de Salarios system with one important modification. Adhering to the framework of Law 14,409/1943 regarding the tripartite character of the Consejos and their sectorial scope, the new regime retained the state's authority (imposed by DINACOPRIN) to formally announce through executive decree all wage increases negotiated in the Consejos. Agreements reached in the Consejos de Salarios would have to be ratified by the state to be legally binding. This locked labor and capital into abiding by the agreement's terms under penalty of law. The government thus ensured that wage increases would not surpass or interfere with the requirements of the government's economic stabilization and anti-inflationary program and that agreements would not be modified or violated ex post facto.[41]

COSUSAL then turned to classifying categories of production and occupations (known as wage groups) according to function. These served as points of reference in wage negotiations for employees in different sectors. Given the changes in the structure and relations of production wrought by the authoritarian regime, the classification of such groups was a particularly important issue.[42]

The previous classification scheme had been drawn up in 1968, when more than sixty wage groups were recognized. The new scheme proposed by the MTSS reduced the number to thirty-five. After two months of review and discussion, the three parties agreed to a classification scheme composed of forty-eight wage groups for occupational or productive sectors and two hundred and twenty specific subgroups. That system remains in force today.[43]

The new wage groups were announced by executive decree, which also specified a time frame for concertative wage negotiations (to be held in June, October, and February), and terms for nominating business and labor representatives to each group.[44] "Consensus was reached on a fundamental theme, the structure which would regulate labor situations, based on the basic element of tripartism. . . . This agreement [established] the primary basis [of the labor relations system]: tripartism, negotiation by wage group, and quarterly negotiations."[45]

The Consejo Superior de Salarios (COSUSAL) did not disband once this wage negotiation framework was established. As a sign that the government was looking for ongoing cooperation on the full range of policy issues, high-ranking officials (including the minister of labor and social security, the minister of economy and finance, and the director of planning and budget) continued to meet regularly with the CSC to brief sectorial agents on matters of general policy, receive their feedback, and establish by consensus the macroeconomic parameters for wage negotiations. The recourse to the overarching tripartite agency demonstrated the Colorado government's desire for concertative interaction at the highest levels of policy making, even if the ultimate decision-making authority in economic policy continued to rest with the executive branch.

Due to delay in redefining the wage groups and convoking sectorial representatives, the Consejos de Salarios did not begin to function until late May. The time frame covered by the initial negotiations was June–September 1985, and the original baselines were the wage rates established by the government on March 1, adjusted for inflation during the ensuing interval. Where negotiations continued into the period covered by the agreement, the wage rate was retroactive.

Power to convoke the Consejos rested exclusively with the MTSS. The basic parameters of the Consejos, according to the 1943 and 1985 laws, can be summarized as follows: they establish a minimum wage for all workers in private industrial, manufacturing, and commercial establishments, including the service sector; they do so by "sectorializing" the economy by branch of productive activity; they operate according to tripartite formulas, with the state, labor, and capital represented in a 3-2-2 voting scheme, where decisions are reached by majority or unanimous vote; labor and capital nominate their representatives to each Consejo, although other actors may impugn the nomination of any candidate deemed unrepresentative; nominees are confirmed by the MTSS; state representatives are selected by the MTSS; each Consejo establishes subgroups of occupational categories within its domain that serve as primary referents when establishing wages for specific categories of workers; decisions are announced as legally binding rulings (decrees); and the Consejos are completely independent of each other — that is, each fixes salaries within its own sphere without taking into account the results of other Consejos.

To have legal authority, all wage agreements must be reached through the Consejos and ratified by their constituencies (the union's rank and file, firms in a given sector). Ratification procedures must be democratic (secret ballot) and must result in an absolute majority. Agreements are then enacted as law by the executive branch (see figure 7.1).

In total, more than 340,000 workers are covered by the Consejos. Each subgroup has its own Consejo. Each Consejo is made up of seven members, with three representatives of the executive branch (all Labor Ministry officials), and two each representing labor and capital (workers and employers in each functional subgroup). The senior representative of national labor administration serves as the president of the Consejo and presides over six to eight such groups, while the junior state representatives conduct each Consejo's day-to-day negotiations and serve as permanent staff. All told, there are 100 state representatives, 500 employer representatives, and 500 union representatives in the Consejo system.

The state retains a numerical majority within each Consejo, but unlike the COPRIN system, the reestablished tripartite arrangement gives labor and capital the absolute majority in each

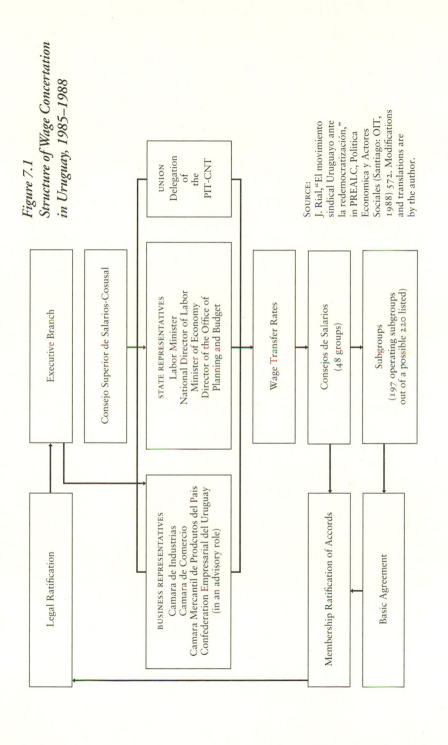

Figure 7.1
Structure of Wage Concertation in Uruguay, 1985–1988

Executive Branch

Legal Ratification

Consejo Superior de Salarios-Cosusal

STATE REPRESENTATIVES
Labor Minister
National Director of Labor
Minister of Economy
Director of the Office of
Planning and Budget

BUSINESS REPRESENTATIVES
Camara de Industrias
Camara de Comercio
Camara Mercantil de Prodcutos del Pais
Confederation Empresarial del Uruguay
(in an advisory role)

UNION
Delegation
of
the
PIT-CNT

Wage Transfer Rates

Consejos de Salarios
(48 groups)

Subgroups
(197 operating subgroups
out of a possible 220 listed)

Membership Ratification of Accords

Basic Agreement

SOURCE:
J. Rial, "El movimiento
sindical Uruguayo ante
la redemocratización,"
in PREALC, Politica
Economica y Actores
Sociales (Santiago: OIT,
1988) 572. Modifications
and translations are
by the author.

instance, leading to voting situations in which they can join forces against the state representatives. This has led to five possible voting patterns: a tripartite unanimous consensus has most often been the result.

In a modification of the 1943 regime, the geographic scope of the Consejo was expanded to cover all workers in a given occupational category. Thus, wage rates are applied uniformly across the nation rather than by departments. Special provisions allow for specific exceptions where pertinent (for example, in hotels and restaurants located in tourist centers). As a result, the Consejos often establish differential wage rates for workers grouped in the same category but residing in different departments, responding to the different cost and price structures of industries located in large and small cities, urban and rural areas, etc.[46]

The role of the state, particularly of its representatives in each Consejo, is crucial. State delegates to the Consejos are instructed to pressure both sides for an agreement during the first half of the month, and to closely monitor the negotiating posture of both sides to determine their "honesty." The state refuses to fix a time limit on negotiations and reserves the right to fix wage rates, if and when appropriate, when negotiations stall. The state's imposition of wage rates could come early or late in the month, and these rates can vary considerably. This makes it very difficult for sectors to calculate whether state-imposed rates will favor them or not.

As a result, sectorial agents have adopted more "honest" negotiating postures to avoid the uncertainty of a state-imposed increase. Averse as they are to risk, sectorial agents in the Consejos often abandon their first-choice strategies and move to negotiate on second-best terms as quickly as possible. Thus, although negotiations in subsequent rounds of the Consejos have often been contentious, they have not been blocked by the stalling tactics seen in the June 1985 round, and agreements tend to be reached in twenty to forty-five days. Thus the state's strategic posture, coupled with its role as mediator and enforcer, concretely influences institutional conditions in a way conducive to a class compromise on material issues.

Because of its overall responsibility to fight the inflationary cycle and stabilize the economy, the executive branch established parameters for wage negotiations within the Consejos. Without such parameters, sectorial agents could engage in bipartite exchanges that merely translated wage increases into price hikes. This would neither help the stabilization program nor result in real wage increases.

Therefore, labor administration established a baseline of transferrable wage increases. A certain percentage of the increase could be transferred to prices, after which the employer would have to absorb the costs, compensate for them by increasing sales or reducing other expenses or utilities, or negotiate for labor concessions in the form of increased productivity, additional hours, or the like. In this way wage hikes would not fuel the inflationary spiral.

A close monitoring program was established to ensure that price ceilings were enforced, with administrative penalties (fines, closures, etc.) for violators. With this mechanism, the Colorado government hoped to slow the rate of inflation while simultaneously allowing the sectorial agents to determine, through strategic interaction, the precise mixture of increases in real wages and labor concessions required to promote the economic reactivation of various sectors.

Initially, both union and business representatives objected to this framework, citing four reasons for their views. First, imposition of a such a ceiling was not included in the original charter of the Consejos de Salarios issued in 1943 and hence violated legal precedent. Second, it constituted state interference in sectorial negotiations, since it went beyond the role of mediator called for in the original Consejo statutes. Given the history of pluralism and sectorial autonomy existing before the authoritarian regime, both labor and capital were loathe to see the state retain broad powers to determine the "proper" range of wage hikes. Third, labor believed that employers would agree to increases only up to the level that the government established as transferrable. As a result, there would be no real salary recuperation.[47] Finally, business preferred to negotiate at the firm level, if at all, since firms believed they could better defend their position if they did not have to share information with sectorial competitors or confront the possibility of mobilization by sectorial union federations.

The government remained firm in its position, noting that other aspects of the 1943 Ley de Consejos de Salarios had been modified in light of changing national realities (such as the classification of wage groups), and that the macroeconomic situation in 1943 was very different from (and much better than) that of 1985.

The government proved correct in its calculations. The average wage increase granted during the first round of the Consejos was 29 percent, with some sectors obtaining 32 percent increases. In addition, the government urged that minimum wage standards be set for each occupational category and that wage increases for the lowest-paid segments of each category exceed those of the highest paid (since the authoritarian regime had provoked serious salary distortions within each occupational category because of the different wage rates established for workers in individual firms). With these guidelines, unions were able to obtain minimum wage standards for each occupational category over the course of the first two rounds of the Consejos. This allowed wage rates to gradually equalize even as the least-advantaged workers moved away from the "submerged" condition they had been in when the formal transfer of authority took place.[48]

Labor had underestimated its bargaining strength. Once engaged in negotiations, it was able to extract increases in real wages and greater wage parity from employers in each sector, within the guidelines provided by the government. This framework, and the state's specific role in it, brought labor back to the negotiating table in a position of relative parity with capital. In other words, labor was formally reincorporated by this mechanism as a socioeconomic agent in Uruguay.

Business representatives were particularly loathe to accept the "ceilings" and "floors" in the government's wage proposals, preferring that wages be directly imposed by government decree, making it easier for business representatives to confront labor without having to make concessions. Labor, on the other hand, despite benefits gained in the first round of the Consejos, continued to be wary of the government's motives and its economic data, fearing that the Colorado leadership would deliberately underestimate the cost of living to prevent an overly rapid increase in real wages that might trigger inflation. Since labor was most concerned with recuperating the wage levels it had enjoyed before the authoritarian regime, it was not partial to the idea of a gradual increase in real wages over an extended period. As a result of these differences, the Consejo Superior de Salarios (COSUSAL) never reached an accord on the transference rates to be used in each round, and the government ultimately established the rates on its own.

It was more difficult to institutionalize a class compromise at the macroeconomic level, among national peak associations, than at the level of the Consejos. After three unsuccessful attempts to reach macroeconomic consensus, the COSUSAL stopped meeting in February 1986. This demonstrates the utility of "bottom up" institutionalization based on sectorial segmentation, which parallels partisan competition in the political arena at the national level. In spite of the failure of "top down" efforts at institutionalization, the COSUSAL served well as an initial rule-making device, that is, as the vehicle that established the procedural parameters within which the initial labor-capital interaction occurred.

The second round of the Consejos extended from October 1985 through January 1986. At that time, the transference rate was set at 18 percent, since the July–September 1985 inflation rate had been 18.2 percent. With discussions lasting little over a month, the average wage increase awarded was 22 percent. As a result, from March to December 1985, real wage rates rose an average of 15 percent for all organized workers in the private sector. This constituted a restoration of wages to pre-1984 levels (although wages were still considerably lower than the historically high rates of 1968–1971).

Employer representatives were better prepared during the second round of the Consejos. In the first round, they had conceded more than they anticipated, because of a well-organized, coherently formulated negotiating posture on the part of labor. Union representatives came to the Consejos with data on productivity, costs, and other economic issues to support their position, whereas business representatives often arrived at the Consejos with little more than note pads.

Since in the first round business was generally ill prepared, economic data provided by labor were often used as the base for establishing wage parameters, particularly since the government agreed that labor had been unfairly punished and that capital had disproportionately benefited from the policies of the military regime. Thus, business representatives approached the second round of the Consejos more seriously and with much better preparation. Hence, while the average wage increase in the second round exceeded the transference "ceiling," the amount of additional increases dropped compared to the first round, from an average of 7 percent to an average of 4 percent.[49]

Unions were also forced to alter their negotiating posture. Although uniformly opposed to capitalism, Uruguayan unions displayed different currents of Marxist ideology. Internal disputes often emerged in negotiations with employers during the first round of the Consejos.

The need to establish a firm negotiating position based on a command of economic data forced unions to educate themselves on a wide range of economic subjects and receive expert advice on specific issues (the relation of wages to investment and productivity, for example). As a result, they worked out their tactical differences and toned down the level of ideological discourse in the Consejos in favor of a more neutral, technical assessment of their position and demands. The de-ideologization of negotiations (save for perfunctory opening statements condemning capitalism in general and Uruguayan capitalism in particular) increased the other actors' respect for labor's competence in economic matters. De facto acceptance of the technical requirements of the capitalist logic of production on the part of unions thus contributed to the increased fluidity of negotiations during subsequent rounds of Consejo negotiations.

Despite the success of the Consejos in 1985, the government

feared that the inflationary cycle was not slowing as it should. Hence, it proposed to determine the wage ceiling according to the projected rate of inflation during the next quarter rather than the rate of inflation of the quarter immediately ended. Labor immediately protested this change while business representatives sided with the government.

With the impasse, the government decided not to convoke the Consejos for the third round scheduled for February 1986, and instead unilaterally fixed the transference ceiling. Labor then called a successful twenty-four-hour general strike and abandoned the CONSUSAL. Refusing to modify its position, the government used the powers awarded it by the 1978 DINACOPRIN law to establish the wage increase for the February–May 1986 quarter. The rate of inflation for that period eventually amounted to 17.4 percent, more than the government's projections, but less than the wage ceiling it had established for that period. Even so, no gains in real wages were made at this time, and in fact labor lost some of its purchasing power as a result of changed criteria for setting the wage rate.

Labor accepted the government's invitation to return to the tripartite forums in June 1986. This round of the Consejos had three special characteristics that mark it as a turning point in consolidating the labor relations partial regime. First, the negotiations were clearly the most fluid and least contentious held up to that time. The success of the Consejos, even with the hiatus produced by the February 1986 impasse and imposition of wages by decree, served to convince the sectorial agents that the institutional forum gave *them* the most viable means for achieving a mutually beneficial material compromise. This was evident in the second important factor, the agreement on "long" accords covering wages, benefits, and working conditions that extended beyond the quarterly period.

Most of these accords contained no-strike and productivity clauses in exchange for regular wage readjustments tied to the cost-of-living index or other means of calculating inflation. The long accords represented "a compromise on real salary growth for the covered workers, and also incorporated criteria on sectoral growth, productivity, and salary participation in both."[50] Finally, the incorporation of non-wage issues in the "long accords" marked the passage from the first, "economistic" phase of the Consejos to the second, "socially mature" phase, where the full range of workplace concerns became the subject of discussion.

Many of the "long" accords were negotiated outside the framework of the Consejos. The government was not enthusiastic about this development but did not declare such bilateral negotiations illegal or otherwise intervene to prevent agreements from being reached. It merely cautioned the actors involved that it would not accept major deviations from the economic clauses used in the Consejos.

This should not be surprising, since the government retained the authority to enact wage rates by decree according to the DINACOPRIN legislation. Contracts reached outside the Consejos were introduced ex post facto for ratification by the state. Although the government was formally interested only in the wage aspects of these agreements, the use of this "hybrid" model served to legitimize the entire scope of the collective agreements reached bilaterally, in a style reminiscent of the Austrian labor relations system and, more pointedly, of the original Consejos de Salarios.

The long accords reached as part of the June 1986 round of negotiations covered fourteen sectors and 70,000 workers. The average increase in real wages for many sectors came to 8.6 percent for the period between January 1, 1986, and May 31, 1987, which corresponded to a similar increase in industrial output. Many of these accords made use of a device for calculating inflation known as the *semi-suma*, which averaged the combined rate of inflation for the last quarter and that anticipated for the following quarter. The government adopted this system at the October 1986 round of Consejo negotiations. Areas of contention between the government and social agents diminished as a result, as did industrial conflict.

The October 1986 round of the Consejos brought two important innovations. First, the PIT-CNT instructed each union to negotiate its own agreement within each wage group based on its capacity for mobilization and negotiation. This was due to the fact that many unions were not participating in subsequent rounds until the terms of their agreements expired.[51]

This had various effects, not the least of which was the growth of income differences within sectors (since the weaker unions were unable to match the gains made by their stronger counterparts), as well as a search for longer-term agreements by a growing number of unions. In addition, changed criteria for adjusting wages, the use of differential pay scales, and the longer duration of many agreements combined to slow the rate of growth in real wages in the second half of 1986 and early 1987.

The architects of the Colorado government's economic program were not happy with the long accords. They proposed that all accords signed up to October be declared void and that all be renegotiated according to the *semi-suma* criteria. They were opposed by leading officials in the labor administration hierarchy. After much cabinet debate, an agreement was reached to allow existing accords to remain in force, while all collective bargaining after October 1, 1986, would have to abide by the inflation-wage transference criteria adopted by the economic team. Here we see the internal replaying of sectorial positions within the apex of the Uruguayan state apparatus: when the economic and ideological costs of social reproduction came into conflict, labor administration and economic management officials adopted opposing positions on the most important policy priority to be pursued. The fact that the debate was resolved by compromise also indicates that the state replayed internally the sectorial interaction taking place outside.

In the fourth round, which covered the period between October 1986 and January 1987, the government used the *semi-suma* criteria to establish a 17 percent transference rate (the previous inflation rate was 21.5 percent and the projected rate was 15 percent).

Initially, the fifth round of the Consejos, covering June–September 1987, was jeopardized by the employers' refusal to recognize the labor representatives (who were appointed rather than elected). They refused to participate in the Consejos until the 1943 law was completely rewritten and a new Law of Professional Associations drafted. The employers' action came in response to increased strike activity in certain sectors, much of which had overtly political overtones.

However, when the government refused to heed its demands, business abandoned its intransigent posture and returned to the concertative forums. The negotiations concluded with an unusually high average wage increase, attesting once again to labor's negotiating abilities within the tripartite forums. The next two rounds were uneventful, with transferable rates used in an effort to close the gap between projected and real rates of inflation.

As mentioned earlier, there were five possible voting outcomes in the Consejos. The evolution of the voting pattern shows a marked trend toward unanimous resolutions.[52] The fifth round (June 1987) witnessed the emergence of the first worker-employer majority decisions in the form of the fourteen long accords reached outside the Consejo framework but ratified within it. This pattern continued through the next rounds, as employers and unions found that autonomous collective bargaining was the most beneficial form of strategic interaction, even when decisions reached were subsequently submitted for state ratification within the Consejo framework.

Beginning with the June 1987 round of negotiations, autonomous collective bargaining increasingly became the preferred form of interaction, with or without state ratification. The fact that most of these agreements stayed close to the wage-transference guidelines established for the Consejos, and thus were easily ratified by the government, attests to the social agents' moderation and desire to project an image of "responsibility" to retain the levels of sectorial autonomy and prerogatives that had been achieved.[53] There was a clear trend toward increased cooperation and a "concertative vocation" on the part of both the state and sectorial agents.[54] This was reaffirmed by the long accords, which, when ratified by the state, pushed the number of unanimous agreements close to 100 percent.

The state's role in negotiating for the public sector, in which 20 percent of the economically active population is employed (275,000 workers), remains paramount. As both an employer and the regulator of macroeconomics, the government saw the need to combine efficiency in wage matters with basic social justice. Union representatives and administration officials in the public sector discuss (but do not negotiate) wage rates and working conditions within bipartite (state and labor) committees constituted for each branch, enterprise, or department of the state apparatus. However, an emergency services law prevented public sector unions from striking in specific areas.

Unions have generally been dissatisfied with this arrangement, which they feel merely places a concertative gloss on what are essentially unilateral economic decisions by the executive branch. From time to time, they have withdrawn from the committees entirely, though the negotiations have been useful in non-wage areas.

Wage adjustments and tariffs throughout the public sector were consequently made via executive decree on a quarterly basis, using the same criteria of adjustment (past inflation, predicted inflation, *semi-suma*) used in the Consejos, with the transference rate serving as the adjustment rate in the public sector. The quarterly adjustments are staggered with the Consejo rounds, occurring in March, July, and November. The overall effect of this arrangement has been to slow the rate of real wage growth in the public sector compared to the private sector.[55] Subsequent real wage gains in 1986–1987 occurred almost exclusively in the private sector, while public sector wages remained in constant terms close to the December 1985 levels.[56]

Nonetheless, increased consensus within the Consejos and in the collective bargaining between sectorial agents, coupled with the state's obvious concern to protect salaries in the face of inflation, were reflected in the gradual drop in the number of strikes throughout the 1985–1988 period. From March 1, 1985, to September 30, 1986, there were 949 strikes, as unions used the opportunity provided by redemocratization to forcefully press their economic and political demands after a long period of enforced silence. By all indicators — number of strikes, worker hours lost, number of workers involved — strike activity declined in the following years.[57]

Efforts to stabilize wage rates in the public sector in the face of inflation, agreements reached in the Consejos, and (as of 1986) the long accords containing anti-strike clauses, not only helped diminish the total number and duration of strikes during the first three years of the democratic regime (particularly in the public sector), but also altered their character. At both the material and the institutional levels, the bases of working-class consent were gradually and incrementally being established.

When we consider the overall role of the Consejos de Salarios in the Uruguayan process of democratic consolidation, it is apparent that, as the nexus in which the articulation of organized labor's social and economic concerns was promoted,

> their very existence contributed to favor some of the functional requisites of a pluralist system in the process of restructuring: affirmation of collective identities, establishment of rules of play, definition and redefinition of interests, identification of the adversary, mutual recognition of groups in the system, and a better evaluation of the forces at play, of the power of one's group and that of opponents; . . . it seems clear that in the process of democratic consolidation the rapid reconstitution of actors and arenas was a necessity, and the re-creation of the Consejos de Salarios a success.[58]

The Consejos served both to restore *and* to renovate, linking the institutional vestiges of the democratic past in economic relations with the necessities of consolidation, in an exercise of mutual sectorial legitimation and procedural reaffirmation that paralleled a complementary process of reconstitution in Parliament. A major reason for this success was the effectiveness of the state representatives involved in the Consejos in achieving concrete results. Beyond the recognition by agents of labor and capital that mutual substantive gains and legitimation could be realized in this concertative framework, another element that had a great importance, with regards to the success of the instrument of the *Consejos* . . . was the confidence that both professional parties had with regard to the equidistance of the delegates of the Executive Branch in each one of the *Consejos*. . . . The concern of those who supervised the [work] of the government delegates was [that they] operated with independent criteria [with respect to the sectorial agents].[59]

This was particularly true because negotiations in the Consejos were reinforced by two separate strategic "tracks." On one track, sectorial agents used their organizational resources to pressure both the state and the other actor in the Consejos. This was a favorite tactic of labor, which used its power to mobilize through strikes, coupled with an extremely classist, noncooperative rhetorical stance, to open space for itself within the concertative forums.

On the other hand, the employers' negotiating positions were hampered by a near-classic problem of collective action: disorganization and heterogeneity of interests. Employers preferred to negotiate collectively at the firm level and were loathe to provide information on the situation of firms for fear that competitors would exploit the situation. When their appeals to fix collective bargaining at the firm level were rejected in favor of sectorial negotiations within the Consejos, employers had little left in the way of a "threat in reserve" with which to pressure the other actors. Prevented by law from engaging in lockouts, employers had few external bargaining chips tied to organizational capacity or resource endowment. At most, they could refuse to attend meetings (as they threatened to do in 1986). In this sense, the relative ideological solidarity and organizational discipline of organized labor worked to its advantage, particularly during the first rounds of negotiations.

The second strategic track was the informal, ad hoc meetings held between the sectorial agents and high labor administration officials, particularly the minister of labor and social security, the national director of labor relations, and close advisers. In practice, supervision of the 220 Consejos ultimately rests in the hands of a half dozen officials, including those mentioned above and the coordinator of the Consejos de Salarios, who is directly responsible to the national director of labor relations. This small group of political appointees works closely with the government delegates to each Consejo, and when necessary, is directly involved in negotiations.

In many cases these officials have dealt directly with union and business representatives, by-passing the government delegates to the Consejos. These meetings were held outside the concertative forum and involved discussions with a similarly reduced number of labor and business representatives. Thus, informal negotiations among small groups, based on the personal relationship between labor administration officials and leading representatives of the sectorial agents, helped lubricate the negotiation process within the Consejos by promoting informal "understandings" that could later be codified as agreements in the concertative forums. This lent agility and efficiency to the system and demonstrates the value of personal bonds in Uruguayan labor relations.[60]

In addition to restoring the system of Consejos de Salarios and using the Consejo Superior de Salarios (COSUSAL) as an institution regulating national-level concertative approaches toward labor-capital interaction, the Sanguinetti government attempted to promote broader compromises among all social groups and political parties that followed on the heels of CONAPRO and played on its success.

The theme of a macrosocietal political-economic "pact" was resurrected periodically by the government, but a generalized consensus emerged that concertation was best promoted segmentally on specific economic and social issues, rather than at the macrosocietal (including the economic) level. This left actors free to pursue their national projects in the political market, specifically through the party system and competition for seats in Parliament and the executive branch, where the broad contours of national policy are determined. In effect, the segmental pursuit of sectorial material interests through neocorporatist concertative vehicles is paralleled by the pluralistic pursuit of ideological interests through the party system.

This suggests that, at least in Uruguay (given its historical legacy and present context), the institutionalization of democratic class compromise occurs incrementally at the meso- or microlevel, through agencies concerned solely with the basic substantive issues involved in the relationship between capital and labor, divided into productive sectors and occupations. With the basic material compromise achieved at this institutional level, labor and capital can wage broader campaigns in pursuit of their (contending) national projects in the political arena.

The segmental, microsocial nature of concertation in Uruguay is precisely what the labor movement desires. For the leaders of the PIT-CNT, the notion of a broad macrosocial pact such as the Spanish Pacto de Moncloa is anathema. So, for that matter, are notions of firm-level concertation in the form of codetermination and worker participation in management decisions popularized by advanced capitalist nations. For leaders of unions dominated by the PC, the usefulness of the Consejos lies in their ability to achieve material benefits for the rank and file: there is no compromise with capital and the bourgeois state, no reconciliation of class differences, no diminishing of class conflict, just a material agreement based on the second-best choice. For this reason, union representatives are not interested in having a voice in investment decisions or in the right to examine the firms' books. Making investment decisions is seen not as a step toward workplace democracy and an incremental move toward socialism, but rather as an open concession to the capitalist order. Looking at the books, on the other hand, is believed to promote cleavages within the working class based on increased salary differences within each sector.

Individual unions negotiate autonomous bilateral agreements with employers based on their constituents' approval, but making broad intersectorial pacts is tantamount to accepting the government's economic policy (which, the unions believe, is dictated by the IMF), therefore an act of antiproletarian complicity. Given the radical challenges to the PC's domination of the union movement, and the rank and file's power to approve or disapprove the agreements reached in the Consejos, the concept of broad concertation is clearly unappealing.

Thus the Marxist view of irreconcilable class differences — and hence class struggle — remains the political norm for labor leaders. However, given the failure of the frontal assaults associated with the revolutionary wars of maneuver attempted by the Tupamaros and their allies in the late 1960s and early 1970s, the strategy of the left has reverted to fighting an incremental war of position in the political, economic, and social fields.

The Consejos are the "trenches" where the battle is fought in the economic sphere. In the political sphere, the Frente Amplio concentrates on expanding its electoral base of support within the middle class, while in the social sphere both the PC and the remnants of the Tupamaros have redirected efforts to promote counterhegemonic apparatuses via the formation of cooperatives, housing associations, neighborhood groups, and related grassroots organizations among the poorest segments of the population.

Rhetorical militancy on the part of labor leaders and the regular flexing of the unions' muscles through strikes are seen as instruments for promoting class solidarity and establishing favorable negotiating positions within the Consejos. Unions trade off wage restraint not for increased investment but for employment guarantees, and may at times (depending on the union) exchange productivity increases for hikes in real wages. In the unions' view, it is the specific "relation of forces" that determines the particular choice of tactics, use of instruments, and outcomes of the segmented labor-capital strategic "game." To this end, and in order to play on capitalist contradictions, labor uses its own economic analyses to present its case in the most technical, neutral, depoliticized terms possible (though this produces internal contradictions, particularly in the acceptance of the capitalist logic of reproduction).[61]

Although the reconstitution of the Consejos de Salarios represented the linchpin of the democratic government's approach to labor relations, several policy areas also have a strong impact on the material and physical fortunes of the working classes. Issues such as social security, housing, nutrition, and cooperatives have been given particular attention by the labor administration, and traditional support services, advice, and training have been a mainstay of the MTSS's approach to the individual aspects of labor relations.

The state's preoccupation with providing social security and welfare services takes on added importance given the fact that, unlike Argentina and Brazil, Uruguay has no union-operated benefit programs. Responding to the orthodox Marxist dictates of its leaders, unions are seen strictly as instruments of economic defense and occupational protection; that is, they defend the position of the working classes in the productive process. Social services sponsored by the left come through the parties, particularly the PC and the Tupamaros, as the most important counterhegemonic apparatuses. For the leadership of these parties, the unions' usefulness is limited to instrumental defensive postures, and remains subordinated to the larger dictates of the party's strategic objectives.

As a result, the Uruguayan state has traditionally assumed full responsibility for providing for the basic welfare needs of the population. This has made it all the more imperative that the democratic regime reorganize and invigorate a system for providing benefits that stagnated in the late 1950s and early 1960s, and was eviscerated by the military regime in the 1970s.

In social security, the major concern was to reestablish basic levels of service and operative autonomy to the agencies that had been systematically closed or ignored by the military regime. The Colorado government reinforced the tripartite character of the foremost distributor of social security benefits, the Banco de Previsión Social (social welfare bank, or BPS) by enacting a new electoral law covering sectorial representation in directorship positions, which had been eliminated and replaced by a military directorship during the previous regime.

The state's contribution to the BPS was increased in order to expand the benefits package for individual recipients. By 1988, 23 percent of the GNP went for social expenditures, of which 70 percent went toward providing social security.

The government passed legislation that made minimum retirement benefits no lower than the minimum national wage, and as a complement, implemented an emergency solidarity plan through which food, clothing, and fuel were distributed to the poorest sectors of the population.[62] As a follow-up, a basic nutritional insurance plan, later termed the "National Program of Alimentary Complementation," was adopted, which ensured that families making less than the minimum wage would have access to the basic food products and hygienic necessities of daily life (the so-called *canasta familiar*, or family basket). Such families amounted to 10 percent of the population in 1985.[63]

Labor administration officials involved in this effort stressed that the program was an investment in the social and productive capital of the population, adopting the rationale that a well-fed (or at least adequately fed) work force is a more productive work force. Over 95 percent of the MTSS's budget for materials and supplies was channeled to agencies charged with administering the food program, attesting to the priority granted it by national labor administration. Overall, these agencies received 70 percent of the entire MTSS budget.[64]

In addition, the MTSS supervised an interagency program that operated 150 family support centers throughout the country, dedicated to preschool care services and primary preventive health care. The Colorado government also promoted cooperatives as a communal form of production.

The traditional areas of emphasis within national labor administration, the so-called individual aspects of labor relations, also received significant upgrading. Under the auspices of the Inspeción General de Trabajo (General Inspectorate of Labor, or IGT), the MTSS's responsibilities for labor hygiene and workplace inspection were restored to traditional positions of prominence. A new system of fines was installed, more inspectors recruited and trained for specific productive areas, and a number of courses offered to both managers and workers on labor, health, and safety issues. Over eighty-five such courses were taught in 1985–1987, including separate ten-day courses on labor safety and hygiene for syndicalists and mid-level managers.

Labor market support is handled by the National Employment Service, which does not in fact operate as an employment service, but instead conducts courses in vocational training, retraining, and assistance, and performs duties connected with labor market research, data collection, unemployment statistics, etc. The structural dislocations promoted by the military regime's economic policies made this an area of immediate priority, since the program was used to train and direct workers to new sources of employment, particularly when they required technical skills. As a result of this program and economic growth after 1985, unemployment dropped from a record high of 16.5 percent in 1984 to 13.51 percent in 1985, 9 percent by the end of 1986, and 8 percent in 1988 (only 1.07 percent of which was involuntary).

The government instituted a Fondo de Garantias de Insolvencia Patronal (Employer Insolvency Guarantee Fund), a special bankruptcy fund derived from a tax on corporate profits, which was designed to provide unemployment benefits to workers displaced by business closures. All firms were required to pay into this fund. Although the fund was not used extensively, over 100,000 workers used the labor administration's vocational training programs, and were successfully reincorporated into the work force.

The MTSS's legal assistance program expanded its services, providing free advice and counseling to individual workers, firms, and unions on matters related to individual grievances. In addition, it operated a mediation board to arbitrate disputes between individual workers and firms. Between 1985 and 1986, over 40,000 workers made use of the advisory services, as did 4,500 firms. The legal assistance services held 15,000 mediation sessions, of which 10,000 resulted in agreements by both parties. There were, in addition, registration, matriculation, and incidental services in this area.[65]

Other related areas received considerable attention as well. The national health system was revamped and given an infusion of funds.[66] Using international funds and the network of family assistance centers, the public health administration system moved to continue expanding coverage so that the population not receiving health services, particularly the elderly and the young, would receive proper care.[67]

In education, emphasis was placed on upgrading funding for the entire system and ensuring that the basic elementary school cycle was provided throughout the country. Public education received 15.65 percent of the central administrative budget by 1987, the largest amount allocated to any non-military ministry. The total allocated to public education from 1985 to 1988 represented a 10 percent increase over the expenditure levels of the military regime. As with the other aspects of the network for distributing public goods, the public education administration opted for centralized formulation but decentralized implementation, and gave priority to teacher training programs and programs for developing rural schools. This responded to the calls for community participation in local educational projects endorsed by the Colorado Party's Statement of Principles.[68]

In addition to the areas for which national labor administration was directly responsible and those public goods that constituted the larger institutional framework in which lower- and working-class needs were addressed, we need to mention the labor-related macroeconomic policy measures implemented by the democratic government. Although an exhaustive review of fiscal policy, exchange policy, and the like cannot be undertaken here, we can highlight the government's economic program to show its relevance to the operation of national labor administration.

The democratic regime inherited an economic crisis. In 1985 Uruguay's gross national product was 16.7 percent lower than it was in 1981, with a 50 percent drop in construction activities, a 20.6 percent drop in manufacturing, and a 12 percent drop in agriculture. Investments and capital stocks depreciated 55.7 percent in the same period, and the real wage was half that of 1968, with a full 20 percent of the decline occurring between 1982 and 1985. Salaries fell from 59 percent of total national income in 1967 to 43.2 percent in 1983, and unemployment reached record high levels of 16.5 percent (16 percent in Montevideo) in 1984.

The consumer price index rose by 50 percent in 1983, and another 66.1 percent in 1984. By 1984 the foreign debt amounted to $5 billion, or five times the total worth of national exports, and the interest on the debt absorbed 48.5 percent of export revenues. Beginning in 1980 and accelerating in 1982, capital flight amounted to almost one-fourth of the funds for repaying foreign loans. There was a corresponding increase in the rate of domestic debt and bankruptcies. Spending on public services, education and health in particular, dropped dramatically, and income distribution was compressed so that the top 5 percent of the population saw their income levels grow from 17 percent to 31 percent of the total national income in the period 1973–1978 (this percentage remained relatively constant thereafter).[69]

The agreements reached in the CONAPRO outlined the broad parameters of the government's economic recovery program: gradually increasing real wages as part of the revitalization of the domestic market; reducing interest rates; renegotiating the terms of the foreign debt; reestablishing the role of the state in providing public goods and orienting private investment; restructuring the incentive and taxation regime for exports; and returning exports to the center of the economy by offering a state-funded prefinancing system to the export sector. Interest rate ceilings were removed and the exchange system freed up, while the Central Bank reestablished its role as the macroeconomic manager of the financial system.

The Blanco Party and the Frente Amplio condemned these policies as a continuation of the neoliberal project of the authoritarian regime, which had been subordinated to the dictates of the IMF. The absence of a competing project on the part of these groups and the heterodox nature of this program, however, produced tangible results during the first three years of the democratic regime.[70]

The new economic program brought about a 14.6 percent national growth rate from 1985 to 1987, with the manufacturing sector rising fastest, by 15.3 percent annually. Exports reached record volumes in 1986, and by 1987 had increased in dollar terms 41 percent compared to the June 1985 rates. Although still below pre-1980 levels, public and private investment began to grow as well, moving from a low of $19 million in the second quarter of 1985 to a high of $65 million in the second quarter of 1987, averaging $129 million per year during this period (the level of investment reached $200 million in 1987).

These rates of investment surpassed those of the last years of the authoritarian regime, and began to approach the record levels of 1979–1980 (before the recession). All this pointed to renewed confidence among investors in Uruguay's political and economic situation. In addition, there was the repatriation of $429 million in 1985–1986, almost half the amount sent abroad during 1981–1984, amounting to approximately 8 percent of the GNP. Inflation dropped from 83.2 percent in 1985 to 57.3 percent in 1987, showing that the government's program of incrementalism in hikes in real wages and in prices was having the desired decelerating effect on the consumer price index. After a small increase in 1985 (0.7 percent), the GNP grew 7.43 percent in 1986 and 6.5 percent in 1987, while both the public deficit and private debt slowly decreased.[71]

It is clear that exogenous events, such as lower oil prices and interest rates on the international market and the opening of the Brazilian market with the announcement of the Plano Cruzado in 1986, considerably aided the recovery process. It is also undeniable that institutionalizing and stabilizing the labor relations regime contributed to renewed investor confidence.

To summarize the external dimension of Uruguay's labor administration in the restored democratic regime: The Colorado government sought to provide institutional guarantees for social reproduction in general by reemphasizing and invigorating the welfare state, to reaffirm and extend the basic citizenship rights that had been denied by the authoritarian regime. These rights were considered the underlying bases of society's consent to democratic capitalist rule. National labor administration, more strictly focused on the organized working classes, reconstituted the institutional mechanisms by which these classes, exercising autonomous sectorial prerogatives through their collective agents, could negotiate the specific material terms of the class compromise sector by sector.

The segmental nature of the class compromise promoted by the structure of tripartite concertation known as the Consejos de Salarios served a dual ideological and economic purpose. On the one hand, it gave to organized labor procedural equality when addressing capital on issues of material concern, with the state serving as a mediator, arbitrator, and enforcer. Even if not always prone to vote in favor of labor's interests, the state was sufficiently detached from capital so that its response was never assured. This forced social agents to negotiate more seriously with each other — a prerogative institutionally guaranteed by the state — rather than seek assistance from the state or run the risk of interference.

·Acceptance of these institutional mechanisms promoted a de facto substantive compromise based on labor's contingent and segmented consent to the material terms negotiated, which increasingly became the basis for longer-term agreements. The successful establishment of an equitable procedural framework for negotiating material interests reaffirmed workers' support for the democratic system, and particularly for the channeling of political demands through elections and parliamentary representation, precisely because these concertative vehicles were able to satisfy those material interests at an immediate level. Politics and economics became two separate fields of play for the rank and file; as a result, workers pursued dual strategies for aggregating sectorial interests. Class conflict was confined to the political arena, and class compromise became the norm in the economic sphere. These were the institutional bases of the new hegemonic system.

The segmental nature of the tripartite concertative forums disarticulated the working classes economically, removing some of the material grounds for class solidarity. Given the segmental and sectorial scope of the Consejos, the autonomy unions enjoyed as bargaining agents served as the root of this disarticulation, as each union's primary responsibility was to satisfy the immediate material needs of its members. Here counterhegemonic class consciousness bowed to sectorial imperatives for material self-improvement. Incremental economic satisfaction through procedurally democratic, segmental, and sectorial concertative mechanisms, coupled with a class-based political voice in Parliament, were the conditions for the working class's consent to bourgeois hegemony in Uruguay.

The Internal Dimension of National Labor Administration, 1985–1988

ORGANIZATION

Like Brazil and unlike Argentina, Uruguay did not suffer major organizational changes in its national labor administration when the democratic regime came into power. This was due in part to the gradual nature of the transition, which allowed the MTSS to adjust its bureaucracy to manage the rising tide of labor demands before the formal transfer of power, and in part to the nature of the MTSS itself under the military regime. From 1981 onward the basic orientation of the labor administration began to change, moving from the exclusionary state-corporatist posture of the 1970s to a more neutral administrative posture that emphasized the individual worker-related aspects of the labor relations regime, including labor inspection, legal advice, human resources, statistics, and research pertinent to that area of state activity.

The modifications made in Uruguayan labor administration in the 1970s and the state-corporatist aspirations of the military leadership notwithstanding, the basic features of labor relations during authoritarian rule were repression and silence, since the authoritarians were never able to reconstruct a lasting labor relations regime along the exclusionary lines envisioned. As a result, it was easily dismantled once the regime's foundational project was rejected and the process of voluntary withdrawal from power began.

The Colorado government inherited the organizational framework outlined by Institutional Act N.9/1979, Law 14,800/1978, and related decrees. The effect of this law was to expand the MTSS's powers to register unions and intervene in collective labor relations while simultaneously diminishing its role as monitor of individual workers's rights and narrowing or eliminating social security and welfare services. The Banco de Previsión Social (BPS) was eliminated along with a host of other decentralized agencies, and their responsibilities were delegated to the newly created Dirección Nacional de Seguridad Social in the MTSS. These areas received primary attention once the new government went about reconstructing the labor relations regime.

In 1985, the new organization of the MTSS was announced by ministerial decree. It was part of a general budgetary reform program that the government implemented to shift the areas of priority in the state's scheme for distributing finances. The MTSS was divided into three hierarchical levels: political, advisory, and operative. Each had its own set of lead agencies and dependencies. At the *political level* (Nivel Político) are the primary formulative agencies of the MTSS, responsible for crafting the broad outlines of labor policy under the Colorado administration. At the *advisory level* (Unidades de Asesoria) are the (division-level) agencies charged with advising the minister and his political cadre. At the *operative level* (Unidades de Linea) are the agencies responsible for implementing labor policy in their respective areas. There are eight operative "lines" in all, each led by an agency with the status of directorate.[72]

Each directorate or similarly ranked agency is considered the lead agency for implementation in its field and includes a general or national director as well as an office of the vice-director and an office of legal advice. Sections and departments can interact and consult with one another on issues of specific concern to each functional area, but the chain of authority requires them to answer through designated superiors when addressing matters of general policy.[73]

This division of labor in the MTSS results in three operative dimensions: labor-related activities, human resources and social welfare, and internal administrative tasks. Labor-related agencies do not occupy as much organizational "space" as agencies for promoting human resources and social welfare, but given the revitalization of the Consejos de Salarios and renewed collective bargaining and union activity at all levels, they enjoy disproportionate importance within the MTSS hierarchy. Otherwise, at the political, advisory, and operative levels, the organization of the MTSS hierarchy remains unchanged.[74]

Responsibilities of the operative branches of the MTSS were expanded considerably under the democratic regime. The number of agencies assigned to each implementing agency was increased, with a new compartmentalization of responsibilities to provide more rapid, reliable, and efficient support within the MTSS. These additions and changes responded to a need for an encompassing yet technically defined, functionally limited division of labor, to avoid overlapping and duplication of functions while promoting better provision of basic services in each area.[75]

The main agency for administering the collective aspects of the external dimension of the government's labor policy, the National Directorate of Labor (DINATRA), also experienced this compartmentalization and technical diversification of functional responsibilities. The primary change was the creation of two directorates below the national director's office, which added an entirely new level in the MTSS hierarchy. The DINATRA was the only operative branch to receive this new level because of its critical importance in national labor administration. The two new directorates were in Relaciones Laborales (Directorate of Labor Relations, or DRLR) and in Salarios y Administración de Trabajo (Salaries and Labor Administration, or DSAT).

Organizational changes were made to better integrate the work of the COSUSAL and the Consejos de Salarios within the MTSS. The new division of labor was designed to separate administration of salary negotiations, conducted through the tripartite forums, from the ongoing monitoring, conciliation, mediation, advice, and documentation functions of the MTSS in the field of labor relations strictly defined (that is, activities unrelated to human resources and the promotion of social welfare, and aspects of the labor relations system not associated with workplace inspection). National labor administration was thus permanently linked to the Consejos, in order to provide the administrative continuity, expertise, and facilities for successfully reproducing the tripartite forums. The logistical problems of these forums should not be overlooked. Several authors have noted the difficulty of locating permanent facilities for holding the Consejos.[76]

Through its restructured format, DINATRA represents a link to the historical mission of Uruguayan labor administration, providing legal advice, mediation and conciliation, union registration and classification, and general documentation services through the Directorate of Labor Relations. At the same time, it responds to the challenges of a new era in labor relations, being an entirely new institutional framework where the core of the labor relations system — the Consejos de Salarios — can be supported and reproduced by the state, specifically through the Directorate of Salaries and Labor Administration. In addition to the centralized agencies already mentioned, several agencies connected to the labor administration, like the BPS, provide autonomous services in the labor relations field.

In general, division of the MTSS into labor-specific concerns, human resource and welfare activities, and internal administrative tasks, with a move toward technical compartmentalization and specialization of functions in both externally and internally oriented branches, has resulted in the expansion of lower-level agencies. This indicates the growth of labor administration's presence and role in carrying out the external dimension of labor policy under the democratic regime.

BUDGET

The military regime had reduced expenditures on national labor administration to less than 1 percent of the central administrative budget, just as it was eliminating many public services provided by labor administration. The Colorado government moved to rectify this situation, which resulted in a dramatic increase in provision of services that had been cut by the authoritarian regime. The proportion of the central budget allocated to national labor administration rose to between 1.36 percent and 1.50 percent for the period 1985–1988. With the drop in the inflation rate, the real value of the funds allocated to national labor administration was maintained.[77]

Unlike the situation in the Argentine and Brazilian labor administrations (and virtually every other labor ministry in Latin

America), materials and supplies, rather than personnel expenditures, constituted the largest single allocation category in the MTSS. This was due to two factors: first, Uruguayan labor administration offered an unusually high level of public services in proportion to its size, especially nutritional programs; and second, the salaries of state delegates to the Consejos de Salarios were not funded by the MTSS, thereby eliminating a major source of personnel expenditures. Other than reversing the proportions of material and personnel expenditures, the resource distribution pattern within the MTSS and linked agencies was very similar to that of other national labor administrations in Latin America, and in fact matched nicely the type of distributional scheme advocated by international labor advisory agencies such as the ILO and the CIAT.[78]

As for the distribution of funds within the MTSS, activities related to human resources and social welfare consumed 73 percent of the MTSS's budget, while labor-specific activities (inspection, mediation, advice, etc.) accounted for 10 percent of the total allocated during 1985–1988.[79] Budget data confirm that the majority of the MTSS's budget is oriented toward providing public goods and services assigned to it by the division of labor within the state apparatus, while the bulk of expenditures in those branches not responsible for providing public goods (in the form of material services) is assigned to personnel.[80]

What is striking about the MTSS's budget, compared to the budgets of its Argentine and Brazilian counterparts, is that, while as a percentage of the central administrative budget it has maintained a level similar to that in the other two countries, it has far more responsibilities for providing public goods than either of the others. Not only is the usual financial distribution pattern reversed in the MTSS compared to the Argentine and Brazilian labor administrations, with material expenditures surpassing personnel allocations; the MTSS also provides public goods that neither of the other two systems offers, even though they have the same general budgetary parameters. Moreover, the services provided that are not public goods are essentially the same in each case, with the labor relations branch having the highest priority within the hier-archy, followed by occupational health and safety inspection ser-vices, administrative agencies, research, and advisory functions. Internal administrative agencies have the highest percentage of non-personnel allocations.

Closer analysis of budgetary allocations within the Argentine and Brazilian labor administrations reveals a disproportionately higher amount allocated to personnel-related expenses (which may indicate a certain level of featherbedding tied to the use of personal patronage networks); it also shows that the amount des-tined for general grants and/or discretionary funds is many times higher than that found in Uruguayan labor administration. Although it is unfair to speculate on what is not absolutely verifiable, it seems plausible that the use of discretionary alloca-tions in Argentina and Brazil remains another hallmark of labor administrations with historically strong state-corporatist tradi-tions (whether inclusionary or exclusionary), where co-option and control continue to characterize the labor relations partial regime even after the authoritarian regime is removed from power.

The MTSS's finances may be better accounted for in part because of the process for formulating the agency's budget. As with all cabinet portfolios, the MTSS contains a sectorial office of planning and budget attached to the minister's office. This adviso-ry agency is responsible for drawing up the ministerial budget, which is then made final in discussions with the political team con-stituted by the minister's closest advisers. Once formulated, the budget is forwarded to the president's office where it is debated, refined, increased, or cut in cabinet meetings. Macroeconomic cri-teria, particularly public sector rationalization schemes, are used to adjust the central administrative budget to economic realities.

Instrumental in this regard are the president's Office of Plan-ning and Budget, which is the senior agency of its kind in the nation and to which all the sectorial planning and budget offices located in the various ministries answer, using the same type of financial classification schemes and criteria employed by the super-ordinate agency. The Ministry of Economy also has a strong voice in determining the final budget submitted by the president to Congress.

Once the budget reaches Congress, various subcommittees and committees debate and amend it, responding to partisan concerns and constituent demands. After votes in various subcommittees and committees responsible for specific areas, a vote on the entire document is taken in full session of both houses. This is a lengthy process covering several months, so budgets formulated by the MTSS in November are not usually approved by Congress until the next April. In the interim, the entire state apparatus operates on contingency funds drawn against accounts approved by Congress in what sometimes culminates in a risky game of financial chicken for the agency administrators involved.[81]

Because of a budgeting agency linked to an overarching budget and planning department outside the MTSS, and because the budget must pass through the multiple levels of scrutiny before final approval, the Uruguayan labor administration budget has not seen the type of discretionary allocations that are commonplace in financial statements of its northern and southern neighbors. In this instance, the efficientist and technical criteria for rationalizing the state apparatus appear to have taken root, at least nominally.

PERSONNEL

The number of employees involved in national labor administration under Uruguay's democratic regime averaged 1,072 for the period 1985–1988, an increase of approximately 200 over that of the military regime. In some agencies (Interior Affairs and Cooperatives), the low number of employees in the MTSS was offset by the number working on contract in various departments of the interior and in cooperative development programs tied to municipal and provincial governments. Including these positions, the number of employees connected with national labor administration (but not financed by the MTSS) would rise to nearly 1,200.[82]

Most of those employed in the MTSS were classified according to civil service criteria, with the largest number falling into the clerical-technical category. Beyond that, significant numbers of employees were also classified as specialists in various fields, particularly nutrition and occupational health and safety, attesting to the importance granted those two branches of the MTSS. The sex distribution pattern within national labor administration shows 60 percent women to 40 percent men, with the majority of women occupied in clerical and technical positions. A disproportionate number of men were in the highest echelons of the hierarchy. The one area where this was not the case was among the state representatives to the Consejos de Salarios, of whom 60 percent were women. Otherwise, with some noticeable exceptions, the leadership cadre of the MTSS, as in the cases of Argentina and Brazil, was dominated by men.

Above the clerical-technical and specialist levels, the MTSS employed in advising or directing capacities a significant number of lawyers, accountants, economists, sociologists, social workers, and, in areas pertinent to their specialties, medical doctors, psychiatrists, and architects. Since the MTSS is responsible for formulating as well as implementing labor policy, a broad variety of specialists were brought into the MTSS hierarchy. If we recall the unique nature of the MTSS's activities related to human resources and social welfare and the division of labor in the implementing branches, employment of architects, nutritionists, doctors, and psychologists is not surprising. In the same light and following a more traditional pattern, the employment of lawyers, economists, accountants, sociologists, and the like in the leading agencies of the labor-specific branches (DINATRA, IGTSS in particular) responded to the obvious need for human expertise in these areas, since through such expertise were interpretations of labor legislation, labor market data, organizational dynamics, etc., brought to bear on the external dimension of the labor administration.

The mixture of merit-based and purely political positions at the highest levels of the MTSS was approximately fifty-fifty. The leading figures in the MTSS — the minister, vice-minister, and most of the directors general — were Colorado Party members drawn from the more progressive wings of that party. The same was true of the advisory staffs to the minister and his principal subordinates. In other areas, particularly below the political level of organization, expertise in a given field served as the criterion for selection. Many employees held responsible positions throughout the MTSS who did not belong to the Colorado Party. On the other hand, because of the overwhelmingly Marxist nature of Uruguayan unionism, no unionists were employed on the staff of national labor administration.[83]

A striking aspect in the personnel of Uruguayan labor administration was the relative youth of those employed in this area, even in high-ranking posts and among representatives to the Consejos de Salarios. Most of the Consejos representatives were under thirty, with university training in law, accounting, or labor-related fields. Likewise, the team in charge of the National Nutrition Institute (Instituto Nacional de Alimentación, or INDA) was made up entirely of young health professionals, as was the fifteen-person advisory team on social policy.

Virtually none of the delegates to the Consejos, except for a few of its presidents, had any experience with the Consejos held before 1968. Few were even in high school, much less in public service, in 1968, when the last pre-authoritarian Consejo negotiations were held. The new cadre of state representatives had to be trained in their mediatory and negotiating functions and instructed in the sectorial economics and productive characteristics of the sectors they were responsible for.

The president of each Consejo (the senior member of the three-person state delegation to the Consejos) was always a political appointee directly attached to the DINATRA director's office, but the two junior state representatives were most often selected on the basis of superior academic records in fields pertinent to labor. They either applied in open competitions for those positions or were nominated from within the MTSS. This added another measure of neutrality to the state's role in the tripartite forums. State representatives to the Consejos reported to the DINATRA hierarchy (in particular, to the coordinator of the Consejos) and to the minister's office. In many cases, these representatives were joined during particularly thorny negotiations by leaders of the MTSS themselves.

While Consejo presidents were responsible for presiding over six to eight Consejos in the same round, the day-to-day negotiations and logistics of the Consejos were handled by the two junior state representatives who reported to the Consejo coordinator and who, in effect, become the glue holding each Consejo together. Coupled with the "open door" policy of the MTSS leadership regarding dialogue with both the union and business leadership, this proved to be a successful way of reproducing the Consejos over the course of three years.[84]

The functional compartmentalization and technical specialization promoted at the organizational level had its corollary in the area of personnel, with numerous functionally defined specialists in various implementing branches. At the leadership level, strong partisanship (liberal Colorado) with merit-based selection criteria, particularly in areas in direct contact with the social agents, were the norms for personnel recruitment. The same criteria applied for the junior advisory corps, which proved instrumental in the MTSS's success.

The pattern of relative youth and multiple roles was repeated throughout the MTSS, even among influential members of the hierarchy. Minister Faingold himself was only forty-two years old at the time of his appointment.

Thus, the MTSS leaders represented a new generation of functionaries without links to the Colorado debacles of 1968–1973. They shared their opposition to the military regime with the younger generation of unionists. Although their ideological perspectives differed and were even opposed in many cases, this new generation of officials and unionists in a country as small as Uruguay, where personal relationships take on added importance, represented a rupture with the past and a reorientation for the future. As a result, employees in national labor administration showed a fresh approach toward the resumed democratic forms of strategic interaction that lie at the heart of the labor-capital relationship. Untainted by association with the past, sobered by formative years spent under dictatorial rule, these officials represented the living foundation of the new labor relations system in Uruguay.

Finally, turnover rates in the MTSS were extremely low, with just one upper-echelon shift in the first three years of the democratic regime. Save for normal attrition due to retirement and the wholesale purge of political appointees from the military regime immediately following the inauguration of the new government, the leadership cadre at the helm of national labor administration remained constant from 1985 to 1989.

That can be attributed to the strong sense of partisan loyalty binding the majority of these functionaries together and to their common perspective on labor relations that allowed for a uniform front before political adversaries inside and outside the labor movement. Based on a belief in tripartism, concertation, cooperative development, and *co-gestión* (roughly translated, co-tenure), this vision offered the ideological and programmatic cement that kept labor administration intact during Uruguay's first phase of democratic consolidation. Coupled with the success at macroeconomic stabilization and the equally successful reproduction of the Consejos de Salarios as wage negotiation forums, this gave the MTSS's political cadre a basis for job security that was lacking in its neighbor, Argentina, and that was far more stable than the ministerial leadership in Brazil.

Conclusion

Uruguay is the exception that proves the rule. Small and homogeneous in size, geography, and population, blessed with a long democratic tradition with both procedural and substantive roots prior to the authoritarian episode, Uruguay has restored and reconstituted a modified version of the traditional political system after a gradual, incremental process of top-down regime transition. Nonetheless, the transition culminated in the military's full return to the barracks (unlike the situation in Brazil), and was guided by a strong and ideologically united government party that was capable of negotiating from a position of strength with both its political opponents and the reactivated labor movement. Ultimately, national labor administration in Uruguay was able to reconstitute and reproduce the institutional bases of a democratic class compromise. Even though it is embryonic in its present state, this augers well for its full maturation in years to come.

In this, the pragmatic Marxist orientation of the union leaders, the emergence of the Frente Amplio as a viable political outlet for the left, and the continuation of a dualist strategy by the rank and file helped to restore democracy. Labor gained an ideological champion and an arena for political action. Simultaneously, the working classes received the best possible collective agents for segmentally negotiating the material bases of class compromise. Added to the restored and reformed welfare statism practiced by the Colorado government, the strategic posture of labor unions in postwar Western Europe under Social Democratic or Christian Democratic leadership come to mind as a basis for comparison. In fact, Uruguay appears to confirm some of the observations made about the importance that small size, economic location, and a homogeneity of population have had in successfully reproducing democratic class compromise in European capitalist democracies, which tend to have as a functional axis the institutionalization of neocorporatist, concertative mechanisms for formulating income policy.[85]

All this is perfectly captured in the external and internal dimensions of Uruguayan national labor administration. Externally, reassertion of its traditional interest in the individual aspects of the labor relations system was coupled with new, innovative programs for providing human resources and promoting social welfare, particularly through nutritional programs. Restoring autonomy to the BPS enhanced the provision of social security benefits after a long period of decline, while promoting cooperative projects, vocational training, occupational health and safety programs, and provision of legal assistance to workers all pointed toward the restoration of a broad network of state-provided services for the working and lower classes.

In parallel, the core of the restored democratic labor relations system has revolved around the reconstituted Consejos de Salarios, now under the tutelage of the state, and coordinated, however informally and episodically, with the umbrella tripartite organization, the Consejo Superior de Salarios. In disarticulating the working classes into wage groups to negotiate the material bases of class compromise sector by sector, the Consejos de Salarios have been the neocorporatist linchpin of the new hegemonic system. They offer democratic procedure (in the form of tripartite negotiation with neutral state mediation and unbiased voting formulas) coupled with substantive benefits (incremental gains in real wages) as a way of commodifying strategic interactions among various sectors. This activity has complemented the role of the Frente Amplio, where organized labor occupies a prominent position, in reinserting labor as a political actor into the democratic regime. Together, both vehicles have fostered the incorporation of the working classes, however much their agents may have resisted it on ideological grounds.

One proof of the success of this project was the gradual move toward longer-term agreements that combined moderate and incremental wage gains with labor peace in order to promote a more productive and stable investment climate. With gains in productivity increasingly exchanged for wage hikes, and employment stability exchanged for wage moderation, workers were gradually reinserted into the economic system as their material stake in it grew.

At the same time, the economic and political spheres of union action were increasingly distanced from each other, which is precisely what labor relations systems in the capitalist world have been oriented to all along.

By using a hybrid labor relations system in which neocorporatist arrangements (the Consejos) were coupled with the pluralist organization of autonomous sectorial interests, open competition in a loose bipartisan political system, and heavy state involvement as macroeconomic manager, political articulator, neutral guarantor, arbiter, and social welfare provider, Uruguayan labor administration successfully reconstituted the institutional bases of the working class's consent to bourgeois rule during the Colorado administration. As such, it stands as a beacon of stability in an otherwise uncertain and often bleak landscape of democratic consolidation efforts in the Southern Cone.

8

CONCLUSION

REGIME TYPE and regime change have a significant impact on public policy in the Southern Cone, particularly in "core" areas of state activity such as interest group mediation. This impact has been manifested in two interrelated areas. Externally, as Oszlak and O'Donnell theorized several years ago, the content of public policy shifts according to different regime objectives in specific policy areas. In the cases examined here, the shift was from an exclusionary to an inclusionary state-corporatist or pluralist approach toward national labor administration. In addition, particular nuances distinguished these attempts from earlier populist authoritarian and democratic experiments with inclusionary state corporatism. Internally, the state apparatus shifted in its organization to better pursue external policy objectives. Reorganization of the state apparatus is an integral part of regime change, since it is considered a necessary complement to implementing major shifts in public policy.

National labor administration adopted similar organizational features in Brazil, Uruguay, and Argentina. The process of decentralizing technical responsibilities defined by function at an organizational level and separating the functions of labor relations, welfare provision, and administration (in that order of priority), was cloaked in a procedurally neutral and clientelist legal mantle. Union recognition, legislative oversight, collective bargaining, and conflict mediation constituted the key functional "clusters" in the labor relations branches, while medical and welfare responsibilities occupied the bulk of the social welfare branches.

The functional decentralization of administrative tasks and the procedural neutrality of national labor administration contrasted sharply with the centralized, overtly coercive, and exclusionary state-corporatist labor administrations of the military regimes, and with earlier experiments with a populist, inclusionary state-corporatist labor administration (also characterized by centralized administration).[1]

Upper-echelon personnel showed a strong orientation toward the government party (initially a center-right party with several internal *tendencias*), though they represented its most pro-worker sectors. State managers employed in labor administration had expertise as labor lawyers, medical or technical experts in occupational health and safety, or labor economists. They had a clientelist orientation toward moderate labor demands, though more often they served as subordinate cabinet voices of union interests and bearers of bad news to labor from the capitalist-oriented cabinet portfolios. The common use of executive decrees to impose economic policies unilaterally reduced national labor administration's role in formulating macroeconomic strategy to promoting the labor pluralism needed to apply programs for free-market "liberal" austerity and structural adjustment.

Budget allocations to labor administration never surpassed 5 percent of central administrative expenditures, and the bulk of this was divided between the social welfare and labor relations branches. Even so, this was nearly double the allocations of the military regimes. The relatively equal balance of budgetary outlays between labor relations and social welfare branches in Argentina and Brazil suggests that the process of recognizing the unions and reconstructing the labor relations partial regime had a strong material basis in those cases. State managers focused as much (if not more) on the needs of working-class collective agents as those of union members. This focus was similar to that found in inclusionary corporatist systems, which rely heavily on patronage politics. The primary approach to labor policy emphasized inducements over exclusionary constraints, but this time with more procedural neutrality on the part of the state.

Institutionalizing non–zero-sum forms of class conflict was a fundamental objective of all governments that followed the authoritarian regimes. Although the strategies and specific institutional mechanisms varied from country to country and the process is still uncertain, incremental, and susceptible to reversal, the move toward substantive democratization of class relations in the Southern Cone ultimately turned on the institutionalized participation of labor as an important actor in political and economic decision making.

Thus, organized labor's political presence was revitalized among the working classes. Yet subsumed under the general resurgence of collective action among subordinate groups were shifts in the content and practice of social policy coming from the state, which opened institutional space to previously excluded sectors while reinforcing the ideological message that served as the cultural dimension of the new democratic projects.

Labor's economic participation revolved around the hard choices involved in negotiating mutually satisfactory exchange, wage, price, and investment strategies between sectorial peak associations. In post-authoritarian environments of crisis and austerity such as those of the Southern Cone, establishing mutually acceptable vehicles for economic negotiation and rebuilding labor organizations were in themselves major bones of contention between the state, labor, and capital. Procedural disagreements made it difficult to address the substantive bases of class conflict, thereby impeding the democratic consolidation process in Argentina and Brazil. The exception was Uruguay.

Despite the failure to promote national-level concertative agreements in Argentina and Brazil, all three regimes attempted to create institutional frameworks through which to negotiate the substantive terms of a reproducible class compromise. They initially used an external strategic approach that promoted tripartite negotiations at the national level. These complemented attempts to promote pluralist peak associations and more issue-specific or limited forms of bi- or tripartite concertation.

In each case, national labor administration took the lead in promoting democratic consolidation at the level of the labor relations partial regime. This is because, in the end, the economic terms, political arrangements, and related organizational conditions that frame democratic class relations all depend on the state apparatus — in the guise of functionally specified state agencies such as labor administration — as the ultimate enforcement mechanism. Over time, these elements together constitute the institutional bases of democratic class relations in capitalist societies.

With that in mind, we turn to an assessment of the reconstruction of the labor relations partial regime in the Southern Cone. In doing so, we also return to the central theoretical concern addressed in this study: the role of national labor administration as a core hegemonic apparatus of democratic capitalist regimes.

The Post-Authoritarian Moment

The democratic capitalist hegemonic projects that emerged in the 1980s in South America have structural and ideological roots in the military-bureaucratic authoritarian regimes of the previous two decades. The departed *dictaduras* applied two forms of "shock" to the body politic, one political and one structural. This prepared the social terrain on which hegemonic projects based on combinations of pluralism and free-market strategies could be pursued. The systematic application of coercion at the structural and superstructural levels, and the concomitant (and necessary) expansion of the repressive state apparatus at the expense of ideological state apparatuses,[2] "cleaned the slate" of the militant counterhegemonic projects voiced by increasingly empowered organizations of subordinate groups (workers, students, revolutionary guerrillas) during the 1960s and early 1970s. The fear of repression promoted varied degrees of individual atomization and infantilization which, coupled with the forcible disarticulation of networks of subordinate interest groups, resulted in the decomposition of collective identities into what amounted to an authoritarian "vacuum."[3]

The engineered decline in the working class's material standards of living was coupled with a sharp increase in the levels of

exploitation by foreign and domestic capitalists, who were attracted by the favorable investment terms of labor quiescence, low
import tariffs, and reduced domestic content quotas. Under the
umbrella of repression, foreign-trained architects of economic policy sought to restructure national economies to make them internationally competitive under the guidance of new "power blocs"
made up of international finance capital allied with transnational-
ized domestic entrepreneurial sectors. At the same time, they
sought to break once and for all the structural bases of working-
class power. Only in Brazil was this project moderated by nation-
alist economic interests and elite self-restraint.

The combination of the international economic and political
moment and the dialectics of class conflict and other social dynamics over the previous three decades framed the parameters in which
the new hegemonic projects were advanced. Yet seldom have environmental conditions so favored the reassertion of bourgeois
supremacy worldwide. The dissolution of Stalinist regimes and the
apparent nonviability of socialist development gave undisputed
primacy to market-oriented solutions coupled with the mechanisms of procedural democracy.

Having shown that they could dominate in concert with the
military, the principal economic interests of the Southern Cone
have now moved toward exercising ideological leadership, the
basis for hegemonic rule. We can highlight the microfoundations
of this process by illuminating the mutually reinforcing network of
overlapping institutional features promoted at the international,
national, and internal labor administrative levels.

Pluralism in Civil Society

If organized labor power is a function of the working class's standard of living, level of information, political resources, and collective representation, the material and ideological thresholds for
securing the consent of the subordinate classes to a class compromise in the Southern Cone were lowered substantially by the atomizing effects of military authoritarian repression.[4] Authoritarianism cleared civil society of the class-based militancy of the 1960s

and 1970s and sowed the seeds for reconstituting collective identities around pluralist ideals. With the rupture with the militant past completed, the reforging of new hegemonic projects could begin.

A pluralist ideological discourse tied to free-market (so-called neoliberal and heterodox) capitalist modernization strategies exalted the "freedom of choice" available in post-authoritarian settings. The political-cultural and economic dimensions of these projects were based on the ideological championing and structural reinforcement of non-class forms of mediation between subordinate interest groups. The primacy of the individual, exalted both at the social level and in the marketplace, was encouraged by the subordinate group's adoption of survivalist strategies during the *dictaduras*, which, coupled with structural shifts of the authoritarian regimes, heavily disrupted and altered collective identity, particularly subordinate groups' notions of citizenship and class solidarity.

These constraints accompanied the contraction of the formal economy around agriculture, finance, and tertiary and service industries, which were part of a dialectic that produced a highly diverse and stratified informal sector throughout the region. This informal sector resulted directly from the social and economic dislocations produced by the authoritarian regimes. So was the widespread rise in crime — also the result of the combined effects of economic crisis, relative relaxation of the repressive apparatus as it reverted to police functions under civilian rule, and the atomizing effects of the "limited citizen" survivalist concepts of social identity promoted by the dictatorships, in which social responsibility took a back seat to near-primal self-interest on the part of many individuals and social groups.[5]

The narrowing of notions of citizenship and class identity under the dictatorships included limiting the acceptable range of public discourse. What were public, collective issues became strictly private, individual matters, since there were severe sanctions on publicly airing private opinions on the rights of classes or citizens. Reading and writing between the lines was a common form of public discourse among subordinate groups, because any overt form of dissent in the military regime's climate of censorship brought reprisals. This was as true for Brazil, with its traditional distinction between "public" and "private" life,[6] as for the other Southern Cone nations, where historically the private and public aspects of citizenship and class relations have been more closely intertwined.

Only as the dictatorships waned did public discourse flourish anew, but even then, structural constraints made public expression more symbolic than substantive. The very expression of a public voice, codified in the transitional or foundational elections that ushered in the civilian regimes, was the most pressing issue of that time.

Expansion of what was properly construed as "private" life semantically and psychologically eased the way for the use of "privatization" to reduce the size of the state and stabilize the economy under the new democracies. State enterprises were auctioned off to private interests, most often consortiums of diversified foreign and domestic investors structurally buttressed by the dictatorships' economic policies. Significant cutbacks in state-provided public goods added to the reduced concept of citizenship — particularly in its public dimension — and helped lower individual expectations of public rights under the law. This reaffirmed the "minimalist" basis for securing the consent of subordinate groups to the democratic capitalist political form. Only in Uruguay did the process of redemocratization take a less feral path.

Under these conditions, the citizenship ties of the subordinate class were disrupted to the point that reconstituting them continues to be a project on its own. More pointedly, this apparent anomie has had a structural and ideological role to play in the reconstruction of bourgeois hegemony in post-authoritarian settings. Materially, it has provided labor market conditions (a large surplus of highly exploitable unorganized labor) conducive to foreign investment and justified the continued use of the repressive apparatus for overt social control. Ideologically, it has enhanced the value of participation and having a political voice of any sort. In the partial regime of state-labor relations, this has been manifested by encouraging the right to unionize and economism over collective strategies of class-based militancy. In pluralist labor relations systems, unions seldom engage in direct political action at the production level, preferring instead to use the party system and

Parliament for such purposes while confining collective action in production to the decentralized pursuit of economic objectives realizable within capitalist parameters.

Whatever the intent of the original labor projects studied here, since 1989 relatively successful strategies for stabilizing democratic capitalism have been based on policies that promote the atomization of labor and its exclusion from macroeconomic decision making. These have been pursued in lieu of a national-level, institutionalized class compromise between labor and capital.[7]

Marketplace hegemony and policy reform based on the so-called Washington consensus may succeed in sharply reducing the necessity for broad-based "consent" to bourgeois rule by the subaltern classes by weakening labor-backed parties, disarticulating civil society, and undermining labor's traditional strategies and bases of support. Here capitalist democracy may be possible without the institutionalization of labor's expanded participation along the lines of a European-style class compromise. Instead, it may be secured on the basis of a segmental, sectorial, piece-by-piece approach toward negotiating substantive agreements between labor and capital organized under pluralist guidelines. In increasingly stratified and heterogeneous societies, social integration and labor's subordination based on market discipline — with relatively few "economic-corporate sacrifices" by "leading groups" — along the lines of a post-Fordist "American model," may succeed in stabilizing procedural democracy, even if it is an elitist, exclusionary, and "hollow" version of it. Hence, limited democratic stability could possibly be based on the pluralist incorporation of labor as a completely subordinate actor.[8] The reproduction of a pluralist ideological discourse in the Southern Cone meshes well with the rebirth of civil societies marked by economically and politically weak subordinate groups and by "survivalist" atomization and individual alienation.

The Hegemonic Debate

As a mixture of concessions by the dominant group and consent by the subordinate group, bourgeois hegemony can be construed as a dynamic yet hierarchical debate[9] — at times one-sided, at other times more balanced — about the material and ideological terms of the class compromise that is the foundation of democratic capitalism.[10] According to Gramsci's conception of hegemony, the state's role in the debate is to aid the power bloc (the hegemonic class or class faction) in shaping the interests and needs of subordinate groups, to reproduce the relations of production on which the state's survival (as a socioeconomic and political institution) depends.

Capitalist democracy is a contingent outcome of the institutionalized conflicts that determine subordinate group consent to bourgeois rule. The combination of sectorial strategies determines the range of possible outcomes of these mediated conflicts qua "debates." "Democratic" institutions promote negotiated, mutual second-best (Pareto-optimal) outcomes based on notions of concession and compromise in order to secure and reproduce on an iterative basis contingent sectorial consent to elected civilian rule.

The hegemonic debate affects and reproduces not only a narrow part of the production process itself, but all social and cultural relations on which this process is imposed. The goal is to reproduce capitalism, but the audience extends beyond the working class. Hegemony also seeks to reproduce, at a micro level, the hierarchies of gender, ethnicity, religion, and race that underpin capitalism.

The debate may be arranged in different ways, with different strategies defining its limits and its topics. Some topics must remain outside the debate. "Touching the essential," that is, bringing about a fundamental transformation of the economic system, is "outside" the debate.[11] Likewise, militant sectors (e.g., guerrilla movements) are excluded (often by choice), and various other disorganized or marginalized groups (peasants, indigenous peoples, women) are excluded against their will.

Yet issues or sectors that are *outside* the debate may define what can be included *within* the debate. As long as certain topics are not broached and certain actors not admitted, there may be a broad freedom to promote and achieve consent on "legitimate" issues, because within the limits of debate there is "room" for corporate concessions. On the other hand, outside those limits, dialogue is not possible and negotiation is not an option. Should "forbidden" topics (such as the possibility of socialism or radical land reform that changes the proprietary rights of landowners) become an issue, the latitude for sectorial negotiation narrows significantly, since they threaten the economic and political system. Likewise, should previously excluded groups press for inclusion before the elite is prepared to admit them, the limits of tolerance may be breached, and institutionalized dialogue may break down.

The fundamental rule of the hegemonic debate is that, however inclusionary, it is between *unequal* actors. This inequality is structurally based on the dependence of all actors on the decisions of capitalists.[12] If the working class grows in strength, or the capitalist/state alliance weakens such that the participants threaten to become relatively equal actors, the "debate" stops and the move to a hegemonic impasse or stalemate begins. At that point the state moves toward an organic crisis where Caesarism prevails and *dominio* becomes the form of rule.

Labor Administration as Hegemonic Apparatus and Lens

No state apparatus is as critical to maintaining and reproducing democratic capitalist regimes as national labor administration. That is because only labor administration simultaneously fulfills the repressive economic and political functions necessary to secure and reproduce the working class's contingent consent to capitalist rule.

It is the "core" institutional nexus within which the hegemonic debate is joined. It is the forum where the basic material and ideological terms of capitalist concession and working-class consent to democratic capitalism are worked out, administered, and enforced by a procedurally "neutral," "autonomous," and "legalistic" state. The utility of national labor administration as a core hegemonic apparatus is not affected by reduced unionization in the post-authoritarian period, because this is still the only area where the working class appears "as a class" before the state and capital.

In its hegemonic role, the democratic capitalist state adopts a mediating and arbitrating role in the class conflict, ameliorating and mystifying class relations through a web of institutional mechanisms based on principles of procedural equality and commonweal. Contrary to Marx's belief that the combination of the universal franchise and private ownership of the means of production was inherently doomed to self-destruction, it is the state-mediated and regulated exchange of political and economic concessions and consent on the part of capital and labor that makes bourgeois rule palatable to the subordinate classes, and hence self-reproducing over the long term.

Ideological apparatuses (family, schools, the media, Parliament, etc.) play important roles as cultural "transmission belts" reproducing the hegemonic message throughout society in both the material and political dimensions of the social relations of production. Yet however much the cultural aspects of the hegemonic project, administered and mystified by these other ideological state apparatuses, may complement the labor relations partial regime, it is this regime that spotlights the essence of class relations — and the forms of class conflict involved. No amount of ideological mystification produced by other "transmission belts" can obscure this core functional task, and here the hegemonic project is most clearly observed.

In that light, and recognizing that it does not encompass the totality of the hegemonic experience, we can assert that national labor administration represents at the microfoundational level the clearest lens on the hegemonic system. Here working-class demands regarding relations in production (politics of production) and the social relations of production (politics of reproduction) are realized through institutional vehicles of political and economic representation and state-enforced guarantees of material and occupational standards. Within this web, national labor administration manages the political, economic, and repressive tasks necessary for securing the working class's consent to capitalist rule.

Hegemony as a Form of Rule

For Gramsci, hegemony (*egemonia*) was contrasted to *dominio*, or domination, where one social group or class alliance exercised power by force.[13] Hegemonic rule is a consensual political regime whereby the economically dominant classes (the hegemonic "bloc") exercise ideological "leadership" over the subordinate classes. Socialized in the ideas of the elite, the subordinated masses actively consent to be governed by a system in which they renounce class militancy in exchange for material and ideological payoffs such as a better standard of living and access to participation in government and politics. This exchange constitutes the base of democratic legitimacy in capitalist societies.

Whereas capitalist consent is an integral feature of any form of bourgeois rule, only democratic capitalism strives to cultivate and reproduce the working class's consent. This is the basic difference between *egemonia* and *dominio*, even if the latter is of the top-down, co-optive, passive revolutionary sort (e.g., fascism and populism). Regardless of their public or private character under bourgeois law (though the importance of this distinction as a device for mystification cannot be overlooked), all hegemonic apparatuses are rooted in the state (or at least regulated by it), which has both ideological and repressive functions. It is here that the importance of national labor administration as a hegemonic apparatus becomes clear.

Althusser pointed out that the democratic rule of capital is perpetuated by ideological and repressive means. Ideology inculcates citizens' acceptance of, if not consent to, the economic and political status quo. Repression constrains those who would challenge the foundations of that rule. Working in concert, ideology and repression serve to reproduce over time, mutatis mutandis, a given set of political, economic, and social relations. To fully understand the workings of the system, we must functionally "unpack" or disaggregate the state apparatuses to grasp their separate components, features that together add nuances — and strength — to the hegemonic project.

There is a clear distinction between overt and subtle coercion by repressive state apparatuses. On the one hand, there is the naked application of physical punishment to those who violate established norms of individual and collective conduct. This includes imprisonment, execution, torture, and other forms of applied duress, though the degree of acceptable punishment varies according to country and circumstance. Subtle coercion, on the other hand, includes the law, the formal codification of "common sense," and universally accepted standards of behavior. Civil law exerts very little repression, while criminal law uses it as both punishment and deterrent. Yet the imposition of fines, taxes, proscriptions, prohibitions, sanctions, and other nonrepressive restraints are all designed to punish unacceptable forms of conduct and enforce compliance.

Ideological state apparatuses operate on at least two levels of discourse. The economic discourse is the specific type of economic logic underpinning the capitalist project at a given time. The political-cultural discourse is the accepted terrain of individual and collective interaction outside the sphere of production. Here again, both dimensions overlap, and an "inner core" of coercion inhabits each one, yet they are analytically distinct spheres with autonomous features.

The more the ideological dimensions overlap with each other and mesh with the two levels of coercion, offering to citizens a semblance of congruence and coherence, the more likely that the hegemonic system will endure. The less the congruence, the more likely the possibility of hegemonic breakdown and organic crisis. The exact circumstances under which this might occur vary. In all cases, the stability of the hegemonic system rests not on the bifurcated actions of ideological and repressive state apparatuses conceptualized *grosso modo*, but on the complex dynamics of a network of apparatuses of both types spanning several levels of interaction.

Parliament and the party system — overlapping but distinct partial regimes — clearly play a role in all reproductive dimensions and are an important apparatus for securing the working class's consent to capitalist socioeconomic relations. However, these partisan and parliamentary partial regimes play strictly the roles of formulation and oversight. That is, they are vehicles through which the general bases of labor-capital interaction are periodically debated and ratified. Having no role in implementation, they are not involved in the ongoing daily administration of the specific, microfoundational terms on which working-class consent is founded. Nor are they the first point of contact between labor and the state at the levels of production and the social relations of (re)production. These are the exclusive province of national labor administration.

National labor administration alone manages the political, economic, and repressive microfoundational dimensions necessary for securing the working class's day-by-day consent to capitalist rule. As such, it exhibits distinctive traits in its use of coercion and concession vis-à-vis the working classes. At the repressive level, regulations governing union recognition, collective negotiation, mandatory arbitration, and strike legislation, which includes the government's strike-breaking powers, are all coercive disincentives or constraints that keep labor's demands within "proper" institutional channels. At the political and economic levels, minimum wage legislation and wage categorization by occupational stratum, procedural arrangements governing union organization and representation (both internal and vis-à-vis capitalist agents), occupational health and safety standards, mechanisms for redressing workers' grievances, and the provision of public goods all provide ideological concessions or inducements for labor to use institutional channels.

The iterative negotiation of political and economic concessions represents the organized system of trade-offs between coercion and consent that is the core of capitalist hegemony. Capital's corporate concessions to the demands of labor or of the subordinate classes mystify the aspect of coercion inherent in an economic system that requires workers to sell their labor to survive. In turn, subordinate classes consent to structural and political inequalities that privilege the dominant classes. This exchange constitutes the basis of a regime's legitimacy in democratic capitalist societies.

Institutionalizing labor's demands constrains capital by determining the minimum wage, working conditions, and benefits. Employers' capacity to exploit workers is reduced. At the same time, the state mollifies capital by forestalling challenges to the socioeconomic parameters of society by an overly militant or revolutionary working class. The institutional system reaffirms these parameters by guaranteeing certain procedural and substantive rights in exchange for workers' acceptance of the bourgeois status quo.

Although the policies and instruments for promoting democratic class compromise vary by national context and circumstance, it should not be surprising that the role and organization of national labor administration is extraordinarily similar under all democratic capitalist regimes. Its essential reproductive functions are to secure the ongoing institutional bases and microfoundational terms guaranteeing the material and ideological conditions for workers' consent to capitalist rule.

Labor Pluralism in a Hegemonic System

Pluralist labor relations systems are to the working classes what free-market economies are to capitalists: both systems promote increased intrasectorial competition, thereby contributing to overall economic efficiency. Yet economic efficiency so defined benefits capitalists, not workers, because it depresses the relative gains achievable by the working classes *in toto*. Pluralist labor relations systems combine with market economies to lower the overall wage bill, particularly in times of high unemployment (excess labor) and a growing informal sector. This level of exploitation is surpassed only in a regime where a totally unorganized labor force is subjected to the direct depredation of employers. Such superexploitation was the original intent of labor-related edicts enacted by the military-bureaucratic regimes that governed the Southern Cone in the 1970s.

Given the resurgence of free-market economic ideologies, especially in Latin America, and the depressed post-authoritarian economies of the Southern Cone in the 1980s, pluralist labor relations systems are now seen as an *apertura* by labor and a benefit to capital. However, this *apertura* reinforces the subordination of the working class to the interests of capital under an ideological mantle of equality that increases the legitimacy of capitalism.

Labor pluralism functions as a mechanism of hegemonic reconstruction on three interlocking levels: administrative, national, and international. National labor administration (the administrative level) is subject to global pressures to reorganize in a pluralist fashion. International demands are filtered through the state and translated into national policies that, in parallel, are influenced by internal pressures dictated by capitalist concerns and the various agencies involved in the labor relations partial regime.

Capitalists' concern with securing institutional bases for reproducing the working class's consent to bourgeois rule on a global scale is evident in the work of the International Labor Organization. The ILO began with an explicitly anticommunist orientation that over the years was combined with a "pluralist" focus designed to preserve the unions' autonomy and the freedom of organizations representing the working classes to organize and bargain collectively. The ILO's interest in fostering pluralism has compounded efforts to atomize working-class movements along economic or ideological lines. The strategic approach behind this procedural concern with "collective" rights keeps the labor movement segmentally focused and internally divided. Unions act as sectorial rather than class agents, and are therefore less prone to question — much less challenge — the rule of capital.

The ILO champions the pluralist aggregation of interest groups coupled with tri- or bipartite concertative bargaining at the micro (shop), meso (industry or region) and macro (national) levels. This leads to forms of interest mediation along materially or functionally defined terms that cut across class lines. Such forms of sectorial bargaining leave class representation to the parliament, where parties representing labor and other subordinate groups are relegated to a minority role behind mainstream, heterogeneous procapitalist parties. Lacking a united economic voice and a dominant political agent to represent them, the working class and subordinate groups can defend their interests only in a segmental, disarticulated, and often myopic manner. This belies the "freedom of choice" so often ascribed to pluralism. Simultaneously empowering the propertied classes and disempowering nonpropertied groups, pluralism exploits and reinforces the material hierarchy that is the structural foundation of capitalist systems.

Since 1983, a majority of ILO conventions have been legally ratified in the Southern Cone. All the regimes studied here advocate and use the ILO's standards of labor rights and freedoms. In particular, promoting ideological plurality within labor federations and confederations — achieved by labor legislation that guaranteed minority representation in union elections — was a common concern of all three governments.

This helped undermine the ideological homogeneity of labor leaders that had allowed them to use the labor movements and their main weapon — national strikes — as political vehicles. Political demands were shunted toward the parliamentary arena and voiced through parties, while unions themselves, and the (con)federations that grouped them together by sector or function at the regional and national levels, began to make more economic and material demands. As a result, unions redirected their attention toward employers and away from the state, thereby "privatizing" labor relations, which followed the general trend in the national economy. Thus, while the number of decisional sites to which labor had access increased, the substantive discourse in those sites was segmental rather than integrated, thereby reducing overall working-class power within the political and economic systems.

In all cases, there was a great temptation to use the vestiges of authoritarian institutions, and legal uncertainties in interpreting different labor codes allowed specific privileges to be accorded by law. With the exception of Uruguay, the problem of reconstructing the partial regime of labor relations also ran into the legacy of state-corporatist labor administrations inherited from the previous regimes, which made automatic adoption of the ILO's pluralist standards all the more difficult. Many in the Argentine and Brazilian labor movements — to say nothing of various business leaders and public officials — resisted them. Sectorial conflict over the ILO's pluralist standards resulted from the knowledge that state-corporatist labor codes offered something that no pluralist system could provide: a measure of control over other actors' behavior, coupled with specific sectorial prerogatives.

From the standpoint of the state and capital, pluralism is the best hedge against unrestrained working-class sectorial *unity*. The combination of state-corporatist legislation governing *collective* labor rights and pluralist labor codes governing *individual* workers' rights thus promoted the greatest amount of ideological leadership (and state control) of the working class. This integrated an *etatist* administrative approach to collective action issues coupled with a market-oriented approach toward individual material gains that would promote the disarticulation of subordinate interest groups and sectorial diversification not based on class. Only in Uruguay was this not entirely the case.

In every case, progress was made toward adopting more open and autonomous labor relations frameworks, not only when compared to those of the departed dictatorships, but also with regard to the pre-authoritarian labor relations systems. This was true for pluralist Uruguay and for state-corporatist Argentina and Brazil, since the reconstitution of the labor relations partial regime in Uruguay was complemented by the emergence of the labor-based Frente Amplio as the third political force in the country. Coupled with the continued strength of the Peronist Party in Argentina and the emergence of the Partido dos Trabalhadores (PT) in Brazil, the rise of the Frente Amplio as a viable political agent in Uruguay gave labor in the Southern Cone a parliamentary presence that expanded the number of class agents *and* decisional sites to which the working class had access in attempting to influence the course of state-labor relations. In this regard progress was made, albeit to different degrees, toward institutionalizing democratic class relations in all three countries.

The utter disruption of the models of accumulation displaced by the authoritarian regimes was an obstacle in all three nations. Somewhat perversely, it actually strengthened the move toward consolidating a democratic partial regime of labor relations. Rather than push the limits of their material demands (as would occur in expanding economies characterized by excess demand

and full employment), sectorial agents concentrated on negotiating the material "floor" — most often wages and prices, but also issues of health and welfare, social security, investment support, tariffs, and exchange rates — needed to stabilize their productive sectors and pacify increasingly restive members. More important (and more successful), the lack of structural grounds on which to create a material base for generalized working-class consent in all three countries opened space for negotiation with the state on the political agreements and institutional mechanisms to be used in the pursuit of substantive (material) compromises. Thus the common interest in pressing for a definition regarding the labor codes and related legislation from Parliament and the labor courts.

Labor Pluralism at the National Level

In addition to legislative reform in Parliament, labor courts were set up according to neutral legal criteria that would recognize the autonomy of agents for labor and capital, and the need for state mediation and oversight of enforcement in the labor relations system.[14]

In most of the cases studied, state agencies (led by labor ministries) negotiated the legal boundaries of the new labor relations system, while economic and political agents defended their class and organizational interests. In these negotiations, the combined effects of previous labor relations frameworks and union characteristics led to different strategic perspectives by the labor movements in each country. State approaches remained relatively constant in promoting labor's pluralism and using economic *dirigismo* on the part of the executive branch.[15]

Where there was a legacy of a state-corporatist labor administration and a divided labor movement (Brazil), labor attempted to unify at the federational or sectorial level, using pluralist procedures for representation at the shop level to achieve a societal corporatist presence in the labor relations system. Where a legacy of pluralism in both labor administration and the unions had led to unified classist control of the labor movement (Uruguay), the move was to restore the status quo ante at the institutional level. Where there was a state-corporatist legacy in the labor administration and labor had been relatively unified under a party-dominated, vertical, and centralized union structure (Argentina), labor preferences gravitated toward restoring the corporatist framework, albeit with an inclusionary slant.

The greatest degree of consensus was between the Uruguayan state, labor, and capital in favor of reconstituting the pre-1968 labor relations partial regime centered on the tripartite, concertative Consejos de Salarios. This approach was based on strategies of cooperation that focused on "minimizing losses" over "maximizing gains" and led to reforms that have kept all actors playing the game but have made no sector entirely happy. This is the essence of pluralism.

In Argentina and Brazil, negotiations over procedural frameworks have been more contentious, owing to the combined effects of the ingrained authoritarian attitudes and ongoing political strength of many capitalists, entrenched authoritarian institutions in both the state and labor, and the political and economic divisions within the labor movement, among business leaders, and in the government, which made tactical opportunism rather than strategic uniformity a preferred way to secure political advantage. Thus substantive democratization in these countries is less advanced than in Uruguay. This highlights the importance of a pre-authoritarian democratic legacy as an institutional precondition for class compromise — or at least democratizing class conflict — in post-authoritarian contexts.

Initially, maintaining capitalists' consent to democratic rule was at least as big an issue as securing the consent of subordinate groups, since the withdrawal of capitalist consent invites a regression to authoritarianism. This checked the government's ability to accede to the demands of subordinate groups to gain their consent and restricted the nature of these demands. Only in Uruguay has capital's consent been less assiduously pursued than labor's consent.

Yet both types of sectorial consent are necessary for bourgeois hegemony. While capitalists' consent is needed for the transition to elected government and initial, short-term democratic consolidation, the long-term stable reproduction of democratic capitalism hinges on securing, and contingently reproducing, the consent of subordinate groups. Thus, whereas the recent pluralist projects may promote the disarticulated acquiescence of subordinate groups over the short term, the long-term consolidation of these regimes will ultimately depend on the substantive incorporation of organized labor as a full social actor. Anything short of this invites the withdrawal of working-class consent to the project of pluralization.

Summary

Global and national changes in the 1980s offered unprecedented environmental conditions for promoting new hegemonic projects of capitalist democracy in the Southern Cone.[16] The consolidation of these projects hinges on bringing the collective agents of the working classes, organized labor in particular, into the socioeconomic and political systems as full, but subordinate, social actors by institutionalizing the ideological and material terms of a class compromise.

National labor administration is at the core of any such project, being a hegemonic apparatus that simultaneously fulfills the institutionalized ideological and repressive functions required to secure the working class's consent to bourgeois rule. The chances of democratic consolidation in Latin America's Southern Cone rest on the extent to which national labor administration is used to promote new hegemonic projects construed along these lines.

These state apparatuses have become key sites for reproducing a "new pluralism" in the Southern Cone. The microfoundations of the new hegemonic projects related to class conflict are generating self-sustaining dynamics that make it unlikely that these regimes will regress to authoritarianism. The process of democratic consolidation has begun, uprooting the tradition of authoritarianism so deeply inscribed in the collective memory. Yet this process is extremely complex and delicate, fraught with contradictions and trade-offs, and nowhere assumed simply because a "democratic vocation" exists among citizens of countries previously dominated by authoritarianism.

Of course, the possibilities for class compromise, while encouraging in the political realm, continue to be based on capital's willingness to offer structural concessions. A legacy of capitalist super-exploitation, followed by the current economic austerity, indicates that capital is able to make limited procedural and substantive agreements (or concessions) to workers; it does not prove, however, that it will keep them indefinitely, or in the same measure. For such compromises to succeed, long-term substantive material exchanges must be promoted and renegotiated within the labor relations partial regimes, adding structural microfoundations to the democratic consolidation.

The emerging ideological consensus on the institutional dimensions of class compromise is manifested in the creation of pluralist, democratic partial regimes of labor relations. Nevertheless, as I have argued here, even though class compromise is managed by "legalistic" and "neutral" labor administrations, the post-authoritarian context of the pluralist projects strips labor relations of any semblance of "equilibrium" between labor and capital. While the pluralist projects offer workers the right to unionize and therefore to participate, they simultaneously undermine workers' collective efforts in support of their class interests.

This highlights the subordination of workers to capital, particularly on the uneven material terrain reinforced by the authoritarian regimes, but even under procedurally democratic capitalism. While this last type of rule may lead to liberal democratization, which would be no small success for the post-authoritarian regimes, it is still a far cry from *substantive* democracy in its economic, social, and political dimensions.

The question is whether to look at the Southern Cone as a glass half empty or half full. Optimists may regard the post-authoritarian openings as an opportunity to wage counterhegemonic wars of position within the ISAs, sowing the seeds for a peaceful move toward democratic socialism. Pessimists will note that the prospects for socialism in Latin America have seldom been dimmer, and that where peaceful electoral transitions to democratic socialist regimes have occurred (e.g., Chile in 1970), they were overthrown by force. Whatever the outlook, bourgeois hegemony is clearly being reconstructed in the Southern Cone on the micro-foundations of a pluralist ideology that is institutionalized at multiple levels. As seen through the lens of state-labor relations, this project combines with authoritarian legacies of individual atomization to mystify the very class weakness it perpetrates.

We end on a wary note, acknowledging that much progress in labor relations has been made in all three cases (and elsewhere for that matter, such as in Chile), even as we shy away from offering a prognosis for the long-term success of the regimes in question. Through trial and error, learning from past mistakes, and adapting extrahemispheric examples to the realities of the Southern Cone, these countries are well on their way to consolidating democratic partial regimes of labor relations using national labor administration as the institutional core of the hegemonic project. That move appears increasingly irreversible.

A new generation of working-class leaders, capitalists, government officials, and the public at large have slowly begun to explore the fruitful possibilities of adopting nonmaximalist, mutual second-best strategic postures and negotiated forms of conflict resolution in virtually all social contexts (including those of crisis). With hegemonic and counterhegemonic projects overlapping to such a degree, the room for sectorial compromise broadens considerably and may lead to the stable reproduction of society.

Here lies a new basis for hope, for these orientations are the essence of democratic discourse at all levels of interaction, from relations between individuals to relations between classes. Reinforced through institutional mechanisms throughout the partial regime network, such "minimax" sectorial strategies underpin the broader web of relational practices that ultimately form the ideological basis for democratic political culture. Above and beyond the material constraints and specific ideological objectives of the moment, this is what underrides the long-term possibility for hegemonic reproduction.

We are expectant about the future, hoping that through a combination of *virtu* and *fortuna* we will see the microfoundations of the new hegemonic projects related to class conflict in the Southern Cone generate self-sustaining dynamics that make the prospect of regression to authoritarianism remote, if not impossible. If such is the case, the process of consolidating substantive democracy has begun, thereby altering the tradition of authoritarianism and exploitation so deeply inscribed in the collective memory. Turning away from this dark past, we look to a brighter future.

NOTES

BIBLIOGRAPHY

INDEX

NOTES

1. Class Compromise and Democratic Consolidation in the Southern Cone

1.   The literature on redemocratization has grown exponentially over the last fifteen years and cannot be cited in full here. A good overview of the major points addressed by this body of work can be found in C. Acuña and R. Barros, "Issues on Democracy and Democratization: North and South. A Rapporteur's Report," working paper 30, Kellogg Institute, October 1984. As for the literature itself, see G. A. O'Donnell, "Notas para el estudio de procesos de democratización política a partir del estado burocratico-autoritario," *Estudio CEDES* 2, 5 (1979); E. Baloyra, ed., *Comparing New Democracies* (Boulder: Westview Press, 1987); J. Malloy and M. Seligson, eds., *Authoritarians and Democrats* (Pittsburgh: University of Pittsburgh Press, 1987); G. A. O'Donnell, P. Schmitter, and L. Whitehead, eds., *Transitions from Authoritarian Rule: Prospects for Democracy*, 4 vols. (Baltimore: Johns Hopkins University Press, 1986); L. Diamond, J. Linz, and S. M. Lipset, eds., *Democracy in Developing Countries: Africa, Asia, and Latin America* (Boulder: Lynne Rienner, 1988); L. Diamond and G. Manks, eds., *Comparative Perspectives on Democracy* (Newbury Park: Calif.: Sage Publications, 1992); K. Middlebrook, "Prospects for Democracy: Regime Transformation and Transitions from Authoritarian Rule," working paper 62, Wilson Center Latin American Program, 1980; Middlebrook, "Notes on Transitions from Authoritarian Rule in Latin America and Latin Europe," working paper 82, Wilson Center Latin American Program, 1981; R. Scholk, "Comparative Aspects of the Transitions from Authoritarian Rule," working paper 114, Wilson Center Latin American Program, 1982; K. Remmer, "Redemocratization and the Impact of Authoritarian Rule in Latin America," *Comparative Politics* 17, 3 (April 1985): 253–76; E. Viola and S. Mainwaring, "Transitions to Democracy: Brazil and Argentina in the 1980's," *Journal of International Affairs* 38, 2 (Winter 1985): 193-

219; C. Gillespie, "Review Essay: From Authoritarian Crises to Democratic Transitions," *Latin American Research Review* 22, 3 (Fall 1987); and, for a study of the role of social movements in these processes, E. Viola and S. Mainwaring, "New Social Movements, Political Culture, and Democracy: Brazil and Argentina in the 1980's," *Telos* 61 (Fall 1984). For a more descriptive survey of the Southern Cone, see the special issue of *Government and Opposition* 19, 2 (Spring 1984), titled "From Authoritarian to Representative Government in Brazil and Argentina."

2. See L. Diamond, "Crisis, Choice and Structure: Reconciling Alternative Models for Explaining Democratic Success and Failure in the Third World," in Diamond, Linz, and Lipset, eds., *Democracy in Developing Countries*.

3. Besides the now classic work by G. A. O'Donnell, *Modernization and Bureaucratic Authoritarianism: Studies in South American Politics* (Berkeley: University of California, 1973), see idem, *El Estado burocrati-co-autoritario* (Buenos Aires: Editorial de Belgrano, 1982). Other good examinations of military-bureaucratic authoritarianism and its impact on the state are found in J. Malloy, ed., *Authoritarianism and Corporatism in Latin America* (Pittsburgh: University of Pittsburgh Press, 1977); and D. Collier, ed., *The New Authoritarianism in Latin America* (Princeton: Princeton University Press, 1979).

4. The best works to date on modern democratic consolidation in the wake of authoritarian transitions are those produced by the SSRC-Kellogg Institute project on "Dilemmas and Opportunities in the Consolidation of Democracy in Contemporary Latin America," which also included the participation of CLADE (Argentina), CEBRAP (Brazil), CEDYS (Peru), and CIESU (Uruguay). These include: J. Nun and J. C. Portantiero, eds., *Ensayos sobre la transición democrática en la Argentina* (Buenos Aires: Editores Puntosur, 1987); F. W. Reis and G. A. O'Donnell, eds., *A democracia no Brasil: Dilemas e perspectivas* (São Paulo: Edições Vertice, 1988); L. Pásara and J. Parodi, eds., *Democracia, sociedad y gobierno en el Peru* (Lima: CEDYS, 1988); and several shorter monographs and journal essays by Juan Rial and Carina Perelli on Uruguay, published by CIESU as part of their Documento de Trabajo series. In English, see S. Mainwaring, G. A. O'Donnell, and J. Valenzuela, eds., *Issues in Democratic Consolidation* (South Bend: University of Notre Dame Press, 1992).

5. By structural bases of class compromise, I am referring to the economic and material benefits awarded the organized working classes in return for their acceptance of liberal democratic rule (i.e., in exchange for these benefits, they agree to renounce class-based revolutionary struggle designed to bring about fundamental change in the political and economic

systems). These structural bases are most often worked out via collective bargaining, state mediation, and political agreements between organized labor, employers associations, and the political authorities. In effect, these structural bases are both institutional and substantive. The notion that the maintenance of democracy requires structural bases is derived from arguments offered in A. Przeworski and M. Wallerstein, "The Structure of Class Conflict in Democratic Capitalist Societies," *American Political Science Review* 76 (June 1982): 215–38; A. Przeworski, "Class Compromise and the State: Western Europe and Latin America," unpublished paper, University of Chicago, June 1980 (a Spanish version of this essay can be found in N. Lechner, ed., *Estado y política en America Latina* (Mexico City: Siglo XXI, 1981); and idem, "Economic Conditions of Class Compromise," unpublished paper, University of Chicago, December 1979 (a revised version appears under the title "Material Interests, Class Compromise, and the Transition to Socialism," *Politics and Society* 19 (1980): 125–53). Przeworski has compiled his extensive thoughts on this and many other subjects in two recent books: *Democracy and the Market: Political and Economic Reform in Eastern Europe and Latin America* (New York: Cambridge University Press, 1991), and *The State and Economy Under Capitalism* (New York: Harwood Academic Publishers, 1992). The ideological bases of democratic capitalism are explained by L. Althusser in *For Marx* (London: Penguin Books, 1969); and *Lenin and Philosophy and Other Essays* (New York: Monthly Review Press, 1971).

6. This passage is derived from comments made by Fabio Wanderley Reis at the Conference on Microfoundations of Democracy, University of Chicago, April 29, 1988. Any misinterpretations are my own.

7. It is not possible here to delve at length into the full range of implications inherent in notions of economic democracy. For a brief look into the applications such notions have for the workplace, see chap. 2, n. 11.

8. For a discussion of the differences between various democratic systems and how they apply to the transitions to democracy in Argentina and Brazil, see Viola and Mainwaring, "New Social Movements." On inclusionary versus exclusionary democracy as a regime type, see K. Remmer, "Exclusionary Democracy," *Studies in Comparative International Development* 20, 4 (Winter 1985–1986): 64–85. For a general survey of the different levels of democracy, particularly the differences between "state" and "societal" democracy, see R. Perez, "La articulación de la sociedad y el Estado: Una sugerencia metodológica," *Cuadernos del CLAEH* 37, 1 (1986): 57–73.

9. C. Offe, "Societal Preconditions of Corporatism and Some Current Dilemmas of Democratic Theory," working paper, Kellogg Institute, 1984, 17.

10. See Robert Barros, "The Left and Democracy: Recent Debates in Latin America," *TELOS* 68 (Summer 1986): 68.

11. José Nun, "Democracia y socialismo: Etapas o niveles?" in *Los caminos de la democracia en America Latina* (Madrid: Pablo Iglesias, 1984), 257ff; cited in Barros, "The Left and Democracy," 68.

12. On the notions of "horizontal" versus "vertical" dialogue, see G. A. O'Donnell, "On the Fruitful Convergence of Hirschman's *Exit, Voice and Loyalty* and *Shifting Involvements*: Reflections from the Recent Argentine Experience," working paper 58, Kellogg Institute, February 1986.

13. Liberalization is a process of transition via managed reform (*reforma*) which often involves negotiation by elites of exit agreements with the opposition (a transition through transaction or *reforma pactada*). It involves a gradual softening of authoritarian rule, as in relaxation of censorship, but is not to be confused with democratization.

14. These and many other dimensions of peaceful authoritarian demise are vigorously explored in O'Donnell, Schmitter, and Whitehead, eds., *Transitions from Authoritarian Rule*, esp. vols. 3 and 4. For a critique, see D. Levine, "Paradigm Lost: Dependence to Democracy," *World Politics* 40, 3 (April 1988): 377–94.

15. A stronger case can be made for Chile in 1989, though it remains outside the scope of this study. On the Chilean transition and its impact on labor-state relations, see E. M. Putnam, "Deconstructing Hegemony: The State/Labor Partial Regime in Chile" (M.A. thesis, University of Arizona, 1992).

16. For a comparative view of top-down transitions to democracy, see D. Share and S. Mainwaring, "Transitions from Above: Democratization in Brazil and Portugal," working paper 32, Kellogg Institute, December 1984; and Mainwaring and Share, "Transitions through Transaction: Democratization in Brazil and Spain," in W. Selcher, ed., *Political Liberalization in Brazil* (Boulder: Westview Press, 1986). The notion of democratic transition as a political bargain is taken from A. Przeworski, "Suggestions for an Empirical Agenda," paper presented at the Conference on Democratic Consolidation, Saõ Paulo, December 25–27, 1985, 5–6.

17. On the general notion of political language as it pertains to social and interpersonal discourse, with particular reference to the Southern Cone, see O. Landi, "Sobre lenguajes, identidades y ciudadanias políticas," in Lechner, *Estado y política en America Latina*, 172–98; and G. A. O'Donnell "*y a mí, que me importa?* Notas sobre sociabilidad y política en Argentina y Brasil," working paper, Kellogg Institute, January 1984.

18. Here, the fact that institutionalizing democracy occurs after procedural democracy is achieved makes the question more rather than less interesting. It highlights the fact that the timing of the consolidation of substantive democracy is not linearly related to its procedural aspect.

19. On this point, see M. A. Garretón, "The Failure of Dictatorships in the Southern Cone," *TELOS* 68 (Summer 1986): 71–78.

20. On the military's penetration of Chilean institutional life, see C. Huneeus and J. Olave, "A participação dos militares nos novos autoritarismos: O Chile en una perspectiva comparada," *DADOS* 30, 3 (1987): 275–310.

21. It is interesting to note that in Uruguay a popular referendum was held on the issue, with 52 percent of the voters favoring amnesty for the military leaders of the authoritarian regime. The vote was split along generational rather than partisan lines, with those over the age of thirty-five favoring amnesty. The issue of post-authoritarian military legacies, including the questions of military contestation and self-perceived "prerogatives," is discussed in A. Stepan, *Rethinking Military Politics: Brazil and the Southern Cone* (Princeton: Princeton University Press, 1988). See also L. W. Goodman, J. S. R. Mendelson, and J. Rial, eds., *The Military and Democracy: The Future of Civil-Military Relations in Latin America* (Lexington, Mass.: Lexington Books, 1990).

22. The term "secular communion" is attributed to an unnamed Chilean politician by Peter Winn, an observer of the Latin American Studies Association to the 1988 Chilean national plebescite, recounted at the Conference on the United States and Latin American Democracy, University of Southern California, April 6–9, 1989.

23. Although the existence of a pre-authoritarian democratic political culture by no means assures democratic consolidation in the wake of authoritarian withdrawal. Robert Barros argues that the pre-authoritarian character of the Chilean party system and the uneven survival of political parties frustrated the transition to civilian rule. See "A Democratic Past, Strong Political Parties, But No Transition to Democracy: The Paradox of Chile Explored," paper presented to the Latin American Studies Association Fourteenth International Congress, New Orleans, March 1988. On the other hand, the experience with factory-level salary councils (the Consejos de Salarios) dating back to 1943 in Uruguay provided tangible institutional foundations for securing sectorial agreements under the new regime. See H. Rodriguez, *Nuestros sindicatos* (Montevideo: Centro Estudiantes de Derecho, 1966).

24. M. A. Kaplan, "Recent Trends of the Nation-State in Contemporary Latin America," *International Political Science Review* 6, 2 (1985): 96.

25. For an example of working-class socialization as an authoritarian legacy, see Y. Cohen, "The Benevolent Leviathan: Political Consciousness Among Urban Workers Under State Corporatism," *American Political Science Review* 76, 1 (March 1982).

26. For a more detailed look at the impact of authoritarianism on sub-

sequent processes of democratization, see Remmer, "Redemocratization and Authoritarian Rule"; and G. A. O'Donnell, "Democracia en la Argentina: Micro y macro," working paper 2, Kellogg Institute, December 1983. Given the historically high levels of state tutelage of sectorial interests in the Southern Cone — often formalized via state corporatist arrangements that incorporated sectorial hierarchies into the state bureaucratic apparatus — the degree of political closure imposed by the military-bureaucratic regimes paradoxically encouraged the emergence of autonomous, representative currents within various excluded sectors, particularly organized labor. The elimination of traditional institutional channels of sectorial representation, coupled with the use of a high degree of coercion to enforce authoritarian exclusionary programs, encouraged the formation (however surreptitiously at first) of more representative currents closely tied to the constituent bases of each sector. Unbeholden to traditional modes of interest group representation, these new currents repudiate both the pre-authoritarian and the authoritarian status quo, and are much more responsive to their constituencies. However, the impact of such groups is evident only after the procedural transfer has taken place. The visibility and weight of traditional political actors and sectorial agents force new currents to join established vehicles in the initial phase of (re)democratization. Having done that, these new currents must wage an internal battle to reorient the perspective (and often the composition) of the established vehicles or break away and compete as separate agencies. Again, this happens after the procedural transition to democracy has occurred, and constitutes part of the effort to overcome authoritarian legacies and consolidate the institutional bases of substantive democracy.

27. A. Viña, "Democracia liberada en un pais bloqueado," *Cuadernos del CLAEH* 32 (1984): 29–38. See also Barros, "A Democratic Past."

28. O'Donnell, Schmitter, and Whitehead have been accused of being unduly pessimistic when assessing these factors, and for undervaluing actors' intrinsic (as opposed to tactical) interest in liberal democracy. See Levine, "Paradigm Lost."

29. The results of different societal equations in post-authoritarian situations can be formulated as follows. Where democratic values (DV) in civil society are greater than elitist-corporatist/authoritarian values (E-C/A) a simultaneous consolidation of procedural and at least two substantive (institutional and societal) levels is possible: (DV > E-C/A —>P+(IS)E). Where DV-E-C/A, the sequential consolidation of democracy is more likely: DV-E-C/A —>P+(I+S+E). Where DV < E-C/A, a new era of "hollow" democracy based on elitist institutions ensues (DV < E-C/A —>P+I*, where I* = elitist institutions). To this last scenario (DV < E-C/A) we can add, again, the outcome that would preclude or abort democratic consolidation at all levels, namely, regression to authoritarianism.

An alternative way of conceptualizing the potential for democratic consolidation, again in very general terms, might be as follows:

$$C^* = D\text{-}A(F)/E$$

where C^* = democratic consolidation (both procedural and substantive); D = Democratic culture; A = Authoritarian tradition or vestiges; F = Form of regime change; and E = Macroeconomic context. Where A>D, and F is top-down, the chances of substantive democratic consolidation are low; where D>A, and F is bottom-up, the chances of successful substantive democratic consolidation are higher; where D-A, (F) takes on special importance in determining the chances of C^*.

The product of the superstructural variables (D-A(F)) is divided by the structural variable (E), because of the universally recognized importance economic factors have in determining the viability of democratic regimes. This structural dependence is accentuated in dependent capitalist contexts of crisis. It should be underscored that the specifics of this equation and its modification in the direction of C^* rest on institutional factors. That is, the weight of authoritarian legacies, democratic practices, macroeconomic conditions, and forms of regime change all have a specific institutional manifestation that can aid or hinder the process of democratic consolidation.

The problems in measuring these different ethos are obvious, and I make no claim to be able to respond to them adequately. One might use public opinion polls and survey data to arrive at some assessment of societal values, but even that would inadequately explain the gradations and subtle changes at play in the polity. An appraisal of this issue is offered in Perez, "La articulación de la sociedad," esp. 58–59.

30. See A. Przeworski, "Democracy as a Contingent Outcome of Conflicts" (unpublished manuscript, University of Chicago, 1983). It is reprinted in Portuguese under the title "Ama a incerteza e serás democrático," *Novos Estudos CEBRAP* 9 (July 1984): 26–46.

31. The notion of partial regimes is derived from P. C. Schmitter, "The Consolidation of Political Democracy in Southern Europe" (unpublished manuscript, Stanford University, July 1987).

32. Ibid., 54–57.

33. Legitimacy can be seen as *organized* consent, where consent is defined as acquiescence motivated by objective agreement with (and preference for) a given set of values, norms, and rules governing sectorial competition. A. Przeworski, "Some Problems in the Study of the Transition to Democracy." In O'Donnell, Schmitter, and Whitehead, eds. *Transitions from Authoritarian Rule*, 3:11.

34. D. Rostow, "Transitions to Democracy," *Comparative Politics* 2, 3 (April 1970): 357. Rostow is referring to J. Bryce, *Modern Democracies*, vol. 2 (London: n.p., 1921).

35. It should be noted here that competition is more political than economic. P. C. Schmitter nicely summarizes the political dimension of contingent consent as follows: "Political actors agree to compete in such a way that those who win greater electoral support will exercise their temporary superiority and incumbency in government in such a way as not to prevent their opponents who may win greater support in the future from taking office, and those who lose in the present agree to respect the authority of the winners to make binding decisions on everyone, in exchange for being allowed to take office and make similar decisions in the future." P. C. Schmitter, "Organized Interests and Democratic Consolidation in Southern Europe (and Latin America)," (draft research proposal, European University Institute, November 1984), 10.

36. For a discussion of the concept of "contingent outcome," see Przeworski, "Democracy as a Contingent Outcome of Conflicts."

37. M. Carnoy, *The State and Political Theory* (Princeton: Princeton University Press, 1984), 245.

38. The term, of course, is Lenin's. See *Selected Works,* vol. 2 (Moscow: Progress Publishers, 1970).

39. S. Prates, "Cambios estructurales y movimientos populares: Reflexiones sobre la concertación social en el Uruguay post-autoritario," in CIESU, *Enfoques sobre la concertación* (Montevideo: Ediciones de la Banda Oriental, 1984), 115.

40. On the notion of "pact sequence" and its application in Venezuela, see J. McCoy, "Labor and the State in a Party-Mediated Democracy: Institutional Change in Venezuela," *Latin American Research Review* 24 (1989): 35–67. See also K. Neuhowser, "Democratic Stability in Venezuela: Elite Consensus or Class Compromise?" *American Sociological Review* 57 (February 1992): 117–35.

41. Witness as an example the secret military-orthodox Peronist rapprochement initiated in 1983 in Argentina, which was hastily abandoned once public attention to the subject was raised by the press and the Radical Party, and was criticized by "renovating" Peronist factions. Speculation had the orthodox Peronist leadership offering guarantees of continued budgetary discretion and immunity from prosecution for military officers involved in the "dirty war" in exchange for military noninterference in future political affairs and support for the Peronist candidates in the 1983 elections. The *górila* factions in the military and among the Peronists continued to pose the most serious authoritarian challenges to the Radical government throughout its tenure, and are believed to have forged an alliance behind the Peronist presidential candidate in 1989, Carlos Menem.

42. The role of elite pacts is discussed in J. Higley and R. Gunther, eds.,

Elites and Democratic Consolidation in Latin American and Southern Europe (New York: Cambridge University Press, 1992).

43. N. Bobbio, *El futuro de la democracia* (Barcelona: Plaza y Janés, 1986), quoted in A. Abós, *El Posperonismo* (Buenos Aires: Editorial Legasa, 1986), 139.

44. Przeworski, "Economic Conditions of Class Compromise," 20.

45. A. Przeworski, "Capitalism, Democracy, Pacts: Revisited," paper presented at the Conference on the Microfoundations of Democracy, University of Chicago, April 29–May 1, 1988, 6.

46. For an introduction to game theory, see M. Shubik, *A Game-Theoretic Approach to Political Economy* (Cambridge: MIT Press, 1984); and R. Hardin, *Collective Action* (Baltimore: Johns Hopkins University Press, 1982).

47. For use of game theory constructs along these lines, see G. A. O'Donnell and P. C. Schmitter, "Tentative Conclusions about Uncertain Democracies," in O'Donnell, Schmitter, and Whitehead, eds., *Transitions from Authoritarian Rule*, vol. 4; and F. W. Scharpf, "The Political Calculus of Inflations and Unemployment in Western Europe: A Game Theoretic Interpretation," paper presented at the Conference on the Microfoundations of Democracy, University of Chicago, April 29–May 1, 1988.

48. See W. C. Smith, "Heterodox Shocks and the Political Economy of Democratic Transition in Argentina and Brazil," in W. W. Conack, ed., *Debt, Austerity and Development in Latin America* (Boulder: Westview Press, 1989), 139–40; and idem, "Democracy, Distributional Conflicts and Macroeconomic Policy-Making in Argentina, 1983–89," *Journal of Interamerican and World Affairs* 32, 2 (1990): 1–42.

2. The Political Economy and Institutional Bases of Democratic Class Relations

1. On notions of structural dependence, see C. Lindblom, *Politics and Markets* (New York: Basic Books, 1977), 173–75; C. Offe, "The Capitalist State and the Problem of Policy Formation," in L. Lindberg et al., *Stress and Contradiction in Contemporary Capitalism* (Lexington, Mass.: Lexington Books, 1975); A. Przeworski, *Capitalism and Social Democracy* (Cambridge: Cambridge University Press, 1985), esp. chap. 5; idem, "Marxism and Rational Choice," *Politics and Society* 14, 4 (1985), esp. 393–95; A. Przeworski and M. Wallerstein, "Popular Sovereignty, State Autonomy, and Private Property" (paper prepared for the Conference on Policy Dilemmas in Front of the Crisis of State Regulatory Capacities in Europe and Latin America, Instituto de Investigaciones Europeo-Latinoamericanas, Buenos Aires, October 14–16, 1985); and idem, "Struc-

tural Dependence of the State on Capital," *American Political Science Review* 82, 1 (1988): 11–29.

2. See Przeworski and Wallenstein, "Structural Dependence of the State on Capital," and idem, "Popular Sovereignty."

3. A. Przeworski, "Toward a Theory of Capitalist Democracy," (University of Chicago, 1977, mimeographed), 7.

4. Jungwoon Choi, "The English Ten-hours Act: Official Knowledge and the Collective Interest of the Ruling Class," *Politics and Society* 13, 4 (1984): 456.

5. A. Gramsci, *Selections from the Prison Notebooks*, ed. and trans. Quintin Hoare and Geoffrey Norwell Smith (New York: International Publishers, 1971), 61.

6. J. Nun, "La Teoria política y la transición democrática," in Nun and Portantiero, eds., *Ensayos sobre la transición*, esp. 36–47. "Social accumulation regime" refers to the assemblage of social and economic practices rooted in a given productive structure. As such, it is very much a fluid entity with its own particular set of dynamics, contradictions, and evolutionary characteristics.

7. M. F. Masters and J. D. Robertson, "Class Compromise in Industrial Democracies," *American Political Science Review* 82, 4 (December 1988): 1185.

8. Ibid., 1188, 1185, and 1184.

9. L. Panitch, "Trade Unions and the Capitalist State," *New Left Review* 125 (1981): 26.

10. Competition between workers as "teams" rather than as individuals on the assembly line has the effect of reducing worker solidarity both at the individual level and vis-à-vis management as a whole. Labor and management are ostensibly made "partners in production," thereby ensuring overall capitalist reproduction based on a restrained rate of profit. Obviously, exploitative methods of capitalist control are becoming more opaque, both in the workplace and in the modern labor administration.

11. It should be emphasized that the focus here is on the macroeconomic level, and deliberately omits discussion of the now extensive debate over economic democracy in the workplace (e.g., employee participation in management, producer cooperatives, wage-earner investment funds, worker-management "codetermination," etc.). Nonetheless, it should be intuitively apparent that economic democratization of the workplace gives workers a larger stake in the productive process, and hence would strongly support, at a microeconomic level, the establishment of the structural bases of democratic class compromise envisioned here. That is, cooperative management, labor integration into the deci-

sion making of the controlling group, etc., lend themselves more readily to joint control over investment decisions at a macroeconomic level both within and across economic sectors. It has been suggested that workers involved in cooperative management schemes are more disposed toward wage restraint because of their more apparent self-interest in increased profitability, higher rates of investment, expansion, productivity, and consequent long-term material gains. Moreover, the solidarities and material interests across sectors generated by such arrangements work to increase mutual calculations of self-advantage and diminish the perceptions of risk of both sides when negotiating the precise terms of the compromise. In any case, our attention here is directed toward the role of particular branches of the state in providing an institutional framework that at a macroeconomic (and political) level is conducive to establishing the structural bases of democratic class compromise. For a succinct discussion of the concept of economic democracy (though sketchy in its presentation of neo-Marxist views on the subject), see Drew Christie, "Recent Calls for Economic Democracy," *Ethics* 95, 1 (October 1984): 112–18. For a more complete analysis, see Michael Burowoy, "Marxism Without Microfoundations," *Socialist Review* 89, 2 (1989); idem, "The Contours of Production Politics," in C. Berquist, ed., *Labor in the Capitalist World Economy* (Beverly Hills: Sage Publications, 1984); and idem, *The Politics of Production* (London: Verso; New York: Schocken Books, 1985). For an intriguing view of how economic democratization of the workplace in advanced capitalist societies potentially creates the structural conditions for a transition to socialism, see P. G. Schervish and A. Herman, "On the Road: Conceptualizing Class Structure in the Transition to Socialism," *Work and Occupations* 13, 2 (May 1986): 264–91; and A. Herman, "Conceptualizing Control: Domination and Hegemony in the Capitalist Labor Process," *Insurgent Sociologist* 11, 3 (1982): 7–22.

12. The argument made in this paragraph (including definitions of controlling and noncontrolling groups) is drawn from C. N. Pitelis, "Corporate Control, Social Choice, and Capital Accumulation: An Asymmetrical Choice Approach," *Review of Radical Political Economics* 18, 3 (1986): 85–100. Any errors and modifications are my own.

13. On the range of state activities used to this effect in Latin America, see Kaplan, "Recent Trends," 89.

14. Przeworski, "Capitalism, Democracy, Pacts: Revisited," 31.

15. International Labour Organization, *Public Labor Administration and Its Role in Economic and Social Development*, report 2, Eleventh Conference of American States Members of the International Labour Organization, Medellín, Colombia, September–October, 1979 (Geneva: International Labour Office, 1979), 46.

In general, the substantive terms upon which democratic class compromise is based include "immediate salary issues and indirect benefits, public goods and services, [improved or stable] perspectives on questions of employment and job stability, the `equitative' distribution of [economic] costs, the immediate demands and longer-term expectations in which social and economic programs weigh heavily, the specific orientation of private and public investment, the focus of production and amplitude of the market, in so far as they all point towards more promising forms of development and a more adequate distribution [of resources]." J. L. Lanzaro, "Movimiento obrero y reconstitución democrática. Convencionalidad neocorporativa o aplicaciones neoliberales?" *Revista Mexicana de Sociologia* 17, 2 (1987): 203.

16. M. B. Rosenberg and J. M. Malloy, "Indirect Participation Versus Social Equity in the Evolution of Latin American Social Security Policy," in J. Booth and M. Seligson, eds., *Political Participation in Latin America*, vol. 1, *Citizen and State* (New York: Holmes and Meier, 1978), 168. For an overview of social security programs in Latin America, see C. Mesa-Lago, *Social Security in Latin America* (Pittsburgh: University of Pittsburgh Press, 1978), which includes discussions of Argentina and Uruguay. For Brazil, see J. M. Malloy, "Social Security Policy and the Working Class in Twentieth Century Brazil," *Journal of Interamerican Studies and World Affairs* 19, 1 February 1977): 33–60; and idem, *The Politics of Social Security in Brazil* (Pittsburgh: University of Pittsburgh Press, 1979).

17. I am indebted to Darren Greybill for calling my attention to this point.

18. For a concrete Latin American example, see K. Neuhowser, "Democratic Stability in Venezuela: Elite Consensus or Class Compromise?" *American Sociological Review* 57, 1 (February 1992): 117–35. Events in 1992 suggest that neither alternative exists any longer.

19. Although the withdrawal of capitalist consent has been well discussed in the literature on the demise of democratic regimes and the rise of bureaucratic-authoritarianism in Latin America, less attention has been devoted to the withdrawal of labor's consent as a precipitating factor in these processes. In the three countries studied here, it was precisely the withdrawal of organized labor's consent before the capitalist defection that signaled the crisis of the pre-authoritarian regimes. No matter how they responded, the regimes were unable to reform-monger a new base of labor consent, which led to the popular mobilizations that, as O'Donnell has noted, breached the threshold of capitalists' perception and tolerance of threat. On this, see J. Linz and A. Stepan, eds., *The Breakdown of Democratic Regimes: Latin America* (Baltimore: Johns

Hopkins University Press, 1978); G. A. O'Donnell, *Modernization and Bureaucratic Authoritarianism: Studies in South American Politics* (Berkeley: University of California Press, 1973); Collier, ed., *The New Authoritarianism*; and Malloy, ed., *Authoritarianism and Corporatism*.

20. On the contradictions of this exchange, see C. Offe, "Societal Preconditions of Corporatism,," 18.

21. It should be clear that I am referring here to organized labor as a whole, that is, as a collective agent and social actor, and not to individual workers, whose individual strategies may well differ. For a discussion of workers' strategies, see the sources cited in chap. 3.

22. Offe, "Societal Preconditions of Corporatism," 11.

23. Among many others, see L. Panitch, "Recent Theorizations of Corporatism: Reflections on a Growth Industry," *British Journal of Sociology* 31 (1980).

24. The preceding discussion of labor strategies and figure 2.1 are drawn from C. Crouch, *Trade Unions: The Logic of Collective Action* (London: Fontana Books, 1983), 111–14.

25. This typology is derived from that offered by A. Przeworski in a lecture presented at CEDES, Buenos Aires, November 11, 1986.

26. W. Smith, "Heterodox Shocks," 151.

27. See J. Elster, *Ulysses and the Sirens* (New York: Cambridge University Press, 1983).

28. This outline of the general obstacles to democratic class compromise is drawn from Przeworski and Wallerstein, "The Structure of Class Conflict."

29. Schmitter, "Organized Interests and Democratic Consolidation," 10. It should be noted that there is a difficulty inherent in Schmitter's view. Having an institutional ability to diminish uncertainties of an economic type is one thing; having an institutional ability to diminish expectations is quite another, and, I would guess, a far more complex issue.

30. The literature is too vast to cite here. For good reviews and summaries of the main themes, see G. Lehmbruch, "Concertation and the Structure of Corporatist Networks" and M. Regini, "The Conditions for Political Exchange: How Concertation Emerged and Collapsed in Italy and Great Britain," both in J. Goldthorpe, ed., *Order and Conflict in Contemporary Capitalism* (Oxford: Oxford University Press, 1985).

31. For a more recent approach, see Schmitter, "Organized Interests and Democratic Consolidation."

32. The most obvious difference are that, while in advanced capitalist societies concertation serves as a mediating and stabilizing mechanism that ameliorates the effects of stop-and-go cycles associated with the internationalization of the economy, in dependent capitalist countries the

state is often confronted with situations of economic stagnation and severe fiscal crisis. This necessarily changes the orientation of concertation and complicates its mission. On concertation in the Southern Cone, see C. Pareja, "Las instancias de concertación. Sus presupuestos, sus modalidades, y su articulación con las formas clásicas de democracia representativa," *Cuadernos del CLAEH* 32 (1984); M. Grossi and M. R. Dos Santos, "La concertación social: Una perspectiva sobre instrumentos de regulación económico-social en procesos de redemocratización," *Crítica y Utopia* 9 (1982): 127–47; M. Cavarozzi, L. de Riz, and V. Feldman, *Concertación, Estado, y sindicatos en la Argentina contemporanea* (Buenos Aires: CEDES, 1986); *Novos Estudos CEBRAP* 13 (October 1985): 2–44 (special section on social pacts and redemocratization, with emphasis on Brazil); P. Mieres, "Concertación en Uruguay: Expectativas elevadas y consensos escasos," *Cuadernos del CLAEH* 36 (1985): 29–44; N. Lechner, *Pacto social en los procesos de democratización. La experiencia Latinoamericana* (Santiago: FLACSO, 1985); A. Canitrot, "Sobre concertación y la política economica. Reflexiones en relación a la experiencia argentina de 1984" (Buenos Aires, 1985, mimeographed); and G. A. O'Donnell, "Pactos políticos y pactos económico sociales. Por que sí y por que no" (Buenos Aires, 1985, mimeographed).

33. C. Pareja, "Las instancias de concertación," 39–41.

34. J. A. Silva Michelena and H. R. Sontag, *El proceso electoral de 1978* (Caracas: Editorial El Ateneo de Caracas, 1979), 51; cited in C. I. Davis and K. L. Coleman, "Labor and the State: Union Incorporation and Working Class Politization in Latin America," *Comparative Political Studies* 18, 4 (January 1986): 401.

35. For the most thorough review of the recent process of democratic transition experienced by Uruguay, see C. Gillespie, et al., *Uruguay y la democracia*, 3 vols. (Montevideo: Ediciones de la Banda Oriental, 1984–1985).

36. For a lengthy discussion of the factors involved in transitions from authoritarian regimes, see G. A. O'Donnell and P. C. Schmitter, *Tentative Conclusions About Uncertain Democracies*, vol. 4 of *Transitions From Authoritarian Rule*.

37. For an excellent conceptualization of concertation during processes of transition, and of organized labor's role in it, see Lanzaro, "Movimiento obrero y reconstitución democrática," 173–209.

38. Using Venezuelan and Mexican labor as case studies, Davis and Coleman (in "Labor and the State") argue that participation in inclusionary corporatist labor relations systems (they do not say whether of the state or societal variety) does not significantly alter workers' attitudes toward the political regimes they are subject to. Avoiding discussion of

the issue of individual strategies of choice based on materially calculated grounds of self-interest versus the binding properties of professed attitudes, they conclude that these systems provide no guarantees against a future labor revolt. That is to say, at some point the labor relations systems will no longer be able to fulfill their functional imperative (as defined by the authors) of *controlling* organized labor. This makes organized labor a "dormant volcano" in each of these countries. One could argue that *control* of organized labor is the functional imperative of *exclusionary*, rather than inclusionary corporatist labor relations systems. Inclusionary corporatism is based on co-opting, if not incorporating, sectorial interests such as organized labor. The differences between the two systems are evident in the number of constraints imposed by the state on the activities of the labor movement, the penalties levied against those who violate these constraints, and their specific mixture with state-provided inducements for cooperation (and eventual incorporation). Exclusionary systems emphasize constraints and hence control. Inclusionary systems emphasize inducements that are designed to secure labor's cooperation. The difference in functional imperative is manifested at the organizational level in the structure and functions of the national labor administration. Moreover, while one can readily agree with their general conclusion and find their specific findings of interest, Davis and Coleman's focus appears to be misplaced. It is the institutional arrangements governing the interaction among "peak" sectorial associations that condition the range of choices made available to their affiliates, and hence they ultimately determine individual workers' degree of loyalty to a given system. In fact, if the attitudes of workers in inclusionary systems are basically similar regardless of the formal status of their unions, the location of their industry, and the type of political regime that governs them, then it seems reasonable to believe that something else — possibly rationally calculated grounds of material self-interest — determine workers' affiliation and their seemingly passive acceptance of the political and economic status quo. In any case, specific institutional arrangements underpin each of these regimes, and account for their differences and their relative stability.

I leave for another time a discussion of the implications inherent in the uniformly negative appraisal given by all workers in both countries of the political regimes in question. Despite the location of their industry, the type of regimes governing them, and whether or not their unions are incorporated into inclusionary labor relations systems, it seems that workers in Mexico and Venezuela are, *as a class*, disaffected with the prevailing order, something that augers potential trouble for the current political elites.

39. Institutionalized concertation oriented toward crisis resolution dif-

fers from less formal sectorial agreements produced by growth, which have been the core of certain Keynesian projects. Such agreements have been reached in expansionist economies such as those of Venezuela in the 1960s. The material bases of the class compromise underriding the "pacted" democracy in Venezuela after 1958 were provided by revenues from an average overall yearly investment rate of 28.3 percent, the bulk of which was provided by revenues from state-controlled oil production. The immediate dependence of these pacts on the material payouts derived from revenues accrued by rapid growth underscores their inherent fragility (as the Venezuelan crises of 1991–1992 would suggest), and points to the need to establish more flexible and durable institutional bases for ongoing concertative interaction on a broad range of economic, social, and political issues.

40. On this, see Przeworski, "Capitalism, Democracy, Pacts: Revisited," 33.

41. C. Offe, "Competitive Party Democracy and Keynesian Welfare State: Some Reflections Upon its Historical Limits," in J. Keane, ed., *Contradictons of the Welfare State* (London: n.p., 1984); cited in Grossi and Dos Santos, "La concertación social," 130.

42. P. C. Schmitter, "Neo-corporatism and the State," in W. Grant, ed., *The Political Economy of Corporatism* (London: Macmillan, 1985), 36.

43. Panitch, "Trade Unions and the Capitalist State," 36.

44. On this concern, see P. C. Schmitter, "Democratic Theory and Neo-Corporatist Practice," working paper 106, European University Institute, Florence, 1983.

45. This schematic representation of types of concertative insertion into democratic political systems is taken from Mieres, "Concertación en Uruguay," 32–33.

46. G. Lehmbruch, "Liberal Corporatism and Party Government," in P. C. Schmitter and G. Lehmbruch, eds., *Trends Towards Corporatist Intermediation* (Beverly Hills: Sage Publications, 1979), 155.

47. Lehmbruch, "Concertation and the Structure of Corporatist Networks," 68. This essay also provides a good overview and discussion of the varieties of European concertation.

48. Panitch, "Trade Unions and the Capitalist State," 37.

49. *Pagina 12* (Buenos Aires), June 29, 1988, 3 (my translation).

50. See A. Gramsci, *Prison Notebooks*, ed. G. Howard, G. Smith (New York: International Publishers, 1970), 210–63.

51. Grossi and Dos Santos, "La concertación social," 136.

52. A. Thompson, "Sindicatos y Estado en la Argentina: El fracaso de la concertación social desde 1983," *Boletin Informativo Technit* 251 (January–March 1988): 22.

53. Smith, "Heterodox Shocks," 152. Smith quotes L. De Ris, M. Cavarozzi, and V. Feldman, "El contexto y los dilemas de la concertación en la Argentina actual," in M. Dos Santos, *Concertación político-social y democratización* (Buenos Aires: CLASCO, 1987), 192–93. The notion of attributing public status to private interests has been raised by C. Offe, "The Attribution of Public Status to Interest Groups," in S. Berger, ed., *Organizing Interests in Western Europe* (Cambridge: Cambridge University Press, 1981), 123–58.

54. *Pagina 12* (Buenos Aires), June 29, 1988, 2.

55. C. Offe, "Societal Preconditions of Corporatism," 9.

56. Mieres, "Concertación en Uruguay," 33–37.

57. Ibid., 37–40.

58. Ibid., 32.

59. Margaret E. Keck, "Labor, Social Policy, and Transition in Brazil: Some Dilemmas"(paper presented at the Latin American Studies Association Fourteenth International Congress, New Orleans, March 17–19, 1988), 6. See also her *The Workers Party and Democratization in Brazil* (New Haven: Yale University Press, 1992). On decisional sites and currencies, see B. Ames, *Political Survival: Politicians and Public Policy in Latin America* (Berkeley: University of California Press, 1987), 35–40.

60. A. Flisfisch, "Reflexiones algo oblicuas sobre el tema de la concertación," *Desarrollo Económico* 26, 61 (April–June 1986), 16.

61. CIESE, *Documento básico preparado para el seminario sobre concertación* (Quito, 1968), 2. Cited in S. Prates, "Cambios estructurales," 115.

62. See Przeworski and Wallerstein, "The Structure of class conflict in Democratic Capitalist Societies," 235–36; and Przeworski, "Class Compromise and the State," 23–26.

63. J. L. Lanzaro, "Movimiento obrero y reconstitución democrática," 198 (my translation).

3. Labor Collective Action, Regime Type, Political Incorporation, and the State

1. Schmitter, "Organized Interests and Democratic Consolidation," 2.

2. For a more detailed description of "peak associations" (of an economic-functional kind), see ibid., 6–17.

3. P. C. Schmitter and D. Brand, "Organizing Capitalists in the United States: The Advantages and Disadvantages of Exceptionalism" (paper presented at the APSA Annual Meetings, Chicago, 1979); quoted in Przeworski, "Marxism and Rational Choice," 392.

4. R. Hardin, *Collective Action* (Baltimore: Johns Hopkins University Press, 1982). A classic statement of the two logics employed by labor and

capital is provided by C. Offe and H. Wiesenthal, "Two Logics of Collective Action: Theoretical Notes on Social Class and Organizational Form," in *Political Power and Social Theory*, ed. M. Zeitlin (Greenwood, Conn.: JAI Press, 1980). See also M. Wallerstein, "Unions and Firms as Rational Actors," in "Working Class Solidarity and Rational Behavior" (Ph.D. diss., University of Chicago, 1985). It should be noted that Przeworski has argued that if both labor and capital rely on cost-benefit analyses in formulating their preferences and strategies, then no matter what their specific reasons for doing so or what precisely is being calculated, both logics are essentially the same; hence, there is only one logic of collective action once sectorial organization has occurred. His point is also well taken with regard to the initial question of organizing, which has generally been seen as stemming from very different logics tied to different material and nonmaterial interests.

5. International Labour Organization, *Growth, Employment, and Basic Needs in Latin America and the Caribbean*, report of the general director, Eleventh Conference of American State Members of the International Labour Organization, Medellín, Colombia, September–October 1979 (Geneva: International Labour Office, 1979), 75.

6. Offe, "Societal Preconditions of Corporatism," 11.

7. Agustín Tosco, interview published in *Primera Plana*, June 20, 1972.

8. The discussion of the logic of union organizing and strategies is based on a reading of the following: C. Crouch, *Trade Unions: The Logic of Collective Action* (London: Fontana Books, 1983); C. Offe and H. Wiesenthal, "Two Logics of Collective Action," 1:69–117; A. Errandonea and D. Constabile, *Sindicato y sociedad en el Uruguay* (Montevideo: Biblioteca de Cultura Universitaria, 1969); M. Olson, *The Logic of Collective Action* (Cambridge: Harvard University Press, 1965); W. Streek, "Interest Heterogeneity and Organizing Capacity: Two Class Logics of Collective Action?" (paper presented at the conference on "Political Institutions and Interest Intermediation," University of Constance, April 20–21, 1988); M. Wallerstein, "Working Class Solidarity and Rational Behavior"; and A. Przeworski and M. Wallerstein, "Unionization as a Union Strategy" (March 1986, mimeographed).

9. M. H. Tavares de Almeida, comments made at the Conference on Microfoundations of Democracy, University of Chicago, April 30, 1988.

10. Increasing internationalization and technological innovation among capitalist economies have given rise to new productive methods, such as quality circles and workers councils, which are designed to give workers more autonomy over their jobs (it should be stressed, however, that they rarely get to participate in productivity and investment deci-

sions). Coupled with other employee-participation devices such as employee stock option plans (ESOPs), recreational and nursery facilities, and the extension of health and pension benefits, the move toward "workplace democracy" has eroded the structural foundations of industrial unionism while shifting the locus of labor-capital interaction back to the factory or firm level, via either concertative or collective bargaining strategies. Hence, the changing nature of the structure of production and the attendant modifications in the social relations of production brought about by capitalists' strategic shifts constantly redefine labor's approaches to conflict resolution, the forms in which sectorial interaction occurs, and the vehicles and terms through which class compromise can be reached. The relationship between the structure of production and labor organization has been explored at length by Alain Touraine. I am indebted to Floreal Forni for calling my attention to this point.

11. Panitch, "Trade Unions and the Capitalist State," 29 (citing Giovanni Arrighi).

12. W. Wiarda, *The Corporative Origins of the Iberian and Latin American Labor Relations System* (Amherst: University of Massachusetts Labor Relations and Research Center, 1976).

13. See D. Collier and R. B. Collier, *Shaping the Political Arena* (Princeton: Princeton University Press, 1992).

14. See W. Streek, "Interest Heterogeneity and Organizing Capacity" esp. 29–33.

15. H. Rebhan, speech given at the Fourth International Federation of Industrial Metalworkers Conference on Latinamerican Autoworkers, September 17–19, 1987, 23 and 10–11.

16. On the subject of vanguardism, see, among others, J. E. Connor, ed., *Lenin On Politics and Revolution: Selected Writings* (New York: Pegasus, 1968); Q. Hoare, ed., *Antonio Gramsci: Selections from Political Writings (1910–1920)* (London: Lawrence & Wishart, 1977); and M. Rejal, ed., *Mao Tse-Tung on Revolution and War* (Garden City, N.Y.: Doubleday, 1969). With due respect to those higher intellects, my point is simple: in democratic capitalist societies, most of the major gains made by the working classes on the three dimensions of citizenship have been the result of trade union militancy (not always Marxist in orientation) rather that the efforts of vanguard parties.

17. J. Taiana, "El movimiento obrero (1973–1988)" *Cuadernos de Crisis* (Buenos Aires), 34 (1989): 40 (my translation).

18. M. Olson, "A Theory of Incentives Facing Political Organizations: Neo-Corporatism and the Hegemonic State," *International Political Science Review* 7, 2 (April 1986):184.

19. We do not consider "yellow" agents created by the company and

controlled by management, such as the "solidarismo" organizations recently erected in Costa Rica, Venezuela, and other Central American countries, to be authentic labor unions. Here union autonomy and freedom of action (especially with regard to strikes and other forms of withholding labor service) — which are the ultimate determinants of union independence and legitimacy — are forsaken in exchange for specific material benefits at the moment of their creation. Although an interesting variant of the late twentieth century's social relations of production, these types of labor organization are excluded from consideration due to their patently unrepresentative nature.

20. A. Gorz, *Farewell to the Working Class* (Boston: South End Press, 1982), 80; cited in P. Ranis, "Redemocratization and the Argentine Working Class," *Canadian Journal of Development Studies* 10, 2 (1989): 301. I am indebted to Ranis for calling my attention to this dimension of working-class identities.

21. I owe thanks to Roberto DaMatta for alerting me to the relational aspects of group behavior and Weber's notion of ethical dualism or duality. This particular interpretation, however, is my own.

22. A. Przeworski, "Material Bases of Consent: Economics and Politics in a Hegemonic System," *Political Power and Social Theory* 1:28–29.

23. Panitch, "Trade Unions and the Capitalist State," 33.

24. It should be noted that labor's ability to bring the productive process to a halt is contingent on a number of external variables, of which we can mention, as just four examples, new technologies, the composition of the labor force, unemployment levels, and demographic change. This necessarily complicates strategic calculations on the part of union leadership.

25. In Spanish-speaking countries, a linguistic difference gives a precise character to various types of strikes. *Huelgas* are strikes of indefinite duration, while *paros* are strikes of fixed duration. *Paros* are used for political purposes or as devices of mobilization, warning, and threat, while *huelgas* tend to be labor's response to breakdowns in collective bargaining or an expression of its utter disenchantment with the prevalent socioeconomic or political conditions. Other forms of political and economic pressure (boycotts, etc.) are also used, particularly where labor has a strong formal influence in government, where it has the support of established political parties, or where it commands significant organizational resources.

26. Przeworski, "Material Bases of Consent," 12.

27. See Crouch, *Trade Unions*, for a discussion of these points.

28. Offe and Wiesenthal, "Two Logics of Collective Action," 85–86 and 94–95. The term "market coup" is explained in *Ambito Financiero* (Buenos Aires), December 15, 1989, 1–2.

29. H. H. T. de Souze Martins, O *Estado e a burocratizão do sindicato no Brasil* (São Paulo: Editora Hucitec, 1979), 185.

30. Quoted ibid., 120.

31. On capitalist interest aggregation in the Southern Cone, see C. H. Acuña and L. Golbert, *Los empresarios y sus organizaciones: Actitudes y reacciones on relación al Plan Austral y su interacción con el mercado de trabajo* (Buenos Aires: OIT-PREALC, 1988), esp. chap. 1; C. H. Acuña, M. R. Dos Santos, and L. Golbert, "Relación Estado-empresarios y políticas concertadas de ingresos. El caso Argentino," in *Política económica y actores sociales: La concertación de ingresos y empleo* (Santiago: ILO, 1988). On capitalist collective action more generally, see J. R. Bowman, *Capitalist Collective Action: Conflict and Cooperation in the Coal Industry* (New York: Cambridge University Press, 1989); idem, "The Logic of Capitalist Collective Action," *Social Science Information* 21 (1982); idem, "The Politics of the Market: Economic Competition and the Organization of Capitalists," *Political Power and Social Theory* 5 (1985).

32. On this point, with specific reference to labor-based parties, see P. W. Drake, "Los movimientos urbanos de trabajadores bajo el capitalismo autoritario en el Cono Sur y Brasil, 1964–1983," *Cuadernos del Claeh* 40 (1986): 27.

33. On this, see for example, Drake, "Los movimientos urbanos," 25–53.

34. See, for example, Collier and Collier, *Shaping the Political Arena*; and idem, "The Initial Incorporation of the Labor Movement in Latin America: A Comparative Perspective" (paper presented at the Western Political Science Association Annual Meetings, March 1986). See also Gregory M. Luebbert, "Origins of Modern Capitalists' Polities and Labor Markets in Western Europe" (paper presented at the Fifth International Conference of Europeanists of the Council of European Studies, October 1985).

35. Collier and Collier, *Shaping the Political Arena*; and sources cited therein.

36. This summary of the expanded notion of incorporation is drawn from the critique of Collier and Collier's *Shaping the Political Arena* offered by I. Roxborough, "Dependent Development and Fragile Institutions: The Dynamics of Incorporation" (paper presented at the Seventeenth Latin American Studies Association International Congress, September 1992), esp. 2–8.

37. On this, see I. Roxborough, "The Analysis of Labor Movements in Latin America: Typologies and Theories," *Bulletin of Latin American Research* 1, 1 (1981): 81–96.

38. The notion of "historic memory" refers to the collective conscious-

ness of particular social groups, particularly as it applies to interpretations of past events. In the case of organized labor, a central part of the historic memory revolves around the initial period of incorporation, since that is what brought labor into the political and economic arena in a way that had not been seen before. In the cases studied here, this is a relatively privileged period (at least when compared to more recent experiences) to which current unionists can hark back.

39. J. Samuel Valenzuela, "Movimientos obreros y sistemas políticos: Un análisis conceptual y tipológico," *Desarrollo Económico* 23, 91 (October–December 1983): 339–68.

40. Ibid., 367–68.

41. Drake, "Los movimientos urbanos," 28.

42. Valenzuela, "Movimientos obreros," 339–41 and passim. Another study that undertakes a disaggregation of variables that influence the role and character of organized labor under the recent authoritarian (and to a lesser extent, the new democratic) regimes in the Southern Cone is G. Falabella, "Un `nuevo sindicalismo'? El gran ABC bajo régimenes militares," *Serie de Estudios Sociológicos* (Santiago de Chile), 54 (October 1986).

43. S. Valenzuela, "Labor Movement in Transitions to Democracy: A Framework for Analysis," *Comparative Politics* 21, 2 (1989): 445–72.

44. Ibid.

45. Roxborough, "Analysis of Labor Movements," 84–90.

46. B. Loveman, "Political Participation and Rural Labor in Chile," in M. A. Seligson and J. Booth, eds., *Political Participation in Latin America* (New York: Holmes and Meier, 1979); and Putnam, "Deconstructing Hegemony" (master's thesis, University of Arizona, 1992).

47. For an extended discussion of these issues, see J. McGuire, "Labor in Contemporary Latin America: An Agenda for Research — A Rapporteur's Report," working paper 61, Kellogg Institute, February 1986.

48. On this point, see N. Mouzelis, "On the Rise of Postwar Military Dictatorships: Argentina, Chile, Greece," *Comparative Studies in Society and History* 28 (1986): 68–72.

49. Ibid., 70.

50. Lanzaro, "Movimiento obrero y reconstitución democratica," 203 (my translation).

51. On the status of labor under the military regimes, see among others Drake, "Los movimientos urbanos"; and D. R. Decker, *The Political, Economic, and Labor Climate in Argentina* (Philadelphia: Industrial Research Unit, The Wharton School, University of Pennsylvania, 1983), esp. 75–107; F. Delich, "Después del diluvio, la clase obrera," in A. Rouquié, ed., *Argentina Hoy* (Buenos Aires: Siglo XXI, 1982); B. Gallitelli and A. Thompson, eds., *Sindicalismo y régimenes militares en*

Argentina Y Chile (Amsterdam: CEDLA, 1982); J. L. Schlagheck, *The Political, Economic, and Labor Climate in Brazil* (Philadelphia: Industrial Research Unit, The Wharton School, 1977), esp. 52–94; A. da Souza and B. Lamounier, "Governo e sindicatos no Brazil: A perspectiva dos años 80," *Dados* 4, 2 (1980); K. P. Erickson, *The Brazilian Corporative State and Working Class Politics* (Berkeley: University of California Press, 1977); idem, *Sindicalismo no proceso político no Brazil* (São Paulo: Brasiliense, 1979); H. Handelman, "Class Conflict and the Repression of The Uruguayan Working Class" (paper presented at the conference on "Contemporary Trends in Latin American Politics," University of New Mexico, 1977); and idem, "Labor-Industrial Conflict and the Collapse of Uruguayan Democracy," *Journal of Interamerican Studies and World Affairs* 23, 4 (November 1981).

52. Schmitter, "Organized Interests and Democratic Consolidation," 13.

53. Crouch, *Trade Unions*, 217.

54. For an extended discussion of the effects of institutions on the framing of choice and strategic interaction between social groups, see Jack Knight, *Institutions and Social Conflict* (New York: Cambridge University Press, 1992).

55. On O'Donnell's conceptualization of democratic consolidation (particularly the different "games" played by C (committed democratic) and B (committed authoritarian) actors, and the critiques it has received, see S. Mainwaring, "The Consolidation of Democracy in Latin America — A Rapporteur's Report," working paper 73, Kellogg Institute, July 1986). Adam Przeworski has offered an analogy that aptly captures the importance of institutional parameters as "rules of the game." According to him, the chances of success of a team of six-footers playing basketball against a team of seven-footers hinges not on the height of the players (i.e., their relative capabilities), but on the height of the basket (i.e., the rules of the game). Przeworski offers another analogy to show how universalistic laws actually affect different sectors of the population differently: a law banning all Frenchmen from sleeping under bridges in fact prevents only some Frenchmen from doing so. Sadly, exactly this type of municipal ordinance was passed in New York City in 1989, where it is now illegal to sleep overnight on park benches. It is left for the reader to speculate on the motivations behind such a measure, though it is clear which social strata were targeted.

56. Przeworski, "Material Bases of Consent," 14.

57. This discussion of relative power is drawn from J. Knight, "How Unobservable Can 'Power' Be?" in S. Lukes, ed., *Power* (London: Macmillan, 1991).

58. By way of brief definition, an institution is here considered to be the network of substantive rules, procedural mechanisms, and organizational frameworks that over time aggregate in regularized fashion self-defined collectivities around specific ideals or particular material and nonmaterial objectives. Institutions can therefore be large or small, broad or narrow in scope, hierarchical or egalitarian with regard to organizational procedure, highly formalized and bureaucratic, or relatively informal and unroutinized, charismatic or rational-technocratic in orientation, public, private, or a mixture of both, self-regulating or externally enforcing, and can exhibit highly concrete features (such as the national state apparatus) or more amorphous traits (e.g. laws). Obviously, there are many variations on the theme and degrees of approximation to the ideal-type posited in each category. The point is that it is the assemblage of norms, ongoing organization, and regularized practice that constitute what are generically considered to be institutions.

59. The general contours of this argument can be found in Althusser, *Lenin and Philosophy*; N. Poulantzas, *Political Power and Social Classes* (London: New Left Books, 1974); and idem, *State, Power, Socialism* (London, New Left Books, 1978). See also C. Buci-Glucksman, *Gramsci and the State* (London: Lawrence and Wishart, 1980). For a general survey, see M. Carnoy, *The State and Political Theory*, esp. chaps. 3–4.

60. See, e.g., P. G. Buchanan, "State Corporatism in Argentina: Labor Administration under Perón and Onganía," *Latin American Research Review* 20, 1 (Spring 1985).

61. For a recent historical-political-sociological comparative enterprise that addresses this point (among many others), see P. Evans, D. Rueschemeyer, and T. Skocpol, eds., *Bringing the State Back In* (Cambridge: Cambridge University Press, 1985). For a classic interpretation, see Poulantzas, *Political Power and Social Classes*.

62. G. A. O'Donnell, "Apuntes para una teoria de Estado," *Documento CEDES/G.E. CLACSO* 9 (1977); G. A. O'Donnell and O. Oszlak, "Estado y políticas estatales en America Latina: Hacia una estrategia de investigación," *Documento CEDES/G.E. CLACSO* 4 (1976); O. Oszlak, "Políticas publicas y régimenes políticos: Reflexiones a partir de algunas experiencias Latinoamericanas," *Estudios CEDES* 3, 2 (1980); idem, "Notas críticas para una teoria de la burocracia estatal," *Documento CEDES/G.E. ClACSO* 8 (1977); and idem, "Formación historica del estado en America Latina: Elementos teórico-metodológicos para su estudio," *Estudios CEDES* 1, 3 (1978).

63. The "core" functional areas of state activity that occupy central attention under virtually all modern political regimes are: providing national defense and internal security; conducting international diplomat-

ic relations; exploiting national resources (both natural and human); providing basic public goods and services; formulating national economic policy; and administering the interests of important social groups. I recognize there is considerable overlapping between areas, and that the emphasis given to each varies according to regime type. This is precisely why study of these areas under different regimes is important. More generally, these functional areas are those of economic and political management, social control and socialization, resource extraction, integration, security, and distribution of benefits; they encompass both ideological (if not hegemonic) and coercive state apparatuses. A more lengthy discussions of this point is found in P. G. Buchanan, "Regime Change and State Development in Postwar Argentina" (Ph.D. diss., University of Chicago, 1985), chap. 1.

64. P. G. Buchanan, "State Organization as a Political Indicator," technical report 1 (56-87-008), Western Hemisphere Area Studies, Department of National Security Affairs, Naval Postgraduate School, March 1986.

65. For example, it is clear the Argentine BA of 1976–1983 was much more military in nature than its predecessor, in power from 1966 to 1973. The Brazilian and Uruguayan BAs were both less militarized than either Argentine BA, and the Chilean BA of 1973–1989 was the most militarized of all. The term "colonization" comes from A. Rouquié, interview published in *Resumen de la Actualidad* 88 (March 23, 1983): 23. On relative militarization of the state apparatus, see P. G. Buchanan and R. Looney, "Relative Militarization and Its Impact on Public Policy: Budgetary Shifts in Argentina, 1963–1982," technical report 7 (56-88-002), Western Hemisphere Area Studies, Department of National Security Affairs, Naval Postgraduate School, July 1988.

66. The general characteristics of the state apparatus under different regime types outlined here are drawn from Oszlak, "Políticas publicas y régimenes políticos," 15 and passim.

67. Buchanan, *Regime Change and State Development*, chaps. 3 and 4.

68. T. J. Bossert, "Can We Return to the Regime for Comparative Policy Analysis?" *Comparative Politics* 15, 4 (July 1983): 419–41; Benjamin A. Most, "Authoritarianism and the Growth of the State in Latin America: An Assessment of Their Impacts on Argentine Public Policy, 1930–1970," *Comparative Political Studies* 13, 2 (July 1980): 173–203. On the relationship of regime type to public policy more generally, see O'Donnell and Oszlak, "Estado y políticas estatales"; and Oszlak, "Políticas publicas y régimenes políticos."

69. See, for example, T. Skocpol, "Bringing the State Back In: Strategies of Analysis in Current Research," in Evans, Reuschemeyer, and Skocpol, eds., *Bringing the State Back In*, 3–37.

70. For an excellent review of the concept of state autonomy in the Marxist literature, see Carnoy, *The State and Political Theory*, esp. chap. 5.

71. Skocpol, "Bringing the State Back In," 3–37.

72. Oszlak, "Políticas publicas y régimenes políticos"; and Buchanan, *Regime Change and State Development*.

73. Kaplan, "Recent Trends," 93.

74. On this, see G. Esping-Andersen, R. Friedland, and E. D. Wright, "Modes of Class Struggle and the Capitalist State," *Kapitalstate* 4–5 (1976): 186–220.

75. This is not to imply that I am unaware of the generally negative evaluations of such "incumbents of technocratic roles" (i.e. technocrats) who, along with "specialists in coercion" (the military hierarchy), constituted the nucleus of political authority in the preceding BA regimes. The point is that under democratic regimes the orientation and roles of these public servants must change significantly. See Offe, "The Capitalist State and Policy Formation." The theme of "state managers" in capitalist democracies has been refined by several authors, most notably F. Block. See his "The Ruling Class Does Not Rule," *Socialist Revolution* 7, 3 (1977): 6–28; and idem, "Beyond Relative Autonomy: State Managers as Historical Subjects," in R. Miliband and J. Saville, eds., *Socialist Register* (London: Merlin Press, 1980).

76. Kaplan, "Recent Trends," 93.

77. For specific evidence of this in the Argentine case, see Buchanan, *Regime Change and State Development*, chap. 3.

78. One area that warrants separate attention is the impact of external systemic influences on these processes of redemocratization. In particular, the constraining parameters imposed in each case by the repayment conditions of large foreign debts makes the task of institutionalizing democratic class compromise especially difficult. This is particularly significant in cases such as these, where the legacy of zero-sum authoritarian solutions weighs heavily on the new democratic regimes. In that light, the role of lender-nation government policies in fostering or preventing a resolution to the debt crisis that allows for the institutionalization of democratic class compromise in the Southern Cone deserves closer scrutiny.

79. On this point, see L. I. Rudolph and S. H. Rudolph, "Authority and Power in Bureaucratic and Patrimonial Administration: A Revisionist Interpretation of Weber on Bureaucracy," *World Politics* 31, 2 (January 1979): 195–227.

4. National Labor Administration as a State Apparatus

1. Among others, see V. Alba, *Historia del movimiento obrero en*

America Latina (Mexico City: Libreria Mexicanos Unidos, 1964); R. Alexander, *Labor Relations in Argentina, Brazil, and Chile* (New York: McGraw-Hill, 1962); S. M. Davis and L. W. Goodman, eds., *Workers and Managers in Latin America* (Lexington, Mass.: D. C. Heath, 1972); J. Godio, *Sindicalismo y política en America Latina* (Caracas: ILDIS, 1983); H. Spaulding, *Organized Labor in Latin America: Historical Case Studies of Workers in Dependent Societies* (New York: Harper and Row, 1977); and Wiarda, *Corporative Origins*.

2. See for example E. Cordoba, *Las relaciones colectivas de trabajo en America Latina* (Geneva: ILO, 1981), esp. 65–82; Centro Interamericano de Administración del Trabajo (OIT/PNUD), *La administración publica del trabajo: Concepto, principios, organización y evolución* (Lima: CIAT/OIT, 1980); Centro Interamericano de Administración del Trabajo/Organización Internacional del Trabajo, *La administración publica del trabajo y su papel en el desarrollo económico y social* (Lima: CIAT/OIT, 1980); J. A. Difieri, *Planificación global, reforma administrativa, y administración del trabajo* (Lima: CIAT, 1982); J. I. Husband, *Introducción a la administración del trabajo* (Geneva: ILO, 1982); M. Poblete Troncoso and B. G. Barnett, *The Rise of the Latin American Labor Movement* (New York: Bookman, 1960); and M. Poblete Troncoso, *El movimiento obrero Latinoamericano* (Mexico City: Biblioteca del trabajador Mexicano, 1976).

3. Besides the work of Wiarda cited above, other essays that attempt cross-national comparisons are R. B. Collier and D. Collier, "Inducements Versus Constraints: Disaggregating `Corporatism,'" *American Political Science Review* 73, 4 (December 1979): 967–86; Davis and Coleman, "Labor and the State"; F. Zapata, "Structural Bases of the Organization of the Latin American Labor Movement: Some Notes for Discussion," working paper 31, Center for Developing Area Studies, McGill University, August 1975; and C. Bergquist, *Labor in Latin America: Comparative Essays on Chile, Argentina, Venezuela and Columbia* (Stanford: Stanford University Press, 1986).

4. Schmitter and Lehmbruch, eds., *Trends Towards Corporatist Intermediation*; idem, *Patterns of Corporatist Policy-Making* (Beverly Hills: Sage Publications, 1982); A. Cawson, ed., *Organized Interests and the State: Studies in Meso-Corporatism* (Beverly Hills: Sage Publications, 1985); S. Berger, ed., *Organizing Interests in Western Europe: Pluralism, Corporatism, and the Transformation of Politics* (Cambridge: Cambridge University Press, 1981); and Goldthorpe, ed., *Order and Conflict in Contemporary Capitalism*.

5. See Przeworski and Wallerstein, "The Structure of Class Conflict," 232.

6. The following summary of the historical development of Latin American labor administrations is derived from Cordoba, *Las relaciones colectivas*; and Wiarda, *Corporative Origins*. For additional information, consult these works and those cited in notes 1 and 2.

7. Wiarda, *Corporative Origins*, 8.

8. For one such shift, see P. G. Buchanan, "State Corporatism in Argentina."

9. Cordoba, *Las relaciones colectivas*, 68–69.

10. ILO, *Public Labor Administration*, 43.

11. Centro Interamericano de Administración de Trabajo, *Reunión técnica regional sobre el Convenio 150 y la Recomendación 158 de la OIT relativos a la administración de trabajo*, informe final, vol. 1 (Mexico City, 1981; Lima: CIAT, 1982), 75 (my translation).

12. Among the measures I have in mind are laws governing collective bargaining, mediation in labor disputes, welfare services, pensions, and insurance plans for unionized workers, dues deductions from wages, the right to strike, formal recognition of unions as bargaining agents in specific industries, etc. See Collier and Collier, "Inducements Versus Constraints," for a good description and categorization of these measures.

13. I have used this analytical framework in previous work, including *Regime Change and State Development*; "State Corporatism in Argentina"; and "State Organization as a Political Indicator."

14. For reasons of economy, and because others are engaged in such research, I shall not delve extensively into the organization of capitalist interests and their administration by the state in these countries. Moreover, I do not claim that organized labor, even with a monopoly of collective representation, enjoys an absolute monopoly over individual workers' range of choices. As Peter Lange explains, there can exist several situations in which the rank and file adopt economic strategies that differ from those of their leaders. This is even more the case for unorganized labor, where the urge to "free ride" to secure short-term material gains is strongest. Even so, as Lange points out, workers have powerful rational motives, on material grounds, for accepting the wage regulation necessary for class compromise. See Peter Lange, "Unions, Workers and Wage Regulation: The Rational Bases of Consent," in Goldthorpe, ed., *Order and Conflict in Contemporary Capitalism*, 98–123. For a succinct discussion of the logic and dynamics of collective action in unions, firms, and business associations, see M. Wallerstein, "Unions and Firms as Rational Actors."

5. *Argentine Labor Administration Under the Radical Government*

1. The literature on this subject is extensive. For a succinct exposi-

tion, see M. Cavarozzi, *Autoritarismo y democracia (1955–1983)* (Buenos Aires: Centro Editor de America Latina, 1983); and G. Wynia, *Argentina in the Postwar Era* (Albuquerque: University of New Mexico Press, 1978).

2. P. G. Buchanan, "The Varied Faces of Domination: State Terror, Economic Policy, and Social Rupture during the Argentine 'Proceso,'" *American Journal of Political Science* 31, 2 (1987): 336–82; J. Corradi, "The Mode of Destruction: Terror in Argentina," *TELOS* 54 (1982–1983): 61–76; G. A. O'Donnell, "La cosecha del miedo," *NEXOS* 6 (1983): 6–12; and A. Smith, "State Terror in Argentina. A Frankfurt School Perspective," *Praxis International* 6, 4 (January 1987): 477–87.

3. D. Pion-Berlin, "The Fall of Military Rule in Argentina, 1976–1983," *Journal of Interamerican Studies and World Affairs* 27, 1 (1985); A. Fontana, "Fuerzas armadas, partidos políticos, y transición a la democracia en Argentina, 1981–1982," working paper 28, Kellogg Institute, July 1984; idem, "De la crísis de Malvinas a la subordinación condicionada: Conflictos intramilitares y transición política en Argentina," working paper 74, Kellogg Institute, August 1986.

4. On this point, see Abós, *El Posperonismo*.

5. A. Abós, *La columna vertebral: Sindicatos y Peronismo* (Buenos Aires: Editorial Hispanoamerica, 1986).

6. A. Canitrot, "La disciplina como objectivo de la política economica. Un ensayo sobre el programa del gobierno argentino desde 1976," *ESTUDIOS CEDES* 12 (1980); J. Schwarzer, *Argentina, 1976–1981. El endeudamiento externo como pivote de la especulación financiera* (Buenos Aires: CISEA, 1983); and W. Smith, *Authoritarianism and the Crisis of the Argentine Political Economy* (Stanford: Stanford University Press, 1989).

7. Abós, *El Posperonismo*, 185–90; Taiana, "El movimiento obrero," 20–21.

8. P. G. Buchanan, "Exorcising Collective Ghosts: Recent Argentine Writings on Politics, Economics, Social Movements, and Popular Culture," *Latin American Research Review* 25, 2 (1990): 184.

9. O. Oszlak, "La conquista del orden publico y formación histórica del Estado Argentino 1862–1880." *Estudios CEDES* 4, 2 (1982); and idem, *La formación del Estado Argentino* (Buenos Aires: Editorial Belgrano, 1982).

10. *Boletin de la Dirección General de Trabajo* 1 (June 1907): 5–30; Ley Organica N.8999/October 8, 1912, cited in J. M. G. Pujato, "El ministerio de trabajo en la Republica Argentina," *Derecho de Trabajo* 10, 1 (1950): 5–34.

11. E. J. Bilsky, *La Semana Tragica* (Buenos Aires: n.p., 1984).

12. V. Alba, *Historia del movimiento obrero*, 343–57; Alexander, *Labor Relations in Argentina, Brazil, and Chile*; and S. Baily, *Labor, Nationalism, and Politics in Argentina* (New Brunswick: Rutgers University Press, 1967).

13. Wynia, *Argentina in the Postwar Era*, 31–42.

14. The literature is too vast to cite here. For a good summary of the critiques, see P. Klaren and T. Bossert, *The Promise of Development* (Boulder: Westview Press, 1987).

15. L. Doyon, "El crecimiento sindical bajo el peronismo," *Desarrollo Económico* 15, 57 (April–June 1975); M. Murmis and J. C. Portantiero, *Estudios sobre los origines del Peronismo* (Buenos Aires: Siglo XXI, 1972); W. Little, "La organización obrera y el estado peronista, 1943–1955," *Desarrollo Económico* 18, 75 (October–December 1979); J. Horowitz, *Argentine Unions, the State, and the Rise of Perón, 1930–1945* (Berkeley: Institute of International Studies, 1990); and D. Tamarin, *The Argentine Labor Movement, 1930–1945* (Albuquerque: University of New Mexico Press, 1985).

16. Decreto 15,074 (law 12,921)/November 27, 1943, *Anales de Legislación Argentina* 3 (1943): 4591.

17. P. G. Buchanan, "State Corporatism in Argentina," 61–95.

18. Alba, *Historia del movimiento obrero*, 363.

19. Nor was it limited to organized labor. Cf. S. Mainwaring, "The State and the Industrial Bourgeoisie in Perón's Argentina, 1945–1955," *Studies in Comparative International Development* 21, 3 (Fall 1986), 3–31.

20. This approach failed because intralabor conflicts grew increasingly violent, leading to the deaths of many cooperative labor leaders and the increased radicalization of the labor opposition. This in turn set the stage for increased labor conflicts, a rising wave of strikes, and ultimately the week-long series of worker- and student-led violent demonstrations in the industrial city of Cordoba in 1968, which came to be known as the "Cordobazo." All this had the effect of increasing struggles within the regime over how to approach labor, which eventually led to General Onganía's ouster in a palace coup in 1970 and the ultimate withdrawal of the regime in 1973, all against a backdrop of escalating guerilla warfare and civil strife. See G. A. O'Donnell, *El Estado burocratico-autoritario 1966–1973: Triunfos, derrotos y crisis* (Buenos Aires: Editorial de Belgrano, 1982), esp. chaps. 6–9.

21. This discussion of the national labor administration during the postwar period is drawn from Buchanan, *State Development and Regime Change*, chap. 3.

22. On bifrontal and segmental state corporatism, see G. A. O'Don-

nell, "Corporatism and the Question of the State," in Malloy, ed., *Authoritarianism and Corporatism.*

23. G. A. O'Donnell, "Estado y alianzas en Argentina, 1955–1970," *Documento CEDES/G.E. CLASCO* 5 (1976); O. Oszlak, "Políticas publicas y régimenes políticos."

24. For a discussion of the Proceso's labor policies and its impact on labor administration, see Buchanan, *Regime Change and State Development,* 170–81, 230–35, 260–63; idem, "The Varied Faces of Domination"; A. Abós, *Las organizaciones sindicales y el poder militar (1976–1983)* (Buenos Aires: Centro Editor de America, 1984); and Gallitelli and Thompson, eds., *Sindicalismo y regimenes militares,* part 2, 91–225.

25. *La Nación,* July 28, 1986, 2.

26. "Mensaje del Sr. Presidente de la Nación, Dr. Raúl R. Alfonsín, a la Honorable Asamblea Legislativa el dia 10 de diciembre de 1983," *Discursos Presidenciales* (Buenos Aires: Secretariá de Información Pública, 1984), 17.

27. *La Nación,* March 24, 1986, 3.

28. On the vertical structure of the Argentine labor movement, see Abós, *La columna vertebral;* R. Zorrilla, *Estructura y dinámica del sindicalismo* (Buenos Aires: Editorial La Playade, 1974); R. Rotundaro, *Realidad y cambio en el sindicalismo* (Buenos Aires: Editorial Pleamar, 1973); D. James, *Resistance and Integration: Peronism and the Argentine Working Class* (New York: Cambridge University Press, 1988); M. Cavarozzi, *Sindicatos y política en Argentina* (Buenos Aires: Estudios CEDES, 1984); J. Godio, H. Palomino, and A. Wachendorfer, *El movimiento sindical Argentino (1880–1987)* (Buenos Aires: Puntosur Editores, 1988); and T. S. Di Tella, *Política y clase obrera* (Buenos Aires: Centro Editor de America, 1983).

29. The best analysis of these authoritarian and corrupt tendencies is found in J. Correa, *Los jerarcas sindicales* (Buenos Aires: Editorial Obrador, 1975).

30. See the comments of Radical leaders in *La Nación,* July 25, 1986, 7, and July 30, 1986, 6.

31. Law 23,071/1984, *Regimen de Elecciones: Asociaciones Profesionales de Trabajadores* (Buenos Aires: Ministerio de Trabajo y Seguridad Social, 1984); *Sindicatos: Elecciones, 1984–1986* (Buenos Aires: Ministerio de Trabajo y Seguridad Social, 1988); R. Gaudio and H. Domeniconi, "Las primeras elecciones sindicales en la transición democratica," *Desarrollo Económico* 26, 103 (October–December 1986); idem, *El proceso de normalización sindical bajo el gobierno radical* (Buenos Aires: Mimeo, 1986); and Ministerio de Trabajo y Seguridad Social, *Estructura Sindical*

en la Argentina (Buenos Aires: Dirección Nacional de Recursos Humanos y Empleo, 1987).

32. P. Ranis, *Argentine Workers: Peronism and Contemporary Values* (Pittsburgh: University of Pittsburgh Press, 1992), 61.

33. Law 23,551/March 23, 1988 and Decree 465/April 14, 1988, *Asociaciones de Uniones de Trabajadores* (Buenos Aires: Ministerio de Trabajo y Seguridad Social, 1988). Most modifications concerned electoral requirements in unions, employment guarantees for shop stewards, minority representation on electoral slates and in the Obras Sociales, and timetables for leadership turnover.

34. Law 23, 545/January 1988. See also Law 14,250/October 1953. On the evolution of collective bargaining in Argentina, see J. Slodky, *La negociación colectiva en la Argentina* (Buenos Aires: Puntosur, 1988); and J. Godio and J. Slodky, *El regreso de la negociación colectiva* (Buenos Aires: Fundación Friedrich Ebert, 1988).

35. On this, see Ranis, *Argentine Workers*, chap. 3.

36. This point is discussed in S. Senén Gonzáles, *Breve historia del sindicalismo Argentino, 1874–1974* (Buenos Aires: Alzamor Editores, 1974).

37. On strike characteristics during the Alfonsín administration, see H. Palomino, "Movimiento social e instituciones," *El Bimestre* 38 (March–April 1988), 17; Ranis, *Argentine Workers*, chaps. 3–4; and J. McGuire, "Union Political Tactics and Democratic Consolidation in Alfonsin's Argentina, 1983–1989" *Latin American Research Review* 27, 1 (1992): 37–74.

38. Given the state's extensive role in labor relations, this should not be surprising. The rationale for this state-centered union perspective is discussed in Senen Gonzalez, *Breve historia*, and the sources cited in note 37.

39. For a discussion of labor's position on strikes, see J. Taiana, "El movimiento obrero," 30.

40. The Committee on Labor Legislation in the Cámara de Diputados included ten Peronists and thirteen Radicals on its twenty-four-member roster; the Committee on Welfare and Social Security had twelve Radicals and ten Peronists out of twenty-four members; and the Committee on Social Assistance and Public Health had thirteen Radicals and ten Peronists on its roster. The remaining seats were held by minority parties, including the pro-labor *Partido Intransigente* and provincial parties. See Camara de Diputados, Republica Argentina, *Reseña 1985* (Buenos Aires: Dirección Secretariá de la Camara de Diputados, 1985).

41. *La Nación*, May 26, 1986, 2.

42. On the Obras Sociales, see J. C. D'Abate, "Trade Unions and Peronism," in F. Turner and J. Miguens, eds., *Juan Perón and the Reshaping of*

Argentina (Pittsburgh: University of Pittsburgh Press, 1976); *Informes DIL (Documentación e Información Laboral)* 216 (August 1984); A. Fernandez, *Las practicas sociales del sindicalismo, 1* (Buenos Aires: Centro Editor de America Latina, 1986); and J. C. Torre, *Los sindicatos en el gobierno, 1973–1976* (Buenos Aires: Centro Editor de America Latina, 1983).

43. Decreto 353/December 30, 1983, *Boletín Informativo Anales de Legislación Argentina* 1 (1984).

44. *La Nación,* June 16, 1986, 8. On concertation under Alfonsín, see de Riz, Cavarozzi, and Feldman, *Concertación, estado y sindicatos,* 38–55; Thompson, "Sindicatos y Estado en la Argentina"; and M. Cavarozzi, "Sindicatos, Estado y política en la Argentina: 1986–1987" (paper presented to PREALC, Santiago, August 1988).

45. See for example, International Labor Conference, *Final List of Delegations, 77th Session* (Geneva: ILO, 1986), 6–8.

46. A. Thompson, "Will the New Bill Work?" *Argentine News,* May–June 1988, 11–12.

47. *La Nación,* March 17, 1986, 2. See also de Riz, Cavarozzi, and Feldman, *Concertación, Estado y sindicatos*; Thompson, "Sindicatos y Estado"; and Cavarozzi, "Sindicatos, Estado y política."

48. *La Nación,* March 24, 1986, 2.

49. Ibid.

50. "Propuesta de acuerdo social," and "Propuesta de crecimiento en libertad y con justicia social," February 8, 1985. José Pedraza, *renovador* Peronist, CGT executive council member, and leader of *Union Ferroviaria,* the railroad workers union, claimed that the government did not want to share information with the labor movement because workers would then be able to make a rational calculation of macroeconomic prospects. This lack of trust was considered crucial in the failure of concertative approaches to income policy. Speech given at the Instituto Italiano de Cultura, Buenos Aires, June 29, 1988.

51. See the speech by Labor Minister Barrionuevo, cited in *La Nación,* March 24, 1986, 2.

52. *La Nación,* August 4, 1986, 2.

53. Ibid., March 24, 1986, 2. See also United States Department of Labor, *Foreign Labor Trends: Argentina* (Washington: Bureau of International Labor Affairs, 1985), 13–14.

54. Ministry of Economy and Central Bank of the Argentine Republic, *Argentine Economic Program 1984/1985* (Buenos Aires: Ministry of Economy and Central Bank of the Argentine Republic, 1984), 16.

55. Labor Minister Barrionuevo, quoted in *La Nación,* March 24, 1986, 2.

56. This was the result of bitter internecine conflicts within the CGT that dated back to the early 1960s, and became increasingly violent after 1968, culminating in the fratricidal warfare that followed Perón's death in 1974. On this point, see Godio, Palomino, and Wachendorfer, *El movimiento sindical Argentino*. For more on the origins and initial contours of this factional dispute, see S. Senen Gonzalez, *Diez años de sindicalismo argentino: De Perón al Proceso* (Buenos Aires: Ediciones Corregidor, 1984); J. M. Candia, "Argentina: Proceso militar y clase obrera," *Cuadernos del Sur* 2 (April–June 1985); F. Delich, "Desmovilización sindical, reestructuración obrera y cambio sindical," *Crítica y Utopia* 6 (1981); and H. Palomino, "El movimiento de democratización sindical," in E. Jelin, ed., *Los nuevos movimientos sociales* (Buenos Aires: Centro Editor de America Latina, 1985). For accounts in English, see P. Pozzi, "Argentina 1976–1982: Labour Leadership and Military Government," *Journal of Latin American Studies* 20 (May 1988); and, in a more journalistic vein, P. G. Buchanan, "The Argentine Labor Movement, 1982," *Washington Report on the Hemisphere* 3, 3 (November 2, 1982): 4–5.

57. For descriptions of these unions see *La Nación*, July 25, 1986, 7 and July 30, 1986, 6. Also see United States Department of Labor, *Directory of Foreign Labor Organizations: Argentina* (Washington: Bureau of International Labor Affairs, 1986); and A. Abós, *Los sindicatos Argentinos: Cuadro de situación. 1984* (Buenos Aires: CEPNA, 1985).

58. *La Nación*, March 17, 1986, 4.

59. Thompson, "Sindicatos y Estado" 24, 26.

60. On the heterodox nature of the Austral Plan and the move to orthodox stabilization policies, see W. Smith, "Hyperinflation, Macroeconomic Instability, and Neoliberal Restructuring in Democratic Argentina," in E. Epstein, ed., *The New Democracy in Argentina* (New York: Praeger, 1993).

61. *La Nación*, July 14, 1986, 2.

62. Ibid., July 30, 1986, 6.

63. On the historical utility of such an approach, see Taiana, "El movimiento obrero."

64. H. Gambarotta, A. LaMadrid, and A. Orsatti, *Propuestas económicas del sindicalismo Argentino, guia temática y recopilación* (Buenos Aires: CEDEL, 1988), 3.

65. The Ubaldinista-Movimiento Sindical Peronista Renovador (MSPR) bloc offered a broad socioeconomic and political critique cum stabilization program, outlined in the 26 *Puntos*, that spoke for a fundamental break with the economic legacy of the Proceso and a return to a more efficient and responsive *estado de bienstar* attuned to the needs of the masses. Ubaldini himself increasingly adopted a "messianic" posture

as the individual champion of subordinate group interests. The dialoguist "15" and other unions of the "62 Organizations" preferred to accept the government's economic logic of austerity in exchange for certain sectorial or organizational privileges. De facto wage restraint resulting from the acceptance of government-imposed salary rates was traded for control of the Obras Sociales, the government's absorption of union debts incurred under the Proceso, and episodic free riding. The objective here was to move the "ceilings" and "floors" for wages incrementally upward, in an exercise of partial sectorial restraint that was supposed to be replicated by employers, who would do the same for prices.

The "messianic" posture belied Ubaldini's relatively circumscribed sphere of influence within the labor movement itself, since the organizational basis of his support was derived from small unions such as his own. For their part, the *renovador* unions had totally committed themselves to a strategy oriented toward Parliament, and thus saw no possibility of cooperation with the Radical government, a view Alfonsín's advisers shared.

66. See C. Berquist, *Labor in Latin America* (Stanford: Stanford University Press, 1986), esp. 149–81 (where he discusses the role of another important union, the Meatworkers, and the government's approach to it).

67. R. T. Alemann, "La retroalimentación," *La Nación*, July 27, 1986, section 3, p. 1.

68. For an excellent depiction of the strategic terrain of this coordination game, see Smith, "Hyperinflation, Macroeconomic Instability."

69. *La Nación*, May 19, 1986, 2.

70. Roberto Bigatti, quoted in *La Nación*, July 14, 1986, 2.

71. Interview by the author with José A. Caro Figueroa, Secretario de Trabajo, MTSS, January 10, 1987.

72. For an exploration of this theme, see Buchanan, "Exorcising Collective Ghosts," esp. 180–185 and 200. A fuller analysis is offered in Smith, *Authoritarianism and the Crisis*, esp. chap. 9.

73. J. J. Lopez, "Determinants of Private Investment in Argentina" (paper presented at the Latin American Studies Association Sixteenth International Congress, April 1991), 19.

74. Law 22,520–December 21, 1981, *Boletin Oficial* (1981).

75. Law 23,023–December 10, 1983; Decree 15–December 10, 1983; and Decree 132–December 10, 1983, article 4, *Boletín Informativo Anales de Legislación Argentina* 1 (1984) 79–93.

76. Decree 132–December 10, 1983, ibid., article 23, p. 90.

77. The term "cluster" rather than "branch" is used to give more dimension to the concept, as it accounts for roles and patterns of internal interaction that more linear descriptions overlook.

78. Decree 2,907–December 10, 1988; Law 23,023–December 8, 1983, article 27, paragraphs 1, 2, 4–16, and 18; Decrees 15 and 134–December 10, 1983.

79. The Peronist shift to crude patronage politics after the withdrawal of the military bureaucratic regime in 1973 constituted the institutional equivalent of a 180-degree turn, and other Radical governments of the postwar period moved to a legalistic and technically neutral stance similar to Alfonsín's. Whenever in power, the military and its civilian allies predominately opted to repress labor, particularly its more militant branches. See Buchanan, *Regime Change and State Development*, chap. 3.

80. Figures are from the *Presupuesto General de la Administración Central* (Buenos Aires: Congreso de la Nación), for the years cited. For a historical overview of Argentine labor administration budgets, see ibid.

81. Buchanan and Looney, "Relative Militarization and Its Impact."

82. As an example, compare the figures offered in note 80 to those offered in Centro Interamericano de Administración del Trabajo (OIT–PNUD), *Estructura orgánica del Ministerio de Trabajo de Argentina, Decreto 2097, del 10 de diciembre de 1981* (Lima: CIAT/, 1983).

83. Interview by the author with Dr. Ferraro, Director General de Planeamiento, MTSS, December 19, 1986.

84. Decree 2,097–December 1, 1981, anexo 3a and 4. See also Buchanan, *Regime Change and State Development*, chap. 3.

85. This would support Offe's inference that recognized specialization among state managers is important for the autonomy of the democratic state, at least in Argentina.

86. For example, the Subsecretario de Trabajo y Seguridad Social (assistant secretary of labor and social security) existed as a direct political conduit to the minister, bypassing the secretariats of labor and social security. Acting as a screen or filter for the minister, the undersecretary was less constrained by the neutral and legalistic criteria that constituted the obligations and criteria for secretarial conduct outlined in the reorganizational decrees of December 1983. The regional delegations were also top heavy with "professionals," usually experts in local labor codes or political appointees with contacts in local union networks.

87. The effort to establish personal bases for a rapprochement with organized labor was also evident in the appointment of German López as secretary-general of the presidency, which was the closest advisory position to the president. Prior to his dismissal in June 1986 as a result of an unrelated scandal, Lopez was an active participant on the labor scene, and had long-standing (though often acrimonious) ties to the Peronist Party and the CGT. Among many other positions, he had previously occupied posts in the labor ministry under Frondizi and Illia.

88. Ferraro interview.

89. *La Nación*, March 17, 1986, 5.

90. Ibid., emphasis added.

91. On sectorial representation in government and the issue of concertation, see de Riz, Cavarozzi, and Feldman, *Concertación, estado y sindicatos*; Thompson, "Sindicatos y Estado en la Argentina"; and Acuña et al., "Relación Estado-empresarios."

92. For an early discussion of this problem, see *El Periodista* 3, 107 (September 26–October 2, 1986): 2–3, 8, and 12.

93. S. A. Hewitt, *The Cruel Dilemmas of Development: Twentieth Century Brazil* (New York: Basic Books, 1980); see also Ames, *Political Survival*.

94. On this, see Cavarozzi, de Riz, and Feldman, *Concertación, estado y sindicatos*, 31–36; R. Ayres, "The `Social Pact' as Anti-Inflationary Policy: The Argentine Experience Since 1973," *World Politics* 28, 4 (July 1975), 473–501; and B. Capeletti, *La concertación en la Argentina: Antecedentes y experiencias* (Buenos Aires: CEPNA, 1985).

95. On Menem's economic project, see J. Corradi, "The Argentina of Carlos Saul Menem," *Current History* 91, 562 (February 1992); G. Wynia, "Argentina's Economic Reform," *Current History* 90, 553 (February 1991); W. Smith, "State, Market, and Neoliberalism in Post-Transition Argentina: The Menem Experiment," *Journal of Interamerican and World Affairs* 33, 4 (Winter 1991); and idem, "Hyperinflation, Macroeconomic Instability," 20–60. On Menem's approach to labor policy, particularly regarding union control of the Obras Sociales, see "Rival CGT Factions to Bury Hatchet," *Latin American Weekly Report* 27 (February 1992): WR 92-08, p. 10.

6. National Labor Administration and Democracy in Post-Authoritarian Brazil

An earlier version of this chapter appeared in *DADOS* 32, 1 (1989): 75–124.

1. For the early history of Brazilian labor administration, see S. S. Vianna, "Direito Administrativo do Trabalho," in A. Sussekind et al., *Instituções de Direito de Trabalho*, 8th ed. (Rio de Janeiro: Livreria Freitas Bastos, S.A., 1981), 2:1, 117–33.

2. Decree 19,433, November 26, 1930; and Decree 19,667–February 4, 1931 in Sussekind et al., *Instituções de Direito de Trabalho*, 2:1, 117–33.

3. For a discussion of Brazilian corporatism and its effect on labor relations, see P. C. Schmitter, *Interest Conflict and Political Change in Brazil* (Stanford: Stanford University Press, 1971); K. Mericle, "Conflict

Regulation and the Brazilian Industrial Relations System" (Ph.D. diss., University of Wisconsin, 1974); idem, "Corporatist Control of the Working Class: Authoritarian Brazil Since 1964," in Malloy, ed., *Authoritarianism and Corporatism*; Erickson, *The Brazilian Corporative State*; and J. Humphrey, *Capitalist Control and Workers' Struggle in the Brazilian Auto Industry* (Princeton: Princeton University Press, 1982).

4.   L. Besouchet, *Historia da criação do Ministério do Trabalho: Ensaio de intepretaão* (Rio de Janeiro: Imprensa Nacional Coleção Lindolfo Collor, 1952), 78–79, 62.

5.   Alexander, *Labor Relations in Argentina, Brazil, and Chile*, 45–60.

6.   Decree Law 5422–May 1, 1943, articles 511–610 (titulo 5), in A. C. Costa, I. Ferrari, and N. B. Correa, *Consolidação das leis do trabalho*, 9th ed. (São Paulo: Edições LTR, 1979), 69–80.

7.   "Quadro de actividades e professões a que se refere o Artigo 577 do consolidação das leis do trabalho," annex to *Consolidação das leis do trabalho*, 2d ed. (São Paulo, 1956).

8.   For a succinct analysis of the major features of inclusionary and exclusionary corporatism, see R. B. Collier and D. Collier, "Inducements Versus Constraints: Disaggregating ̀Corporatism.'"

9.   Prior to October 1988, prohibitions on strikes were formally extended to essential industries such as petrochemicals, maritime transportation, banking, and most public services. Recent history has proved that formal restrictions do little to deter strikes, at least under democratic conditions.

10. The DNT was responsible for recognizing worker and employer organizations, initially mediating labor disputes (through the regional labor delegations), enforcing labor legislation (including intervention in unions), supervising union elections and finances, collecting labor statistics, and overseeing the activities of regional labor delegates, which, besides the arbitration responsibilities mentioned above, were also charged with most duties for workplace inspection and union control. The DGPS supervised the national social security system and individual union benefit programs. This included accounting for the uses to which the *imposto sindical* was put.

11. Sussekind et al., *Instituções de Direito de Trabalho*, 1118.

12. On this point, see Cohen, "The Benevolent Leviathan," 46–59.

13. Alexander, *Labor Relations in Argentina, Brazil, and Chile*, 66, 79.

14. Ibid., 88.

15. E. de Moraes Filho, *O direito e a ordem democrática* (São Paulo: Editora LTR, 1984), 135.

16. Ibid., 41–42.

17. M. H. Moreira Alves, *State and Opposition in Military Brazil* (Austin: University of Texas Press, 1985), 51.

18. On factors contributing to authoritarian liberalization and eventual democratization, see O'Donnell and Schmitter, *Tentative Conclusions about Uncertain Democracies*, vol. 4 of *Political Life After Authoritarian Rule*.

19. For a comparative view of the Brazilian process of *abertura* leading to redemocratization, see D. Share and S. Mainwaring, "Transitions From Above"; S. Mainwaring, "The Transition to Democracy in Brazil," *Journal of Interamerican Studies and World Affairs* 28, 3 (May 1986): 149–79; F. Hagopian and S. Mainwaring, "Democracy in Brazil: Origins, Problems, Prospects," *World Policy Journal* 4, 3 (summer 1987): 485–514; and L. Martins, "The 'Liberalization' of Authoritarian Rule in Brazil," in O'Donnell, Schmitter, and Whitehead, *Transitions from Authoritarian Rule*, vol. 2, *Latin America*, 72–94.

20. Decree 81,663–May 16, 1978, in *Consolidação das leis do trabalho*, 9th ed., 403–05.

21. For an extended discussion of this point, see Buchanan, "State Organization as a Political Indicator."

22. For further discussion of these corporatist traits, see Schmitter, *Interest Conflict*; Mericle, "Conflict Regulation"; Erickson, *The Brazilian Corporative State*; and Humphrey, *Capitalist Control and Workers' Struggle*.

23. *Correio Brasilense*, May 2, 1986.

24. The struggle between the new and old labor elites was visibly manifest in the competition between the most important labor confederations — the militant Central Unica dos Trabalhdores (CUT), the *pelego* (lackey)-dominated Confederacão General de Trabalho (CGT), and the business-oriented Union Sindical Independiente (USI) for the position of organized labor's national representative.

25. *O Globo*, April 4, 1987, 2.

26. On DIEESE's role and background, see *O Globo*, April 5, 1987, 8; *O Globo*, April 11, 1987, 24; and *O Globo*, April 12, 1987, 43. On labor integration in the other agencies, see *Correio Brasilense*, May 2, 1986, and the president's telegram to the labor confederations after his March 1987 meetings with them, reprinted in *O Globo*, April 11, 1987, 24.

27. Interview by the author with Plínio Sarti, Secretário de Relações do Trabalho do Ministério do Trabalho, March 16, 1987.

28. *Clarín* (Buenos Aires), April 6, 1987, 25. See also the declarations of Jair Meneguelli and the editorial critique of his position in *O Globo*, April 7, 1987, 4.

29. Ministério do Trabalho, "Exposição de Motivos No 24 e Projeto de Lei que regula a negociação coletiva de trabalho e o exercício do direito de greve" (draft proposal, Brasilia, August 1986), 4–8.

30. Ibid., 1–4. Also see *Correio Brasilense*, June 26, 11.

31. *O Globo*, April 7, 1987, 6.

32. Ibid., April 10, 1987, 18.

33. Both statements are by Senator Carols Chiarelli, member of the president's Conselho Político and leader of the Partido do Frente Liberal (PDF); in *Correio Brasilense*, June 26, 1986, 11; and *O Globo*, April 17, 1987, 5.

34. For the pros and cons of the proposed ratification of ILO Convention N. 87 and the elimination of the *imposto sindical*, see "Dois pontos: O imposto sindical," *O Globo*, March 31, 1987, 4; and "Dois pontos: A reforma sindical," *O Globo*, April 13, 1987, 4.

35. This was notable in a country in which 29.3 percent of the economically active population were working more than eight hours daily without overtime pay and where the minimum legal work week prior to 1988 was forty-eight hours.

36. On the specifics of these rights, see titles 1 and 5–7 of the ANC.

37. These included the Partido dos Trabalhadores (PT), Partido Democrático Trabalhista (PDT), Partido Trabalhista do Brasil (PTB), Partido Comunista do Brasil (PCB), Partido Socialista Brasileiro (PSB), and the left wing of the dominant party, the PMDB (who are collectively known as the Grupo Auténtico. Some of them eventually broke away to form the Partido Social Democrático Brasileiro [PSDB]).

38. *O Globo*, March 5, 1987, 17.

39. Ibid., March 30, 1987, 12; and April 3, 1987, 16.

40. See the analysis offered ibid., March 30, 1987, 12.

41. A. Pazzianoto, "Pronunciamento do Ministro do Trabalho," given at the Escola Superior de Guerra, August 1986, and published that year by the Ministério do Trabalho as an informational pamphlet, 8–10.

42. *O Globo*, February 18, 1987, 17–18.

43. Ibid., April 18, 1987, 21; *Latin American Weekly Report*, July 16, 1987 (We-87-27), 1; *Veja*, June 24, 1987, 34–41; and *Boletim IBASE*, August 1987, 7.

44. Additional information on real wages, the effects of the Novo Plano Cruzado, and labor's response is available in *Latin America Weekly Report*, June 25, 1987 (WR-87-24), 4; *Brazil Report*, June 4, 1987 (RB-87-05); and *Boletim IBASE*, August 1987, 7–9 and 20–26.

45. M. H. Tavares de Almeida, "A Difficult Path," 5–6.

46. Sarti interview, March 16, 1987. Also see A. Pazzianoto, "Discurso do Ministro do Trabalho," given to the 72d Meeting of the International Labor Conference, Geneva, 1986, and published that year by the Ministério do Trabalho as an informational pamphlet, 5–6.

47. *O Globo*, March 5, 1987, 17.

48. Ibid., February 18, 1987, 19.

49. For a discussion of the *seguro desemprego* and its economic impact, see J. P. Zeetano Chahad, "O seguro-desemprego e o mercado de trabalho no Brasil," *Trabalho para discussão interna* (São Paulo: Universidade de São Paulo, 1986).

50. A. Pazzianoto, "Discurso," 4–5. See also the statements of Secretária de Emprego e Salarios Dorothea Wernek in *O Globo*, February 18, 1987, 19.

51. *O Globo*, March 9, 1987, 13.

52. Ibid., March 3, 1987, 17.

53. See the advertisement placed in *O Globo*, April 8, 1987, 24–25.

54. Interview by the author with Eros de Almeida, Secretário-Geral do Ministério do Trabalho, March 17, 1987.

55. Thus a public transportation strike in São Paulo was rapidly declared illegal in mid-April 1987 and subjected to prompt MTb intervention, whereupon it collapsed in two days. A similar scenario occurred during the August 20, 1987, general strike, where the government and employers combined selective intervention and repression (most often on the part of state governments) with economic incentives (in the form of a 250-cruzado across-the-board wage increase decreed by the government and employer-provided wage readjustments for cooperative unions on the eve of the strike) in order to weaken rank-and-file support for the strike — a tactic widely considered to have been successful.

56. IBASE, *Politicas governmentais*, December 1987–January 1988, 12, seperata; and DIEESE, internal memorandum, 1988. Also see *O Globo*, March 9, 1987, 13, and ibid., March 29, 1987, 40.

57. *Folha do São Paulo*, March 18, 1987, cited in *Boletim IBASE*, March 1987, 16.

58. A. Pazzianotto, interviewed in *O Globo*, April 12, 1987, 16.

59. Tavares de Almeida, "A Difficult Path," 6.

60. According to Ricardo Bladino, president of the CGT, the reason for the reluctance to call general strikes was that they played into the hands of international banks and the far right by destabilizing the government at a time when it needed united domestic support (*O Globo*, March 1, 1987, 2). The CUT leadership, however, saw the situation quite differently. For the CUT, the decision to suspend interest payments on the foreign debt was little more than a "populist game on the part of a government that lacked the courage to make the fundamentally political decision to suspend debt payments entirely" (statement by CUT Vice-President Arelino Ganzer, cited in ibid.) Hence, the underlying causes for the lack of national mobilization lie elsewhere.

In the view of Jair Meneguelli, president of the CUT, the moment for general strikes was problematic because "there exists an incapacity for mobilization. The rank and file are preoccupied with their immediate needs and with the climate of recession and unemployment that grips the country, all of which contributes to demobilization" (*O Globo*, March 30, 1987, 9).

The depth of the economic crisis forced the rank and file to engage in daily survival strategies that worked against support for politically symbolic, general strikes (or for any prolonged work stoppage for that matter). Instead, the pattern of strikes after 1985 suggests that the rank and file and national labor administration shared a perspective with regard to fundamental concerns — employment stability and protecting real wage levels — which in terms of labor strategy removed union members' support of general strikes that were political referendums rather than attempts at economic revindication.

61. See the results of a Gallup Poll survey published in *O Globo*, April 26, 1987, 12.

62. One positive result of these efforts and the attempts to establish a concertative sectorial dialogue may have been the 1988 initiatives promoted by FIESP to jointly formulate an anti-inflation package with major industrial union representatives. There is increasingly an inclination on the part of both labor and business to negotiate independently of the state, something that does not mesh well with the government's attempts at economic stabilization via anti-inflationary programs such as the Plano Cruzado and the Novo Plano Cruzado announced in January 1989. On the attempts of FIESP to promote concertative, bipartite anti-inflation packages with the São Paulo labor unions, see the reports offered in the *Journal do Brasil* and *Folha do São Paulo* in July and August 1988.

63. For a succinct exposition of these views, see the interviews with Julio Lobos, labor adviser to several major industries, in *Veja*, September 24, 1986, 5–8.

64. *Boletim IBASE*, March 1987, 16.

65. *Latin American Weekly Report*, July 2, 1987 (WR-87-25).

66. For exanple, during the petrochemical workers' strikes of the March 1987, army troops were sent in to guard refineries and other installations. This pattern was repeated several times, as in late September 1987, when the army sent troops into the Itaipú Dam complex on the Paraná River to break up a strike, with the ensuing clashes with workers resulting in several serious injuries, and in the November 1988 army raid on a steel plant occupied by striking metalworkers in Volta Redonda, in which several workers were killed and many others injured (despite the recently passed law guaranteeing a constitutional right to strike!).

67. For a sympathetic view of this type of labor approach, see *Boletim IBASE*, March 1987, and *Boletim Nacional CUT*, December 1986–January 1987.

68. Pazzianotto, "Discurso," 4.

69. *Consolidação das leis do trabalho*, 9th ed., 403–05. The discussion of organizational structure that follows is drawn from this source.

70. For example, with regard to professional training programs, the CFMO (Conselho Federal de Mão-de Obra) and CCA (Comissão Consultativa do Artesanato) draw up policies, which are implemented by the SMO (Secretaría de Mão-de Obra); wage, labor market, and employment policies are formulated in the CNPS (Conselho Nacional de Política Salerial) and CNPE (Conselho Nacional de Política de Emprego), then implemented by the SES (Secretaría de Emprego e Salarios); labor legislation interpretation and reform (including issues involving union recognition, collective bargaining, etc.) is carried out and formulated by the CDT (Comissão de Direito do Trabalho) and enforced by the SRT (Secretaría de Relações do Trabalho).

71. In terms of specific implementation responsibilities, the SMO handles all federal job training programs; the SES constitutes the center of the Sistema Nacional de Emprego (national employment system), and has a major role in determining income policy (since it is the agency charged with primary responsibilities for determining when wage adjustments should be implemented); the SSMT (Secretaría de Segurança e Medicina do Trabalho) is charged with all matters related to labor medicine, safety, and hygiene, and therefore has major inspection and control responsibilities; the SPS (Secretaría de Promoção Social) oversees syndical social promotion activities (i.e., educational, cultural, and recreational facilities, etc.); and the SIMIG (Secretaría de Immigração) is responsible for labor-related matters connected with immigration and migration. The SRT has the primary tasks of union registration and recognition, collective bargaining, mediation, arbitration, electoral and financial oversight, and, in conjunction with the SSMT through the Delegacias Regionais, workplace inspection. As a result, it is the main institutional referent for organized labor's professional concerns, and thus is a major instrument in the structuring of working-class interests in Brazil. As such, the SRT is the first among equals in the external functional area, in a scaled-down version of the centralized structure inherited from the Estado Novo.

72. Interview by the author with Dr. Renaldo Estelis, Secretário de Orçamento e Finanças do Ministério de Trabalho, March 17, 1987.

73. This phenomenon was particularly evident under the military-bureacratic regime. See D. Collier, "Corporatism and the Question of the State," in *The New Authoritarianism*, ed. Collier.

74. Sarti interview, March 16, 1987.

75. It is worth noting that none of those interviewed for this study wished to discuss the DSI on record, and many avoided discussion of the subject altogether. Those who did agree to talk all concurred that the

prevalent attitude within the MTb toward the DSI was one of active neglect, with hopes for a future organizational reform that would bring about its elimination. All agreed that such a prospect was remote in the foreseeable future.

76. Figures supplied by Dr. Renaldo Estelis, March 17, 1987.

77. Ministério do Trabalho, "Dotação, 1984–1985," internal memorandum, n.d., 5–6.

78. "Demostrativo do Orçamento Annual," 1.

79. Ibid.

80. Ministério do Trabalho, "Orçamento 1986–1987: Outras despesas de custeio e capital — Atividade fim, quadro comparativo," internal memorandum, n.d.

81. Estelis interview, March 17, 1987.

82. Ministério do Trabalho, "Distribuição da Força de Trabalho — MTb," internal memorandum, October 1986. This discussion of personnel factors in labor administration is also derived from information gathered during an interview with Dr. Mauro Moreira Filho, Director of Personnel of the MTb, March 17, 1987.

83. Ministério do Trabalho, "Situação Empregos, Orgaos Regionais—DRT's Actualização–DP: 02–07–86," internal memorandum, Departmento de Pessoal, 1986.

84. Ministério do Trabalho, "Situação Empregos, SEDE, Actualização–DP: 02–07–86," internal memorandum, Departamento de Pessoal, 1986; and "Situação Empregos, Orgaos Regionais — DRT's."

85. Interview with Argeu Quintanilha, Director Regional de Trabalho, Estado do São Paulo, in *O Estado de São Paulo*, April 23, 1987, 30.

86. "Situação Empregos, SEDE," 5.

87. Estelis interview, March 17, 1987.

88. De Almeida interview.

7. Uruguayan Labor Administration, 1985–1988

1. On the history of Uruguay, see T. Halperin Donghi, *Historia de los Orientales*, 4th ed. (Montevideo: Ediciones de la Banda Oriental, 1984).

2. Law 13,640–November 26, 1968, CIAT, *La administración pública del trabajo y su papel en el desarollo económico y social*, serie documentos 79–1, 1980, 528–29.

3. M. Gargiulo, "El movimiento sindical Uruguayo en los '80: Concertación o confrontación?" in *El sindicalismo Latinoamericano en los Ochenta* (Santiago: CLACSO, 1968), 167; see idem, "El desafio de la democracia. La izquierda política y sindical en el Uruguay post-autoritario," *Cuadernos del CLAEH* 38, 11, 2 (1986): 19; and A. Errandonea and D. Constabile, *Sindicato y sociedad en el Uruguay* (Montevideo: Cuadernos del Sur, 1969); esp. chaps. 3, 4, 6, 7.

4. Interview by the author with Alfonso Vivo, adviser to the labor minister, Montevideo, January 26, 1987.

5. For a good review and analysis of the original Consejos de Salarios, see A. Fraga, M. Maronna, and Y. Trochón, "Los Consejos de Salarios como experiencia de concertación," *Cuadernos del CLAEH* 33, 10, 1 (1985): 27–36.

6. C. Real de Azua, "Politica, poder y partidos en el Uruguay de hoy," in C. Benvenuto et al., *Uruguay de Hoy* (Mexico City: Siglo XXI, 1971), 181–82. See also J. Rial, "Estado, partidos políticos, y concertación social en el Uruguay de la transición," in CIESU, *7 enfoques sobre la concertación* (Montevideo: Ediciones de la Banda Oriental, 1984), 131–56.

7. R. Franco, "El Estado Uruguayo en la transición a la democracia," in Gillespie et al., *Uruguay y la democracia* 3:82.

8. The nature of the political spoils system is yet another unique characteristic of Uruguayan democracy. In the 1930s more than 22,000 positions were created in the public sector, a 73-percent increase over the 1920s. By 1957 the Uruguayan state employed 17.2 percent of the economically active population, with the total number of public servants exceeding 170,600. In the period 1956–1960, 30,000 additional jobs were created; another 50,000 positions were added from 1961 to 1969.

9. H. Handelman, "Labor-Industrial Conflict," 384–86.

10. On the economic crisis and its impact, see M. Weinstein, *Uruguay: The Politics of Failure* (Westport, Conn.: Greenwood Press, 1975), esp. 118–20; I LO, *Relaciones de Trabajo en el Uruguay* (Geneva: ILO, 1987), 8–10; and Handelman, "Labor-Industrial Conflict," 374–76.

11. Law 13,720–December 16, 1968, *Diario Oficial*, December 19, 1968. On the scope and effects of the COPRIN, see United State Department of Labor, *Labor Law and Practice in Uruguay* (Washington: Government Printing Office, 1971), 41. On the changes in the labor relations system in the 1960s, see ILO, *Relaciones*, chaps. 3, 5–6.

12. ILO, *Relaciones*, 19.

13. See Handelman, "Labor-Industrial Conflict," 387–88; and ILO, *Relaciones*, 10–12.

14. Handelman, "Labor-Industrial Conflict," 390; A. Melgar and W. Cancela, "Concentración del ingreso y desarticulación productiva: Un desafio al proceso de democratización," *Revista Mexicana de Sociologia* 47, 2 (1985): 215, 219–24.

15. V. Corbo and J. de Melo, "Lessons from the Southern Cone Reforms," *The World Bank Research Observer* 2, 2 (1987): 116–17.

16. The number of women in the work force increased 35 percent from 1968 to 1977, while the number of young people employed increased 15 percent. The emigration figures totalled 8 percent of the Uruguayan population from 1967 to 1975, with 100,000 more leaving the country dur-

ing the period 1975–1982, for a total of 300,000, or 10 percent of the population. This number included 12 percent of the population of Montevideo prior to 1975, and 11 percent of the economically active population. The number of self-employed increased from between 1.5 and 9 percent depending on the sector of production. For these and other detailed figures, see J. C. Fortuna, "Los cambios en el escenario estructural de los movimientos laborales," *Revista Mexicana de Sociologia* 47, 2 (1985): 233–48. See also Melgar and Cancela, "Concentración del ingreso," 222; S. Prates, "El trabajo informal o las relaciones contradictorias entre la reproducción, la producción, y el Estado," *Documento de Trabajo* (CIESU) 73 (1987); S. Prates, "El trabajo de la mujer en una epoca de crísis (o cuando se pierde ganando)," in GRECMU (Grupo de Estudios sobre la Condición de la Mujer en el Uruguay), *La Mujer en Uruguay: Ayer y Hoy* (Montevideo: Ediciones de la Banda Oriental, 1983); and M. Boado, "La juventud en el empleo," internal research note, CIESU, 1983.

17. Melgar and Cancela, "Concentración del ingreso," 220, 223, 225.

18. Ibid., 225 (investment); ILO, *Relaciones*, 10–11 (growth); and N. Aragones, "Entre la `fatalidad' de la decadencia y la creación de alternativas viables: Notas sobre estilos alternativos de desarrollo y concertación estratégica en el Uruguay," *Cuadernos del CLAEH* 34, 10, 2 (1985): 24 (capital flight).

19. CIAT, *Reunión Téchnica*, 529.

20. Law 14,106–March 14, 1973, cited in ibid., 530–31.

21. Decree 574–July 12, 1974 and Law 14,218–1974, replacing Decree 160– March 1, 1967, cited ibid., 532–33. On the general orientation of the MTSS under the military regime, see E. Heguey Terra, *Estudios sobre la administración del trabajo en el Uruguay*, 2 vols. (Montevideo: MTSS and Universidad de la Republica, 1979).

22. CIAT, *Reunión Técnica*, 534–35.

23. Ibid., 540–41.

24. Law 15,137–May 21, 1981 and Decree 513–October 9, 1981. For Decree 622–1973, see A. Plá Rodriguez, *La reglamentación sindical en Uruguay* (Montevideo: Biblioteca de "Marcha," 1973). On this and Law 15,137–May 21, 1981, see ILO, *Relaciones*, 36.

25. The IGTSS was demoted to the position of "subprogram" in the newly created general directorate of the secretariat. The Dirección Nacional de Costos, Precios e Ingresos (national directorate of costs, prices, and income, or DINACOPRIN) was established as an institutional successor to the COPRIN.

26. On the DINACOPRIN, see Law 14,791–June 8, 1978, Decree 371–June 30, 1978, and Resolution 991–June 30, 1978 (creating, specifying the functions of, and ratifying the structure of the DINACOPRIN). The text of Law 14,791 can be found in *Diario Oficial*, June 21, 1978.

On the effects of these measures see ILO, *Relaciones*, 83–85.

27. This included those linked to food programs; programs for the protection and promotion of the family, youth, and the elderly; cooperative projects; handicapped and rehabilitation programs; the social and labor aspects of housing and community development; labor problems specific to women; and all other questions relevant to the promotion of social welfare not explicitly assigned to other portfolios.

28. E. Cordoba, *Las relaciones colectivas*, 69.

29. The most complete analysis of the transition is available in C. Gillespie, et al., *Uruguay y la democracia*. Two excellent studies of the varied aspects of concertative approaches towards the Uruguayan redemocratization process can be found in CIESU, *7 Enfoques sobre la Concertación*; R. Jacob et al., *Concertación y democracia* (Montevideo: CLASCO, 1984). Good summaries in English of the transition are also available in G. Gillespie, "Uruguay's Transition from Collegial Military-Technocratic Rule," in O'Donnell, Schmitter, and Whitehead, eds., *Latin America*, vol. 2 of *Transitions from Authoritarianism*; and J. Rial, "Political Parties and Elections in the Process of Transition in Uruguay," in E. Baloyra, ed., *Comparing New Democracies* (Boulder: Westview Press, 1987).

30. C. H. Filgueria, "Mediacion política y apertura democrática en el Uruguay," *Revista Mexicana de Sociologia* 47, 2 (1985): 48–49; see also ILO, *Relaciones*, 74–77.

31. L. A. Brezzo and E. Vispo, "Experiencia de la concertación de políticas de ingreso en Uruguay: Formas de negociación, función de los Consejos de Salarios, resultados" (paper presented at the Grupo de Trabajo sobre Políticas de Ingreso y Empleo Concertadas, PREALC, Santiago, Chile, September 2–3, 1986), 2.

32. On this, see J. Rial, "Post Scriptun," in C. Gillespie et al., *Uruguay y la democracia* 3:139–46; and Filgueria, "Mediación política."

33. The scope and effects of the CONAPRO are well described in Filgueria, "Mediación política"; Brezzo and Vispo, "Experiencia de la concertación"; and ILO, *Relaciones*, 73–77.

34. For an excellent analysis of the evolution of the Uruguayan party system and its role in the transition, see L. E. Gonzalez, "Los partidos y la redemocratización en Uruguay," *Cuardenos del CLAEH* 37, 11, 1 (1986): 25–56. See also Rial, "Political Parties and Elections."

35. ILO, *Relaciones*, 85–86; Brezzo and Vispo, "Experiencia de la concertación," 2–4; R. Muiño and R. Rossi Albert, "La materia laboral en la concertación nacional programmática," in *La concertación social* (Montevideo: Ediciones Jurídicos Amalio Fernandez, 1985), 273–74.

36. *Programa de Principios del Partido Colorado* (Montevideo, n.p., 1984), 54.

37. Ibid., 54–55.

38. Ibid., 55.

39. Ibid., 55–58.

40. ILO, *Relaciones*, 85–87 and 97, n. 14; Brezzo and Vispo, "Experiencia de la concertación," 5; and C. H. Filgueria, "Organizaciones sindicales y empresariales ante las programas de estabilización: Uruguay, 1985–1987" (paper presented at the Seminario-Taller sobre Políticas Anti-ínflacionarias y Mercado de Trabajo, PREALC, Santiago, Chile, August 2–4, 1988), 9.

41. Brezzo and Vispo, "Experiencia de la concertación," 5–9.

42. The decline of industries for durable consumer goods, the rise of the service sector, and the increase in clerical forms of labor associated with the expansion of the financial sector and the automation of the workplace required a reclassification of wage groups to better accommodate and represent the new categories of employees present in the work force (such as computer operators). Labor tried to include in various wage groups several categories of unorganized or weakly organized workers (like those in the agricultural sector), while business was staunchly opposed to including such workers in unions with well-established organizational bases.

43. Brezzo and Vispo, "Experiencia de la concertación," 9–10.

44. Decree 178–May 10, 1985, article 5.

45. Brezzo and Vispo, "Experiencia de la concertación," 11.

46. Ibid., 13–15.

47. Ibid., 15–22.

48. Ibid., 23–25.

49. ILO, *Relaciones*, 89–92; Brezzo and Vispo, "Experiencia de la concertación," 28, 33–34.

50. Brezzo and Vispo, "Experiencia de la concertación," 31.

51. On the "long accords," see ILO, *Relaciones*, 92–124; Brezzo and Vispo, "Experiencia de la concertación," 31–32; Filgueria, "Organizaciones sindicales y empresariales," 36–37; and M. Rama, "Políticas de estabilización y Mercado de Trabajo: El Caso Uruguayo" (paper presented at the Seminario-Taller sobre Políticas Antiínflacionarias y Mercado de Trabajo, PREALC, Santiago, Chile, August 2–4, 1988), 24–25.

52. In the June 1985 round there were sixty-nine unanimous agreements reached in the Consejos, with three majority decisions by the state and employers, one by the state and workers, none by workers and employers, and twenty-seven unresolvable conflicts (whereupon the state fixed salaries by decree). In October 1985 the number of unanimous decisions rose to seventy-nine, state-employer majorities increased to ten, state-worker majorities to four. There were no worker-employer majorities and the number of unresolved negotiations dropped to seven.

In the third round, that of June 1986, the degree of unanimity dropped by one to seventy-eight, the number of state-employer majority decisions rose to fifteen, and the number of state-worker majority decisions dropped to one. There were no worker-employer majority decisions and six unresolved disputes. In the fourth round, in October 1986, the number of unanimous decisions rose to ninety-two and state-employer majorities drop to six. There were no state-worker or worker-employer agreements, and the number of unresolved negotiations dropped to two.

53. Unanimous decisions in the Consejos amounted to 90 percent of the total agreements reached during this period, with state-employer majorities at 8.5 percent, state-worker majorities at 1.5 percent, and, prior to the "long accords," worker-employer majorities at zero. The number of unresolved negotiations dropped from 27 percent during the first round to under 3 percent for the fourth round.

54. On voting patterns in the Consejos, see Brezzo and Vispo, "Experiencia de la concertación," 50–51; Filgueria, "Organizaciones sindicales y empresariales," 35–39; and Rama, "Políticas de estabilización," 30a (chart 6). The notion of "vocación concertativa" is repeatedly expressed in these works as a fundamental trait shared by all Uruguayan social and political actors, although the approach toward different concertative arenas differs in each case.

55. Thus, where real wages in the private sector grew an average of 15 percent in 1985, they grew only 14.1 percent in the public sector.

56. Rama, "Políticas de estabilización," 12a (chart 1); CEPAL, "Problemas estructurales de la crísis económica en el desarrollo social del Uruguay y respuestas en las estrategias de las políticas del gobierno democrático" (paper prepared for the "Reunión sobre Crísis Externa: Proceso de Ajuste y su Impacto Imediato y de Largo Plazo en el Desarrollo Social: Que Hacer?" CEPAL–UNICEF–OIT, Lima, November, 25–29, 1986), 28. In "Evolución de precios e ingresos 1985–1986," *Cuadernos del CLAEH* 39, 11, 3 (1986): 95, P. M. Bengochea and A. Melgar show a 15.06-percent growth rate growth in real wages in the private sector and a 12.64-percent growth in real wages in the public sector.

57. Whereas the total number of strikes called during the period 1985–1987 amounted to well over fifteen hundred, 43.5 percent of these occurred in 1985, with 31.0 percent in 1986 and 25.5 percent in 1987. In the private sector, the distribution of strikes showed a slightly different pattern, with 41.3 percent of the total occurring in 1985, 27.8 percent in 1986, and a rise to 30.9 percent in 1987. As for the public sector, the trend was more accentuated, with 46.2 percent of the total strikes called in that sector occurring in 1985, 35.2 percent in 1986 (including five general strikes involving unions in the public sector) and 18.5 percent in

1987. Strike data are from ILO, *Relaciones*, 101–02 (for the period March 1, 1985–September 30, 1986), while percentages come from Filgueria, "Organizaciones sindicales y empresariales," 30a (chart 1).

58. Filgueria, "Organizaciones sindicales y empresariales," 42 (my translation).

59. Brezzo and Vispo, "Experiencia de la concertación," 49.

60. Ibid., 25–26; ILO, *Relaciones*, 29 and 94. From my own observations, the importance of personal relations in the conduct of the labor administration is not limited to Uruguay, and in fact seems to be a common feature of labor relations systems throughout the Southern Cone.

61. This outline of labor's position is derived from interviews by the author with Jose D'Elia, president of the PIT-CNT, and Ruben Villaverde, propaganda secretary of the PIT-CNT, conducted on July 5, 1988. For excellent overviews of labor's strategic posture(s), see M. Gargiulo, "La izquierda política y sindical en el Uruguay post-autoritario," *Cuadernos del CLAEH* 38, 11, 2 (1986): 17–46; and J. Rial, "El movimiento sindical Uruguayo ante la redemocratización," in PREALC, *Política económica y actores sociales* (Santiago: ILO, 1988), 511–92.

62. Under the MTSS's administration, these goods were distributed to 306,423 persons (10 percent of the population), of which 112,769 were retirees, with the remainder schoolchildren, pregnant women, and those unemployed for a period of more than six months. The total cost of this plan reached $9.8 million.

63. CEPAL, "Problemas estructurales," 15; information on this program was also provided during an interview by the author with Dr. Luis Gonzalez Machado, Director de Política Social (social policy director) of the MTSS, January 27, 1987.

64. MTSS, *Resumen de rubros de retribuciones personales y gastos de funcionamiento e inversión*, internal memorandum, Montevideo, 1987.

65. Law 15,809–April 8, 1986, insert 13, p. 6.

66. In 1987 the ministry of public health (Ministerio de Salud Pública, or MSP) received 10.6 percent of the central administrative budget, and had extended its services (via a program of distributing cards for national health service assistance) to 600,947 individuals. Nonetheless, with an estimated 19.9 percent of the Uruguayan population lacking health insurance or the ability to pay for private care, this left at least 400,000 people without access to proper medical attention, of which 121,496 were immediately eligible for public health benefits. Budget figures are from the Oficina Sectorial de Planeamiento y Presupuesto, *Presupuesto Nacional 1987* (Montevideo: Presidencia de la Nación, MTSS, 1986), 18–19. Figures on the population lacking health coverage come from MTSS, *Projecto políticas publicas y desarrollo social: Uruguay, documento de trabajo* (Montevideo: Programa de las Naciones Unidas para el

Desarrollo, Proyecto Regional "Pobreza Crítica," RLA–86–004 (February 1987), 19, 79–80.

67. MTSS, *Projecto políticas públicas*, 111–12. Among other things, this helped reduce the infant mortality rate from a high in modern times of 47 percent in 1977 to 31.8 percent in 1986: MTSS, *Projecto políticas publicas*, map 4.

68. Partido Colorado, *Programa de Principios*, 58–59; budget information comes from the Oficina Sectorial de Planeamiento y Presupuesto, *Presupuesto Nacional*, 1.

69. Economic figures are from Filgueria, "Organizaciones sindicales y empresariales," 4–5; MTSS, *Proyecto políticas públicas*, 38; and Rama, "Políticas de estabilización," 17–26.

70. On the objections voiced by the Blanco Party and the Frente Amplio to the Colorado economic program, see Filgueria, "Organizaciones sindicales y empresariales," 4–5.

71. Figures are from Rama, "Políticas de estabilización," 7a (chart 1), 27a (chart 5), 27, and passim.

72. Information of the MTSS organizational framework is drawn from MTSS, *Organigrama actual* (Montevideo: Oficina Sectorial de Planeamiento y Presupuesto, 1987); and Law 15,809–April 8, 1986, article 53, insert 13.

73. MTSS, *Organigrama actual*.

74. MTSS, *Organigrama: Estructura Orgánica Proyectada* (Montevideo: Oficina Sectorial de Planeamiento y Presupuesto, 1986), under guidelines provided by article 53 of Law 15,809–April 8, 1986.

75. Ibid., 6, 9–9.6.

76. See among others, Brezzo and Vispo, "Experiencia de la concertación," 13; and ILO, *Relaciones*, 94, 99, n. 26.

77. Budget figures during the military-bureaucratic regime are from E. Cordoba, *Las relaciones colectivas*, 68–70; 1985–1988 budget figures are from ILO, *Relaciones*, 51–52; and MTSS, *Presupuesto Nacional* (1987), 1.

78. MTSS, "Resumen de rubros de retribuciones personales y gastos de funcionamiento e inversión," OSPP, internal memorandum 133–86 (November 14, 1986), 2.

79. Ibid.; ILO, *Relaciones*, 52.

80. MTSS, "Resumen de rubros."

81. This description of the budgetary process was provided by Ricardo Stilling, director de la Oficina Sectorial de Planeamiento y Presupuesto, MTSS, during an interview by the author, conducted on January 27, 1987.

82. MTSS, "Nomina de Cargos Ocupados por Programa," OSPP internal memorandum 133–November 14, 1996, 3.

83. Personnel characteristics are drawn from an interview by the

author with Jorge Capellini, Director General de Secretaria, MTSS, January 27, 1987.

84. On the "open door" policy and the youth of state representatives, see Brezzo and Vispo, "Experiencia de la concertación," 13–14, 16, 49; and ILO, *Relaciones*, 29, 94.

85. P. Katzenstein, *Small States in World Markets* (Ithaca: Cornell University Press, 1985).

8. Conclusion

1. On this, see P. G. Buchanan, "State Corporatism in Argentina"; idem, "Plus ça change? A administração nacional do trabalho e a democracia no Brasil, 1985–1987," *DADOS* 32, 1 (1989).

2. The so-called shrinking of the state cited by analysts of Latin American authoritarianism, whereby the populist or welfare states that had evolved over the previous fifty years were reduced to their coercive-administrative cores, stripped of most ideological reproductive functions, and outweighed by authoritarian instruments of social control and domination.

3. J. E. Corradi, "The Culture of Fear in Civil Society," in *From Military Rule to Liberal Democracy in Argentina*, ed. M. P. Ramos and C. H. Weisman (Boulder: Westview Press, 1987); J. E. Corradi, "The Mode of Destruction: Terror in Argentina," *TELOS* 54 (winter 1982–1983); G. A. O'Donnell, "La cosecha del miedo," *NEXOS* 6 (1983).

4. The exception to this is the Novo Sindicalismo movement born in 1979 in the industrial belts of São Paulo, which continue to be the engine of the Brazilian economy. The dynamism of that industrial bloc gave the emerging labor unions strategic importance, which they used to press relatively militant political and economic demands upon both the state and employers well before the authoritarian elite was disposed to relinquish power.

5. The motives behind actors' self-interested strategies differed: in the case of the working classes and other subordinate groups, individual and collective survival as social entities was at stake. Therefore, they maximized defensive rationales (of self-preservation). For the dominant factions of capital, the goal was to maximize an immediate advantage by using offensive rationales of self-enrichment (greed).

6. R. DaMatta, *A casa e a rua* (São Paulo: Editora Brasiliense, 1985).

7. The far-reaching projects of neoliberal restructuring in Argentina and Brazil initiated by the Menem and Collor governments rejected national-level class compromise in favor of securing working-class consent to capitalist rule through the creation and strengthening of environmental political and societal backing (across classes) for free-market poli-

cies and the preservation of economic stability. They did not pressure the propertied classes into collective bargaining aimed at improving the material conditions of the working sectors.

8. This account of recent events is (quite literally) informed by the comments of William Smith and Aldo Vacs, to whom I am indebted.

9. I have been influenced by Betts Putnam's thinking on the conceptualization of hegemony as a hierarchical debate.

10. A. Przeworski and M. Wallerstein, "The Structure of Class Conflict"; Przeworski, "Material Bases of Consent."

11. According to Gramsci,

hegemony presupposes that account be taken of the interests and the tendencies of the groups over which hegemony is exercised, and that a certain compromise equilibrium should be formed — in other words that the leading group should make sacrifices of an economic-corporate kind. But there is also no doubt that such sacrifices and such a compromise cannot touch the essential; for though hegemony is ethical-political, it must also be economic, and must necessarily be based on the decisive function exercised by the leading group in the decisive nucleus of economic activity.

Selections from the Prison Notebooks, 161. See also N. Poulantzas, *Political Power and Social Classes* (London: New Left Books, 1974), 279.

12. A. Przeworski and M. Wallerstein, "Structural Dependence of the State on Capital."

13. This is what separates Lenin's and Gramsci's notions of hegemony, since Lenin equated hegemonic rule with class dictatorship and hence downplayed the consent-versus-coercion aspects of different forms of rule.

14. The importance of labor courts in these processes of redemocratization should be noted, particularly in Argentina and Brazil, where authoritarian labor relations have been the historical norm. The need to redraw the legal boundaries framing state-labor-capital interaction made the system of labor courts one of the front lines of interaction (along with Parliament) between the three strategic actors in these countries. In Uruguay, the role of labor courts is circumscribed by individual grievance petitions, since the readoption of the concertative pluralist pre-authoritarian labor codes removed the need for legal definition of collective labor rights.

15. Remarkable in this regard are the attempts by the Peronist government of Carlos Menem (ostensibly worker-based) to transfer union-operated health and welfare systems (Obras Sociales) to state or private control while simultaneously pushing legislation that fosters collective

bargaining at the factory or shop level rather than at the industry level, which has been the (corporatist) norm in Argentina since 1946. Thus, not only are the benefits accrued by union membership reduced; so is the structural (sectorial and strategic) bargaining power of unions themselves. Ironically, the preceding Alfonsín administration, a government not based on labor's support, failed to do exactly this because it attempted to legislatively disarticulate organized labor as a political agent by promoting a dissolution of the national labor confederation, the CGT. Although structurally weakened at that time (1984), the CGT remained politically powerful, with a strong parliamentary presence, and was able to defeat the move in Congress. The fact that these new attempts are occurring under an ostensibly pro-labor government is all the more proof that pluralist ideologies are the dominant labor relations paradigm of the post-authoritarian moment. On this, see "Rival CGT Factions to Bury Hatchet," 10.

16. These changes were: the new international division of labor; the enormous structural problems confronting Latin America; the global move toward political democracy; the critical reappraisal of socialist prescriptions for national development; and the recognition on the part of Latin Americans that the authoritarian solutions of the past offer little in the way of long-term stability or national self-realization.

BIBLIOGRAPHY

Books

Abós, A. *El Posperonismo*. Buenos Aires: Editorial Legasa, 1986.

———. *La columna vertebral: Sindicatos y Peronismo*. Buenos Aires: Editorial Hispanoamérica, 1986.

———. *Las organizaciones sindicales y el poder militar (1976–1983)*. Buenos Aires: Centro Editor de América, 1984.

———. *Los sindicatos Argentinos: Cuadro de situación. 1984*. Buenos Aires: CEPNA, 1985.

Alba, V. *Historia del movimiento obrero en América Latina*. México, D.F.: Librería Mexicanos Unidos, 1964.

Alexander, R. *Labor Relations in Argentina, Brazil, and Chile*. New York: McGraw Hill, 1962.

Althusser, L. *For Marx*. London: Penguin Books, 1969.

———. *Lenin and Philosophy and Other Essays*. New York: Monthly Review Press, 1971.

Ames, B. *Political Survival: Politicians and Public Policy in Latin America*. Berkeley: University of California Press, 1987.

Baily, S. *Labor, Nationalism, and Politics in Argentina*. New Brunswick: Rutgers University Press, 1966.

Baloyra, E., ed. *Comparing New Democracies*. Boulder: Westview Press, 1987.

Berger, S., ed. *Organizing Interests in Western Europe: Pluralism, Corporatism, and the Transformation of Politics*. Cambridge: Cambridge University Press, 1981.

Bergquist, C. *Labor in Latin America: Comparative Essays on Chile, Argentina, Venezuela and Columbia*. Stanford: Stanford University Press, 1986.

Besouchet, L. *Historia da criação do Ministério do Trabalho: Ensaio de intepretação*. Rio de Janeiro: Imprensa Nacional Coleção Lindolfo Collor, 1952.

Bilsky, E. J. *La semana trágica*. Buenos Aires: n.p., 1984.

Blau, P. *Exchange and Power in Social Life*. New York: Wiley and Sons, 1964.

Bobbio, N. *El futuro de la democracia*. Barcelona: Plaza y Janés, 1986.

Bowman, J. R. *Capitalist Collective Action: Conflict and Cooperation in the Coal Industry*. New York: Cambridge University Press, 1989.

Bryce, J. *Modern Democracies*. Vol. 2. London: n.p., 1921.

Buci-Glucksman, C. *Gramsci and the State*. London: Lawrence and Wishart, 1980.

Burowoy, M. *The Politics of Production*. London: Verso, 1985.

Calderón, F., and E. Jelin, eds. *Los nuevos movimientos sociales*. Buenos Aires: Centro Editor de América Latina, 1985.

Capeletti, B. *La concertación en la Argentina: Antecedentes y experiencias*. Buenos Aires: CEPNA, 1985.

Carnoy, M. *The State and Political Theory*. Princeton: Princeton University Press, 1984.

Cavarozzi, M. *Sindicatos y política en Argentina*. Buenos Aires: Estudios CEDES, 1984.

―――. *Autoritarismo y democracia (1955–1983)*. Buenos Aires: Centro Editor de América Latina, 1983.

Cavarozzi, M., L. de Riz, and V. Feldman. *Concertación, Estado, y sindicatos en la Argentina contemporánea*. Buenos Aires: CEDES, 1986.

Cawson, A., ed. *Organized Interests and the State: Studies in Meso-Corporatism*. Beverly Hills: Sage Publications, 1985.

CIESU. *7 enfoques sorba la concertación*. Montevideo: Ediciones de la Banda Oriental, 1984.

Collier, D. ed. *The New Authoritarianism in Latin America*. Princeton: Princeton University Press, 1979.

Collier, D., and R. B. Collier. *Shaping the Political Arena*. Princeton: Princeton University Press, 1992.

Connor, J. E., ed. *Lenin On Politics and Revolution: Selected Writings*. New York: Pegasus, 1968.

Córdoba, E. *Las relaciones colectivas de trabajo en América Latina*. Geneva: ILO, 1981.

Correa, J. *Los jerarcas sindicales*. Buenos Aires: Editorial Obrador, 1975.

Costa, A. C., I. Ferrari, and N. B. Correa. *Consolidação das leis do trabalho*. 2d ed. São Paulo: n.p., 1956.

―――. *Consolidação das leis do trabalho*. 9th ed. São Paulo: Edições LTR, 1979.

Crouch, C. *Trade Unions: The Logic of Collective Action.* London: Fontana Books, 1983.

DaMatta, R. *A casa e a rua.* São Paulo: Editora Brasiliense, 1985.

Davis, S. M., and L. W. Goodman, eds. *Workers and Managers in Latin America.* Lexington, Mass.: D.C. Heath, 1972.

De Ferrari, F. *Derecho del trabajo.* 2d ed. Vol. 1. Buenos Aires: DePalma Editores, 1968.

Diamond, L., and G. Marks, eds. *Comparative Perspectives on Democracy.* Newbury Park: Calif.: Sage Publications, 1992.

Diamond, L., J. Linz, and S. M. Lipset, eds. *Democracy in Developing Countries: Africa, Asia, and Latin America.* Boulder: Lynne Rienner Publishers, 1988.

Di Tella, G. *Argentina Under Peron, 1973–1976: The Nation's Experiment with a Labor-Based Government.* New York: St. Martin's Press, 1983.

Di Tella, T. S. *Política y clase obrera.* Buenos Aires: Centro Editor de América, 1983.

Elster, J. *Ulysses and the Sirens.* New York: Cambridge University Press, 1983.

Erickson, K. P. *The Brazilian Corporative State and Working Class Politics.* Berkeley: University of California Press, 1977.

———. *Sindicalismo no proceso político no Brazil.* São Paulo: Brasiliense, 1979.

Errandonea, A., and D. Constabile. *Sindicato y sociedad en el Uruguay.* Montevideo: Biblioteca de Cultura Universitaria, 1969.

Evans, P., D. Rueschemeyer, and T. Skocpol, eds. *Bringing the State Back In.* Cambridge: Cambridge University Press, 1985.

Fernández, A. *Las prácticas sociales del sindicalismo, 1.* Buenos Aires: Centro Editor de América Latina, 1986.

Gallitelli B., and A. Thompson, eds. *Sindicalismo y regímenes militares en Argentina y Chile.* Amsterdam: CEDLA, 1982.

Gambarotta, H., A. LaMadrid, and A. Orsatti. *Propuestas económicas del sindicalismo Argentino, guia temática y recopilación.* Buenos Aires: CEDEL, 1988.

Gillespie, C. et al. *Uruguay y la democracia.* 3 vols. Montevideo: Ediciones de la Banda Oriental, 1984–1985.

Godio, J. *Sindicalismo y política en América Latina.* Caracas: ILDIS, 1983.

Godio, J., H. Palomino, and A. Wachendorfer. *El movimiento sindical Argentino (1880–1987).* Buenos Aires: Puntosur Editores, 1988.

Godio, J., and J. Slodky. *El regreso de la negociación colectiva.* Buenos Aires: Fundación Friedrich Ebert, 1988.

Goldthorpe, J., ed. *Order and Conflict in Contemporary Capitalism.* Oxford: Clarendon Press, 1985.

Goodman, L. W., J. S. R. Mendelson, and J. Rial, eds. *The Military and Democracy: The Future of Civil-Military Relations in Latin America.* Lexington, Mass.: Lexington Books, 1990.

Gorz, A. *Farewell to the Working Class.* Boston: South End Press, 1982.

Gramsci, A. *Selections from the Prison Notebooks.* Ed. and trans. Quintin Hoare and Geoffrey Norwell Smith. New York: International Publishers, 1971.

Halperin Donghi, T. *Historia de los Orientales.* 4th ed. Montevideo: Ediciones de la Banda Oriental, 1984.

Hardin, R. *Collective Action.* Baltimore: Johns Hopkins University Press, 1982.

Heguey Terra, E. *Estudios sobre la administración del trabajo en el Uruguay.* 2 vols. Montevideo: MTSS and Universidad de la República, 1979.

Hewitt, S. A. *The Cruel Dilemmas of Development: Twentieth Century Brazil.* New York: Basic Books, 1980.

Higley J., and R. Gunther, eds. *Elites and Democratic Consolidation in Latin American and Southern Europe.* New York: Cambridge University Press, 1992.

Hoare, Q., ed. *Antonio Gramsci: Selections from Political Writings (1910–1920).* London: Lawrence & Wishart, 1977.

Horowitz, J. *Argentine Unions, the State, and the Rise of Perón, 1930–1945.* Berkeley: Institute of International Studies, 1990.

Humphrey, J. *Capitalist Control and Worker's Struggle in the Brazilian Auto Industry.* Princeton: Princeton University Press, 1982.

Jacob, R. et al. *Concertación y democracia.* Montevideo: CLASCO, 1984.

James, D. *Resistance and Integration: Peronism and the Argentine Working Class.* New York: Cambridge University Press, 1988.

Katzenstein, P. *Small States in World Markets.* Ithaca: Cornell University Press, 1985.

Keck, Margaret E. *The Workers Party and Democratization in Brazil.* New Haven: Yale University Press, 1992.

Keynes, J. M. *La teoria general de empleo, interés, y dinero.* México City: Fondo de Cultura Económica, 1943.

Klaren, P., and T. Bossert. *The Promise of Development.* Boulder: Westview Press, 1987.

Knight, J. *Institutions and Social Conflict.* New York: Cambridge University Press, 1992.

Lechner, N. *Pacto social en los procesos de democratización. La experiencia Latinoamericana.* Santiago: FLACSO, 1985.

Lechner, N., ed. *Estado y política en America Latina*. México, City: Siglo XXI, 1981.

Lehembruch, G., and P. C. Schmitter, eds. *Patterns of Corporatist Policy-Making*. Beverly Hills: Sage Publications, 1982.

Lenin, V. I. *Selected Works*. Vol. 2. Moscow: Progress Publishers, 1970.

Lindblom, C. *Politics and Markets*. New York: Basic Books, 1977.

Linz, J., and A. Stepan, eds. *The Breakdown of Democratic Regimes: Latin America*. Baltimore: Johns Hopkins University Press, 1978.

Maier, C. S. *Recasting Bourgeois Europe*. Princeton: Princeton University Press, 1975.

Mainwaring, S., G. A. O'Donnell, and J. Valenzuela, eds. *Issues in Democratic Consolidation*. South Bend: University of Notre Dame Press, 1992.

Malloy, J. *The Politics of Social Security in Brazil*. Pittsburgh: University of Pittsburgh Press, 1979.

Malloy, J., ed. *Authoritarianism and Corporatism in Latin America*. Pittsburgh: University of Pittsburgh Press, 1977.

Malloy, J., and M. Seligson, eds. *Authoritarians and Democrats*. Pittsburgh: University of Pittsburgh Press, 1987.

Matushita, H. *Movimiento obrero argentino 1930–1945. Sus proyecciones en los orígines del Peronismo*. Buenos Aires: Siglo XXI, 1983.

Mesa-Lago, C. *Social Security in Latin America*. Pittsburgh: University of Pittsburgh Press, 1978.

Michels, R. *Political Parties*. Trans. E. Paul and Cedar Paul. New York: Dover Publications, 1959.

Moraes Filho, E. de. *O direito e a ordem democrática*. São Paulo: Editora LTR, 1984.

Moreira Alves, M. H. *State and Opposition in Military Brazil*. Austin: University of Texas Press, 1985.

Murmis, M., and J. C. Portantiero. *Estudios sobre los origines del peronismo*. Buenos Aires: Siglo XXI, 1972.

Nun, J., and J. C. Portantiero, eds. *Ensayos sobre la transición democrática en la Argentina*. Buenos Aires: Editores Puntosur, 1987.

O'Donnell, G. A. *El Estado burocrático-autoritario 1966–1973: Triunfos, derrotas y crisis*. Buenos Aires: Editorial de Belgrano, 1982.

———. *Modernization and Bureaucratic Authoritarianism: Studies in South American Politics*. Berkeley: University of California Press, 1973.

O'Donnell, G. A., P. C. Schmitter, and L. Whitehead, eds. *Transitions from Authoritarian Rule: Prospects for Democratization*. 4 vols. Baltimore: Johns Hopkins University Press, 1986.

Olson, M. *The Logic of Collective Action*. Cambridge: Harvard University Press, 1965.

Oszlak, O. *Políticas públicas y regímenes políticos: Reflexiones a partir de algunas experiencias Latino-americanas*. Buenos Aires: ESTUDIOS CEDES, 1980.

———. *La formación del Estado Argentino*. Buenos Aires: Editorial Belgrano, 1982.

Pásara L., and J. Parodi, eds. *Democracia, sociedad y gobierno en el Perú*. Lima: CEDYS, 1988.

Paulón, C. A. *Direito Administrativo do Trabalho*. São Paulo: Editora LTR, 1984.

Peralta-Ramos, M. *Etapas de acumulación y alianzas de clases en Argentina*. Buenos Aires: Siglo XXI, 1972.

Peralta-Ramos, M., and C. Weisman, eds. *From Military Rule to Liberal Democracy in Argentina*. Boulder: Westview Press, 1987.

Perón, J. D. *La organización a través del pensamiento de Perón*. Buenos Aires: Editorial Freeland, 1973.

Plá Rodriguez, A. *La reglamentación sindical en Uruguay*. Montevideo: Biblioteca de "Marcha," 1973.

Poblete Troncoso, M. *El movimiento obrero Latinoamericano*. México City: Biblioteca del Trabajador Mexicano, 1976.

Poblete Troncoso, M., and B. G. Barnett. *The Rise of the Latin American Labor Movement*. New York: Bookman, 1960.

Potash, R. *The Army and Politics in Argentina: 1928–1945*. Stanford: Stanford University Press, 1969.

Poulantzas, N. *Fascism and Dictatorship*. London: Verso Editions, 1979.

———. *Political Power and Social Classes*. London: New Left Books, 1974.

———. *State, Power, Socialism*. London: New Left Books, 1978.

Prado, P. E. *Leyes y decretos de trabajo y previsión*. 2d ed. Buenos Aires: Librería y Editora Alsina, 1949.

Przeworski, A. *Capitalism and Social Democracy*. Cambridge: Cambridge University Press, 1985.

———. *Democracy and the Market: Political and Economic Reform in Eastern Europe and Latin America*. New York: Cambridge University Press, 1991.

———. *The State and Economy Under Capitalism*. New York: Harwood Academic Publishers, 1992.

Ranis, P. *Argentine Workers: Peronism and Contemporary Values*. Pittsburgh: University of Pittsburgh Press, 1992.

Reis, F. W., and G. A. O'Donnell, eds. *A democracia no Brasil: Dilemas e Perspectivas*. São Paulo: Edições Vertice, 1988.

Rejal, M., ed. *Mao Tse-Tung on Revolution and War*. Garden City, New York: Doubleday, 1969.

Riz, L. de, M. Cavarozzi, and V. Feldman. *Concertación, estado y sindicatos en la Argentina contemporánea*. Buenos Aires: Estudios CEDES, 1987.

Rock, D. *Argentina, 1516–1982: From Spanish Colonialism to the Falklands*. Berkeley: University of California Press, 1985.

Rodriguez, H. *Nuestros sindicatos*. Montevideo: Centro Estudiantes de Derecho, 1966.

Rotundaro, R. *Realidad y cambio en el sindicalismo*. Buenos Aires: Editorial Pleamar, 1973.

Rouquié, A. *Argentine Hoy*. Buenos Aires: Siglo XXI, 1982.

Schmitter, P. C. *Interest Conflict and Political Change in Brazil*. Stanford: Stanford University Press, 1971.

Schmitter P. C., and G. Lehembruch, eds. *Trends Towards Corporatist Intermediation*. Beverly Hills: Sage Publications, 1979.

Schvarzer, J. *Martinez de Hoz: La lógica política de la política económica*. Buenos Aires: CISEA, 1983.

———. *Argentina, 1976–1981. El endeudamiento externo como pivote de la especulación financiera*. Buenos Aires: CISEA, 1983.

Senén Gonzáles, S. *Breve historia del sindicalismo Argentino, 1874–1974*. Buenos Aires: Alzamor Editores, 1974.

———. *Diez años de sindicalismo argentino: De Perón al Proceso*. Buenos Aires: Ediciones Corregidor, 1984.

Shubik, M. *A Game-Theoretic Approach to Political Economy*. Cambridge: MIT Press, 1984.

Silva Michelena, J. A., and H. R. Sontag. *El proceso electoral de 1978*. Caracas: Editorial El Ateneo de Caracas, 1979.

Slodky, J. *La negociación colectiva en la Argentina*. Buenos Aires: Puntosur, 1988.

Smith, W. C. *Authoritarianism and the Crisis of the Argentine Political Economy*. Stanford: Stanford University Press, 1989.

Souze Martins, H. H. T. de. *O Estado e a burocratizão do sindicato no Brasil*. São Paulo: Editora Hucitec, 1979.

Spaulding, H. *Organized Labor in Latin America: Historical Case Studies of Workers in Dependent Societies*. New York: Harper and Row, 1977.

Stepan, A. *Rethinking Military Politics: Brazil and the Southern Cone*. Princeton: Princeton University Press, 1988.

Sussekind, A. et al. *Instituções de Direito de Trabalho*. 8th ed. Rio de Janeiro: Livreria Freitas Bastos S/A, 1981.

Taiana, J. *El movimiento obrero (1973–1988)*. Buenos Aires: Cuadernos de Crisis 34, 1988.

Tamarin, D. *The Argentine Labor Movement, 1930–1945*. Albuquerque:

University of New Mexico Press, 1985.

Torre, J. C. *Los sindicatos en el gobierno, 1973–1976*. Buenos Aires: Centro Editor de América Latina, 1983.

Weinstein, M. *Uruguay: The Politics of Failure*. Westport, Conn.: Greenwood Press, 1975.

Wiarda, W. *The Corporative Origins of the Iberian and Latin American Labor Relations System*. Amherst: University of Massachusetts Labor Relations and Research Center, 1976.

Wynia, G. *Argentina in the Postwar Era*. Albuquerque: University of New Mexico Press, 1978.

Zorrilla, R. *Estructura y dinámica del sindicalismo*. Buenos Aires: Editorial La Playade, 1974.

Articles and Chapters

Acuña, C. H., M. R. Dos Santos, D. García, and L. Golbert. "Relación Estado-empresarios y políticas concertadas de ingresos. El caso Argentino." In PREALC, *Política económica y actores sociales: La concertación de ingresos y empleo*. Santiago: ILO, 1988.

Alemann, R. T. "La Retroalimentación." *La Nación*, July 27, 1986.

Aragonés, N. "Entre la `fatalidad' de la decadencia y la creación de alternativas viables: Notas sobre estilos alternativos de desarrollo y concertación estratégica en el Uruguay." *Cuadernos del CLAEH* 34, 10, 2 (1985).

Ayres R. "The `Social Pact' as Anti-Inflationary Policy: The Argentine Experience Since 1973." *World Politics* 28, 4 (July 1975).

Barros, Robert. "The Left and Democracy: Recent Debates in Latin America." *TELOS* 68 (Summer 1986).

Bengochea P. M., and A. Melgar. "Evolución de precios e ingresos 1985–1986." *Cuadernos del CLAEH* 39, 11, 3 (1986).

Block, F. "Beyond Relative Autonomy: State Managers as Historical Subjects." In R. Miliband and J. Saville, eds. *Socialist Register*. London: Merlin Press, 1980.

———. "The Ruling Class Does Not Rule," *Socialist Revolution* 7, 3 (1977).

Bossert, T. J. "Can We Return to the Regime for Comparative Policy Analysis?" *Comparative Politics* 15, 4 (July 1983).

Bowman, J. "The Logic of Capitalist Collective Action," *Social Science Information* 21 (1982).

———. "The Politics of the Market: Economic Competition and the Organization of Capitalists." *Political Power and Social Theory* 5 (1985).

Buchanan, P. G. "The Argentine Labor Movement, 1982." *Washington Report on the Hemisphere* 3, 3 (November 2, 1982).

———. "Exorcising Collective Ghosts: Recent Argentine Writings on Politics, Economics, Social Movements, and Popular Culture." *Latin American Research Review* 25, 2 (1990).

———. "Plus ça change? A Administração Nacional do Trabalho E a democracia no Brasil, 1985–1987." *DADOS* 32,1 (1989).

———. "State Corporatism in Argentina: Labor Administration Under Perón and Onganía." *Latin American Research Review* 20, 1 (Spring 1985).

———. "The Varied Faces of Domination: State Terror, Economic Policy, and Social Rupture during the Argentine 'Proceso.'" *American Journal of Political Science* 31, 2 (1987).

Burowoy, M. "Marxism without Microfoundations." *Socialist Review* 89, 2 (1989).

———. "The Contours of Production Politics." In C. Berquist, ed. *Labor in the Capitalist World Economy*. Beverly Hills: Sage Publications, 1984.

Candia, J. M. "Argentina: Proceso militar y clase obrera." *Cuadernos del Sur* 2 (April–June 1985).

Canitrot, A. "La vialidad económica de la democracia: Un análisis de la experiencia peronista, 1973–1976." *Estudios Sociales* 11 (1978).

Christie, Drew. "Recent Calls for Economic Democracy." *Ethics* 95, 1 (October 1984).

Cohen, Y. "The Benevolent Leviathan: Political Consciousness Among Urban Workers Under State Corporatism." *American Political Science Review* 76, 1 (March 1982).

Collier, D., and R. B. Collier. "Inducements Versus Constraints: Disaggregating 'Corporatism.'" *American Political Science Review* 73, 4 (December 1979).

Corbo, V., and J. de Melo. "Lessons from the Southern Cone Reforms." *The World Bank Research Observer* 2, 2 (1987).

Corradi, J. E. "The Argentina of Carlos Saul Menem." *Current History* 91, 562 (February 1992).

———. "The Culture of Fear in Civil Society." In M. Peralta Ramos and C. H. Weisman, eds. *From Military Rule to Liberal Democracy in Argentina*. Boulder: Westview Press, 1987.

———. "The Mode of Destruction: Terror in Argentina," *TELOS* 54 (Winter 1982–1983).

D'Abate, J. C. "Trade Unions and Peronism." In F. Turner and J. Miguens, eds. *Juan Perón and the Reshaping of Argentina*. Pittsburgh: University of Pittsburgh Press, 1976.

Davis, C. I., and K. L. Coleman. "Labor and the State: Union Incorporation and Working Class Politization in Latin America." *Comparative Political Studies* 18, 4 (January 1986).

Delich, F. "Después del diluvio, la clase obrera." In A. Rouquié, ed. *Argentina Hoy*. Buenos Aires: Siglo XXI, 1982.

———. "Desmovilización sindical, reestructuración obrera y cambio sindical." *Crítica y Utopia* 6 (1981).

Diamond, L. "Crisis Choice and Structure: Reconciling Alternative Models for Explaining Democratic Success and Failure in the Third World." In L. Diamond, J. Linz, and S. M. Lipset, eds. *Democracy in Developing Countries: Comparing Experiences with Democracy*. New York: Lynne Rienner, 1990.

Diamond, L., S. M. Lipset, and J. Linz. "Introduction: Comparing Experiences with Democracy." In *Democracy in Developing Countries*.

Doyon, L. "El crecimiento sindical bajo el peronismo." *Desarrollo Económico* 15, 57 (April–June 1975).

Drake, P. W. "Los movimientos urbanos de trabajadores bajo el capitalismo autoritario en el Cono Sur y Brasil, 1964–1983." *Cuadernos del Claeh* 40 (1986): 27.

Esping-Andersen, G., R. Friedland, and E. D. Wright. "Modes of Class Struggle and the Capitalist State." *Kapitalstate* 4–5 (1976).

Falabella, G. "Un `nuevo sindicalismo'? El gran ABC bajo régimenes militares." *Serie de Estudios Sociológicos* 54 (October 1986).

Filgueria, C. H. "Mediación política y apertura democrática en el Uruguay." *Revista Mexicana de Sociología* 47, 2 (1985).

Flisfisch, A. "Reflexiones algo oblicuas sobre el tema de la concertación." *Desarrollo Económico* 26, 61 (April–June 1986).

Fortuna, J. C. "Los cambios en el escenario estructural de los movimientos laborales." *Revista Mexicana de Sociología* 47, 2 (1985).

Foweraker, J. "Corporatist Strategies and the Transition to Democracy in Spain." *Comparative Politics* 20, 1 (October 1987).

Fraga, A., M. Maronna, and Y. Trochón. "Los Consejos de Salarios como experiencia de concertación." *Cuadernos del CLAEH* 33, 10, 1 (1985).

Franco, R. "El Estado Uruguayo en la transición a la democracia." In Gillespie et al. *Uruguay y la democracia*. Vol. 3.

Gargiulo, M. "El movimiento sindical Uruguayo en los '80: Concertación o confrontación?" In *El Sindicalismo Latinoamericano en los Ochenta*. Santiago: CLACSO, 1986.

———. "El desafío de la democracia. La izquierda política y sindical en el Uruguay post-autoritario." *Cuadernos del CLAEH* 38, 11, 2 (1986).

Garretón, M. A. "The Failure of Dictatorships in the Southern Cone." *TELOS* 68 (Summer 1986).

Gaudio, R., and H. Domeniconi. "Las primeras elecciones sindicales en la transición democratica." *Desarrollo Económico* 26, 103 (October–December 1986).

Germani, G. "Democracia y autoritarismo en la sociedad moderna." *Crítica y Utopia* 1 (1979).

Gillespie, C. "Review Essay: From Authoritarian Crises to Democratic Transitions." *Latin American Research Review* 22, 3 (Fall 1987).

Gillespie, G. "Uruguay's Transition from Collegial Military-Technocratic Rule." In G. A. O'Donnell, P. C. Schmitter, and L. Whitehead, eds. *Transitions from Authoritarianism.* Vol. 2, *Latin America.*

Gonzalez, L. E. "Los partidos y la redemocratización en Uruguay." *Cuardenos del CLAEH* 37, 11, 1 (1986).

Government and Opposition 19, 2 (Spring 1984). Issue entitled "From Authoritarian to Representative Government in Brazil and Argentina."

Grossi, M., and M. R. Dos Santos. "La concertación social: Una perspectiva sobre instrumentos de regulación económico-social en procesos de redemocratización." *Crítica y Utopia* 9 (1982).

"Los grupos socioeconómicos y los partidos políticos en el espacio de la concertación." In Documento 2, *Concertación y Democracia.* Montevideo: CIEDUR, 1984.

Hagopian, F., and S. Mainwaring. "Democracy in Brazil: Origins, Problems, Prospects." *World Policy Journal* 4, 3 (Summer 1987).

Handelman, H. "Labor-Industrial Conflict and the Collapse of Uruguayan Democracy." *Journal of Interamerican Studies and World Affairs* 23, 4 (November 1981).

Herman, A. "Conceptualizing Control: Domination and Hegemony in the Capitalist Labor Process." *Insurgent Sociologist* 11, 3 (1982).

Huneeus, C., and J. Olave. "A participação dos militares nos novos autoritarismos: O Chile en una perspectiva comparada." *DADOS* 30, 3 (1987).

Jessop, B. "Capitalism and Democracy: The Best Possible Political Shell?" In G. Littlejohn et al., eds. *Power and the State.* London: Croom Helm, 1978.

Jouval, H. J. "La atención medica en la seguridad social. Brasil 1985." *Cuadernos Médico Sociales* 38 (1986).

Jungwoon Choi. "The English Ten-hours Act: Official Knowledge and the Collective Interest of the Ruling Class." *Politics and Society* 13, 4 (1984).

Kaplan, M. A. "Recent Trends of the Nation-State in Contemporary Latin America." *International Political Science Review* 6, 2 (1985).

Karl, T. "Petroleum and Political Pacts: The Transition to Democracy in Venezuela." In O'Donnell, Schmitter, and Whitehead, eds. *Transitions from Authoritarian Rule: Prospects for Democracy.* Vol. 2, *Latin America.*

Knight, J. "How Unobservable Can 'Power' Be?" In S. Lukes, ed. *Power.* London: Mcmillan Press, 1991.

Landi, O. "Sobre lenguajes, identidades y ciudadanías políticas." In N. Lechner, ed. *Estado y política en América Latina*. México City: Siglo XXI, 1981.

Lange, Peter. "Unions, Workers and Wage Regulation: The Rational Bases of Consent." In John H. Goldthorpe, ed. *Order and Conflict in Contemporary Capitalism*. Oxford: Clarendon Press, 1985.

Lanzaro, J. C. "Movimiento obrero y reconstitución democrática. Convencionalidad neocorporativa o aplicaciones neoliberales?" *Revista Mexicana de Sociología* 47, 2 (1987).

Lehmbruch, G. "Concertation and the Structure of Corporatist Networks." In Goldthorpe, ed. *Order and Conflict in Contemporary Capitalism*.

———. "Liberal Corporatism and Party Government." In P. C. Schmitter and G. Lehmbruch, eds. *Trends Towards Corporatist Intermediation*. Beverly Hills: Sage Publications, 1979.

Levine, D. "Paradigm Lost: Dependence to Democracy." *World Politics* 40, 3 (April 1988).

Little, W. "La organización obrera y el estado peronista, 1943–1955." *Desarrollo Económico* 18, 75 (October–December 1979).

Loveman, B. "Political Participation and Rural Labor in Chile." In M. A. Seligson and J. Booth, eds. *Political Participation in Latin America*. New York: Holmes and Meier, 1979.

Mainwaring, S. "The State and the Industrial Bourgeoisie in Perón's Argentina, 1945–1955." *Studies in Comparative International Development* 21, 3 (Fall 1986), 3–31.

———. "The Transition to Democracy in Brazil." *Journal of Interamerican Studies and World Affairs* 28, 3 (May 1986).

Mainwaring, S., and D. Share. "Transitions through Transaction: Democratization in Brazil and Spain." in W. Selcher, ed. *Political Liberalization in Brazil*. Boulder: Westview Press, 1986.

Malloy, J. M. "Social Security Policy and the Working Class in Twentieth Century Brazil." *Journal of Interamerican Studies and World Affairs* 19, 1 (February 1977).

Manzetti, L., and M. Dell'Aquila. "Economic Stabilization in Argentina: The Austral Plan." *Journal of Latin American Studies* 20 (May 1988): 1–26.

Martins, L. "The `Liberalization' of Authoritarian Rule in Brazil." In O'Donnell, Schmitter, and Whitehead. *Transitions from Authoritarian Rule*. Vol. 2, *Latin America*.

Masters, M. F., and J. D. Robertson. "Class Compromise in Industrial Democracies." *American Political Science Review* 82, 4 (December 1988).

McCoy, J. "Labor and the State in a Party-Mediated Democracy: Institutional Change in Venezuela." *Latin American Research Review* 24, 2 (1989).

McGuire, J. "Union Political Tactics and Democratic Consolidation in Alfonsin's Argentina, 1983–1989." *Latin American Research Review* 27, 1 (1992).

Melgar, A., and W. Cancela. "Concentración del ingreso y desarticulación productiva: Un desafío al proceso de democratización." *Revista Mexicana de Sociología* 47, 2 (1985).

Mericle, K. "Corporatist Control of the Working Class: Authoritarian Brazil Since 1964." In J. Malloy, ed. *Authoritarianism and Corporatism in Latin America*. Pittsburgh: University of Pittsburgh Press, 1977.

Mieres, P. "Concertación en Uruguay: Expectativas elevadas y consensos escasos." *Cuadernos del CLAEH* 36, 4 (1985).

Most, Benjamin A. "Authoritarianism and the Growth of the State in Latin America: An Assessment of Their Impacts on Argentine Public Policy, 1930–1970." *Comparative Political Studies* 13, 2 (July 1980).

Mouzelis, N. "On the Rise of Postwar Military Dictatorships: Argentina, Chile, Greece." *Comparative Studies in Society and History* 28 (1986).

Muiño, R., and R. Rossi Albert. "La materia laboral en la Concertación Nacional Programática." *La Concertación Social*. Montevideo: Ediciones Jurídicas Amalio Fernández, 1985.

Neuhowser, K. "Democratic Stability in Venezuela: Elite Consensus or Class Compromise?" *American Sociological Review* 57, 1 (February 1992).

Novos Estudos CEBRAP 13 (October 1985).

Nun, J. "Democracia y socialismo: Etapas o niveles? in Fundación Pablo Iglesias." *Los caminos de la democracia en America Latina*. Madrid: Pablo Iglesias, 1984.

———. "La teoria política y la transición democrática." In J. Nun and J. C. Portantiero, eds. *Ensayos sobre la transición democrática en la Argentina*. Buenos Aires: Puntosur Editores, 1987.

O'Donnell, G. A. "La cosecha del miedo." *NEXOS* 6 (1983).

———. "Corporatism and the Question of the State." In J. Malloy, ed. *Authoritarianism and Corporatism in Latin America*. Pittsburgh: University of Pittsburgh Press, 1977.

O'Donnell, G. A., and P. C. Schmitter. "Tentative Conclusions About Uncertain Democracies." In O'Donnell, Schmitter, and Whitehead, *Transitions from Authoritarian Rule*. Vol. 4.

Offe, C. "The Capitalist State and the Problem of Policy Formation." In L. Lindberg et al. *Stress and Contradiction in Contemporary Capitalism*. Lexington, Mass.: Lexington Books, 1975.

———. "The Attribution of Public Status to Interest Groups." In S. Berger, ed. *Organizing Interests in Western Europe.* Cambridge: Cambridge University Press, 1981.

———. "Competitive Party Democracy and Keynesian Welfare State: Some Reflections on the Welfare State." In J. Keane, ed. *Contradictions of the Welfare State.* London: n.p.

Offe, C., and H. Wiesenthal. "Two Logics of Collective Action: Theoretical Notes on Social Class and Organizational Form." In M. Zeitlin, ed. *Political Power and Social Theory.* Vol. 1. Greenwood, Conn.: JAI Press, 1980.

Offe, C., and V. Runge. "Theses on the Theory of the State." *New German Critique* (Fall 1975).

Olson, M. "A Theory of Incentives Facing Political Organizations: Neo-Corporatism and the Hegemonic State." *International Political Science Review* 7, 2 (April 1986).

Palomino, H. "El movimiento de democratización sindical." In E. Jelin, ed., *Los nuevos movimientos sociales.* Buenos Aires: Centro Editor de América Latina, 1985.

———. "Movimiento social e instituciones." *El Bimestre* 38 (March–April 1988).

Panitch, L. "Trade Unions and the Capitalist State." *New Left Review* 125 (1981).

———. "Recent Theorizations of Corporatism: Reflections on a Growth Industry." *British Journal of Sociology* 31 (1980).

Pareja, C. "Las instancias de concertación. Sus presupuestos, sus modalidades, y su articulación con las formas clásicas de democracia representativa." *Cuadernos del CLAEH* 32, 4 (1984).

Pérez, R. "La articulación de la sociedad y el Estado: Una sugerencia metodológica." *Cuadernos del CLAEH* 37, 11, 1 (1986).

Pion-Berlin, D. "The Fall of Military Rule in Argentina, 1976–1983." *Journal of Interamerican Studies and World Affairs* 27, 1 (1985).

Pitelis, C. N. "Corporate Control, Social Choice, and Capital Accumulation: An Asymmetrical Choice Approach." *Review of Radical Political Economics* 18, 3 (1986): 85–100.

Pozzi, P. "Argentina 1976–1982: Labour Leadership and Military Government." *Journal of Latin American Studies* 20 (May 1988).

Prates, S. "Cambios estructurales y movimientos populares: Reflexiones sobre la concertación social en el Uruguay post-autoritario." In CIESU, *7 enfoques sobre la concertación.* Montevideo: Ediciones de la Banda Oriental, 1984.

———. "El trabajo de la mujer en una época de crisis (o cuando se pierde ganando)." In GRECMU (Grupo de Estudios sobre la Condición de la Mujer en el Uruguay). *La mujer en Uruguay: Ayer y hoy.* Montevideo: Ediciones de la Banda Oriental, 1983.

Przeworski, A. "Marxism and Rational Choice." *Politics and Society* 14, 4 (1985).

———. "Material Bases of Consent: Economics and Politics in a Hegemonic System." In M. Zeitlin, ed. *Political Power and Social Theory* 1 (1980).

———. "Material Interests, Class Compromise, and the Transition to Socialism." *Politics and Society* 19, 2 (1980).

Przeworski, A., and M. Wallerstein. "Capitalismo y democracia: Una reflexión desde la macroeconomia." *Crítica y Utopia* 8 (November 1982).

———. "Democratic Capitalism at the Crossroads." *Democracy* 2, 3 (July 1982).

———. "Structural Dependence of the State on Capital." *American Political Science Review* 82, 1 (1988).

———. "The Structure of Class Conflict in Democratic Capitalist Societies." *American Political Science Review* 76, 2 (June 1982).

Pujato, J. M. G. "El Ministerio de Trabajo en la República Argentina." *Derecho de Trabajo* 10, 1 (1950).

Ranis, P. "Redemocratization and the Argentine Working Class." *Canadian Journal of Development Studies* 10, 2 (1989).

Real de Azua, C. "Política, poder y partidos en el Uruguay de hoy." In C. Benvenuto et al. *Uruguay de hoy*. Mexico City: Siglo XXI, 1971.

Regini, M. "The Conditions for Political Exchange: How Concertation Emerged and Collapsed in Italy and Great Britain." In Goldthorpe. *Order and Conflict in Contemporary Capitalism*.

Remmer, K. "Exclusionary Democracy." *Studies in Comparative International Development* 20, 4 (Winter 1985–1986).

———. "Redemocratization and the Impact of Authoritarian Rule in Latin America." *Comparative Politics* 17, 3 (April 1985).

Rial, J. "Post Scriptun." In C. Gillespie et al. *Uruguay y la Democracia*. Vol. 3.

———. "El movimiento sindical Uruguayo ante la redemocratización." In PREALC, *Política económica y actores sociales*. Santiago: ILO, 1988.

———. "Political Parties and Elections in the Process of Transition in Uruguay." In E. Baloyra, ed. *Comparing New Democracies*. Boulder: Westview Press, 1987.

———. "Estado, partidos políticos, y concertación social en el Uruguay de la transición." In CIESU, *7 enfoques sobre la concertación*.

Riz, L. de, M. Cavarozzi, and V. Feldman. "El contexto y los dilemas de la concertación en la Argentina actual." In M. Dos Santos. *Concertación político-social y democratización*. Buenos Aires: CLASCO, 1987.

Rosenberg, M. B., and J. M. Malloy. "Indirect Participation Versus Social

Equity in the Evolution of Latin American Social Security Policy." In J. Booth and M. Seligson, eds. *Political Participation in Latin America.* Vol. 1, *Citizen and State.* New York: Holmes and Meier, 1978.

Rostow, D. "Transitions to Democracy." *Comparative Politics* 2, 3 (April 1970).

Roxborough, I. "The Analysis of Labor Movements in Latin America: Typologies and Theories." *Bulletin of Latin American Research* 1, 1 (1981).

Rudolph, L. I., and S. H. Rudolph. "Authority and Power in Bureaucratic and Patrimonial Administration: A Revisionist Interpretation of Weber on Bureaucracy." *World Politics* 31, 2 (January 1979).

Schervish, P. G., and A. Herman. "On the Road: Conceptualizing Class Structure in the Transition to Socialism." *Work and Occupations* 13, 2 (May 1986).

Schmitter, P. C. "Still the Century of Corporatism," *Review of Politics* (1970).

———. "Neo-corporatism and the State." In W. Grant, ed. *The Political Economy of Corporatism.* London: Macmillan, 1985.

Sheahan, J. "Economic Policies and the Prospects for Successful Transition from Authoritarian Rule in Latin America." In O'Donnell, Schmitter, and Whitehead, eds. *Transitions from Authoritarian Rule.* Vol. 3, *Comparative Perspectives.*

Skocpol, T. "Bringing the State Back In: Strategies of Analysis in Current Research." In P. Evans, D. Reuschemeyer, and T. Skocpol, eds. *Bringing the State Back In.* Cambridge: Cambridge University Press, 1985.

Smith, A. "State Terror in Argentina. A Frankfurt School Perspective." *Praxis International* 6, 4 (January 1987).

Smith, W. C. "Democracy, Distributional Conflicts and Macroeconomic Policy-Making in Argentina, 1983–89." *Journal of Interamerican and World Affairs* 32, 2 (1990).

———. "Heterodox Shocks and the Political Economy of Democratic Transition in Argentina and Brazil." in W. L. Canak, ed. *Lost Promises: Debt, Austerity, and Development in Latin America.* Boulder: Westview Press, 1989.

———. "Hyperinflation, Macroeconomic Instability, and Neoliberal Restructuring in Democratic Argentina." in E. Epstein, ed. *The New Argentine Democracy: The Search for a Successful Formula.* New York: Praeger, 1992.

———. "State, Market, and Neoliberalism in Post-Transition Argentina: The Menem Experiment." *Journal of Interamerican and World Affairs* 33, 4 (Winter 1991).

Souza, A. da, and B. Lamounier. "Governo e sindicatos no Brazil: A Perspectiva dos Anos 80." *Dados* 4, 2 (1980).

Stepan, A. "State Power and the Strength of Civil Society in the Southern Cone of Latin America." In Evans et al. *Bringing the State Back In.* Cambridge: Cambridge University Press, 1985.

Taiana, J. "El movimiento obrero (1973–1988)." *Cuadernos de Crisis* 34 (1989).

Thompson, A. "Sindicatos y Estado en la Argentina: El fracaso de la concertación social desde 1983." *Boletín Informativo Technit,* 251 (January–March 1988).

———. "Will the New Bill Work?" *Argentine News* (May–June 1988).

Valenzuela, J. S. "Movimientos obreros y sistemas políticos: Un análisis conceptual y tipológico." *Desarrollo Económico* 23, 91 (October–December 1983).

———. "Labor Movement in Transitions to Democracy: A Framework for Analysis." *Comparative Politics* 21, 2 (1989).

Vianna, S. S. "Direito Administrativo do Trabalho." In A. Sussekind et al. *Instituções de Direito de Trabalho,* 8th ed. Rio de Janeiro: Livreria Freitas Bastos, S.A., 1981. Vol. 2.

Viña, A. "Democracia liberada en un pais bloqueado." *Cuadernos del CLAEH* 32, 4 (1984).

Viola, E., and S. Mainwaring. "New Social Movements, Political Culture, and Democracy: Brazil and Argentina in the 1980's." *Telos* 61 (Fall 1984).

———. "Transitions to Democracy: Brazil and Argentina in the 1980's." *Journal of International Affairs* 38, 2 (Winter 1985).

Wynia, G. "Argentina's Economic Reform." *Current History* 90, 553 (February 1991).

Monographs

Acuña, C., and R. Barros. "Issues on Democracy and Democratization: North and South. A Rapporteur's Report." Working paper 30, Kellogg Institute, October 1984.

Acuña, C. H., and L. Golbert. "Los empresarios y sus organizaciones: Actitudes y reacciones en relación al Plan Austral y su interacción con el mercado de trabajo." Buenos Aires: OIT-PREALC, 1988.

Boletim Nacional CUT, December 1986–January 1987.

Buchanan, P. G. "Regime Change and State Organization in Postwar Argentina." Ph.D. diss., University of Chicago, 1985.

———. "State Organization as a Political Indicator." Technical report 1 (56-87-008), Western Hemisphere Area Studies, Department of National Security Affairs, Naval Postgraduate School, March 1986.

Buchanan, P. G., and R. Looney. "Relative Militarization and Its Impact on Public Policy: Budgetary Shifts in Argentina, 1963–1987." Technical Report 7 (NPS 56-88-002), Western Hemisphere Area Studies,

Department of National Security Affairs, Naval Postgraduate School, July 1988.

Canitrot, A. "La disciplina como objectivo de la política económica. Un ensayo sobre el programa del gobierno argentino desde 1976." *Estudios CEDES* 12 (1980).

Cavarozzi, M. "Sindicatos, Estado y política en la Argentina: 1986–1987." *Estudios CEDES* (1988).

CIESE. *Documento Básico preparado para el Seminario sobre Concertación.* Quito, 1968.

Cumby, R., and R. M. Levich. "On the Definition and Magnitude of Recent Capital Flight," Working paper, series 2275, National Bureau of Economic Research, June 1987.

Decker, D. R. *The Political, Economic, and Labor Climate in Argentina.* Philadelphia: Industrial Research Unit, The Wharton School, University of Pennsylvania, 1983.

Fontana, A. "De la crisis de Malvinas a la subordinación condicionada: Conflictos intramilitares y transición política en Argentina." Working paper 74, Kellogg Institute, August 1986.

———. "Fuerzas armadas, Partidos políticos, y transición a la democracia en Argentina, 1981–1982." Working paper 28, Kellogg Institute, July 1984.

IBASE. *Politicas governmentais*, December 1987–January 1988.

Informes DIL (Documentación e Información Laboral) 216 (August 1984).

International Labour Conference. *Final List of Delegations.* 77th Session. Geneva: ILO, 1986.

Keck, M. "From Movement to Politics: The Workers' Party in the Brazilian Transition." Ph.D. diss., Yale Unversity, 1986.

Mainwaring, S. "The Consolidation of Democracy in Latin America—A Rapporteur's Report." Working Paper 73, Kellogg Institute, July 1986.

McGuire, J. "Labor in Contemporary Latin America: An Agenda for Research—A Rapporteur's Report." Working paper 61, Kellogg Institute, February 1986.

Middlebrook, K. "Notes on Transitions from Authoritarian Rule in Latin America and Latin Europe." Working paper 82, Wilson Center, Latin American Program, 1981.

———. "Prospects for Democracy: Regime Transformation and Transitions from Authoritarian Rule." Working paper 62, Wilson Center, Latin American Program, 1980.

Ministry of Economy and Central Bank of the Argentine Republic. *Argentine Economic Program 1984/1985.* Buenos Aires, December 2, 1984.

O'Donnell, G. A. "Apuntes para una teoría de Estado." *Documento CEDES/G.E. CLACSO* 9 (1977).

———. "Democracia en la Argentina: Micro y macro." Working paper 2, Kellogg Institute, December 1983.

———. "Estado y alianzas en la Argentina, 1956–1976." *Estudios CEDES/C.E. CLACSO* 5 (October 1976).

———. "Notas para el estudio de procesos de democratización política a partir del estado burocrático-autoritario." *Estudio CEDES* 2, 5 (1979).

———. "*y a mí, que me importa?* Notas sobre sociabilidad y política en Argentina y Brasil." Working paper 9, Kellogg Institute, January 1984.

———. "On the Fruitful Convergence of Hirschman's *Exit, Voice and Loyalty* and *Shifting Involvements*: Reflections from the Recent Argentine Experience." Working paper 58, Kellogg Institute, February 1986.

O'Donnell, G. A., and O. Oszlak. "Estado y políticas estatales en América Latina: Hacia una estrategia de investigación." *Documento CEDES/G.E. CLACSO* 4 (1976).

Offe, C. "Societal Preconditions of Corporatism, and Some Current Dilemmas of Democratic Theory." Working paper 14, Kellogg Institute, 1984.

Oszlak, O. "Formación histórica del Estado en América Latina: Elementos teórico-metodológicos para su estudio." *Estudios CEDES* 1, 3 (1978).

———. "La conquista del orden público y formación histórica del Estado Argentino 1862–1880." *Estudios CEDES* 4, 2 (1982).

———. "Notas críticas para una teoría de la burocracia estatal." *Documento CEDES/G.E. CLACSO* 8 (1977).

———. "Políticas públicas y regímenes políticos: Reflexiones a partir de algunas experiencias Latinoamericanas." *Estudios CEDES* 3, 2 (1980).

Prates, S. "El trabajo informal o las relaciones contradictorias entre la reproducción, la producción, y el Estado." *Documento de Trabajo N.73, CIESU,* 1987.

Programa de Principios del Partido Colorado. Montevideo: n.p., 1984.

Putnam, Elizabeth M. "Deconstructing Hegemony: The State/Labor Partial Regime in Chile." Master's thesis, University of Arizona, 1992.

Sánchez, M. A. "Deuda externa, grupos económicos y Estado en Argentina 1976–1987." *Documento de Trabajo N.11* (Buenos Aires), February 1988.

Schlagheck, J. L. *The Political, Economic, and Labor Climate in Brazil.*

Philadelphia: Industrial Research Unit, The Wharton School, University of Pennsylvania, 1977.

Schmitter, P. C. "Democratic Theory and Neo-Corporatist Practice." European University Institute working paper 106, Florence, 1983.

Scholk, R. "Comparative Aspects of the Transitions from Authoritarian Rule." Working paper 114, Wilson Center, Latin American Program, 1982.

Share, D., and S. Mainwaring. "Transitions From Above: Democratization in Brazil and Spain." Working paper 32, Kellogg Institute, December 1984.

Taiana, J. "El movimiento obrero, (1973–1988)." *Cuadernos de Crisis* 34 (1988).

Wallerstein, M. "Working Class Solidarity and Rational Behavior." Ph.D. diss., University of Chicago, 1985.

Zapata, F. "Structural Bases of the Organization of the Latin American Labor Movement: Some Notes for Discussion." Working paper 31, Center for Developing Area Studies, McGill University, August 1975.

Zeetano Chahad, J. P. "O seguro-desemprego e o mercado de trabalho no Brasil." *Trabalho para Discussão Interna*, Universidade de São Paulo, Facultade de Economia e Administração, Instituto de Pesquisas Econômicas–IPE, 1986.

Unpublished Papers and Documents

Barros, Robert. "A Democratic Past, Strong Political Parties, but No Transition to Democracy: The Paradox of Chile Explored." Paper presented to the Latin American Studies Association Fourteenth International Congress, New Orleans, March 1988.

Boado, M. "La juventud en el empleo." Internal research note, CIESU, 1983.

Brezzo, L. A., and E. Vispo. "Experiencia de la concertación de políticas de ingreso en Uruguay: Formas de negociación, función de los Consejos de Salarios, resultados." Paper presented at the Grupo de Trabajo sobre Políticas de Ingreso y Empleo Concertadas, PREALC, Santiago, Chile, September 2–3, 1986.

Canitrot, A. "Sobre concertación y la política económica. Reflexiones en relación a la experiencia argentina de 1984." Buenos Aires,1985, mimeographed.

Cavarozzi, M. "Sindicatos, Estado y política en la Argentina: 1986–1987." Paper presented to PREALC, Santiago, Chile, August 2–4, 1988.

CEPAL. "Problemas estructurales de la crísis económica en el desarrollo social del Uruguay y respuestas en las estrategias de las políticas del gobierno democrático." Paper prepared for the "Reunión sobre Crísis

Externa: Proceso de Ajuste y su Impacto Imediato y de Largo Plazo en el Desarrollo Social: Que Hacer?" CEPAL/UNICEF/OIT, Lima, November 15–29, 1986.

Collier, David, and Ruth Berins Collier. "The Initial Incorporation of the Labor Movement in Latin America: A Comparative Perspective." Paper presented at the Western Political Science Association Annual Meeting, March 1986.

Confederación General de Trabajo, "Propuesta de Acuerdo Social" and "Propuesta de Crecimiento en Libertad y con Justicia Social." Buenos Aires, February 8, 1985.

DIEESE. "Strike Statistics." Internal memorandum, 1988.

Fernández, A. "Sindicalismo y concertación social: La coyuntura argentina actual." Buenos Aires, mimeographed.

Filgueria, C.H. "Organizaciones sindicales y empresariales ante los programas de estabilización: Uruguay, 1985–1987." Paper presented at the "Seminario-Taller Sobre Políticas Anti-inflacionarias y Mercado de Trabajo," PREALC, Santiago, Chile, August 2–4, 1988.

Gaudio, R., and H. Domeniconi. "El proceso de normalización sindical bajo el gobierno radical." Buenos Aires, 1986, mimeographed.

Handelman, H. "Class Conflict and the Repression of The Uruguayan Working Class." Paper presented at the conference on "Contemporary Trends in Latin American Politics," University of New Mexico, 1977.

Keck, M. "Great Expectations: The Workers' Party in Brazil, 1979–1985." Paper delivered at the Eighth International Conference of the Latin American Studies Association, Boston, October 23–25, 1986.

———. "Labor, Social Policy, and Transition in Brazil: Some Dilemmas." Paper presented at the Latin American Studies Association Fourteenth International Congress, New Orleans, March 17–19, 1988.

Levine, D. "On the Nature, Sources, and Future Prospects of Democracy in Venezuela." Paper presented at the Conference on Democracy in Developing Nations, Hoover Institution, Stanford University, December 1985.

López, J. J. "Determinants of Private Investment in Argentina." Paper presented at the Latin American Studies Association Sixteenth International Congress, April 1991.

Luebbert, Gregory M. "Origins of Modern Capitalists' Polities and Labor Markets in Western Europe." Presented at the Fifth International Conference of Europeanists of the Council of European Studies, October 1985.

Mericle, K. "Conflict Regulation and the Brazilian Industrial Relations System." Ph.D. diss., University of Wisconsin, 1974.

O'Donnell, G. A. "Pactos políticos y pactos económico sociales. Por que sí y por que no." Buenos Aires, 1985, mimeographed.

Przeworski, A. "Capitalism, Democracy, Pacts: Revisited." Paper presented at the Conference on the Microfoundations of Democracy, University of Chicago, April 29–May 1, 1988.

———. "Class Compromise and the State: Western Europe and Latin America." Unpublished paper, Department of Political Science, University of Chicago, June 1980.

———. "Democracy as a Contingent Outcome of Conflicts." Unpublished ms., Department of Political Science, University of Chicago, 1983. Reprinted in Portuguese under the title "Ama a incerteza e serás democrático." *Novos Estudos CEBRAP* 9 (July 1984).

———. "Economic Conditions of Class Compromise." Unpublished paper, Dept. of Political Science, University of Chicago, December 1979.

———. "Suggestions for an Empirical Agenda." Paper presented at the Conference on Democratic Consolidation, Saõ Paulo, December 25–27, 1985.

———. "Toward a Theory of Capitalist Democracy." University of Chicago, 1977, mimeographed.

Przeworski, A., and M. Wallerstein. "Popular Sovereignty, State Autonomy, and Private Property." Paper prepared for the conference on "Policy Dilemmas in Front of the Crisis of State Regulatory Capacities in Europe and Latin America," Instituto de Investigaciones Europeo-Latinoamericanas, Buenos Aires, October 14–16, 1985.

———. "Unionization as a Union Strategy." March 1986, mimeographed.

Rama, M. "Políticas de estabilización y mercado de trabajo: El caso Uruguayo." Paper presented at the Seminario-Taller sobre Políticas Anti-inflacionarias y Mercado de Trabajo, PREALC, Santiago, Chile August 2–4, 1988.

Reis, F. W. "Rationality, `Sociology,' and the Consolidation of Democracy." Paper presented at the Conference on Microfoundations of Democracy, University of Chicago, April 29–May 1, 1988.

Roxborough, I. "Dependent Development and Fragile Institutions: The Dynamics of Incorporation." Paper presented at the Seventeenth Latin American Studies Association International Congress, September 1992.

Scharpf, F. W. "The Political Calculus of Inflations and Unemployment in Western Europe: A Game Theoretic Interpretation." Paper presented at the Conference on the Microfoundations of Democracy, University of Chicago, April 29–May 1, 1988.

Schmitter, P. C. "Organized Interests and Democratic Consolidation in

Southern Europe (and Latin America)." Draft research proposal, European University Institute, November 1984.

―――. "The Consolidation of Political Democracy in Southern Europe." Unpublished ms., Department of Political Science, Stanford University, July 1987.

Schmitter, P. C., and D. Brand. "Organizing Capitalists in the United States: The Advantages and Disadvantages of Exceptionalism." Paper presented at the APSA Annual Meeting, Chicago, 1979.

Streek, W. "Interest Heterogeneity and Organizing Capacity: Two Class Logics of Collective Action?" Paper presented at the conference on "Political Institutions and Interest Intermediation," University of Constance, April 20–21, 1988.

Tavares de Almeida, M. H. "A Difficult Path: Unions and Politics in the Construction of Democracy." Unpublished ms., Universidade de São Paulo, 1987.

Laws, Decrees, and Government Documents

LAWS AND DECREES

• *Argentina*

Unless otherwise indicated, all laws and decrees are published in the *Boletín Informativo* and the *Anales de Legislación Argentina*.

Decree 15,074 (law 12,921)/November 27, 1943.

Decree 15/December 10, 1983.

Decree 132/December 10, 1983.

Decree 134/December 10, 1983.

Decree 353/December 30, 1983.

Decree 465/April, 14, 1988. *Asociaciones de Uniones de Trabajadores.* Buenos Aires: Ministerio de Trabajo y Seguridad Social, 1988.

Decree 2,907/December 10, 1988.

Law 22, 105/November 7, 1979. *Boletín de Legislación* 21, 2 (July–December 1979).

Law 22,520/December 21, 1981. *Boletín Oficial*, December 23, 1981.

Law 23,023/December 8, 1983, article 27.

Law 23,023/December 10, 1983.

Law 23,551/March 23, 1988. *Asociaciones de Uniones de Trabajadores.* Buenos Aires: Ministerio de Trabajo y Seguridad Social, 1988.

• *Brazil*

Decree 19,433/November 26, 1930.

Decree 19,667/February 4, 1931.

Decree 81,663/May 16, 1978.

Decree 2,097/December 1, 1981, anexo 3a and 4.

• *Uruguay*

Unless otherwise indicated, all laws and decrees are published in the
   Diario Oficial.
Decree 574/July 12, 1974.
Decree 371/June 30, 1978.
Decree 513/October 9, 1981.
Decree 178/May 10, 1985, article 5.
Law 13,720/December 16, 1968.
Law 14,106/March 14, 1973.
Law 14,218/1974.
Law 14,791/June 8, 1978.
Law 14,800/June 30, 1978 (article 23).
Law 15,137/May 21, 1981.
Law 15,800/January 17, 1986.
Law 15,809/April 8, 1986 (Law of the National Budget), insert 13, pp.
   15–16.
Law 13,640/November 26, 1986.
Resolution 991/June 30, 1978 (creating, specifying the functions of, and
   ratifying the structure of the DINACOPRIN).

GOVERNMENT DOCUMENTS

   • *Argentina*

Boletin de la Dirección General de Trabajo 1 (June 1907).
Cámara de Diputados, República Argentina. *Reseña 1985*. Buenos Aires:
   Dirección Secretaría de la Cámara de Diputados, 1985.
Congreso de la Nación, Cámara de Diputados. *Diario de Sesiones*, Sep-
   tember 24–25, 1984.
———. *Diario de Sesiones*, March 6–7, 1986.
Ministerio de Trabajo y Seguridad Social. *Dotación de Personal: Total
   General*. Internal memorandum. Buenos Aires: Dirección de Personal,
   Ministerio de Trabajo y Seguridad Social, December 1986.
———. *Estructura Sindical en la Argentina*. Buenos Aires: Dirección
   Nacional de Recursos Humanos y Empleo, 1987.
———. *Régimen de Elecciones: Asociaciones Profesionales de Traba-
   jadores (Ley 23,071/1984)*. Buenos Aires: Departmento de Publica-
   ciones y Biblioteca, 1984.
———. *Sindicatos: Elecciones, 1984–1986*. Buenos Aires: 1988.
Ministry of Economy and Central Bank of the Argentine Republic.
   Argentine Economic Program 1984/1985. Buenos Aires: December 2,
   1984.
Presupuesto General de la Administración Central. Buenos Aires: Con-
   greso de la Nación, for the years cited.

• *Brazil*

Ministério do Trabalho. "Demostrativo do Orçamento Annual." Brasilia: 1986.

———. "Demostrativo do Orçamento Anual." Internal Memo, 1987.

———. "Distribução da Força de Trabalho—MTb." Internal Memorandum. Brasilia: October 1986.

———. "Dotação, 1984–1985." Internal Memorandum, n.d.

———. "Exposição de Motivos No 24 e Projeto de Lei que regula a negociação coletiva de trabalho e o exercício do direito de greve." Draft Proposal. Brasilia: August 1986.

———. "Orçamento 1986/1987: Outras despesas de custeio e capital—Atividade fim, quadro comparativo." Internal memorandum, n.d.

———. "Situação Empregos, SEDE, Actualização/DP: 02/07/86." Internal memorandum, Departamento de Pessoal, 1986.

———. "Situação Empregos, orgaos regionais—DRT's Actualização/DP: 02/07/86." Internal memorandum, Departmento de Pessoal, 1986.

Ministério do Trabalho/Instituto de Econômia Industrial (UFRJ). *O Mercado de Trabalho Brasileiro: Estrutura e Conjuntura*. Brasilia: Secretaria de Emprego e Salarios, April 1987, esp. chap. 12.

Ministério do Trabalho, MTb/SG/SOF. "Participação das atividades no Orcamento de ODC/CAP." Internal memorandum, September 1986.

Ministério do Trabalho, SG/SGAT/SOF. "Execução Orcamentaria." Internal Memorandum, September 1986.

Presidencia da Nacão, "Anteprojeito da Nova Constitucão." Brasilia, 1987.

• *United States*

United States Department of Labor. *Directory of Foreign Labor Organizations: Argentina*. Washington: Bureau of International Labor Affairs, 1986.

———. *Foreign Labor Trends: Argentina*. Washington: Bureau of International Labor Affairs, 1985.

———. *Labor Law and Practice in Uruguay*. Washington: Government Printing Office, 1971.

• *Uruguay*

Ministerio de Trabajo y Seguridad Social. "Funcionamiento de los Consejos de Salarios 1985–1987." Montevideo: n.p., 1988.

———. "Identificación de experiencias cooperativas y normativa aplicable." N.p: 1986.

———. "Nómina de cargos ocupados por programa." OSPP internal memorandum 133, November 14, 1986.

———. *Organigrama Actual, 1987*. Montevideo: Oficina Sectorial de

Planeamiento y Presupuesto, Departamento de Racionalización Administrativa, January 1987.

————. *Organigrama: Estructura Orgánica Proyectada, 1987*. Montevideo: Oficina Sectorial de Planeamiento y Presupuesto, Departamento de Racionalización Administrativa.

————.*Proyecto políticas públicas y desarrollo social: Uruguay, documento de trabajo*. Montevideo: Programa de las Naciones Unidas para el Desarrollo, Proyecto Regional "Pobreza Crítica," RLA/86/004, February 1987.

————. "Resúmen de Rubros de Retribuciones Personales y Gastos de Funcionamiento E Inversión." OSPP, Inf. 133/86, November 14, 1986.

————. *Resúmen de Rubros de Retribuciones Personales y Gastos de Funcionamiento e Inversión*. Internal memorandum. Montevideo, 1987.

Oficina Sectorial de Planeamiento y Presupuesto. *Presupuesto Nacional 1987*. Montevideo: Presidencia de la Nación. OSPP internal memorandum 133, November 14, 1986.

Partido Colorado. *Programa de principios*, 1985.

Secretaría de Fomento Cooperativo. *Memoria 1985*. Montevideo: MTSS, 1987.

• United Nations. International Labor Organization

Centro Interamericano de Administración del Trabajo (OIT/PNUD). *Estructura orgánica del Ministerio de Trabajo de Argentina, Decreto 2097, del 10 de diciembre de 1981*. Lima: CIAT/Serie Legislación Laboral 9, 1983.

————. *La administración pública del trabajo: Concepto, principios, organización y evolución*. Lima: CIAT/OIT, 1980.

————. *Reunión técnica regional sobre el convenio 150 y la recomendación 158 de la OIT relativos a la administración de trabajo*. Informe final. Vol. 1. Mexico City, August 10–14, 1981; Lima: CIAT, 1982.

————. *Reunión técnica regional sobre el convenio 150 y la recomendación 158 de la OIT relativos a la administración del trabajo*. Informe final. Vol. 2. Lima: CIAT, 1982.

Centro Interamericano de Administración del Trabajo/Organización Internacional del Trabajo. *La administración pública del trabajo y su papel en el desarrollo económico y social*. CIAT/OIT Serie Documentos 79/1, Lima, 1980.

Difieri, J. A. *Planificación global, reforma administrativa, y administración del trabajo*. Documento de Trabajo CIAT/DT/82/105, Lima, 1982.

Husband, J. I. *Introducción a la administración del trabajo*. Geneva: ILO, 1982.

International Labour Conference. *Final List of Delegations*, 77th session. Geneva: ILO, 1986.

International Labor Organization. *Growth, Employment, and Basic Needs in Latin America and the Caribbean*. Report of the Director-General. Eleventh Conference of American State Members of the International Labor Organization, Medellín, Colombia, September–October 1979. Geneva: ILO, 1979.

———. *Public Labor Administration and Its Role in Economic and Social Development*. Report 2. Eleventh Conference of American States Members of the International Labor Organization, Medellín, Colombia, September–October, 1979. Geneva: International Labour Office, 1979.

———. *Relaciones de trabajo en el Uruguay*. Geneva: ILO, 1987.

Newspapers and Periodicals

ARGENTINA

Ambito Financiero, December 15, 1989.
Clarín, April 6, 1987.
El Periodista, March 28–April 3 and September 26–October 2, 1986.
La Nación, March 17–August 4, 1986, and June 29, 1988.
Página 12, June 29, 1988.
Periodico CGT, August 1986.

BRAZIL

Boletim IBASE, March and August 1987.
Correio Brasilense, May 2 and June 26, 1986.
Folha do São Paulo, March 18, 1987, and July and August 1988.
Journal do Brasil, July and August 1988.
O Globo, February 18–April 26, 1987.
Veja, June 24, 1987.

UNITED STATES

Brazil Report, June 4, 1987.
Latin American Weekly Report, June 25–July 16, 1987, and February 27, 1992.

Interviews, Lectures, and Speeches

ARGENTINA

Alfonsín, Raúl A. "Mensaje del Sr. Presidente de la Nación, Dr. Raúl R. Alfonsín, a la Honorable Asamblea Legislativa el dia 10 de diciembre de 1983." *Discursos Presidenciales*. Buenos Aires: Secretaría de Información Pública, 1984.

Barrionuevo, H., Labor Minister. Speech quoted in *La Nación*, March 24, 1986.

Caro Figueroa, José A., Secretario de Trabajo, MTSS. Interview by the author, January 10, 1987.

Pedraza, José, leader of the Unión Ferroviaria. Speech given at the Instituto Italiano de Cultura, Buenos Aires, June 29, 1988.

Przeworski A. Lecture presented at CEDES, Buenos Aires, November 11, 1986.

Rebhan, Herman. Speech given at the 4th International Federation of Industrial Metalworkers (FITIM) Conference on Latin American Autoworkers, Buenos Aires, Argentina, September 17–19, 1987.

Rouquié, A. Interview published in *Resúmen de la Actualidad* 88 (March 23, 1983), 23.

Tosco, Agustín. Interview published in *Primera Plana*, June 20, 1972.

BRAZIL

Almeida, Eros de, Secretário-Geral do Ministério do Trabalho. Interview with the author, March 17, 1987.

Chiarelli, Carols, Senator, member of the president's Conselho Político, and leader of the Partido do Frente Liberal (PDF). *Correio Brasilense*, June 26, 1986, 11.

———. *O Globo*, April 17, 1987, 5.

Estelis, Dr. Renaldo, Secretário de Orçamento e Finanças do Ministério de Trabalho. Interview with the author, March 17, 1987.

Ganzer, Avelino, Vice President CUT. Statement cited in *O Globo*, February 18, 1987, 19.

Lobos, Julio. Interviews published in *Veja*, September 24, 1986, 5–8.

Moreira Filho, Dr. Mauro, director of personnel of the MTb. Interview with the author, March 17, 1987.

Meneguelli, Jair. Declarations and the editorial critique of his position. *O Globo*, April 7, 1987.

Pachowski Vania, Flavio, press director, CUT Nacional. Interview by the author, March 20, 1987.

Pazzianoto, A. "Discurso do Ministro do Trabalho." Given to the 72d Meeting of the International Labor Conference, Geneva, 1986.

———. Interview in *O Globo*, April 12, 1987, 16.

———. "Pronunciamento do Ministro do Trabalho." Given at the Escola Superior de Guerra, August 1986.

Quintanilha, Argeu, Director Regional de Trabalho, Estado do São Paulo. Interview published in *O Estado de São Paulo*, April 23, 1987, 30.

Rocha Dinitz, director of FIESP (Federação Industrial do Estado de São

Paulo). Comments in O *Estado de São Paulo*, July 19, 1986.

Sarti, Plínio, Secretário de Relações do Trabalho do Ministério do Trabalho. Interview by the author, March 16, 1987.

Wernek, Dorothea, Secretária de Emprego e Salarios. Statements in O *Globo*, February 18, 1987, 19.

UNITED STATES

Schmitter, P. C. Comments made at the Conference on Microfoundations of Democracy, University of Chicago, April 30, 1989.

Tavares de Almeida, M. H. Comments made at the Conference on Microfoundations of Democracy, April 30, 1988.

Wanderley Reis, F. Comments made at the Conference on Microfoundations of Democracy, April 29, 1988.

URUGUAY

Capellini, Director General de Secretaría (general director of the secretariat), MTSS. Interview by the author, January 27, 1987.

D'Elia, José, president of the PIT-CNT. Interview by the author, July 5, 1988.

Ferraro, Dr., Director General de Planeamiento, MTSS. Interview by the author, December 19, 1986.

Gitto, Dr. Carlos, adviser to the Director Nacional de Trabajo (national labor director), MTSS. Interview by the author, January 26, 1987.

Gonzalez Machado, Dr. Luis, Director de Política Social (social policy director) of the MTSS. Interview by the author, January 27, 1987.

Stilling, Ricardo, Director de la Oficina Sectorial de Planeamiento y Presupuesto, MTSS. Interview by the author, January 27, 1987.

Torres, Roberto, Inspector, Jefe de la Oficina de Higiene y Seguridad Industrial (chief of the office of industrial hygiene and safety). Interview by the author, January 27, 1987.

Vidart, Gabriel, adviser to the Director de Política Social (social policy director), MTSS. Interview by the author, July 7, 1988.

Villaverde, Rubén, propaganda secretary of the PIT-CNT. Interview by the author, July 5, 1988.

Vivo, Alfonso, adviser to the labor minister. Interview by the author, Montevideo, January 26, 1987.

INDEX

Aberatura, Apertura (political opening), 7–9, 175, 192, 293

Access, to decision making, 27–28, 63

Agriculture: export, 128–29, 214, 221; as labor sector, 95

Alderete, Carlos, 147

Alfonsín, Raúl: importance of election of, 126, 128-29; labor administration under, 157, 159; labor relations under, 142–43, 146, 151. *See also* Argentina; Radical government

Argentina, 126–66; authoritarianism in, 8–9, 11; concertations in, 59–60; labor administration under authoritarianism, 126–28, 132–33; labor administration under Peronism, 126–28, 131–32; labor administration under Radicals, 133–66; labor movement in, 90, 129–31; politics in, 62, 296

Association, right of, 32, 180–81, 183, 211

Austral Plan (Argentina), 145–46

Authoritarian culture, 9–13, 134–35

Authoritarianism: corporatism in, 115–16; descent into, 216–20; effects of, 110, 282–86, 309n26, 356n2; labor under, 78, 81, 90–91, 93–94, 192, 210, 357n14; legacies of, 62, 176, 199, 298; liberalization of, 7–9, 308n13; movement away from, 7–9, 49–50, 154–55, 175, 210; reversion to, 36, 300–02

Autonomy: of labor administrations, 160–62, 200–01, 205; of unions, 323n19; of workers, 322n10

Banco de Previsión Social (BPS), 259, 266–67, 277

Barrionuevo, Hugo, 135

Batlle y Ordóñez, José, government of, 209, 214

Bipartism: of labor and capital, in Brazil, 187, 190, 346n62; of labor and capital, in Uruguay, 187, 218–19, 250, 252; of labor and state, 253; state with labor and capital separately, 178–79

Blanco Party (Uruguay), 215, 227, 233

Brazil, 60; as authoritarian culture, 11; labor relations in, 90; liberalization in, 7–8, 9; national labor administration in, 167–208; politics in, 62, 296

Budgets: of Argentine labor administration, 158–59, 269–71, 280; of Brazilian labor administration, 171, 197, 199–202, 269–71; of unions, 171, 182–83, 200; of Uruguayan labor administration, 225–26, 260, 269–72

Bureaucracies: federal, 107–09, 203–04; labor's internal, 77–78, 88–89

Bureaucratic-authoritarian regimes, 105, 330n75. *See also* Authoritarianism

Cabinets, federal, 119–20; labor administrations in, 116–18, 202

Capital: control of, 25–26, 37; decline in, 222–23, 263; increase in, 221

Capitalism, 13–14; and labor, 69–70, 92–94, 105–11, 293–94; opposition to, 75–76, 248, 257–58; reproduction of, 124–25, 287; strength of, 35–37, 90–91. *See also* Consent, labor's to capitalism

Capitalists, 29–30, 30, 193; bilateral negotiations with labor, 187, 190, 346n62; in class compromise, 17–20; in concer-